From Russia with Code

FROM
RUSSIA
<with> CODE

PROGRAMMING MIGRATIONS
IN POST-SOVIET TIMES

Edited by Mario Biagioli and Vincent Antonin Lépinay

DUKE UNIVERSITY PRESS
Durham and London | 2019

© 2019 Duke University Press
All rights reserved
Printed in the United States of America on acid-free paper ∞
Designed by Jennifer Hill / Counterspace Design
Typeset in Minion Pro by Westchester Publishing Services

Library of Congress Cataloging-in-Publication Data
Names: Biagioli, Mario, [date] editor. | Lépinay, Vincent Antonin, editor.
Title: From Russia with code : programming migrations in post-Soviet times /
edited by Mario Biagioli and Vincent Antonin Lépinay.
Description: Durham : Duke University Press, 2019. | Includes bibliographical
references and index.
Identifiers: LCCN 2018037346 (print)
LCCN 2018044254 (ebook)
ISBN 9781478003342 (ebook)
ISBN 9781478001843 (hardcover : alk. paper)
ISBN 9781478002994 (pbk. : alk. paper)
Subjects: LCSH: Information technology—Social aspects—Russia (Federation) |
Computer software—Development—Social aspects—Russia (Federation) |
Brain drain—Russia (Federation) | Hacking—Social aspects—Russia
(Federation) | Hacking—Political aspects—Russia (Federation) | Russia
(Federation)—Emigration and immigration.
Classification: LCC HM851 (ebook) | LCC HM851 .F75 2019 (print) |
DDC 303.48/330947—dc23
LC record available at https://lccn.loc.gov/2018037346

CONTENTS

III. Interlude: Russian Maps

IV. Bridges and Mismatches

ACM	Association for Computing Machinery
CIS	Commonwealth of Independent States
CS	computer science
EUSP	European University at Saint Petersburg
FSU	former Soviet Union
IBM	International Business Machines Corporation
ICPC	International Collegiate Programming Contest
ICT	information and communications technology
IT	information technology
KGB	Komitet gosudarstvennoy bezopasnosti (Committee for State Security)
MIT	Massachusetts Institute of Technology
MNC	multinational corporation
NASDAQ	National Association of Securities Dealers Automated Quotation
NATO	North Atlantic Treaty Organization
NGO	nongovernmental organization
OECD	Organisation for Economic Cooperation and Development
PC	personal computer
R&D	research and development
RCS	Russian computer scientists
RVC	Russian Venture Company
Skolkovo	Skolkovo Innovative City
Skoltech	Skolkovo Institute of Science and Technology
SEZ	special economic zone
STS	Science and Technology Studies
USSR	Union of Soviet Socialist Republics

ACKNOWLEDGMENTS

This book is a collective effort in more ways than we can describe. From conceptualizing the project, securing the funding, assembling the team, all the way to developing the international network to support the research and conversations that we wanted to have, we have relied on colleagues and friends in Russia, the US, France, the UK, and the Netherlands, including several we made along the way. *From Russia with Code* is the product of a three-year effort by a team of scholars connected to the Science and Technology Studies (STS) Center at the European University at Saint Petersburg (EUSP), funded by a grant from the Ministry of Education and Science of the Russian Federation for the study of high-skill brain drain. This project would not have been possible without the EUSP's unique intellectual and interdisciplinary environment and the Ministry's support for the extensive and multisited research required by our research topic.

As in all collective enterprises, especially academic ones, the most important persons are not necessarily the most visible. In our case, they do not appear on the book cover nor in the list of contributors, and yet they have been present throughout the book, working next to it, and making it possible. Olga Dragan, EUSP's finance officer, has crucially supported the project from its inception in January 2013, when it was only a grant application, all the way through its slow metamorphosis into the book you are reading. With the help of Natalia Voinova, Olga steered the ship clear of all bureaucratic shoals, even when the political campaigns against the EUSP turned bureaucratic rules into something else.

A relatively recent arrival on the Russian academic landscape, the EUSP is at once a research center and the leading private higher-degree-granting social science institution in Russia, ranking every year in the top five of all Russian universities. A project of this scale would not have been possible without the support that the STS Center was fortunate to receive from the other departments, especially Anthropology, History, Sociology, Political Science, and Economics. While enjoying their support, it has also been a pleasure to witness the "positive spillovers" that our project has enabled, inserting STS questions and approaches into conversations with colleagues across the social sciences and into the research that the graduate students have been conceptualizing and pursuing.

We were fortunate when Zinaida Vasilyeva accepted our invitation to become the executive director of the project. Since the project's inception, she skillfully negotiated the contrasting needs and desires of the academic scholars and of the multilayered bureaucratic world in which the project grew and operated. In this, she was helped throughout by Anastasia Karkacheva, who added to the job description of assistant director her precious and much-appreciated design skills. Diana Kurkovsky West joined the project as a researcher in 2014, quickly moving to direct the STS Center in 2016, with the support of Olga Sezneva who took leave from her faculty position in Amsterdam to help strengthen and broaden the academic agenda and programs of the Center while also connecting it to Saint Petersburg's broader cultural circles and networks. Liliia Zemnukhova was part of the research project from the beginning, always contributing much-appreciated problem-solving skills and contagious energy. Mélanie Feakins generously shared with us her knowledge and experience of Russian offshoring in the IT business, providing crucial fieldwork contacts and suggestions.

In Paris, Sciences Po supported the completion of the book through its Scientific Advisory Board funding in 2014. Medialab was the perfect institution to conduct the project while in Paris. Michel Gardette and Bruno Latour were understanding enough to let Vincent Lépinay finish the project in Saint Petersburg while holding a teaching position in Paris. In Davis, California, the Center for Science and Innovation Studies and the faculty of the Science and Technology Studies Program supported and participated in the project, providing a welcoming intellectual and institutional home to some of our Russian visitors. Martin Kenney lent his expertise in innovation studies and regional development, making him one of our most helpful collaborators, brainstorming with our team both in Saint Petersburg and Davis.

Andrei Mogoutov provided invaluable guidance to the project participants pursuing quantitative analyses of the patterns of collaboration and publication of Russian computer scientists. Michael Gordin, Loren Graham, Alexei Grinbaum, David Kaiser, and Martin Kenney joined our summer school in 2014, providing extensive and insightful comments on the team's work. Their generous presence and critical input were as useful as the inspiration that their work triggered. Harley Balzer, Slava Gerovich, Martin Giraudeau, and Ben Peters kindly discussed with us versions of this book and provided much-needed advice, as did Yuri Takhteyev on the earlier framing of the project. As EUSP's vice-rector, Boris Kolonitsky provided much-needed support and connections. Olga Sezneva, Diana Kurkovsky West, Mikhail Sokolov, Ilya Utekhin, Artemy Magun, Anatoly Pinsky, Stephanie Dick, and Jay West have all supervised and advised students at the STS Center. As the project was reaching its completion, Veljko Vujacic read the book manuscript and provided extensive and incisive comments that contributed to shaping it in its current form. Special thanks go to Beatrice Lewin Dumin whose editing skills turned an assemblage of stylistically unruly essays into a coherent volume.

Preliminary versions of this book's chapters were presented at a variety of conferences: "From Streets to Boardrooms: Internet Activism and Business Strategies," September 18–19, 2013, EUSP; "Crossbreeding STS and Innovation Studies," December 7–8, 2013, EUSP; "Innovating Russia: Computer Science and Entrepreneurship in Historical Perspective," December 9–10, 2013, EUSP; "Explorers and Pirates: Digital Creators and the Creation of Value," June 18–19, 2014, EUSP; "Summer School on Russian Computer Scientists," June 16, 17, and 20, 2014, EUSP; "Garage Innovation," September 26–27, 2014, EUSP; "Central and Eastern European Software Engineering Conference," October 23–25, 2014, Digital October Center, Moscow; "Scientific Diaspora," December 5–6, 2014, EUSP; "Summer School on Russian Computer Scientists," June 22–24, 2015, EUSP; "STS Winter School," January 8–13, 2016, Venice International University, Italy; Association for Slavic, East European and Eurasian Studies Conference, November 20, 2016, Washington, DC; "Soviet Computing Workshop," November 29, 2016, UC Davis; "History of Science Seminar," June 16, 2017, European Institute, Florence, Italy. We wish to thank all those who provided us with comments, criticism, and support during the many discussions we had at these conferences.

This book would not have seen the light of day were it not for the institutional energy and imagination of Oleg Kharkhordin, who served as EUSP's rector during most of the duration of the project. He first invited one of us (Vincent Lépinay) to take the lead of the STS Center he had recently launched at EUSP, and his work on Russian high-tech entrepreneurship has been a constant reference. This book extends those intellectual conversations and the institutional project that framed them. The team of Russian and international scholars and networks that have grown around the "mega-grant" project have contributed to Oleg's goal of solidifying the EUSP Center's role as the premier STS hub in Russia—a country where our already inter-disciplinary field needs to add additional perspectives to make sense of the many different scenarios emerging at the intersection of dramatic historical changes, geographical specificities, and mobilities. While his name does not appear among the book's contributors, Oleg has been a full-fledged collabo-rator, from his early support of our "megagrant" application to innumerable discussions and brainstorming sessions throughout the project. The pleasure associated with the completion of this book is also tinged by the sadness of acknowledging the closure of the project, but we hope that the relations of intellectual kinship with Oleg and the faculty and students of the EUSP will spawn more initiatives and conversations, in Saint Petersburg and elsewhere.

RUSSIAN ECONOMIES OF CODES

Mario Biagioli and Vincent Antonin Lépinay

Three recent vignettes of Russian information technology (IT) education, migration, entrepreneurship, and activism mark the boundaries of this project, as well as some of its analytical foci.

1

"I tell you honestly and openly—if you want to harm the country, invest in training IT specialists in the Russian Federation. You couldn't harm Russia more."[1] With this stunning remark, Dmitry Marinichev, Russia's presidential internet ombudsman, addressed IT entrepreneurs, government officials, and academics in October 2015 at a meeting of the Russian Civic Chamber to discuss import substitution—the replacement (due to Western sanctions) of foreign-produced technologies with Russian ones. Accepting as a fact the isolationist tendencies of the Vladimir Putin government, the West's growing hostility toward Russia, and the lack of a Russian innovation ecosystem that could sustain the production of domestically and internationally competitive digital technologies, Marinichev argued that Russia was already cut off from global innovation networks and that, therefore, "we can give technology to other countries only when we have a military presence [there]. When other countries will not have an alternative option than to get it from us."

Considerable uproar ensued, but Marinichev held his line in a follow-up interview with *Gazeta*:

> I am saying absolutely banal things, which have been well known since the time of the Roman Empire. First an army

comes on a territory, then merchants, and then there is state power and a market. It's only that way, and no other way. Therefore if at a government level we choose the regimen of "Russia against all," then we will have no chance to sell our products and technologies except by conducting geopolitical expansion in the world. (Evstifeyev 2015).

He then continued:

A clearly-expressed confrontation is underway between the Western world and Russia. Whether Russia is guilty here or not is not important. What's important is the status quo, and it is impossible to discuss technological export and import substitution because we must produce everything ourselves totally and completely. In that context, preparing IT specialists for foreign-based technologies is essentially to undermine Russia's sovereignty. . . . I don't want to look at that option because it is unacceptable. We have all managed to live as citizens of the global world, freely moving about—a vacation in Italy, a merry-go-round ride in America. But it could happen that everything will change. And the question of what method of technology transfer to use lies on that plane—who we are and what we want and where. (Evstifeyev 2015)

2

Exploring his company's server in 2015, Dmitry Korobov, a programmer at the Russian company Yandex, found a folder containing the source code of its search engine, which he proceeded to download and then tried to sell. Yandex is not simply a Russian IT company, but more like *the* Russian IT company. Started in 1997, it quickly outperformed Google in Russia (controlling about 60 percent of the market), becoming one of the few darlings of foreign investors and opening its own research center in Silicon Valley. It is considered the fourth-largest search engine in the world.

At first, Korobov looked for buyers on the darknet, but he then openly approached NIX, an electronics retail company where he had acquaintances. Need, not greed, may have motivated Korobov, who claimed to sell the stolen software in order to launch his own startup, leave Yandex, and become an entrepreneur. He seems to have had poor business sense, though, asking $28,000 for software that may have been worth $14 million; apparently equally oblivious to the fact that $28,000 would hardly have paid office rent in Moscow for a year, let alone launched a startup. With the Russian security services (FSB) scouring the darknet on a daily basis to locate signs of suspicious activities, Korobov was easily lured into meeting a prospective buyer who handcuffed him before he could sing the praises of the sophisticated system he was trying to sell. He received a suspended sentence of two years in jail—a lenient punishment that probably reflects the court's perception of Korobov's actions as naively, rather than professionally, criminal (Degeler 2015).

3

Virtual Rynda: The Atlas of Help is a platform "to support and facilitate mutual aid and crowdsourced solutions to different types of problems affecting Russian citizens" (Asmolov 2014). It emerged in the wake of the 2010 wildfires that ravaged the forested areas around Moscow. Help Map (Wildfires.ru) was set up on the model of Ushahidi, a crowdsourcing platform initially developed in Kenya in 2008 to help collect and report evidence of violence and fraud. Help Map succeeded beyond all expectations, leading its founders to consolidate their social experience of mutual help and collective data gathering into a platform that could be used in a variety of situations. As a response to the poor handling of the disaster by local authorities and as an active decision to equip citizens with new modes of coordination, Help Map both facilitated and managed a successful grassroots outpouring of aid and collaboration. In programming and design terms it effectively translated a massive and otherwise disorganized stream of compassion into human action, and in so doing it reenacted an old Soviet political philosophy. Nearly two decades after the collapse of the USSR, it proudly brought back the notion of the public good, this time in the form of a city threatened by smoke.

Interestingly, the people behind Help Map only met in person after the site had already achieved its collaborative goal. Its successor, Virtual Rynda, is one among many such projects harnessing the power of virtual connectedness to address issues that are both local and broadly shared across constituencies—information, needs, and agendas that political authorities would otherwise leave unseen. These citizen-produced digital platforms are, thus, not just tools for emergency management or other forms of practical help but rather vectors of a new public sphere, their very existence a finger that points to a neglectful or willfully blind state.

< / >

Taken together, these three contemporary vignettes function as signposts of the techno-scientific and political field engaged in this book—a field that kept changing as we were studying it. When we started mapping the brain drain and global migrations of Russian computer scientists, software practitioners, and IT specialists to Finland, the UK, Israel, the US, and beyond we expected the diasporic process to be the primary agent of change and hybridization of people who otherwise shared comparable professional profiles, educational backgrounds, and technical skills. However, as soon as we went into the field—a field that was new to us and for which we had limited background literature to guide us—we were confronted with the heterogeneity and fluidity of our subjects *prior* to their diasporas.

One can recognize an academic computer scientist virtually anywhere in the world by reference to standardized forms of academic training, publication venues, professional roles, and disciplinary networks. The relatively stable profile of Russian academic computer scientists was, however, more the exception than the rule among the subjects of our study. Unlike "computer scientist," terms like "software practitioner," "IT entrepreneur," or "hacktivist" were remarkably difficult to specify in the Russian context, not just because they indexed new professions and roles, but because Russia— the sociocultural and political framework in which these changes were taking place—was itself a work in progress (Yurchak 2005). It quickly became apparent, therefore, that defining our subject was going to be an important and ongoing research question—more a heuristic window than a problem. (When we refer to them as "Russian computer scientists," or RCS, we use that term under erasure.)

What is commonly referred to as the collapse of the Soviet Union in the early 1990s was nothing short of a cultural revolution that triggered a rather unique kind of diaspora. Traditional revolutions often trigger migrations of members of the losing faction (people who had clear social identities like, say, aristocrats after the Bolshevik Revolution of 1917), but the transition to post-Soviet Russia spawned a diaspora of subjects that were in the process of refashioning themselves into something else. The "Russian software practitioners" we have been following around were not seeking refuge in other communist enclaves abroad to hold on to their previous identities, but were instead technically skilled people who, while participating in some emergent post-Soviet subjecthood, often found themselves constrained by the post-Soviet context itself. Being a "tech entrepreneur" in post-Soviet Russia does not mean occupying a specific preestablished role, but rather constructing a new subject position—one that is as new as that of the hacktivist and the forms of political participation associated with that term.

After 1991, the country we now call the Russian Federation migrated toward a capitalist economy, enabled the mobility of its citizens both within and beyond its borders, renegotiated its relation with the former Soviet republics, and attempted to pivot from extractive industries to a "knowledge economy," as well as to reorient its famous and extensive techno-scientific apparatus from its traditional centralized, top-down, and military-oriented structure toward a more horizontal and entrepreneurial culture aimed at technologies and products for private industries and the consumer market. The people whose movements we sought to understand were participants and actors in many of these changes, as well as in the emergence of a new political sphere made possible by the internet and digital media. It became clear, then, that we needed to look both at those who opted to refashion themselves in situ, and those who instead engaged that refashioning process in diasporic settings. Rather than simply the opposite of "staying put," moving was a different facet of a process of emergent change that was affecting all post-Soviet subjects. This emphasis on emergence (whether geographically anchored in Russia or not) is reflected in the layout of our chapters, which map both the new post-Soviet configurations of software practitioners, entrepreneurs, and hacktivists from Saint Petersburg to Vladivostok, as well as some of the assemblages they have constructed abroad.

At the same time, while it became difficult or plainly impossible for us to describe exactly what "Russian" meant in the midst of all these changes, it was equally clear that the conditions, resources, constraints, and possible trajectories for all these developments were genealogically specific to "Russia." The global mobility of IT specialists,[2] software theft, and grassroots web-based initiatives is nothing new. Still, the remarkable mobility of IT specialists, especially highly skilled individuals such as those who have traditionally been produced by the Soviet and then Russian pedagogical system, is a particularly thorny issue for this country because it turns a pedagogical strength into an economic and possibly even political threat. In addition to the problems that brain drain poses to all countries, here it is feared to contribute, at least in Marinichev's neo–Cold War perspective, to "undermin[ing] Russian sovereignty." Unlike other countries that have been able to stem the loss of academics and entrepreneurs, create opportunities for returnees, or benefit from networks developed through the back-and-forth mobility of their highly skilled workers, Russia continues to face a one-directional flow, the pace of which seems to be accelerating in response to an increasingly unsettled political environment at home (Balzer 2011; Kuznetsov 2006; Luo and Wang 2001; Saxenian 2007; Wang 2015). Recent surveys show that in 2014 the emigration of Russian scientists and entrepreneurs was by a wide margin the highest since 1999 (Dezhina 2015, 330). It is this trend that Marinichev was addressing in his radical 2015 speech before the Russian Civic Chamber: "All the programmers will instantly move abroad. That is the practice of the last two years" (quoted in Fitzpatrick 2015a).

METHODS FOR MOVING POPULATIONS

From Russia with Code analyzes changing populations of techno-scientific practitioners and entrepreneurs. As indicated by the three vignettes, these are heterogeneous populations without essential features or stable identities. They mutate as they move, in Russia and abroad, turning communist mathematicians into post-Soviet software entrepreneurs, political activists into civic hackers, academic theoreticians into entrepreneurs, Jews in Russia into Russians in Israel, used-car salesmen in Vladivostok into web designers, KGB technicians into US security specialists, nationalists into cosmopolitans, and back to nationalists, etc.

The book is the outcome of over three hundred in-depth interviews conducted over a three-year period (from 2013 through 2015) in Russia and around the world by a team of Russian, US, French, and Dutch scholars.[3] While the practitioners we have studied are regularly covered by popular media (Bowles 2017; Shane, Sanger, and Perlroth 2017), discussed in business publications, and reported upon in foreign-policy think tanks, they have as a whole received scant scholarly attention, and almost none in academic Anglophone literature (Bardham and Kroll 2006; Borjas and Doran 2012; Feakins 2009; Freinkman, Gonchar, and Kuznetsov 2013; Ganguli 2015; Lonkila 2011). The Russian IT sphere is one of successful private enterprises, greatly varying in size. Despite the limited availability of venture capital in Russia, Yandex and Kaspersky have grown into large companies on par with some of their Silicon Valley competitors. At the other end of the spectrum, thousands of self-employed programmers work on projects without formal labor contracts. Despite the efforts of IT trade associations like Russoft to understand market morphology and the population of programmers actually working in Russia, the actual lay of the land for both companies and individual practitioners has been highly speculative. *From Russia with Code* offers a much more granular picture of the specific, often daily practices of these actors than can be provided by statistical aggregations or high-level policy papers. It provides a unique window onto a Russia that lies beyond the headlines of political and economic media reports—a Russia of technicians, but also of civic hackers who are trying to reshape Russian politics from the bottom up, strongly committed to avoiding both old Soviet and neoliberal Western political templates.

Methodologically heterogeneous, our project is inspired by multisited ethnography, though in this case different sites are analyzed by different chapters authored by different scholars. The chapters sample different practices, goals, and sites of Russian computer scientists, software specialists, hackers, and IT entrepreneurs, but are not aimed at constructing a holistic comparative global picture. Rather,

> comparison emerges from putting questions to an emergent object of study whose contours, sites, and relationships are not known beforehand, but are themselves a contribution of making an account that has different, complexly connected real-world sites of investigation. The object of study is ultimately mobile and multiply situated, so any ethnography of such an object will have a comparative dimension that is integral to it, in the form of juxtapositions of phenomena that conventionally have appeared to be (or conceptually have been kept) "worlds apart." Comparison re-enters the very act of ethnographic specification by a research design of juxtapositions in which the global is collapsed into and made an integral of parallel, related local situations rather than something monolithic or external to them. (Marcus 1995, 102)

In particular, we believe that George Marcus's critique of the conception of the global as something monolithic or external to local situations may be usefully applied to Russia itself. The local materials and analyses put forward by the chapters are not framed by a preset relationship with "Russia" as a stable framework that contextualizes these local studies and organizes their comparisons, but are presented as sites in which post-Soviet Russia is constructed through and in relation with those local situations.

The perspectives that we have borrowed both from multisited ethnographies and from science and technology studies turn *From Russia with Code* into a study of mobilities that does not easily fit the template of diaspora studies. A focus on the movement (domestic and global) and on the constantly outward gaze of highly skilled practitioners is central to the book, but it is articulated primarily through an attention to the technological specificity of this population—code, coding skills and practices, and the social assemblages that are sometimes built through and around code—and how that frames both their migration options and their sense of being "Russian" (which often collides with the professional identity that comes with being a programmer, a computer scientist, or an IT person). This is a population in movement and whose movements—as shown by Marinichev's remarks about the challenges that IT brain drain poses to Russian sovereignty—have created issues for a state that has long assigned populations to their specific cities.

While there may seem to be some family resemblance between our chapters and the genre of diaspora studies, the research object is quite different. Our questions do not concern the transformative effects of distance on memories of and connection to the motherland, or on the organization of diasporic communities. That is not only because the Russian motherland is an openly unstable construct, but especially because "distance" is not the right concept to capture the inherently tense relation between two very different modalities of identity formation that we find in our material. One is tied to the specific skills of the migrant practitioners of a technical discipline with inherently fuzzy boundaries and a deterritorialized ethos—skills that are conducive to the formation of distinctly nondiasporic communities and publics, like those associated with the free software and open source movements. The other modality of identity formation is, instead, virtually antithetical to the first one, developed by a state with a long tradition of population control. At the same time, the technical skills that these practitioners are internationally appreciated for and identified with—the same skills that make them highly moveable and put them on a centrifugal trajectory away from the pull of the Russian state—are skills they have developed through the very specific Russian (and formerly Soviet) educational system.

This unavoidable tension questions the meaning of both "diasporic population" and "motherland," but it also complicates in interesting ways the multisited stories told in this volume. Multisited studies have treated seriously the territories of activities that used to be described without attention to their spatiality—hence the typical study of local and distributed deployments of one object, like a drug tracked from the labs of the pharmaceutical company designing it in Cambridge to the offices of the medical doctors prescribing it in Argentina and the websites where patients comment on the effects of its consumption on their health. But despite this grounding and spatialization of the object and its movements and transformations, multisited analyses have tended to treat territories as *relative* coordinates of objects, which are often as emergent as their trajectories.

But while Russian computer scientists and IT specialists are as dispersed across the world as pharmaceutical drugs are, their movements also make visible, and make sense from, a specific coordinate system. These subjects are Russian (in the specifically constructed sense discussed above), looking with either frustration or nostalgia to their motherland (often perceived through the polarized "Russia v. The World" narrative), while simultaneously exploiting and reinforcing the "Russian software specialists" brand that gives them an edge in the global labor market. In this sense, Russia is not just a departure point but a point of reference for their movements, including the decision to stay put. Their Russianness is constructed and ever changing, but it is also the proverbial elephant in the room, large enough to inflect the otherwise uniform coordinate system of multisited ethnographies.

SETTING THE STAGE

Dmitry Marinichev's frustration is somewhat understandable because coding, unlike most other high-tech disciplines, is predominantly labor intensive—a fact that greatly reduces the government's possible policy levers. Software production's low capital requirements are what made Russia one of the most successful countries for the offshoring of high-end coding projects immediately after the collapse of the Soviet Union; all that foreign companies needed to do was send over some laptops and a bit of cash and that might be enough for a Russian techie to start a company.[4] For example, in 1992 you could hire a good programmer for $100 a month. But the other side of this same coin is that the Russian government finds it very difficult to retain IT specialists, as compared to retaining or attracting back physicists, chemists, or biologists. While the latter require sophisticated and generally expensive facilities—and are thus likely to respond to policies that would provide them with these resources[5]—most IT specialists seek jobs rather than laboratories or companies. Because they travel light (and thus easily) the Russian government can do little to control their movement short of restricting emigration, thus effectively treating them as potential defectors. This is most likely what Marinichev had in mind when claiming that "preparing IT specialists for foreign-base technologies is essentially to undermine Russia's sovereignty."

Dmitry Korobov's story also contains specifically Russian elements: while he is certainly not the first software thief we have heard of, his remarks (if we are to believe them) point to a dramatic lack of funding opportunities for tech startups. Coders like Korobov are allegedly reduced to theft in order to become entrepreneurs, pushing the figurative link between pirates and entrepreneurs to a new level (Clay and Phillip 2015; Durant and Vergne 2012; Ramadan et al. 2016). But, setting his piratico-entrepreneurial visions aside, Korobov (if we are to believe the way he has been represented in the media) seemed to have had extraordinarily little sense of the market value of the goods he was selling, or of how to go about planning or executing such a heist. Of course, one may be tempted to discount this vignette as a mere reflection of Korobov's limited skill set, but the presence of a significant gap between technical ability and entrepreneurial skill has emerged in several of our interviews of Russian IT specialists, suggesting a pattern that moves beyond individual specificities.

There are several true success stories in the Russian IT industry—Yandex being a globally prominent one—but they are the results of extraordinarily steep learning curves in business culture, not just technical innovation. In the mid-1990s, for instance, budding Russian IT entrepreneurs lacked not only MBAs but familiarity with basic business practices. Arkadiy Khotin, the founder of Arcadia—one of Saint Petersburg's earliest software companies that is still going strong today—recalls that in 1994, when he began working on projects for foreign clients, "I had no idea about how to speak of the terms of payment. I had no idea of the concept of things like retainers. My Soviet mentality did not allow me to ask. I was waiting for them to offer. . . . [That] was not very good because when someone asked me how much I wanted to be paid for this activity, I had no idea how to arrive at an appropriate figure. . . . In trying to price a small project I had no idea how to say it would be about $500 or it would be in the lower hundreds of dollars" (quoted in Lonkila 2011, 28).

Things were not much different in 1996: "I definitely had raised some interest but I had a [*sic*] zero marketing skills including a lack of understanding of how to follow-up. I even went [to a meeting in Finland] without business cards. They said we will send you something but they did not even know my e-mail address" (Khotin, quoted in Lonkila 2011, 29).[6] This was clearly not the result of a Soviet-style rejection of bourgeois business mentality. On the contrary, what we see in Russia from the 1990s all the way up to the present is a genuine appreciation—often bordering on mythification—of the discourse of innovation and entrepreneurship, though not one that is always coupled with competence in Western entrepreneurial practices and expectations. Since the early 1990s, however, things have dramatically changed. Still, despite a craze for business workshops, online training materials, and translations of Western textbooks, there remains a noticeable gap between the level of available mathematical, technical, and coding skills and the familiarity with entrepreneurial practices and culture, especially at the periphery of the Russian Federation.[7]

This may help to explain why Russian programmers tend to do very well when they move abroad or are hired by the Russian branches of foreign companies, that is, in contexts where their technical skills are put to work in environments that already have their business organization and infrastructure in place.[8] While coding is a skill young Russians can learn at school, in afterschool computer clubs, in coding competitions, or even on the web, business culture is another matter altogether.[9] Those IT entrepreneurs who went into business just after the collapse of the Soviet Union typically credit their business training not to workshops and classes but to interactions with their Western foreign customers—often initiated by informal or simply out-of-the-blue email contacts whose rate of success was only slightly better than spam. It was through early offshoring work that the first post-Soviet generation of coders slowly turned into entrepreneurs, learning their foreign clients' practices and cultures while also learning how to talk to them and understand what their expectations were so as to build trust and, in some cases, long-term business relations.

It goes without saying that given the virtual absence of domestic training resources, neither the informal but remarkably rapid learning process nor business opportunities would have been possible without access first to FidoNet (from the late 1980s on) and then to Relcom, Free-Net, and the internet, which became available in the early 1990s (for those with some affiliation to a university or academic institute, as several first-wave Russian entrepreneurs had) (Peters 2016). In a literal sense, the Russian IT industry was itself a product of IT. One must also credit the cyberinfrastructure for much of the English-language training—however approximate it may have been—that Russian coders were able to access early on.[10] Despite the increased demand for English-language education in Russian schools (where high schoolers are now required to learn two foreign languages) and plans to introduce a nationwide mandatory English test by 2020 (*Moscow Times* 2005), there remains a substantial gap between the English-language proficiency of Russian IT specialists and those from competitor countries such as India, Ireland, Korea, and Israel.

Arcadia's Khotin (who did not seem to know about business cards in 1994 and was taught how to write proper English business letters by a US acquaintance around 1998)[11] was proud to report in 2009 that his company (which now employs close to five hundred people) is "a top notch specialist in major technologies on the Microsoft platform. *But overall our strongest point is people management, project management and business process organization because this is the most important part.* We call it PPP—People, Processes, Projects" (Cook Report 2009, 22; emphasis in the original). The dramatic shift that Arcadia experienced between 1996 and 2009—moving from an emphasis on superior coding and low cost to superior people-management skills, down to the American-style use of acronyms like "PPP"—was the result of many interactions with important clients (like Johnson and Johnson) that lasted over years, turning into quasi-partnerships (Cook Report 2009, 20–21). However, companies doing offshoring work are not uniformly distributed across the Russian Federation, but tend to cluster in cities with major international airports. The opportunity for informal business training through interactions with foreign customers is therefore rarer in the provinces, or for the many IT specialists working for the domestic market.[12]

The widespread imbalance between technical skills and entrepreneurial competence, however, ceases to be a problem when we look at the third vignette about the Virtual Rynda project. There, substantial IT skills are not directed toward the commercial sphere, and platforms and applications are not being developed with an eye to selling or licensing; rather, they are seen as contributions to the establishment of a new body politic. In these cases, business competence becomes relatively irrelevant compared to technical skills and an eye for identifying spaces and windows of opportunity for political intervention.

The connection between IT and democratic movements is quite direct in Russia, going back to the undoing of the August 1991 attempted coup d'état against Mikhail Gorbachev and his reform program. On that occasion, according to Rafal Rohozinski:

> The programmers at one of Russia's private Net providers—Relcom/ Demos—were among the first to testify to the coup from their offices near the Kremlin. Within a few minutes of tanks appearing in Red Square, they began broadcasting information to network nodes across the USSR. . . . Within hours, they had established a temporary network node at the White House and were e-mailing Yeltsin's defiant declaration, rejecting the legitimacy of the coup committee, to Russia's regions and abroad. . . . By evening, the Relcom network was acting as a major channel of information between Moscow and the regions. . . . The information vacuum, a key factor in the coup plotters' game plan, was filled. (Rohozinski 1999, 1–2)[13]

"Civic hackers" remain key players in Russia today, less dramatically but much more pervasively than in 1991. For them, IT innovation and practice is not just a way to develop better and cheaper products or profitable companies, but also a technically sophisticated attempt to develop new forms of politics and democratic participation. From monitoring elections to filing complaints about failing urban infrastructure with the appropriate authorities, their goal is not to achieve "efficiencies" but to change politics. Their projects are simultaneously mundane and utopian, directed at local problems in the present but aimed at rethinking future politics at the national level. One could say, perhaps, that Russian hackers (of both the civic and dark variety) are particularly effective because their practices require virtually no business skills.

This may also explain the specific kind of attraction that young Russian IT specialists have for the free software movement, for hacker culture, and for informal collaborative worksites like hackerspaces (Davies 2017). In most developed countries, these sympathies often index a commitment to alternative business cultures (or plainly antibusiness attitudes), but the Russian love for free software and hackerism may reflect the values of a community that, for better or for worse, has never been part of a traditional business culture. Is the Russian hacker a business idiot savant?

AMBIVALENT EXCELLENCE

Russian computer scientists are globally sought after by major IT firms, their desirability enhanced by the success of teenage Russian "prodigies" who regularly win the IBM-sponsored Association for Computing Machinery's International Collegiate Programming Contest (ACM ICPC) and other computer science competitions organized by major players in the IT global scene, such as Facebook, Microsoft, and Google. (Students from Saint Petersburg State University won the 2016 ICPC, ahead of Harvard [third] and MIT [sixth], with five Russian universities in the top ten finishers. Between 2000 and 2016, Russian universities won the ICPC eleven times.)

The appreciation of the Russians' coding skills is neither new nor limited to academic circles. Back in 2001, the "Whitepaper on Offshore Software Development" by the American Chamber of Commerce in Russia described the "special characteristics" of Russian coders, and their roots: "Russia's major advantage over other common offshore software development locales is the technical skills and education of its workforce. Russia has more personnel working in R&D [research and development] than any other country, and ranks 3rd in the world for per capita number of scientists and engineers.... Initially trained for research careers in physics, engineering, or mathematics, they switched to IT instead, having 'mastered' new programming languages and other skills for which there was demand" (American Chamber 2001, 4; quoted in Gapova 2006). Jason Horowitz, Sun Microsystems' Russian project team manager, is more categorical. In his view the coders whom Sun employs in Ireland, Israel, India, and the Czech Republic "don't have anywhere near the talent [of] the Russians," who are specifically "stronger at tasks that require deeper mathematical backgrounds" (quoted in Peterson 2005).[14]

But RCS are also followed, at times foreshadowed, by a very different kind of reputation: "After the fall of the Soviet Union, most Russian specialists lost their jobs, some went abroad, others turned to criminal activities. Everyone knows that the best viruses are written in Russia."[15] Hackers originating from ex-communist countries—people who might belong to the same communities as those of the international computer science competitions—have been accused of carrying out cyberattacks on various Western targets, most recently against the US Democratic National Committee (DNC). Cold War memories are thus reactivated by the narratives that Europe and the US have recently developed about Russian hackers, narratives that simultaneously celebrate and fear the technical excellence passed down from the Soviet period. The same applies to the other side in the trenches of cyberwarfare. One of the most globally respected cybersecurity firms—the Moscow-based Kaspersky Labs—was founded by a graduate of the Institute of Cryptography, Telecommunications, and Computer Science at the Federal Security Service of Russia—a school that was previously part of the Technical Faculty of the KGB Higher School.

Russian hackers are perceived as a worrisome mix of Soviet rigor and new Cold cyber-War operatives. At the same time, they can also be seen as epitomizing the ultimate non-Soviet subject, not just as embodiments of neoliberal ideology but also as self-trained anarchists with little allegiance to institutions, authorities, and nations. And while that mentality may worry the ruling classes, it could also be a rather valuable business skill. According to the American Chamber of Commerce in Russia (2001, 11; quoted in Gapova 2006, 5), "many Russian software programmers are self-taught, partially explaining their reputation as hackers who can think outside the box."

These polarized narratives about the different figures of the Russian computer scientist are not accidental but rather index the tense political and ideological environment of technological innovation in post-Soviet Russia.

Because of its nature, IT sits exactly at the intersection between technology, business, and politics. At the economic level, it may be the Russians' best option to end what former President (and now Prime Minister) Dmitry Medvedev (2009) called "our country's humiliating dependence on raw materials." At the same time, being so closely connected to communication and to the development of new platforms for political participation, IT is a prime tool for political criticism, activism, and whistleblowing. Russian computer scientists develop software, computational media, and communication networks and do so while inhabiting them at the same time. They are the vectors of information in the Russian Federation not only because they work on information technologies but because they are the sector of the population that is most exposed to the information disseminated by those technologies, much of it coming from outside the Russian Federation. They are techies but, precisely as a result of being techies, they are also carriers and disseminators of new information and modes of thinking.

DREAMS OF INNOVATION ECOLOGIES

During his presidential tenure, Medvedev vowed to return Russian science and technology to their due rank among the most developed nations of the world by making major investments in areas that had been left to their own devices as public funding virtually vanished with the collapse of the Soviet Union in the early 1990s. The restoration of Russian techno-scientific pride, however, was not aimed at recreating the old Russia but at modernizing and democratizing the present one—"modernization" being mobilized as something between a keyword and a magic incantation.

Information technologies were among the "five strategic vectors for the economic modernisation of our country" that Medvedev identified in his famous "Go Russia!" article of September 2009, a manifesto-like text that was perhaps more representative of his own personal views and desires than those of the Russian government as a whole. Brain drain was flagged as a key problem—"Our best specialists are headhunted by the world's largest companies and universities"—and Russian scientists of all stripes were subsequently courted to return to the motherland and participate in a full-fledged national modernization effort. This time, however, the modernization process was cast as neither imperial nor communist but democratic: "Today is the first time in our history that we have a chance to prove to ourselves and the world that Russia can develop in a democratic way." In that grand plan, information technology was part of both a new economic vision and a new political project: "The growth of modern information technologies, something we will do our best to facilitate, gives us unprecedented opportunities for the realisation of fundamental political freedoms, such as freedom of speech and assembly. It allows us to identify and eliminate hotbeds of corruption. . . . It facilitates the direct exchange of views and knowledge between people all around the world. Society is becoming more open and transparent than ever—even if the ruling class does not necessarily like this" (Medvedev 2009).

His frequent references to the "intelligent economy" suggest that Medvedev saw information technologies as paving the way toward both new forms of democratic politics and new forms of economic value production. Rather than the traditional Chicago-style privatization dogma of the young economists who had set Russia on a wild ride to liberalization in the early 1990s, Medvedev and his advisors seemed to model their vision of the new Russian economy after the innovation ecologies of MIT and greater Boston, or Stanford and Silicon Valley. Information technology was thus key to growing the new Russia, both economically and politically and, in Medvedev's view, the state (rather than the market alone) was best situated to propel that transformation, while simultaneously regulating it.

Despite the political rivalry that characterizes American-Russian relations, key figures of the Russian government like Medvedev and other presidential advisors are enamored of Silicon Valley and, more generally, of the US system of science and technology R&D supported by federal agencies and by technology transfer policies from the university to the private sector. During his highly visible 2010 visit to Palo Alto, Medvedev gave a talk at Stanford in which, reading from his iPad, he told his audience: "It is not by chance that I came here. I wanted to see with my own eyes the origins of success" (quoted in Joseph 2010). His goal was to create relations and partnerships to replicate that success at a new Russian "innopolis," which was to be built at Skolkovo, on the outskirts of Moscow. His plans for a new high-tech city that would also include Skoltech, a new university modeled after and developed in partnership with MIT, testified to these hopes for the future and techno-scientific aspirations. Skolkovo's goal was to develop an innovation ecology able to prevent brain drain not just by providing generous funding but by creating the conditions of possibility for making scientists and entrepreneurs *want* to remain in Russia (Braunerhjelm and Feldman 2007; Kenney and Mowery 2014; Lecuyer 2005; Saxenian 2000).

Medvedev's vision, however, has not materialized, not even by a long shot.[16] Skolkovo never took off the way it had been imagined, its relationship with MIT souring after a promising but brief honeymoon. And while the Russian IT sector has kept growing, it has not had the transformative effect the former president hoped for. In particular, the conspicuous, capital-intensive, and forward-looking innovation policies behind the establishment of Skolkovo seem ineffectual at harnessing the potential of the RCS community that, more often than not, continues to opt for emigration. Then, following the 2011–12 mobilization of students and liberal groups demanding transparency during the presidential election and the accountability of political leaders, the government began to exercise growing control on traditional media. The ecosystem of information has changed quite dramatically, to the point that the rare, but thriving, sources of critical information in the Russian Federation (e.g., the TV channel Dozhd' [Russian for "rain"] and the news platform Slon) have nearly all disappeared, thus leaving the web as the sole source of alternative information for people who, by and large, no longer believe in the new democratic modernizing alliance between government, scientists, technologists, and IT specialists articulated in "Go Russia!"

HISTORICAL PRIDE OR PRESENT CURSE?

The RCS provide interesting food for thought because of the technical and emergent entrepreneurial dimensions of their work but also because of the multiple ways in which they embody both the imaginaries about a future Russia and the tense connections between present Russia and its Soviet past.

Russian computer scientists are hailed for ushering modernity into post-Soviet Russia by exemplifying new forms of e-citizenry—the "bright" side of hackerism—and offering some hope for the emergence of a strong IT industry that will help wean the Russian economy off its dominant extractive industries. At the same time, the RCS are firmly connected to the Soviet past through the school system and its curriculum, which formed generations of formidable Soviet mathematicians and physicists and even now continues to provide the foundation of this community's distinctive technical skills—skills that, based on both the results of international coding contests and the opinions of experts, are widely recognized as outstanding.

The Soviet genealogy of today's RCS, however, is unusually specific. Unlike disciplines whose present identity is still framed by their Soviet past through substantial continuities in their institutional and sociopolitical "hardware"—from the Soviet Academy of Sciences, to engineers' factories, biologists' laboratories and agricultural research stations, and physicists' accelerators and weapons labs—the Russian computer scientists' link to the

Soviet period is through "disciplinary software."[17] The RCS are connected to the past much more through pedagogical traditions than brick-and-mortar laboratories, factories, and professional organizations (which, in the case of the software industry, were established only in 1999).[18] We could say, perhaps, that while most disciplines had and still have extensive links to many parts of the state and government apparatus, the only elements of the Soviet system that are still directly traceable to today's RCS are the schools they frequented (especially the *fizmat* high schools that specialized in math and physics), the curriculum they followed, the teachers they had, and the Math Olympiads they went to with their fellow math students.

Nonetheless, as some of our chapters show, while the connection between modern Russian computer scientists and the old Soviet system may be limited in institutional terms—often confined to the students' relationship to their schools—it is also quite tight; it may be a small umbilical cord, but it is a strong one. Several of our interviewees indicate that it was those personal and pedagogical experiences that made them who they are professionally, shaping what they perceive as a uniquely Russian coding style. This is a mark of identity, not just of professional competence, though the two halves often merge, turning "Russian programmer" into a brand that signifies both origin and quality.

Somewhat paradoxically, the RCS who join the flows of the global brain drain do so precisely because they are Russians, because of the distinctive skills they have acquired as Russians. In this sense, the brain drain could be read as both a source of pride and a curse, or as hope for a future of technological and industrial innovation that is simultaneously possibly within reach and possibly already foreclosed. Because of their reputation (and because of their inherent mobility and relatively low need for institutional support) these specialists often flow away like oil and gas—precisely the resources that Russia hopes to wean itself away from by developing a strong IT industry. From the Russian point of view, brain drain may look like a tragic tale of technology transfer.

THE PROJECT

From Russia with Code is a contribution to science, technology, and innovation studies, focusing simultaneously on technological matters like software and IT development and on the difficult emergence of the new Russian public sphere, which is closely tied to the development of an entrepreneurial economy and a new set of related values.[19] Entrepreneurship is about competition (rather than government plans and policies) but it also requires some notion of trust that is not tied to one's place in a rigid social configuration like a Soviet *kollektiv*, or collective (Kharkhordin 1999).[20] As direct proponents of the digital economy, RCS are thus involved in developing new tools and products while also articulating new (and distinctly non-Soviet) forms of collaboration and accountability. Paraphrasing the famous Russian saying that "a poet in Russia is more than a poet," we believe that in the current political Russian context, software is about a lot more than software.

Recent anthropological studies of populations of software developers, hackers, and hacktivists have shown how their ethos is rooted in technical expertise but also in the appreciation of the unique transparency of computer language and the collaborations enabled by that transparency (Coleman 2012; Kelty 2008; Levy 2010; Takhteyev 2012). The traditional Mertonian divide between the openness of scientific knowledge and proprietary views of industrial expertise and secrets ruled out the cultivation of hybrid professional identities and ethos. Whether or not Merton's divide ever existed in the past, it seems to have disappeared today, as demonstrated by the university/industry partnerships that are now the norm in the US and Europe. At the same time, we also find a growing presence of free and open source software in for-profit environments, suggesting that the shareability of code is not seen as antithetical to business and entrepreneurial logic.

The renegotiation of traditional business culture assumptions that often goes under the name of "open innovation"—however hyped and vague that notion may be—is central to the kind of economy associated with the IT industry (Chesbrough 2005). Because of historical contingencies, however, the emergent Russian IT community engages that "renegotiation" from a distinctly different direction. The question is not how to modify the assumptions of a liberal economy and its understanding of how, as Yochai Benkler (2006) has argued, wealth can be produced by networks, but rather to articulate new notions and practices of collective endeavor that bypass the hierarchical and top-down modus operandi of the Marxist Leninist tradition.

A team at the European University at Saint Petersburg (EUSP) has studied at length the organizational forms mobilized by different groups of contemporary Russian technology entrepreneurs (not limited to IT), and the ways they narrativize their goals and values to themselves and others (Gladarev et al. 2013).[21] One of the project's key findings matched the observation shared by many historians of Russian science and technology;[22] namely, that Russian engineers claim to be "taken by their creation" and are driven by the "love of their work-in-progress (*razrabotka*)" (Kharkhordin

2014, 36). Interestingly, this is not a feeling they found expressed in their interviews of tech entrepreneurs from Finland, South Korea, and Taiwan (Kharkhordin 2014, 27–35). Russian tech entrepreneurs (like the earlier Russian scientists and engineers studied by historians) claimed that both the technical work of innovation and the building of a tech startup are labors of love and dedication, quasi-spiritual calls toward the articulation of the new and still embryonic technological system or device.

The emphasis and value, however, is placed on the working prototype or on the launching of a company rather than on the allegedly less creative labor of bringing the product to market, or growing one's company. Or, to reuse the parental metaphors deployed by several interviewees, their narratives emphasize the "delivery" of their children—the "prototypes"—rather than their growing up into mature products or technologies. As "Olga," an academic chemist and entrepreneur, put it:

> [As for] all those people who really swarm into business, especially the high-tech business, you really need to be crazy to decide on doing it. Often, I think, they are driven more by, say, a love of their work-in-progress. . . . So when they start working on something, at first they are driven, naturally, by all kinds of scientific [impulses]—I want to try this, I want to do this. Then, when [they] have done it, [they wonder] what it would be like in manufactured form. And when someone suddenly asks what it would be like in manufactured form, they are stuck. Because then they also have to be involved in commercialization. (Kharkhordin 2014, 37)

The phase between the prototype and the successfully marketed product is where things often come to a halt for aspiring Russian entrepreneurs. Unlike those in business cultures where product development traverses a path that goes all the way to the market phase with considerations of pricing and distribution, Russian technological entrepreneurs tend to insulate their ideas from such business imperatives. The result of this general posture is a long series of failures, from the nineteenth century onward, which Loren Graham compiles in a depressingly long list that would make any venture capitalist think thrice before investing money in Russia (Graham 2013).

Olga's narrative, however, shows an interesting new spin on the "love-for-the-prototype" model. For her, commercialization is part of the same "work-in-progress aesthetics" that motivated her creative work to begin with: "I was more involved in [the] realm of innovation, but I did not give chemistry up . . . perhaps they are now on an equal footing. . . . That is, I both work on my own work-in-progress—I have a research group and various grad students—and there is the commercial part, where as an entrepreneur, I manage this work-in-progress myself and put science into practice. I realize no one else but me is as keen on implementing it" (Kharkhordin 2014, 37).

The many interviews collected by the EUSP team show that today's Russian tech entrepreneurs still represent themselves as different from (and superior to) "normal" business people in that they are not motivated by money but by the "love of the work in progress"—something that has been desired rather than needed, and whose completion is not as compelling as its conception. Of course money is not at all disparaged, and in fact some "fully liberalized" entrepreneurs present money making as their prime incentive. However, other techno-entrepreneurs, perhaps those more connected to their Soviet backgrounds, present money not just as revenue but as a "symbolic reward": "An IPO is when shares are put up for sale. My desire is to get a high valuation from someone for every share. . . . The goal is not to sell . . . [but] more to achieve a certain recognition, that yes, B****'s shares are worth so much today. . . . For a businessman, an IPO is this pure *selfeksperiens* [self-experience]" (Kharkhordin 2014, 10). It is not difficult to see in these narratives the reflection of Soviet notions of personhood and work as separate from individual economic success—traditional notions that are now being merged (largely through the translations of Anglophone business studies literature) with bourgeois concepts of self-realization through creative work (Kharkhordin 2014, 23).

Western liberals or neoliberals may argue that this element of the Soviet heritage—the dismissal or de-emphasizing of monetary incentives—is an obstacle on the path to entrepreneurial culture and should thus be dispensed with, the sooner the better. But if we go back to Olga's remarks we see that there is something else, something more striking than just the emphasis on the "creative purity" of the tech entrepreneur (as opposed to the tech businessperson). Like many of the other Russian interviewees, Olga expresses a clearly individualistic view of innovation—"No one else but me is keen to . . ." This does not seem identical to the "rugged individualism" of Western entrepreneurs, but more like an emphasis on the agency of the individual as distinct from or even opposed to the collectivism of the Soviet period. It may be an extension of her ethos as a scientist who, even in the USSR, cultivated a notion of the individual through creative work (though that work was done in the interest of the collective).

We believe, then, that the much-documented entrepreneurial failures of Russian scientists and engineers throughout history may not be the tragic outcome of the technological creators' absolute commitment to the integrity of their creations, taking them to their grave to make them die pure rather than grow corrupted. In our view this attachment to an uncompromising model of invention may not stem from a chimeric infatuation with purity, but rather signal a mundane lack of trust in collective modes of organization—the kind of collaborative activities necessary to turn an invention into an innovation. Unlike the operations of the inventor's mind, bringing an invention to market requires a collaborative and adaptable ethos able to encompass the love for the inventive process, the love for profit, and the ability to engage and sustain collaborations involving both openness and the production of commercial value.

This was not something that was cultivated in the USSR, when both science and technology were predominantly managed by the state in a centralized fashion, premised on a scientific division of labor and a hierarchical mode of operations. The Soviet system did embody a collective mode of action, but not one of collaboration, at least of the kind that seems to animate the so-called knowledge economy. But even if not flexible enough to foster innovation, it was nonetheless a collective mode of action, and its collapse (coupled with the generally negative feelings that Russians had left for this particular model or experience) seemed to make the very idea of a collective mode of action unpalatable to the post-Soviet generation.

Studying the RCS communities, both in Russia and abroad, has thus allowed us to analyze the processes (and the remarkable challenges) through which a new entrepreneurial culture emerges—not just a technology or "commercial mentality" but the entire skill set required to work with others by developing grassroots norms of both trust and accountability. Comparing RCS operating in Russia with those who migrate abroad or collaborate with foreign colleagues provides additional evidence on the role that the possibility of geographic mobility plays on their decision to bridge science and collective enterprises, and how and where that tends to happen.

TOPICAL CLUSTERS

The volume includes thirteen chapters grouped into four sections: "Coding Collectives"; "Outward-Looking Enclaves"; "Russian Maps"; and "Bridges and Mismatches."

"Coding Collectives" focuses on the relation one finds in today's Russia between certain kinds of coding and certain kinds of professional and political identities, as new social formations are coming into being through a shared concern with the development of computer languages, software, and apps. The relation between code and identity (in this case disciplinary identity) goes all the way back to the establishment of Soviet computer science and its differentiation from both mathematics and cybernetics, but identity issues take very different forms among contemporary Russian civic hackers (for whom code is both a means and a form of politics), as well as among the employees of Yandex, for whom reading and writing code functions as a rite of initiation into the professional culture and coding style of that corporation.

Scholars of computer codes, especially Friedrich Kittler (2008, 40–47), have long pointed to their duality. Computer codes are written in languages that need to be executed by machines, thus leaving no space for semantic ambiguities. At the same time, and for the same reason, there is a specific sociality to code in the sense that it sets specific conditions of possibility for the ways in which people can collaborate with and through it. Programs instructing a computer to perform a certain task may be written in a wide variety of languages, with different individual coding styles. But this remarkable diversity does not imply semantic ambiguity. Any language that is compilable and executable by a computer needs to be ambiguity free, which also means that those humans who collaborate and create new publics through codes and coding are facilitated in doing so by the fact that their codes are unambiguous not only to the computer but to their human partners too. The formal linguistic nonambiguity of code offers a political vector of community formation by providing a platform for collaboration among humans from different places and cultures, and with different values. Of course, ambiguities and negotiations do not disappear but are rather relocated from the site of coding to other moments of the collaboration, like discussions about its design, goal, structure, maintenance, membership, etc. But the nimbleness and collaboration-enabling features of code were not always there.

Just a few decades ago computer science was associated with large vertically managed facilities, with strict access rules, that could be found only in a few countries in the world. In chapter 1, Ksenia Tatarchenko recounts the Soviet history of that trajectory, looking at Andrey Ershov's commitment to fashion computer science as a discipline with an open and collaborative ethos that was rather unusual during the Cold War, possibly foreshadowing later associations between code-based practices, collaboration, and emergent communities and publics. Contrary to today's popular image of Russian programmers as the heirs to the Soviet Union's KGB, Ershov worked hard to promote a distinctly Soviet version of computers, languages, and their programmers that were meant to function as the new pillars of a peaceful civilization uniting the East and the West. Such porous geopolitics are now resurfacing in many new experimental coding practices, like the hackathons that Ksenia Ermoshina discusses in this volume.

Ermoshina's chapter on contemporary Russian hacktivists offers a window on the sharp tension between the libertarian values of the Silicon Valley ethos and long-held principles of communal help that hark back to an idealized Soviet past. Codes and protocols of information gathering, formatting, and sharing have become central to the conversation animating these emergent collectives, providing not just a means but a form for the new modes of political participation they are developing. Codes also enable quick and efficient collaborations by allowing partners to come together around nothing more than a computer screen—a strikingly minimalist scenario compared to the facilities-intensive collaborations one finds in contemporary physics or biology.

In the age of laptops and tablets, the new Russian excellence in coding is no longer tied to large infrastructures or to the strict organizational and planned structure of Soviet science. But the natural experiment that we describe in these chapters goes beyond the immediate effects of this new looser format of practice. The commerce of codes and coders has created economic value that did not and could not exist in the Soviet system, when intangible goods were not recognized sources of national wealth. In her chapter, Marina Fedorova looks at Yandex—the darling of Russian IT companies—and the role of its source codes in the socialization of its employees. Unlike the old Soviet rules and disciplinary practices that charted the coming into being of good communist subjects, the new code is designed not only to instruct machines but also to foster communication between employees—a kind of communication that has disciplining effects but not preset ones. Also, familiarity with code gives employees skills that, far from being exclusively of local use, become assets that are readily fungible in the labor market. Reading and writing a company's code fashions one into a corporate subject, but also makes one easily and quickly movable beyond that company and its geographical location. Computing codes thus have two intriguing features: they are said to be computationally universal (when they can simulate any Turing machine), but such mechanico-algorithmic universality immediately translates into commercial universality. They are inherently mobile in the conceptual, technical, and commercial sense of the term, and for the same reason. Taken together, the chapters of "Coding Collectives" show some of the different ways in which this duality of code plays out in specific Soviet and post-Soviet Russian situations.

"Outward-Looking Enclaves" considers domestic professional IT enclaves that look abroad for business opportunities, modes of collaboration, or just lines of professional escape. These communities are also the direct heirs to the "science cities" that epitomized Soviet science (Josephson 1997).[23] Populated through massive post–World War II internal migrations like those that brought more than fifty thousand scientists and their families to Siberia's Akademgorodok or to smaller communities like Pushchino and Dubna, these cities were usually shielded from some of the hardships of the Soviet system and developed their own cultures as techno-scientific communes, at times transgressive of Soviet dogma (Tatarchenko 2013). Before the actual physical movement of scientists and young entrepreneurs away from Russia, some Soviet science and high-tech communities were already "moving" not only by relocating and concentrating in other parts of the country but also by developing outward-looking perspectives.

Since the collapse of the USSR, Akademgorodok has been dubbed the "Silicon Forest," due to the many IT startups that have emerged around and on the ashes of this former Soviet academic city (Wainwright 2016). These entrepreneurial developments have held on, albeit in mutated form, to their older ethos of autonomy and outward-looking perspectives, developing models that, as Andrey Indukaev argues in chapter 7, are significantly independent of the Russian state while also distinct from the forms of university-industry collaboration one finds in the US.

Aleksandra Simonova's analysis of Skolkovo—the large technopark recently built at the outskirts of Moscow in a collaboration between the Russian government and MIT—summons the image of the Soviet science city, though one that is not just outward looking but actually developed with foreigners to mimic as closely as possible emblematic high-tech sites like the Cambridge-Boston area or Silicon Valley. At the same time, both Skolkovo and the much smaller and more informal hackerspaces also discussed by Simonova are inward and outward looking at the same time. Skolkovo blends the traditional Soviet model of the science city with Western ecologies like Silicon Valley and its many global reproductions. Similarly, the Moscow hackerspaces borrow and exemplify a kind of collaborative space that has become emblematic of the global innovation scene. Still, despite their obvious outward orientation, their goals are distinctly inward: to create suitable environments for Russian IT innovators to occupy at home. They try to bring the West into Russia so that Russian innovators do not feel they have to leave for the West.

In Vladivostok, at Russia's eastern edge, the gaze of the IT community turned outward not as a byproduct of the Soviet government's centralized planning of the military-scientific complex or of the more recent but equally centralized attempts by the Russian government to develop domestic Silicon Valleys. On the shores of the Pacific, looking outward came with the territory, from being at the periphery of the empire, much closer to China, Japan, Korea, and Pacific networks of exchange than to Moscow. As Aleksandra Masalskaya and Zinaida Vasilyeva show in chapter 4, the IT community there emerged from the computing needs of the local burgeoning Japanese car import business, to then grow into a broader Siberian network of practitioners for whom Moscow often remained effectively beyond the horizon. A different genealogy is found in a different periphery, around Kazan—the capital of the largely Muslim Republic of Tatarstan in the Russian Federation's southern Volga region. There, as Kontareva describes, a strong governmental investment in building a Western-style IT innovation ecology (involving technoparks, university incubators, etc.) is part of an attempt to "brand" the Republic of Tatarstan and its capital as an up-and-coming region, connected to Moscow but inspired by the West—a West that is not merely imitated but Russianized, mobilized as part of a branding narrative to turn Tatarstan into an emblem of the new "tech" Russia.

In other places, however, the West is no longer what it used to be, thus confusing in interesting ways what "inward-" and "outward-looking" may mean. Following the collapse of the Soviet Union and the exit of several former republics from the reconstituted Russian Federation, recently independent nations like Estonia have reinvented themselves as essentially Western, in opposition to Russia. Surprisingly, IT has become a crucial element of Estonia's re-invention as a nation, whose figurative birth date is pinned on a series of distributed denial-of-service (DDoS) attacks in 2007 by Russian hackers, who had blocked many of the country's servers, returning Estonians to pre-internet life. This episode was central to the articulation of the figure of the "new Estonia"—a small but strong new country that had to be defended from similar attacks by developing fine computing skills, starting with the code training of elementary school children. Unlike Tatarstan, which borrows Western images of digital innovation ecologies to brand itself as the epitome of the new Russia, Estonia relies on the menacing figure of Russian government hackers to brand itself as e-Estonia, which *Wired* has termed the "the most advanced digital society in the world."[24] In doing so, however, it relies on the skills and pedagogical tradition left behind by the Soviet computer scientists.

The short interlude "Russian Maps" marks the book's transition from domestic post-Soviet scenarios to properly diasporic ones, offering a comprehensive map of the Russian IT industry, its short history and markets, its major players, and its place in the context of the general Russian industrial and policy landscape. Because the previous sections have aimed at specific questions and regions, they have, as a whole, tended to describe some trees or important branches, but not necessarily the forest. Dmitrii Zhikharevich's interlude operates on a different scale, providing a grid on which the previous chapters can be placed, enabling the visibility of their possible mutual connections, as well as those with other areas of the Russian IT territory.

After surveying the ongoing policy debates and initiatives to wean Russia from its dependence on extractive industries (and the perception of IT as a viable alternative or strong complement to oil and gas), Zhikharevich maps the clustering of Russian computer scientists' activities around a few major centers in the Russian Federation. Presenting both the natural economic impulse for the concentration of IT activities in the Moscow area and recent efforts to create centers of academic excellence and technoparks in various more "provincial" cities, he addresses the main strengths, weaknesses, and paradoxes of today's Russian IT industry.

The book's final section is entitled "Bridges and Mismatches." It documents how the Anglo-Saxon way of life and work is central among the models animating the conversations of Russian computer scientists and software practitioners. It can be invoked in different ways, for different purposes. It can be a foil to belittle the US techno-scientific education compared to the pedagogical excellence that Russia claims to have inherited from the Soviet system; but it can also be mobilized in the opposite direction, to point to limitations in the Russian innovation ecosystem, like its relative lack of support for prospective entrepreneurs, its lax attitude toward intellectual property, or the general absence of trust among young professionals that often forces emergent Russian entrepreneurs to pick their business partners from among close friends or people they already know. The aspiration to identify oneself as American or British (or at least aligned with those lifestyles and business cultures that, while virtually global, are effectively Anglophone) is thus not necessarily the manifestation of frustrations about being Russian but rather about trying to operate in today's Russia.

There are few venues through which people can learn how to perform the roles they aspire to except by connecting to the English-based professional communications networks of IT and computer scientists, or by doing contract work for foreign companies offshoring to Russia, which is often a training in the "ways of the West." There, RCS pick up the concepts and tricks of the trade, learning to walk the walk and talk the talk. These newly acquired skills may be deployed at home, to develop new entrepreneurial trajectories that draw from Western models, but they can also function as "professional passports" for those who wish to move abroad.

Compared to the few migration options that occasionally opened up during the Soviet period (which were ethnicity-based, complicated, costly, and possibly dangerous), the path of today's Russian high-skill brain drain may appear to be as easy as crossing a bridge. But there are very many different bridges, depending on the specific professional niche, country, lifestyle expectations, and political inclinations of the émigrés, and on the time of the crossing. And there are also surprises about what one may find at the other end of those bridges. Rather than producing case studies of scenarios that are often covered in the popular media—young, smart, and aggressive Russian hackers flying straight to Silicon Valley or Seattle to join Google or Microsoft, or to London or Berlin to work for Goldman Sachs or Deutsche Bank—this section looks at more complicated, and not necessarily more successful, scenarios, places where the émigrés' "Anglo-Saxon dreams" may not fully match what they find at the other end of the bridge, or where the brain drain, far from being near instantaneous as the image suggests, is a long and complicated affair, as in Irina Antoschyuk's window on the various stages of migration of RCS to British academia in chapter 10.

Differences in professional and institutional culture do not seem to be particularly salient in that specific kind of migration—the journals are the same and, good or bad, a department is a department. What makes a significant difference in the migration process and its aftermath is, instead, the timeline and steps of the migration decision, which typically spreads over a few years, growing through conferences, visits, and short-term fellowships. The specific steps, and their timing, change the conditions under which the move takes (or does not take) place, as well as the émigré's ability to move alone, with a team, or with the possibility to function as a bridgehead for subsequent brain drain waves. More than travel, migration looks like alliance making, both in the UK and back in Russia.

And then there are cases where, because of the time and circumstances of the migration, the "Anglo-Saxon dream" was not part of the equation. Its absence, however, was consequential nevertheless. In chapter 11, Diana Kurkovsky West looks at predominantly Jewish IT practitioners who migrated to Boston during the Soviet period and, while having many of the same technical skills as more recent Russian emigrants, were not familiar with, and thus did not embrace, the Anglo-Saxon vision of the daring high-tech entrepreneur. Uncomfortable with or unskilled in the entrepreneurial and managerial culture they encountered in Boston, they opted for "upper-middle tech" jobs. These careers led to upper-middle-class status and life-style, but not to startup entrepreneurial glory. This earlier population may have had research-grade skills, and in fact often obtained positions in corporate labs, but did not associate startup culture with the "good life," either materially or morally.

In chapter 12, Marina Fedorova analyzes another mismatch involving Russian immigrants' and native Israelis' cultural and professional values. Like the native Israelis, the immigrants prize education, but, reflecting Russian cultural values and expectations, they identify education almost exclusively with university training. Israeli-born teenagers, instead, understand the key role that military tech training plays in the career of future IT engineers, as well as its function as a networking site from which many startups emerge. One of the more manageable migration trajectories for Soviet Jews from the 1970s onward, Israel has paradoxically not been a destination where their technical skills and training have shone, as has instead been the case in virtually all other countries.

After having spanned several countries and continents, the volume comes to an end by almost coming back "home" to look at the shortest and most accessible brain drain path—that between Russia and Finland. But while geographically diminutive, this distance captures specific cultural and political choices. In the final chapter, Lyubava Shatokhina shows that here too migration choices are guided by views of the Anglo-Saxon way of life and work, and how the prospective émigré values them. For instance, a key factor that Russian software specialists consider in relocating to Finland is the appealing combination of professional autonomy and the country's socially liberal context. Autonomy means that scientists and engineers can pursue their work away from the intense pace they associate (based on evidence or imagined scenarios) with Silicon Valley and its privileging of competition over a commitment to the welfare state. What they identify as the desirable social context of their activities is described in terms that resonate with the ideals of Northern European social democracy, as opposed to the cut-throat competition typical both of the Anglo-Saxon models and of the wild "everything-goes" Russia of the 1990s. The ideals of professional and social life espoused by these immigrants are not far removed from those of Soviet society, and the Finnish lifestyle and political culture allow them to feel that they live in a place where at least some of the old Soviet commitment to the collective and to the respect of one's work is preserved, while being articulated in a much more appealing democratic framework.

1. Partial English translations of Marinichev's speech and critical responses are reproduced in Fitzpatrick 2015a and 2015b.
2. Among the vast literature about high-tech and academic migrations and mobility, see Agrawal 2006; Azoulay, Zivin, and Wang 2010; Breschi and Lissoni 2009; Kuznetsov 2006; and Saxenian 1999.
3. The questionnaire used for the interviews was designed to help understand the practice of computer science or information technology in the context of the migration strategies of our informants. One of the questions that we pursued looked at the exchanges between Russians who moved abroad and those who stayed in the Federation. Several of these interviews were transcribed, and some were translated into English. They are accessible at Rcs.eu.spb.ru, after registration.
4. This is effectively identical to what Loren Graham (1994, 127) has called the "blackboard principle," that is, that a discipline that could be effectively pursued with just a blackboard and a piece of chalk could thrive in the Soviet Union. The important difference, however, is that in the case of software, the "blackboard rule" applies to any country, not just the former USSR or modern Russia. For a contrasting account stressing the peculiar "Sovietness" of applied math, see Dalmedico 2004.
5. These policies were not always in place. For example, in the immediate aftermath of the collapse of the USSR the Russian government was unable to provide research funding (or even salaries) within the system that connected techno-scientific research to the military, causing much of the better part of the scientific community to depart for greener pastures (see Gokhberg and Nekipelova 2001).
6. Years later, after the business relation had developed and grown strong, Khotin realized that, in comparable circumstances, he should have received some equity in the Finnish business he had helped to develop rather than simply being paid as a contractor, but "I did not understand that I needed to ask. This is my Russian mentality. I have learned now that you need to ask. But at that time I would look for them to offer and if they did not offer I would not ask. And of course why would they be crazy enough to offer me stock for which I had never asked?" (Khotin, interviewed in Cook Report 2009, 11).
7. Kharkhordin 2014, 21; citing a 2011 interview with "Timur," a techno-entrepreneur from Tatarstan: "I studied, read a lot, and listened to lots of audiobooks."
8. Similarly, Russian businesses that have become successful doing offshore software development for foreign clients have often done so by "becoming local onshore," that is, by hiring local professionals (say, in the US) to inform and align the Russian company with local business practices and legal arrangements (Feakins 2009).
9. There are still only a few business schools in Russia and it is unclear whether a formal training toward an MBA—a degree predicated on the assumption that

graduates will go to work in business contexts that are comparable to those modeled by the curriculum—is needed, or even useful, given the fluidity and emergent quality of Russian business scenarios post-1991.

10. Unlike other countries that have recently emerged as software powerhouses (e.g., India, Ireland, Israel, and China), Russians had very low English proficiency.

11. "But I also came to understand that I needed to establish Arcadia on a proper professional level. I was getting useful feedback . . . from a guy named Ted McMahon from Boston University. Ted came to Russia to teach English and I was using him to teach my programmers English. I hired him to teach me how to write better business letters in English and I took him with me once on a trip to Helsinki to help in my negotiations" (Cook Report 2009, 11).

12. This is a large, if poorly quantified, population. Many Russian software developers work in-house for Russian companies, writing the software products needed by their employers. Because of a combination of low wages and the specificity of Russian legal, business, and accounting practices (and their frequent changes), it is often both cheaper and better to develop one's own software than to purchase off-the-shelf products from European and US software providers (Peterson 2005).

13. For later developments, see Soldatov and Borogan 2015.

14. On the global spread of the software industry, see Aneesh 2006; Arora and Gambardella 2005; Biao 2006; McFarlan, Jia, and Wong 2012; Popkin and Iyengar 2007; Takhteyev 2012.

15. Aleksey Andreyev, chief editor of Webplanet.ru; quoted in RT 2016.

16. The contrast between hopes and realities can be easily grasped by comparing SPIEF 2012 with Appell 2015. See also Balzer 2016.

17. A succinct but comprehensive institutional map of USSR science and technology is in Berry 1988.

18. Russoft (http://russoft.org/), originally named "FortRoss," after a nineteenth-century Russian settlement in Northern California.

19. On the last Soviet generation (or the first generation of Russian entrepreneurs) and how their entrepreneurial skills started to develop during the late 1980s, see Yurchak 2002.

20. On the distrust of collective action in post-1991 Russia, see also Howard 2003.

21. Additional material can be found at https://eu.spb.ru/sts/projects/item/4417-technological-entrepreneurship. The detailed results of this project are in Bychkova, forthcoming.

22. The most recent statement of this position is Graham 2013.

23. In parallel to the science cities, the Soviets also developed closed cities where techno-scientific work was done, mostly for military application, in secrecy, or at least isolation (Brown 2013).

24. https://e-estonia.com/.

Agrawal, Ajay. 2006. "Gone but Not Forgotten: Knowledge Flows, Labor Mobility, and Enduring Social Relationships." *Journal of Economic Geography* 6: 571–91.

American Chamber of Commerce in Russia. 2001. "Whitepaper on Offshore Software Development." October. Accessed July 25, 2018. http://russoft.org/docs /?doc=733.

Aneesh, Arnand. 2006. *Virtual Migration: The Programming of Globalization.* Durham, NC: Duke University Press.

Appell, James. 2015. "The Short Life and Speedy Death of Russia's Silicon Valley." *Foreign Policy*, May 6. http://foreignpolicy.com/2015/05/06/the-short-life-and -speedy-death-of-russias-silicon-valley-medvedev-go-russia-skolkovo/.

Arora, Ashish, and Alfonso Gambardella, eds. 2005. *From Underdogs to Tigers: The Rise and Growth of the Software Industry in Brazil, China, India, Ireland, and Israel.* Oxford: Oxford University Press.

Asmolov, Gregory. 2014. "Virtual Rynda—The Atlas of Help: Mutual Aid as a Form of Social Activism." In *Global Dimensions of Digital Activism*, edited by Ethan Zuckerman and Lorrie LeJeune. Accessed July 20, 2016. http://book .globaldigitalactivism.org/chapter/virtual-rynda-the-atlas-of-help-mutual-aid -as-a-form-of-social-activism/.

Azoulay, Pierre, Joshua Graff Zivin, and Jiavan Wang. 2010. "Superstar Extinction." *Quarterly Journal of Economics* 125, no. 2: 549–89.

Balzer, Harley. 2011. "Learning to Innovate? Education and Knowledge-Based Economies in Russia and China." Mortara Working Paper 2011–17, Mortara Center for International Studies, Georgetown University, December. Accessed July 20, 2016. https://www.sas.upenn.edu/polisci/sites/www.sas.upenn.edu .polisci/files/Balzer.MortaraLearn2Innovate.pdf.

Balzer, Harley. 2016. "Russia's Knowledge Economy Decline: Views from Inside." Jamestown Foundation Russia in Decline Project. Accessed November 10, 2016. https://jamestown.org/wp-content/uploads/2016/09/Balzer_-_Russia_in _Decline_01.pdf.

Bardham, Ashok, and Cynthya Kroll. 2006. "Competitiveness and an Emerging Sector: The Russian Software Industry and Its Global Linkages." *Industry and Innovation* 13: 69–95.

Benkler, Yochai. 2006. *Wealth of Networks: How Social Production Transforms Markets and Freedom.* New Haven, CT: Yale University Press.

Berry, Michael, ed. 1988. *Science and Technology in the USSR.* Longman.

Biao, Xiang. 2006. *Global "Body Shopping": An Indian Labor System in the Information Technology Industry.* Princeton, NJ: Princeton University Press.

Borjas, George, and Kirk B. Doran. 2012. "The Collapse of the Soviet Union and the Productivity of American Mathematicians." Working Paper, National Bureau of Economic Research, February. http://www.nber.org/papers/w17800.

Bowles, Nellie. 2017. "Russians in Silicon Valley Can't Shake Hacking's Shadow." *New York Times*, October 8. https://www.nytimes.com/2017/10/08/technology /russian-election-hacking-silicon-valley.html.

Braunerhjelm, Pontus, and Maryann Feldman, eds. 2007. *Cluster Genesis: Technology-Based Industrial Development.* Oxford: Oxford University Press.

Breschi, Stefano, and Francesco Lissoni. 2009. "Mobility of Skilled Workers and Co-invention Networks: An Anatomy of Localized Knowledge Flows." *Journal of Economic Geography* 9: 439–68.

Brown, Kate. 2013. *Plutopia: Nuclear Families, Atom Cities, and the Great Soviet and American Plutonium Disasters.* Oxford: Oxford University Press.

Bychkova, Olga. Forthcoming. *Fantasticheskii mir rossiiskogo hai-teka* [A fantastic world of Russian high tech]. Moscow: NLO.

Chesbrough, Henry William. 2005. *Open Innovation: The New Imperative for Creating and Profiting from Technology.* Cambridge, MA: Harvard Business Review Press.

Clay, Alexa, and Kyra Maya Phillip. 2015. *Misfit Economy.* New York: Simon and Schuster.

Coleman, Gabriella. 2012. *Coding Freedom: The Ethics and Aesthetics of Hacking.* Princeton, NJ: Princeton University Press.

Cook Report. 2009. "The Cook Report on Internet Protocol." September.

Dalmedico, Amy Dahan. 2004. "Early Developments of Nonlinear Science in Soviet Russia: The Andronov School at Groskiy." *Science in Context* 17, nos. 1–2: 235–65.

Davies, Sarah R. 2017. *Hackerspaces: Making the Maker Movement.* Cambridge: Polity Press.

Degeler, Andri. 2015. "Yandex Worker Stole Search Engine Source Code, Tried Selling for Just $28K." *Ars Technica*, December 28, 2015. Accessed July 25, 2016. http://arstechnica.com/business/2015/12/yandex-employee-stole-search-engine source-code-tried-to-sell-it-for-just-27000-2/.

Dezhina, Irina. 2015. "The State of Science and Innovation in Russia in 2014." In *Russian Economy in 2014: Trends and Outlooks*, edited by Alexander Radygin, 316–38. Moscow: Gaidar Institute for Economic Policy.

Durant, Rodolphe, and Jean-Philippe Vergne. 2012. *The Pirate Organization.* Cambridge, MA: Harvard Business School Press.

Evstifeyev, Dimitry. 2015. "First Comes the Army, and Only Then the Traders." *Gazeta*, November 15, 2015. Accessed July 25, 2018. https://www.gazeta.ru/social /2015/10/15/7822757.shtml.

Feakins, Melanie. 2009. "Offshoring in the Core: Russian Software Firms Onshoring in the US." *Global Networks* 9: 1–19.

Fitzpatrick, Catherine. 2015a. "Internet Ombudsman Provokes Storm of Protest with Comment That Kremlin Shouldn't Train IT and Only Military Dominance Sustains Technology." *The Interpreter*, October 16. Accessed November 26, 2017. https://www.interpretermag.com/russia-update-october-15–2015/.

Fitzpatrick, Catherine. 2015b. "Russia's IT Business Leaders Object to Kremlin Internet Ombudsman's Call to End IT Training." *The Interpreter*, October 16. Accessed November 26, 2017. https://www.interpretermag.com/russia-update -october-15–2015/.

Freinkman, Lev, Ksenia Gonchar, and Yevgeny Kuznetsov. 2013. "Linking Talent Abroad with a Drive for Innovation at Home: A Study of the Russian

Technological Diaspora." In *How Can Talent Abroad Induce Development at Home? Towards a Pragmatic Development Agenda*, edited by Yevgeny Kuznetsov, 207–66. Washington, DC: Migration Policy Institute.

Ganguli, Ina. 2015. "Immigration and Ideas: What Did Russian Scientists 'Bring' to the United States?" *Journal of Labor Economics* 33: 257–88.

Gapova, Elena. 2006. "The Migration of Information Technology Professionals from the Post-Soviet Region." In *Migration Perspectives: Eastern Europe and Central Asia*, edited by Roger Rios, 6–15. Geneva: International Organization for Migration.

Gladarev, Boris, Irina Olimpieva, Oleg Kharkhordin, Zhanna Tsinman, and Anna Chernysh, 2013. *Vliianie modelei indvidualnogo povedeniia na effektivnost' deiatelnosti innovatsionnykh vysokotekhnologichnykh kompanii na primere chetyrekh stran: Rossiia, Finlandiia, Iuzhnaia Koreia, Taivan* [Influence of models of personal behavior on the efficiency of the innovative high-tech companies, the case of four countries: Russia, Finland, South Korea, Taiwan]. Saint Petersburg: EUSP STS Center.

Gokhberg, Leonid, and Elena Nekipelova. 2001. "International Migration of Scientists and Engineers in Russia." In *International Mobility of the Highly Skilled*, OECD Proceedings, 177–87. Paris: OECD.

Graham, Loren. 1994. "Science and Computers in Soviet Society." *Proceedings of the Academy of Political Science* 35: 124–34.

Graham, Loren. 2013. *Lonely Ideas: Can Russia Compete?* Cambridge, MA: MIT Press.

Howard, Marc Morje. 2003. *The Weakness of Civil Society in Post-Communist Europe*. Cambridge: Cambridge University Press.

Joseph, Drew. 2010. "Medvedev Tours Twitter, Silicon Valley." *SFGate*, June 24. Accessed July 26, 2016. https://www.sfgate.com/business/article/Medvedev -tours-Twitter-Silicon-Valley-3184502.php.

Josephson, Paul. 1997. *New Atlantis Revisited*. Princeton, NJ: Princeton University Press.

Kelty, Christopher. 2008. *Two Bits: The Cultural Significance of Free Software*. Durham, NC: Duke University Press.

Kenney, Martin, and David Mowery, eds. 2014. *Public Universities and Regional Growth: Insights from the University of California*. Stanford, CA: Stanford Business Books.

Kharkhordin, Oleg. 1999. *The Collective and the Individual in Russia*. Berkeley: University of California Press.

Kharkhordin, Oleg. 2014. "Are We Doomed to Creativity? Cultural Characteristics of Technological Entrepreneurship in Russia." Working paper. Saint Petersburg: EUSP STS Center. https://www.academia.edu/8609734/Are_We_Doomed_to _Creativity_Cultural_Characteristics_of_Technological_Entrepreneurship_in _Russia.

Kittler, Friedrich. 2008. "Code (or, How You Can Write Something Differently)." In *Software Studies: A Lexicon*, edited by Matthew Fuller, 40–47. Cambridge, MA: MIT Press.

Kuznetsov, Yevgeny, ed. 2006. *Diaspora Networks and the International Migration of Skills: How Countries Can Draw on Their Talent Abroad*. Washington, DC: World Bank Publications.

Lecuyer, Christophe. 2005. *Making Silicon Valley*. Cambridge, MA: MIT Press.

Levy, Steven. 2010. *Hackers: Heroes of the Computer Revolution*. Sebastopol, CA: O'Reilly Media.

Lonkila, Marrku. 2011. *Networks in the Russian Market Economy*. London: Palgrave.

Luo, Yu-Ling, and Wei-Jang Wang. 2001. "High-Skill Migration and Chinese Taipei's Industrial Development." In *International Mobility of the Highly Skilled*, OECD Proceedings, 253–69. Paris: OECD.

Marcus, George. 1995. "Ethnography in/of the World System: The Emergence of Multi-Sited Ethnography." *Annual Review of Anthropology* 24: 24–117.

McFarlan, F. Warren, Ning Jia, and Justin Wong. 2012. "China's Growing IT Services and Software Industry: Challenges and Implications." *MIS Quarterly Executive* 11, no. 1 (March): 1–9.

Medvedev, Dmitry. 2009. "Go Russia!" Official Internet Resources of the President of Russia. September 10. Accessed July 25, 2018. http://en.kremlin.ru /events/president/news/5413.

Moscow Times. 2005. "Russian Schoolchildren to Learn Two Foreign Languages." *Moscow Times*, September 1. Accessed August 20, 2016. http://russialist.org /russian-schoolchildren-to-learn-two-foreign-languages/.

Peters, Benjamin. 2016. *How Not to Network a Nation: The Uneasy History of the Soviet Internet*. Cambridge, MA: MIT Press.

Peterson, D. J. 2005. *Russia and the Information Revolution*. Santa Monica, CA: Rand.

Popkin, James, and Partha Iyengar. 2007. *IT and the East*. Cambridge, MA: Harvard Business School Press.

Ramadan, Al, Dave Peterson, Christopher Lochhead, and Kevin Maney. 2016. *Play Bigger*. New York: Harper.

Rohozinski, Rafal. 1999. "Mapping Russian Cyberspace: Perspectives on Democracy and the Net." United Nations Research Institute for Social Development, Discussion Paper 115, November. Accessed July 25, 2018. http://www.unrisd.org /80256B3C005BCCF9/(httpAuxPages)/879B8965BF0AE0ED80256B67005B73 8A/$file/dp115.pdf.

RT. 2016. "Medvedev Logs into Silicon Valley." RT News, June 24. Accessed July 21, 2016. https://www.rt.com/news/medvedev-visit-silicon-valley/.

Saint Petersburg International Economic Forum (SPIEF). 2012. "Skolkovo: Fast Track to Russian R&D Talent and Innovation." Seminar at SPIEF, June 21–23. http://forumspb.com/bfx-cc/system/uploads/files/site_session_attr/stenogram _en/77/22_skolkovo_fast_track_to_russian_rd_talent_and_innovation_en.pdf.

Saxenian, AnnaLee. 1999. *Silicon Valley's New Immigrant Entrepreneurs*. San Francisco: Public Policy Institute of California.

Saxenian, AnnaLee. 2000. *Regional Region*. Stanford, CA: Stanford Business Books.

Saxenian, AnnaLee. 2007. *The New Argonauts: Regional Advantage in a Global Economy.* Cambridge, MA: Harvard University Press.

Shane, Scott, David Sanger, and Nicole Perlroth. 2017. "New N.S.A. Breach Linked to Popular Russian Antivirus Software." *New York Times*, October 5. https://www.nytimes.com/2017/10/05/us/politics/russia-nsa-hackers-kaspersky.html.

Soldatov, Andrei, and Irina Borogan. 2015. *The Red Web: The Struggle between Russia's Digital Dictators and the New Online Revolutionaries.* New York: Public Affairs.

Takhteyev, Yuri. 2012. *Coding Places: Software Practice in a South American City.* Cambridge, MA: MIT Press.

Tatarchenko, Ksenia. 2013. "A House with the Window to the West: The Akademgorodok Computer Center (1958–1993)." PhD diss., Princeton University, NJ.

Wainwright, Oliver. 2016. "Step into Silicon Forest, Putin's Secret Weapon in the Global Tech Race." *Guardian*, January 5. https://www.theguardian.com/artanddesign/2016/jan/05/silicon-forest-putin-secret-weapon-global-tech-race-siberia-russia.

Wang, Dan. 2015. "Activating Brokerage: Interorganizational Knowledge Transfer through Skilled Return Migration." *Administrative Science Quarterly* 60: 133–76.

Yurchak, Alexei. 2002. "Entrepreneurial Governmentality in Postsocialist Russia: A Cultural Investigation of Business Practices." In *The New Entrepreneurs of Europe and Asia: Patterns of Business Development in Russia, Eastern Europe, and China*, edited by Vicky Bonnell and Thomas Gold, 278–325. Armonk, NY: M. E. Sharpe.

Yurchak, Alexei. 2005. *Everything Was Forever Until It Was No More: The Last Soviet Generation.* Princeton, NJ: Princeton University Press.

CODING COLLECTIVES

CHAPTER ONE

BEFORE THE COLLAPSE

Programming Cultures in the Soviet Union

Ksenia Tatarchenko

"We desperately need a programmer."—"I'll talk to the guys—I promise—I know a few who are unhappy."—"We do not need any programmer—said the hook-nosed.—Programmers—are the sought-after people, and are spoiled, but we need the unspoiled one."

—STRUGATSKY BROTHERS, *Monday Begins on Saturday* (1964)

In the early 1990s, in a typical middle school located in an industrial neighborhood of the city of Novosibirsk, we had an "informatics" class where we learned about the principles of hardware and programming and could play computer games. The machines were not called "computers" but "EVM" (electronic calculating machines); they had a gray and green interface and were all connected to the main computer controlled by the teacher.

My high school was an experimental school endowed with additional funds, and was where I first experienced a modern computer class with "real" personal computers. The classroom itself often stayed closed behind iron doors and barred windows—during the "wild" 1990s the robbery of school computer classrooms supplied with expensive foreign machines was common. This classroom was closed because the informatics teacher I had met during the admission tests left for Israel; she was greatly missed by older students, who said she was very competent. Eventually, the administration found a replacement and we began to learn how to use a text-editing application. By this time it was generally understood that Word and Excel were what informatics classes should be about. In those days, I was busy discovering French existentialism and Russian semiotics and remember cheating on the Excel assignment.

Among other things, the collapse of the Soviet Union wrecked the national education system and opened the country's frontiers: a calamity turned into an opportunity when I got a chance to study abroad. Moving from Russia to France and then to the US, my own personal trajectory impacted my research subject: the history of Soviet computing from a transnational perspective. Working on my PhD thesis and book manuscript (Tatarchenko 2013), I uncovered in the history of computing itself explanations and connections that shed light on what I experienced in my computer classes as compared to those skills taught to my American friends. In this connection, it is worth pointing out that claims stating the Soviets had missed the "Computer Revolution" were at best misleading and that the relative rarity of personal computers in Soviet homes did not represent the absence of a computer industry or professional programmers. I learned that Western and Eastern IT histories were entangled on many levels and that the Iron Curtain simultaneously isolated and connected these two worlds.

To discern the depth of the transnational connections, we need to consider multiple facets of Soviet IT, including: hardware and software as complex technological artifacts; the emergence of a new mathematical discipline called "computer science" in English and *informatika* in Russian; a set of localized practices; and machines as emblems of political legitimacy. The Cold War military and space race was the chief driving force behind the miniaturization of electronic components encapsulated by what is termed "Moore's law." The military origins of American networking systems and the parallel Soviet efforts to computerize their economy into a single "big data" network are other well-known cases of contemporary IT systems that had Cold War origins. If electronics and computer network technology were the material embodiments of competition between the East and West, the capitalist and socialist versions of modernity were equally rooted in a techno-utopian imaginary that led to different visions of the "Information Age." Accordingly, the curricula for school computer education reflected two versions of an "information society": the American one was predicated on a proficient instrumental use of the personal computer as a basic commodity and a data-processing device; the Soviet one aimed at inculcating thought habits and programming skills in an effort to enable self-control and self-expression for a new kind of responsible individual.

The collapse of the party state and the ensuing political transformations put an end to the project of creating a "socialist information society." The invasion of global IT products following the opening of the Russian markets during the 1990s dramatically altered the material landscape of computing in the New Russia. Yet a half century's worth of Soviet experience with computing did not just disappear; instead, important continuities exist across the 1991 fault line. In this chapter, I take a synthetic approach to the history of Soviet programming in order to provide context and genealogy explaining the distinctly national dimensions of the contemporary IT landscape. First, I provide an overview of the pioneering stage of Soviet programming efforts, as shaped by early Soviet hardware and cybernetics. Next, I focus on the commodification of programming work and analyze the professionalization efforts led by Soviet programming experts who came to claim that programming was a form of human and machine brotherhood. I then conclude with reflections on the philosophy behind the 1985 educational reform, which introduced compulsory programming classes within a context where the cloning of Western hardware became the norm.

EXCLUSIVE AND ILLUSIVE: EARLY PROGRAMMERS BETWEEN ENGINEERS AND CYBERNETICIANS

The specificity of Soviet computing history is inextricably linked to key features of the socialist state: its planned economy and the party's ideological guidance. Centralized power and the planned economy did not lead to an absence of inventiveness or competition. On the contrary, from the first days of Soviet digital computing efforts in the late 1940s, the development of Soviet machines was marked by a rivalry between different groups of specialists. Similar to the Anglo-American debates on the "firsts" embroiling the epithets of "digital," "programmable," and "fully operational," a controversy surrounds the status of the "first" Soviet computer. The chief protagonists in the battle for public memory are M-1 and MESM machines (the former built in Moscow, the latter in the suburbs of Kiev), both important less for their performance characteristics than for their influence on the design and training of the workforce involved in two larger, also competing, hardware projects: Strela and BESM. Operational by the mid-1950s, these two computers engendered a new kind of occupation: professional programming.

Western specialists studying Soviet technology during the Cold War era were little concerned by these priority disputes. Instead, they grappled with the issue of technology transfer, asking questions such as: Were the first Soviet computer developments independent of one another? Were the snippets of information in the form of publicity and published overviews really all the Russians had? As the evidence relating to these questions remains partial at best, it seems sensible to turn our attention to the well-known case of the Soviet nuclear bomb project. According to the latest analysis by historian of science and technology Michael Gordin (2009), even such sustained information-collection efforts as were organized by Soviet intelligence under the secret police chief Lavrentiy Beria could not solve the major problem of information fragmentation, management, and trust. In fact, it was the public knowledge about the technical feasibility of the project and various published reports that were most responsible for the astonishing speed of Soviet nuclear efforts. These observations help elucidate the issue of transfer in the case of Soviet digital computing: feasibility was no doubt the most crucial piece of Western knowledge for early Soviet projects.

If the circulation of scientific overviews stimulated the efforts of Soviet engineers and mathematicians interested in calculation problems, the relationship between early Soviet and early Western computer technology was not limited to a unilateral flow of technical information and soon became shaped by an ideological confrontation over technology's place in society. The speed, size, and cost of early computers attracted the attention of the media and fascinated the Western popular imaginary, famously associating computers with "giant brains." However, in Russia what became known as an anticybernetic campaign was founded in a series of publications that appeared in the Soviet press from the spring of 1950 to the winter of 1955. The first publication was a witty analysis of the militarism implied in the anthropomorphic representation of the Harvard Marc III machine on the pages of *Time* magazine, but later articles attacked a specific enemy: the new American science of cybernetics (Peters 2012).

In his book *Cybernetics: Or Control and Communication in the Animal and the Machine* (1948), the American mathematician Norbert Wiener introduced the term and gave it a vague definition as "scientific study." The interdisciplinary and metascientific ambitions involved in drawing connections between biological and man-made systems, as well as the explicit analogies between machines and human institutions articulated in Wiener's bestseller, *The Human Use of Human Beings: Cybernetics and Society* (1950), made cybernetics an inviting ground for ideological contestation. The Soviet publications labeled cybernetics a pseudoscience, a triumph of semantic idealism, and the newest form of mechanical philosophy, all the while stressing its role as a tool of Western militarism. In the wider context of rising geopolitical tensions and Soviet domestic efforts to exert a hold over the creative and scientific intelligentsia (*Zhdanovshchina*), the anticybernetic campaign was peculiar because unlike the infamous case of Lysenkoism and the antigenetic campaign, it was not directed against any Soviet individuals or institutions. The most direct result of the anticybernetic publications—the withdrawal of Wiener's books from Soviet libraries—did not mean that Soviet experts ignored this new Western development.

The Soviet ideologues were not the only Soviet specialists to observe the military roots and implications of the new calculating technologies and cybernetic notions. Wiener's works were held in closed libraries and several unofficial translations circulated among experts. One reader was a young graduate of the Dzerzhinsky Artillery Academy, Anatoliy Kitov. Employed as a military representative at the special construction bureau—the SKB-245—and responsible for the design of the Strela computer, Kitov became an early Soviet programming expert and a proselyte of cybernetic ideas among the Soviet military and scientific elites. Reading and being interested in such ideologically suspicious works was not an act of rebellion but a logical step within a belief system that postulated employing Western technology in a battle against capitalism. Working on secret military projects, early Soviet experts fascinated by cybernetics and digital computing were eager to fight against an imagined Western aggressor, but their immediate threats were much closer—the competitors for state funds offering alternative technical solutions.

Created in 1948 under the auspices of the Soviet Academy of Sciences, the Institute of Precise Mechanics and Computational Technology (ITMiVT) had its mission to develop computational technology inscribed in its very name; tellingly, however, computation did not yet imply "electronic" or "digital" but rather "mechanical." This situation changed in 1950, when the mathematician and explosives expert Mikhail Lavrentyev took over the directorship of the new organization. In his memoirs, Lavrentyev (2000, 57–60) detailed his shrewd solutions for dealing with material scarcity by returning to patronage networks, revealing that no tactic was too dirty. Lavrentyev recounts how he accused leaders of the analogue technology projects of machinations with bureaucratic documents (a common Soviet practice at which Lavrentyev excelled) in order to force them out of the institute. Competitors out, old friends in. Returning to the capital from the Ukrainian Academy of Sciences, Lavrentyev also transferred his protégé and the designer of the MESM computer, Sergey Lebedev, and his team of engineers from Kiev to Moscow.

Lavrentyev's reliance on his prewar Moscow networks also brought to the ITMiVT the mathematician Lazar' Lusternik, an old companion from the famous Luzitanya, a group of mathematicians formed around Nikolay Luzin in the 1920s, and a colleague at the Central AeroHydrodynamic Institute

(TsAGI), the cradle of Soviet aviation during the 1930s. A leading figure in early Soviet programming efforts at the ITMiVT, Lusternik recreated the practices with which he was familiar from his time at the TsAGI: a close cooperation between mathematicians and engineers as well as scientific forms of interaction. In 1950, he organized a seminar on programming where the available literature was read and discussed in a scientific fashion. Lusternik's seminar led to the publication of an influential overview volume: *The Solution of Mathematical Tasks on the Automatic Numerical Machines*, a collective work, with the subtitle *Programming for High-Speed Electronic Calculating Machines* (Lusternik et al. 1952). Over three hundred pages long, it covered all aspects of programming, from a brief introduction to digital computers and numerical systems, to detailed examples of programming techniques for a "hypothetical" three-address machine, which was in fact the BESM computer, which was under development. Circulated under conditions of restricted access, this was the book that introduced most early Soviet programmers to their new craft.

While mathematicians in Lusternik's group considered the problem of how to solve mathematical tasks using computers before any operational Soviet machines even existed, the Soviet science administrators began to work on the crucial question of who would operate them. In 1948, the same year as the creation of the ITMiVT, Moscow State University (MGU) created a new chair in computational mathematics. Here, at the most prestigious school in the country, the mathematics department had few volunteers among its student body willing to abandon their aspirations in pure mathematics for the unknown perspectives of machine mathematics. Assigning students to the chair was the typical top-down solution to the problem of *who* but not the *how* of turning them into specialists of the new machine computation. The logic behind the curriculum—freed from many of the traditional subject areas in mathematics to make room for classes like "Algebra of Relays" and "Theory of Machines and Mechanisms"—implied that in order to program one needed to understand the mechanisms of machines. After struggling through the eclectic curriculum, the first graduates of the computational mathematics chair were to learn their jobs on the fly.

According to graduates' memoirs, they spent their last year as interns at the ITMiVT learning to code on the BESM computer. The actual experience of interaction with the new machine was immersive: its twinkling lights, sounds, and heat combined with the very size of the installation impressed its operators with a sense of almost mysterious power. But it is the human element of interaction, the shared learning and competition between peers on how best to control the machine, that had a deep impact on one's sense of self: "Programmers were counted on fingers, and joining this tribe filled one with a feeling of exclusivity" (Podlovchenko 2003, 372). This tribe, a small group of pioneers bound by the unique experience of working on the first Soviet machines, would influence Soviet programming for several decades to come. The members of the group would go on to lead software projects, consult for new hardware development, and teach many generations of programmers. Unlike the designers of the first machines, they are not in the spotlight of public memory but act as a less visible network transmitting disciplinary mythologies.

The important events that shaped the professional representation of this core group were closely associated with cybernetics, which had radically changed its status from a tool of imperialism to a mathematical metascience in the service of communism. By the fall of 1955—when the existence of Soviet computers was first officially announced in conjunction with an international conference in Darmstadt, West Germany—the scientific reputation of cybernetics had already been publicly redeemed through the appearance of a seminal publication (Sobolev, Kitov, and Lyapunov 1955) titled "Osnovnyye cherty Kibernetiki" (The main features of cybernetics) appearing in the key Soviet ideological journal, *Voprosy filosofii* (Questions of philosophy). The text of the article was drafted by the young colonel Kitov and cosigned by his former teacher from the Dzerzhinsky Artillery Academy, mathematician Aleksey Lyapunov, and Sergei Sobolev, an academician and mathematical prodigy who contributed to the Soviet nuclear bomb project. The article focused on explaining the subject and methods of cybernetics and stressed the legitimate scientific nature of the discipline. According to Slava Gerovitch (2002), the almost decade-long delay in the introduction of cybernetics to the Soviet public had an impact on its very content: unlike the servomechanisms that inspired Norbert Wiener, computers became the machines of reference in the Soviet version of cybernetics, which began to gain popularity in the late 1950s.

I argue that these crucial insights entail yet another observation: by 1955, Kitov, Lyapunov, and Sobolev not only presented computers as the machines of reference for cybernetics but also believed that programming itself was mathematical and a part of a machine's self-regulative process and amenable to automatization. In addition to their highly visible and celebrated role in changing the status of Soviet cybernetics, the three authors played key roles in spreading this vision of programming as pioneer practitioner, mentor, and patron, respectively. Aligning programming with cybernetics by highlighting its mathematical foundations, their publication became the most visible national instantiation of the general international trend toward the development of so-called high-level computer languages and automatic programming systems. The relationship between programming and cybernetics in the 1960s was complicated by the mathematics-based cybernetic orientation on eliminating programming labor by developing system software and the parallel growth of programming as a mass profession. This tension would eventually be resolved with the establishment of a separate disciplinary and professional identity for programmers. However, the visions stipulating the automation of programming labor still animate policy discourses such as that of Dmitry Marinichev (Biagioli and Lépinay, this volume).

IN SEARCH OF IDENTITY: INTEGRATING INTERNATIONAL COMMUNITY, PRODUCING A NEW SOCIALIST COMMODITY

Up to the mid-1950s, programming practice, coding, and notations were highly localized: the craft of an individual programmer was dependent on the intimate knowledge of specific features of a machine and on devising clever tricks to use them efficiently. Proliferation of computers and their transformation from military and scientific calculators into business data-processing machines brought forward the problem of coordinating human efforts and introduced the difficulties of transmitting programs between machines. Across the Atlantic, "hardware" became the colloquial term for computer equipment during the 1950s. The term "software," on the other hand, was initially invented in 1959 and came to denote everything that was not hardware: notation, consulting, and the new programming tools such as assembly systems, compilers, and operating systems. Running parallel to this process of the commodification of programming—encapsulated in the "ware" part of software—the professionalization of programming involved the creation of the first computer science departments in American universities and ongoing debates about their pedagogical mission. Confusion over the meaning of "software" and "program" reflected the ill-defined ontological status of a programmer's work, astutely observed by the historian of computing Thomas Haigh (2002, 6): "Not all 'software' was programs, and not all programs were software."

These Western developments are important to Soviet programming for two reasons—comparison and contextualization. For instance, the fluidity of the better-known American case helps to clarify the paradoxical nature of the Soviet term similar to "software," which came into use in the early 1960s: "mathematical supply" (*obespecheniye*). Starting in the late 1950s, the serial production of computers—such as the lamp-based M-20 and its transistor-based modifications—led to the same problems of coordination from human to human and from machine to machine familiar to the West. In 1960, the Soviet military and scientific organizations that used the M-20 machines met at a conference that resulted in the first user association created to facilitate the exploitation of the machines, and a crucial part of that process became the exchange of programs. Such bottom-up initiatives were soon institutionalized at the state level with a commission on mathematical supply attached to the State Committee for Science and Technology (GKNT). Similar to the vagueness of the English-language "software," the Russian-language "mathematical supply" did not provide for a clear distinction between product and service. However, the epithet of "mathematical" helps trace the direct relationship between Western and Soviet developments in programming—a relationship based on a shared belief in the mathematical nature of programs.

In the political chronology of Cold War interactions, 1955 (the year of the Geneva Summit) appears as an important turning point and a moment when the theory of peaceful coexistence was articulated and enacted. The theory provided a functional framework for the rise of Cold War scientific internationalism, best known for the Atoms for Peace meetings and the spectacular launch of Sputnik during the International Geophysical Year. The early Western-Soviet contacts in computing fit the same larger scheme: spanning activity from participation at international professional conferences and workshops held by the new International Federation for Information Processing (IFIP) to bilateral exchanges. While similar to other strategic technologies, information collection was one of the driving forces behind the exchanges in computing; the dynamic of the first Soviet-American exchanges of computer specialists demonstrates that intellectual coordination and preoccupations with the nature of human-machine interactions were the key elements.

Soviet integration into the international Algol project—a result of visits by American scientists in the late 1950s—provides the best example of mutual efforts triggered by shared beliefs in the power of mathematics for transcending all barriers. By 1960, the project acquired a large set of European participants and an anti-IBM ideology. Unlike the already popular Fortran devised to fit the characteristics of IBM machines, Algol was thought to be a truly universal, machine-independent, and mathematically sound language, empowered not by corporate capital but by scientific internationalism embodied in collective work on its definition and standardization. Considered a practical failure in the US—on the basis of the number of compilers and not its larger influence—and a moderate success in Europe, Algol became the most widely used computer language in the Soviet Union and Eastern Bloc countries during the 1960s.

The puzzle behind Algol's popularity in the East still involves many unknown elements, but the core element on the level of ideas was the conceptualization of the program as a mathematical object, an approach familiar in Soviet circles thanks to the Soviet version of mathematical cybernetics. By the late 1960s, there were at least half a dozen Algol compilers for the M-20 computers in the Soviet Union, along with others for the newer and more powerful Soviet machines, such as the BESM-6. Competing research groups in Moscow, Leningrad, and Novosibirsk made important efforts at distributing and publicizing their work. The particularly rich published accounts and documentary sources produced by the Novosibirsk group—which benefited from the showcase status of the scientific center Akademgorodok, located in Novosibirsk—demonstrate the changing conditions of programmers' work and the emergence of new organizational challenges. These challenges surmounted by Akademgorodok computer pioneers would find an echo in the post-Soviet Siberian initiatives to capitalize upon the region's reputation as an IT hub dating from the 1960s (Indukaev, this volume).

To produce large-scale software systems such as compilers it was not enough to add together individual skills and a labor force. Published by the project leader Andrey Ershov in the local newspaper in January 1965, "The Alpha-Birth" recounted the challenges of producing an automatic programming system competitive in quality to manual programming. The unexpected technical troubles, the missed deadlines, and the doubling of the code volume from the expected twenty thousand to forty thousand lines, were all typical problems that demanded solutions bridging the technical and the social. The coordination of effort was paramount for the ultimate success of the Novosibirsk group and is clearly still a major issue for today's companies, such as in the case of Yandex's emphasis on a shared set of code-writing skills (Fedorova on Yandex, this volume). In Akademgorodok, collective coding became a personally fulfilling experience. "We will keep the gained experience, deep satisfaction with the completed work and the priceless camaraderie," wrote Ershov, "that was born and matured during the years of work on Alpha-system." In other words, the "birth" of a compiler was predicated on the creation of a collective with a family-like cohesion.

The work of Ershov's group is of particular importance not only because of the technical features of the system, but because the creation of a compiling system and the formation of a programming collective came together with the coming of age of a new leader in the field of programming. Riding on the success of his Alpha system, Ershov claimed a professional and disciplinary identity separate from Soviet cybernetics. A talented and ambitious student who participated in Lyapunov's famous class on the principles of programming at MGU, and in 1957 a PhD student and group manager at the new Akademgorodok Computer Center, by the late 1960s Ershov had grown into a pundit and spokesperson for programming on both the national and international level (Kraineva and Cheremnykh 2011).

Ershov was named head of the state commission formed by the GKNT to monitor the development of mathematical supply in the Soviet Union and became the main author of its report submitted in summer 1968 (Ershov 1968). A snapshot of the Soviet programming landscape, the report estimated the number of Soviet system programmers at about one thousand, almost equally distributed between the academic computing centers, the key hardware production facilities, and a series of military-industrial organizations. But the report's most interesting aspect was its language and the policy recommendations that squarely placed the Soviet programming community within the international milieu. In it, Ershov argued for rapid growth and the professionalization of system programming in order to achieve the Soviet computerization goals: the creation of "system programmer" as an established engineering profession; the separation of service and research functions in academic computer centers; and an orientation on borrowing software libraries for the new Soviet family of computers, later known as the United System (ES).

The date of the report, July 1968, is crucial for understanding the full meaning of its content. On the one hand, it captures a moment in time when Soviet experts were still debating the costs and benefits of orientating the new Soviet series on the IBM architecture and the best mechanism for doing so. On the other, the language of and arguments within the report reflected and prefigured the largest concern of the international community at the time, which became encapsulated in the notion of "software crisis." The NATO-sponsored conference on software engineering held in Garmish (West Germany) on October 7–11, 1968, became the epicenter for reflection on software risk and reliability as well as a forum for a very pragmatic preoccupation with the costs of software production, the status of programmers' labor, and the solution to the "software crisis" associated with the creation of "software engineering." To sum up, Ershov's deep integration into the international community, traceable to the Algol group's formal and informal networks, shaped his solutions to peculiar Soviet problems. At the same time, as a Soviet professional, Ershov took on as his responsibility the state's interests in international prestige, the computerization of research and production, and the education of new professionals.

Recognizing that to become an accepted profession programming needed its own mythology, he used the available cultural resources to articulate his vision of an ideal professional for both domestic and foreign audiences. Invited to deliver a prestigious keynote speech at the main American professional conference for computer experts in 1972, Ershov described a universal ideal programmer by creatively combining Soviet rhetorical structure with Western references: "In his work, the programmer is challenged to combine, with the ability of a first class mathematician to deal in logical abstraction, a more practical, a more Edisonian talent, enabling him to build useful engines out of zeros and ones, alone [sic]" (Ershov 1972, 502). To emphasize the transcendent quality of the new profession, Ershov did not shy away from borrowing biblical language and imagery, where a programmer "feels himself to be the father-creator of the program, the son-brother of the machine on which it runs, and the carrier of the spirit which infuses life into the program/ machine combination" (504). The highest aspiration of such an ideal practitioner according to Ershov was to spread the gospel of programming to all humanity in a recognizable logic of both Christian and Marxist worldviews. "Is it not however the highest aesthetic ideal of our profession," concluded the Soviet expert, "to make the art of programming public property, and thereby to submerge our exclusiveness within a mature mankind?" (505).

The reception of the speech, which immediately met with enthusiasm from its Western audience, and its present-day relevance visible in recent citation patterns point to the ongoing elaboration of professional identity in the field of programming. All grandiloquence aside, Ershov nonetheless reflected upon the mundane and concrete aspects of a programmer's labor as shared across the Atlantic and behind the Iron Curtain: their interaction with the machine, between themselves, and with society at large as complicated by the pace of hardware evolution, the status of scientific knowledge, and institutional struggles. At the same time, such shared concerns did not preclude Ershov's and his Western colleagues' awareness of the different political and economic structures that were in place. They considered it their duty to serve the needs of their respective countries. For Ershov, this duty found its utmost expression in his involvement in the 1985 reform introducing computer education into the Soviet school system.

CONTESTED VISIONS OF LATE SOVIET COMPUTERIZATION

While it is beyond the scope of this overview to provide a full account of Soviet programming developments during the 1970s, 1980s, and early 1990s, the following question is nevertheless unavoidable: Is failure the only way to describe late Soviet computer developments? By the early 1970s, there was not only a Soviet computer industry but also a new Soviet profession: the programmer. Although not nearly as numerous as their American colleagues, programmers had specialized journals, professional meetings, and even a public relations coup thanks to the national and international victories of the chess program, Kaissa. Yet when the Cold War ended with the Soviet collapse, Western specialists were quick to observe that the Soviet Union entered the 1990s without computers. Although such observations chiefly referred to the absence of personal computers in Soviet households, they implied a more general Soviet failure to experience what is generally coined the "Computer Revolution" and to enter the "Information Age." The 1968 state decision to make the new Soviet computer series compatible with IBM 360 architecture was considered a major turning point away from original Soviet research and development to systematic illicit borrowing.

In fact, the practice of reverse engineering shaped the materiality of late Soviet computing from ES large-frame computers to minicomputers to Apple and PCs and even to pocket programmable calculators. While there is no single systematic study of the late Soviet computer industry, the common Western perception holds that the planned economy could not handle the sophistication of microelectronics production, and that the party's monopoly on information could not allow for the diffusion of personal computers, a technology that allegedly enabled freedom of expression. To reconstruct the major changes in Soviet programming in this material environment defined by imitation we need to break with the circularity of such explanations and account for the ongoing contestation of Soviet computerization schemas from within.

Several observations are relevant for understanding the professional challenges and aspirations of Soviet programmers during the late Soviet period. On the one hand, changes due to the importation of Western technologies were mitigated by important institutional and social continuities.

For instance, the pioneer computer organization focusing on military computing, the SKB-245, was integrated into the Scientific Research Center for Electronic Computational Technology (NITsEVT), the lead organization supervising the developments of ES computers in the Soviet Union. By the same logic, the NITsEVT software department relied on established academic experts in programming to oversee its projects. On the other hand, major changes appeared due to large-scale diffusion of hardware: by the late 1970s about 70 percent of all computers in the country were ES machines. Although plagued by many delays and reliability issues, the mass production of ES machines (estimated at about sixteen thousand units for the entire period of production) led to the spread of computers across the country, entailing the demand for many more exploitation engineers, system programmers, and operators. New economies of scale led to major changes in the Soviet computing landscape. Yet social continuities also translated these changes into particular hybrid practices on the ground; hybridization not only explains the operation of post-Soviet IT but in a more uncanny away appears to foreshadow the unpredictable outcomes stemming from the Putin-era initiatives to transplant Western forms of innovation onto the Russian soil (Simonova, this volume).

A sketch of the activities of Ershov's department at the Akademgorodok Computer Center elucidates the issue. The work on the original computer research and development never completely stopped. In the early 1970s, Ershov was able to create a production spin-off of his department, a software construction bureau institutionalized as the Novosibirsk branch of the IT-MiVT and charged with developing software for the supercomputer that continued the BESM-6 line, called Elbrus. At the same time, Ershov's group was able to obtain funds under the ES umbrella to work on an extremely ambitious experimental project that was never delivered to its customer—a multilingual translating system called BETA for Algol 68, Simula, and PL/1.

Understanding how various actors adapted to the practice of borrowing on the local level helps us to appreciate the paradoxical characteristics of more general patterns that appear on a national scale: for example, the widespread custom of modifying hardware and programming in machine codes at the institutional level was disrupted, but tinkering with electronics became a common hobbyist practice with the availability of discarded pieces and the mass production of affordable programmable calculators; experts trained in the tradition of Soviet mathematical cybernetics turned into traveling lecturers on the ES operating system, while in the 1970s PL/1 took the place of Algol 60 as the most popular language in civilian computer centers;

Western home computers were sold on the black market and at the closed foreign currency shops, and the network of afterschool education centers carrying programming classes for children led to a wide popularity of Basic by the mid-1980s.

This usage of Western programming languages and software packages and the adoption of corresponding programming practices had its advantages, and its costs. As became apparent to the early critics of the Soviet policy of giving priority to technology transfer over investment in the indigenous projects, the oft-cited argument about the benefits of copying hardware architecture to obtain access to millions of lines of software did not account for two crucial factors: First, there was the inherent difficulty of understanding foreign, often illegally obtained, programs. Without appropriate documentation and human interaction, the economy of labor was questionable. Second, there was the concern for nurturing a critical mass of qualified specialists working on cutting-edge developments in systems' software. The expertise of system programmers was not solely evaluated by a degree or diploma but represented a personal profile built over years of experience and corresponded to a particular mindset. Borrowing software disrupted such dynamics of professional growth. To sum up, the orientation on copying hardware to save on software development led to a radical growth in the number of programmers, but it simultaneously aggravated questions surrounding the status of their work and training.

These implications are best demonstrated following Ershov's and his group's trajectory. While Ershov ascended in the Soviet scientific hierarchies, and as his research on the mathematical nature of compilation became recognized on the national level with the prestigious Krylov Prize, his vision of the professionalization of programming soared. Masses of programmers were trained on the job by the computer industry and dispersed throughout the computer centers of the production ministries. While there were many specialized national and international conferences on the topics of computer science and theoretical programming held in the Soviet Union in the 1970s and 1980s, no meetings followed the two Union-wide professional conferences for programmers held in Kiev (1968) and Novosibirsk (1970). Despite the requests for more specialists, the universities, including the Novosibirsk State University where Ershov taught, resisted classes in computing.

In the context where Soviet scientific hierarchies prioritized the authority of pure science, applications, including programming, became niches for what was considered a less reliable labor force—women—and safe havens for "suspicious" social elements: Jews. As a result, Soviet computer centers were prone to high rates of turnover; there was widespread headhunting for system programmers and women often did not return or had to be retrained after taking maternity leave. In addition, programming was one of the areas directly impacted by the Soviet decision to allow Jewish emigration in the early 1970s (Fedorova on Israel, this volume; West, this volume).

The challenges of the Soviet professionalization of programmers' labor described above provide crucial context for understanding the trajectory of the late Soviet project to universalize programming skills, crystallized in the 1981 slogan "Programming, the second literacy" (Ershov 1981). During the 1970s, Ershov reaffirmed his belief that reliable software is a direct reflection of the personal virtues of the programmer: logic, patience, and discipline. Addressing the young readers of the specialized mathematics journal for youth, *Kvant*, Ershov claimed that "good programmers are people of a special kind" and invited schoolchildren to learn programming to become members of tomorrow's computer centers (Ershov and Zvenigorodskiy 1979). In the following years, Ershov articulated a fully developed pedagogical agenda of computer education whereby the human qualities shared by "good programmers" could be nurtured early on, from childhood, by developing a set of mental habits: "algorithmic thinking." Such an agenda was backed by results of the collective work of his computer education group, which developed experimental pedagogical software and ran successful summer camps and distance-learning experiments throughout the 1970s and 1980s.

Although the educational activities of the Akademgorodok group were not unique per se, they led to very distinct results: Ershov's status as a pundit contributed to the international diffusion of his philosophy of computer education, and his authority within the Soviet hierarchies helped him to integrate Moscow's political networks. Ershov's alliance with the ambitious physicist Yevgeniy Velikhov, known for his close connection with the rising party leader, Mikhail Gorbachev, underlie the transformation of his vision into state policy. Among the first state orders signed by Gorbachev when he entered office in winter 1985 was the computerization of education, including the introduction of compulsory classes in "The Basics of Informatics." Although grounded in the ideas and experiments of the 1970s, within the changing political context of the mid-1980s the reform and its pedagogical agenda became rearticulated in coordination with perestroika and its ideals of democratization.

At the same time, the implementation of the reform was anything but a simple affair: teachers were to be trained, textbooks printed and delivered, computers and software produced and distributed. Characterized by numerous setbacks at every level, the reform became associated with the weaknesses of the Soviet state. The delays with the delivery of computers to schools led to descriptions of the reform as a late Soviet absurdity: learning to program without computers was akin to learning to swim without water. The relative ease of obtaining the Japanese computers in Vladivostok, as documented by Aleksandra Masalskaya and Zinaida Vasilyeva in this volume, was more of an exception to the general scarcity. But the main attack driving numerous discussions in the Soviet press concerned the meaning of "computer literacy" itself. According to many Soviet and international specialists, the proficient use of applications such as word processing and spreadsheet calculations, not programming, should be the goal of computer literacy and should define computer education in school curricula.

For the proponents of the reform's philosophy of universal programming skills there was little contradiction between its goals and the instrumental approach: learning to program does not prevent mastering typing or editing. Agreeing that every child would not grow up to become a professional programmer, Ershov (1988) insisted that interacting with the computer should be an empowering human experience: "The discipline of action is equally necessary for a human, like the discipline of mind and the discipline of speech. Exercising in the control over a computer, a human being elaborates an ability to control himself." Drawing on the cultural baggage of the revolutionary project of making a new man and the early Soviet campaign for eradicating illiteracy, the slogan of "Programming, the second literacy" allowed proponents of the reform to envisage a socialist "information society" where programming fostered personal virtues and social harmony.

Because he died in 1988, Ershov did not witness the fall of the Berlin Wall and the dissolution of the Soviet Union. Even if many computers were eventually delivered to schools and the class on "The Basics of Informatics" remained on the curriculum, the reform's goal of developing special thinking habits—algorithmic thinking via programming—was discredited. While the limited and short-lived 1985 reform does not lend itself to causal claims about the numbers or quality of Russian IT specialists abroad, beyond the specific cases of several model schools in capitals and Novosibirsk, the intense debates it provoked demonstrate the high level of interest in IT technologies in late Soviet society and help situate the radical transformative visions among its post-Soviet heirs from Kazan to Estonia (Kontareva, this volume; Savchenko, this volume). Furthermore, the philosophy and pedagogical experiences that guided the reform did not disappear altogether; they can still be found at Akademgorodok—with its ongoing tradition of annual summer camps for young programmers—and in the present-day work of prominent computer education specialists who started their careers within the reform framework of the 1980s.

CONCLUSIONS

From their place in secret military installations to their use as tools of political legitimacy, computers were at the very core of post–World War II Soviet history. Soviet programming did not appear as an afterthought but was part and parcel of Soviet computing efforts. Its specific features were a product of national structures as well as interactions with the West. Following the radical reappraisal of cybernetics in the Soviet Union in 1955, the early public discourse and professional identification of programmers took place under the umbrella of a new metascience. The technological challenges of software portability and international coordination of expertise shaped the definition of a separate professional identity in the 1960s. The rationale behind the much-contested orientation of the late Soviet computer industry on reproducing Western hardware architecture ranged from scientists' interest in integrating the Western community, to problems of coordination between the military and civil sectors, to the state's goals of mass computerization. However, the numerical growth of Soviet programmers did not lead to a stronger corporate identity as the distance between the aspirations and realities of academic professionals and typical computer centers mounted.

The Soviet expert in automated programming, Andrey Ershov, became the main spokesperson for the profession at home and abroad. According to his vision, the essence of programming was the realization of human intelligence predicated on an intimate connection: the brotherhood of man and machine. Fusing the experiments of American and Soviet educators in the 1970s and Soviet revolutionary aspirations to create a "new man," Ershov developed an original philosophy of computer education that guided the Soviet educational reforms of the 1980s and the attempt to create the socialist "information society." According to the slogan "Programming, the second literacy," programming should become a universal skill and a guarantor of social and political cohesion. Although the reform's goal of human engineering was contested and discredited, the end of the Soviet state did not entirely bring to an end the technocratic visions in post-Soviet societies.

While accounting for the radical novelty and the rapid evolution of digital computer technology associated with the notion of computer generations, the concepts of "Computer Revolution" and more recently "big data" do not answer all our questions; it is equally important to trace the continuity of practices predicated on the much slower change of human generations. The Soviet programming cultures and visions of the socialist "Information Age" reveal overlapping social networks, values, and rhetoric stretching from the early Soviet to the post-Soviet periods. From Lenin's famous declarations that without literacy there is no politics and that communism equals Soviet power and electrification, to Gorbachev's perestroika and education computerization, the communist project was predicated on the re-engineering of nature, humans, and machines. However, unlike pilots and cosmonauts—the iconic Soviet heroes embodying the power of flight gained by a man-machine interaction—Soviet programmers were and remain less visible and members of a potentially disposable occupation caught between mathematical designs to automatize programming and the realities of the laborious and error-prone practice of reading and writing code.

REFERENCES

Ershov, Andrei. 1965. "'Al'fa-rozhdenie' ili kak sozdavalas' sistema avtomaticheskogo programmirovaniia." *Za nauku v Sibiri*, January 18.

Ershov, Andrei. 1968. "Ob urovne matematicheskogo obespecheniia elektronnykh vychislitel'nykh mashin." July. Ershov Archive, f. 298/l. 1–45.

Ershov, Andrei. 1972. "Aesthetic and Human Factors in Programming." *Comm. ACM* 15, no. 7: 501–5.

Ershov, Andrei. 1981. "Programming, the Second Literacy." *Multiprocessors and Multiprogramming* 8, no. 1: 1–9.

Ershov, Andrei. 1988. "Kom'iuterizatsiia shkoly i matematicheskoe obrazovanie." International Congress on Mathematical Education, July. Ershov Archive, f. 334/l. 256.

Ershov, Andrei, and Gennadii Zvenigorodskii. 1979. "Zachem nado umet' programmirovat'?" *Kvant* 9: 47–51.

Gerovitch, Slava. 2002. *From Newspeak to Cyberspeak: A History of Soviet Cybernetics*. Cambridge, MA: MIT Press.

Gordin, Michael. 2009. *Red Cloud at Dawn: Truman, Stalin, and the End of the Atomic Monopoly*. New York: Farrar, Straus and Giroux.

Haigh, Thomas. 2002. "Software in the 1960s as Concept, Service, and Product." *IEEE Annals of the History of Computing* 24, no. 1: 5–13.

Kraineva, Irina, and Nataliia Cheremnykh. 2011. *Put' programmista*. Novosibirsk: Nonparel.'

Lavrentyev, Mikhail. 2000. "Opyty zhizni. 50 let v nauke." In *Vek Lavrentieva*, edited by Nataliia Pritvits, Valerii Ermikov, and Zamira Ibragimova, 30–70. Novosibirsk: Izdatel'stvo SORAN.

Lusternik, Lazar,' Aleksandr Abramov, Viktor Shestakov, and Mikhail Shura-Bura. 1952. *Reshenie matematicheskikh zadach na avtomaticheskikh tsifrovykh mashinakh*. Moscow: Izdatel'stvo Akademii Nauk SSSR.

Peters, Benjamin. 2012. "Normalizing Soviet Cybernetics." *Information and Culture* 47, no. 2: 145–75.

Podlovchenko, Rimma. 2003. "Vospominaniia o pore uchenichestva u Alekseia Andreevicha Liapunova." In *Istoriia Informatiki v Rossii: uchenye i ikh shkoly*, edited by Viktor Zakharov, Rimma Podlovchenko, and Iakov Fet, 370–75. Moscow: Nauka.

Sobolev, Sergei, Anatolii Kitov, and Aleksei Liapunov. 1955. "Osnovnye cherty Kibernetiki." *Voprosy filosofii* 4: 136–48.

Tatarchenko, Ksenia. 2013. "A House with the Window to the West: The Akademgorodok Computer Center (1958–1993)." PhD diss., Princeton University, NJ.

Wiener, Norbert. 1948. *Cybernetics: Or Control and Communication in the Animal and the Machine*. Cambridge, MA: MIT Press.

Wiener, Norbert. 1950. *The Human Use of Human Beings: Cybernetics and Society*. Boston: Houghton Mifflin.

CHAPTER TWO

FROM LURKER TO NINJA
Creating an IT Community at Yandex

Marina Fedorova

No one knows what software needs to do. We have to discover it. That's where a lot of people go wrong is they think this is the way a software system should be designed, how it should work, is knowable. It's not. It is discoverable.

—RICHARD SHERIDAN, CEO and chief storyteller of Menlo Innovations; quoted in
Shane Hastie, "Linda Rising and Richard Sheridan on Creating a Culture of Joy—Part 2"

In the beginning was the Bible. To be more precise, it all started with the Russian Bible search algorithm. In 1995, the future cofounders of Yandex[1]—Ilya Segalovich and Arkadiy Volozh—developed a demonstration product that showcased breakthrough capabilities in search and language processing. The idea was to take a classical text and use it as a database for conducting keyword searches. Why the Bible? Volozh simply answered by saying that everything else was under copyright, while Segalovich explained that the choice was driven by general cultural concerns: "The Bible is the most popular text in the world, and if anyone would need some kind of search for some array of Russian texts, that was just it" (Sokolov-Mitrich 2014, 62). As a result, the software enabled a user to run a context search through the Bible, with the algorithm accounting for the Russian language's complex grammar. Then the algorithm started learning and two years on it became a part of the constantly growing corpus of code that unites Yandex developers today.

What makes Yandex such a unique case worth scholarly attention? It started its search engine a year before Google—in 1997—but the contexts of development in the San Francisco Bay Area and in Moscow were starkly different.[2] Yandex emerged in a difficult if not hostile business environment. Not only were there too few companies to sustain the critical mass for a self-replicating cluster—where firms gain advantage from knowledge circulation and the experiential development of human capital—but other industries were also competing for personnel. In the years that followed, Google outgrew the garage, while Yandex outgrew the very structure of the Russian oil-dependent economy (for an overview of initiatives to wean Russia off its dependence on natural resources, see Zhikharevich, this volume).

Since Russia has indeed been well known for its tech-talented emigrants, one might think that Yandex capitalizes on a large stock of scientists and engineers with significant strengths in mathematics, hence the company's success. But contrary to received opinions, the Russian university system—despite its strong Soviet tradition of education—has largely failed to meet the high demand for programmers through relevant training. As a result, the burden of IT training falls to the IT industry itself; Russian software companies had to become factories for turning analytically minded graduates from noncore fields into skilled software developers. Yandex, in particular, hires not only IT professionals but also mathematicians, engineers, physicists, and other techno-scientific practitioners who all need to be integrated into their corporate community. In this regard, Yandex has the same objective as any other enterprise: to break through the clusters of knowledge held by its employees and create a shared base.

But what makes Yandex, Yandex? Yandex is the idea of a search engine expressed in code. The code, and with it the knowledge that constitutes Yandex, cannot exist independently of the complex technical and physical infrastructures where it is stored. However, the code also encapsulates practices and relationships of collaboration, training, and skill transfer. This social infrastructure, which is embedded into the company's code, is a competitive advantage. Drawing on the case of Yandex, this chapter discusses how routine engagement with code serves to transform a diversified body of newcomers with different educational backgrounds into a coherent body of IT professionals while simultaneously creating a unified community.

What kind of knowledge is cultivated in the poster child of Russian IT companies; and how does Yandex manage to breed a collective of programmers who come from various backgrounds and face the lure of foreign markets? These issues require empirical attention because education, professionalization, and the process of membership within the IT community are usually considered in relation to open source development,[3] while the peculiarities of these processes within the corporate software sector are often understudied.

FROM COMMUNITIES OF PRACTICE TO LANGUAGE COMMUNITIES

The concepts of "communities of practice" (Lave and Wenger 1991) and its variation "networks of practice" (Brown and Duguid 2001) have been popular interpretive tools for studying engineering and software communities; however, I believe that the conceptual shift from "practice" to "language" can help us better understand the social dimension of programming by going beyond its technical level. To illustrate the potential of such reconceptualization, I provide examples from the study of the Yandex community.[4]

The reason why the current analysis is centered on the building of a community is that the unsuccessful attempts to establish standards for the professional development of programmers enabled the industry to consider new venues for training.[5] Indeed, software development often does not fit into bureaucratically organized careers. Developers participate in activities related to the exploration, testing, and sharing of knowledge, which virtually never follows formal standards and methods that are taught in academia. On-site training, instead, helps companies provide their employees with a specific type of knowledge that stems from practice and that is always contextualized. Therefore, studying professionalization from the perspective of community-building is productive, since it helps debunk the academic division of labor and avoid discussions of "prescriptive models" as applied to the shaping of the IT profession (Shapiro 1994).

A lens for understanding how one becomes a community member through practices and interactions as the primary inputs to learning was provided by Jean Lave and Étienne Wenger. They suggest that the process of acquiring professional skills does not necessarily correspond to formal training but is closely connected to the milestones of becoming a competent member of an informal "community of practice." However, there is an important, though often omitted, characteristic of their analysis: Lave and Wenger (1991, 29) initially intended "to rescue the idea of apprenticeship." Therefore, their model has limited application in the case of Yandex, as a developer's training usually lacks the most important elements of apprenticeship learning: the face-to-face interaction with a master and hands-on experience through observation.[6] To explain why the Yandex community cannot be studied as a community of practices, a minor detour into how work is organized at Yandex is in order.

What I noticed during my fieldwork was that newcomers and experienced employees most often worked and communicated on terms of parity. Although horizontal communication is highly encouraged at Yandex on the organizational level, as it fosters collaboration and the free flow of information, experienced workers themselves support this managerial strategy and give novices the chance to express their opinions, involving them in all stages of problem solving. Sometimes novices even without any practical experience have knowledge of the most recent developments in the field, allowing them to make a notable contribution. Since interaction often fosters cross- and reciprocal learning, the type of one-way learning that underlies the master-apprentice model has limitations within this context. Another constraint compromising the use of the concept "communities of practice" is the absence of practice under observation.

Situated cognition emphasizes the context dimension of knowledge, where meaning is inseparable from the situation. However, while learning through practice—as described by Lave and Wenger—requires ostensive training, in Yandex such learning through observation is difficult to find. Here, learning occurs through practice, though not in the situation where a master teaches through actions, thereby passing on tacit knowledge to the novices; instead, it occurs when newcomers learn on their own with the help of written information. One hardly ever finds employees actually *showing* their colleagues anything on the screen or demonstrating how they write and fix modules, while going through lines of code together with their peers. New hires have to *discover* by themselves what the rules of practice and the norms of participation are, since an overwhelming majority of developers' work time is spent alone with their computers. I will discuss below the reasons why the developers' work is mostly isolated.

The main factor that eliminates face-to-face communication is the non-geographic organization of Yandex's development activities; in other words, teams can physically work from different locations: a different floor or building or even from different cities. In most cases, software development at Yandex does not create a situation where face-to-face communication is required. Even when Yandex employees want to discuss some work-related matter, any attempt to do so creates, as some put it, "too much fuss." The fact is that most of the company's workspace is an open office plan, where sound travels freely. Yandex developers are very defensive of their right to work in silence and many of them even prefer to work with their headphones on in order to keep themselves "in the zone" and not be bothered by the constant buzz of clicking keyboards. Being "in the zone" is an integral part of developers' work, as software development demands close attention and it is easy to lose focus on an idea, goal, or particular place within hundreds of lines of code. As the rule of silence is not to be violated, all the communications go online. Developers usually prefer to collaborate sitting in front of their own computers using messengers, the intranet, Jabber, email, or tracking changes in the code directly in the version control system.[7] Usually, though, online communication and face-to-face conversations facilitate information *sharing*, rather than the *transfer of skills*. Furthermore, in the particular case of developers, all kinds of discussions do not involve actual learning-by-doing. Knowledge at Yandex does not come from observation, but comes in the form of code that resembles instruction and is very explicit and visible (rather than unarticulated or inexpressible, as it is in Lave and Wenger's framework). Therefore, practices themselves, if studied through the lens of "communities of practice," often appear as a blind spot in the analysis of software communities. Since such conceptualization does not answer how code-writing practices help to reveal and transfer knowledge within a software community, we need to find an approach that can emphasize the materiality of code-writing practices.

To explore the training modes through which professional expertise and shared understanding of practices can be transmitted, we need to take a closer look at code and programming languages in order to study the practices of code writing that govern a programmer's performance in the virtual milieu. Code writing is a central practice in software development that varies mainly by programming language. However, code writing is not a purely technical skill but a social practice. This is because once exercised, code writing inevitably becomes socially contextualized. I will further explain how on-site training of developers is connected to code writing as a sociolinguistic practice of using the source code.

As previously noted, while practice in "communities of practice" is disembedded from its ostensive power within a digital context, another domain where we can find this referential source is *language*. An important aspect of this approach is that language cannot be understood as the mere transmission of information but is a form of social action. Action-oriented approach to language draws extensively on Ludwig Wittgenstein's philosophy. I give priority to Wittgenstein's work because his theoretical framework simultaneously explains situatedness of practices, their communal nature, and learning in coparticipation. The challenge of using Wittgenstein's theories for interpreting programming practices is the question of whether it can be applied to artificial languages.

The issue here is that the machine can only function with binary logic (operating with values that are either true or false) and cannot access the context-dependent, auxiliary knowledge about the range of meaning that accompanies usage. In order for the machine to "understand" the code written by the developer, a compiler or interpreter "translates" it, i.e., converts it into machine code. In this regard, programming languages have a constitutive role in code-writing practices as their syntax is designed to ensure such transitions. Besides syntax, programming languages predetermine the correct combinations of symbols, data structures, comment density,[8] number of lines, the module concept, and so forth. In other words, any programming language defines a set of actions, otherwise the machine will not understand the commands. Since programming language acts as a criterion for determining meaning, the developer must be deprived of the opportunity to misinterpret and must always use a language correctly. With such emphasis placed on the lack of surplus significance in code and its preciseness of definition, one may assume that programming languages are—in line with Wittgenstein's philosophy—"ideal languages" (Wittgenstein [1922] 2001). If this is true, then code must be something clear cut and bug free—as there can be no misuse of an ideal language, such as, for instance, the one in which the code is written. However, bugs happen and software is not flawless, hence we need to discover what bugs show us: mistakes that are made in the human domain.

An error may occur not only because of some crucial mistake in the system's architecture or the wrong implementation of an algorithm, but it may also creep into software by way of a programmer's simple logical mistake, the misapplication of some technique or component, a misprint or slip-up in actual code writing, or any other failure that occurred unintentionally within the social dimension. Such errors often happen when one developer cannot understand another, or, more precisely, when one developer *misinterprets* the code of another. Therefore, the rules that govern code practices are looser than one might imagine and *misuse* of a programming language is possible. We used to think about code as something that is written for machines, rather than for people, though this issue is controversial and deserves special attention.[9]

Programming languages and code are not purely technical. Yet here I want to make an important distinction: the machine indeed "reads" binary code, but the human reader deals with the source code, which is converted into machine code by a compiler (or interpreter, depending on the programming language). Machine code is an object (an executable file), while source code is a constantly growing "corpus" that includes code itself and comments written in natural language.

Source code is the only stage where a developer can *read* code, even without comments, since it comprises only human-readable and human-written source code files.[10] The readability, when considered as such, varies by programming language as well. For instance, one can read a program in Python nearly as easily as reading this text (or at least grasp the general idea of what the code does). High-level languages closely resemble spoken languages; to some extent, this explains why the entry barriers to learning them are relatively low. One can quickly pick up such languages, since they have syntax that is easy to read and to write and in comparison to other languages one need not know a massive base of specialized commands in order to get started. Another argument is that programming languages (just like natural, spoken ones) are actively developed. This occurs not only through their own evolution but also with the appearance of new languages that incorporate many features of their language predecessor. Therefore, the main reason why I believe that programming languages can achieve recognition as natural languages is that most of them are created in the semantics of spoken languages and inherit their immanent ambiguity. With all the technical rules that programming languages set, there is still room for developers to flexibly use a language, readjusting and interpreting the existing technical regulations that were imposed upon them. The crucial point here is that languages themselves are not compiled (or interpreted); rather, it is their *implementations* that compile code. Therefore, languages are, indeed, unambiguous and standardized as such, but there are innumerable ways of how to *use* a language differently for writing code. Consequently, such relative flexibility creates contradictions, making code less readable for its other users (i.e., developers).

Aside from natural-language comments (which will be discussed later), there are a lot of social elements in code, or, as some of my informants call it, "noise":

> I can immediately spot former Python developers by how they name variables. I've seen a couple of times how people follow Python conventions while writing code in other languages, and their code looks untidy. This noise just strikes my eyes and keeps me from focusing. It's not the end of the world, but it shows that you don't care about me reading it. You can, actually, edit this automatically with source code editors, but you need some add-ons that provide such functionality. And I'd rather not to be concerned with such things. (Yevgeniy, aged twenty-seven)[11]

Such "noise" is completely ignored by the compiler because it is not connected with programming language but related to coding style. Coding styles are guidelines for writing software, but they serve as purely visual devices that commonly deal with the appearance of source code. Coding style is a subjective matter and depends on the preferences of an author, although it may also be a company (project or community) convention that emphasizes the necessity to improve the readability of code in order to ensure collaboration. "Noise" (i.e., differences in style) points to the fact that a convention is being violated and that the code is getting hard to read. The issue is that styles provide languages with variability. In most cases, languages support multiple ways of naming variables, presenting data, locating spaces between functions or indicating whether to put curly braces each on their own line, determining what kind of layout is most comfortable to the eye (how long a line should be, whether lines should be placed compactly or have an empty line as separator), and the list goes on. Styles are often developed for a specific programming language since, for instance, the coding style in C++ is not suitable for Python. Therefore, the code can be written differently according to style, and such an unsettling possibility of bypassing the rules influences how users perceive the meaning of code. Styles govern the process of reading and understanding, either hindering or facilitating these actions.

The difficulty here is not only whether there is (or is not) consensus on a programming style, but rests on the fact that such flexibility in representation creates a space where everything that is written is error prone. For instance, if a symbol has different meanings across languages:

> Sometimes Python developers forget the curly braces and then they're surprised that their code doesn't run as intended. In Python, you don't need curly braces, but in C++ curly braces explain your logic to a compiler. So, if you have more than one operator in a loop and you write this loop without curly braces, a compiler will accept that, but it will lead to a bug. Newcomers make such mistakes a lot, especially if they switch between languages. I mean, they are not stupid, it's about formatting properly. (Evgenii)

This highlights how a small and simple typo may alter the meaning of the code. If a coding convention is being followed, it is easier for the developer's eye to catch such errors within what is an organized rather than "messy" code. It seems a reasonable assumption, therefore, that mistakes can be made by anyone, even experienced programmers, since many typos will inevitable sneak past the compiler. However, following the coding convention not only helps one read the code and detect errors at the earliest possible stage, but also creates meaning. Seen in this light, style has transitioned from a mere visual device to a conductor for meaningful code production. Good style makes meaning "visible" and describes the ways in which a language is used, while the absence of style "hides" meaning and introduces ambiguity. If one has a consistent approach for writing code that corresponds to the understanding of others, then the meaning behind code remains clear and unambiguous. I argue, therefore, that programming style itself represents a liminal zone, where the "sociality" of code unfolds.

The implementation of programming languages is indeed governed by the rules of the language itself, though one cannot be reduced to the other. Instead of being automatic and standardized, the usage of programming language can be voluntarily changed by its users and is inherently problematic as well as negotiated. To collaborate effectively, Yandex employees also need to develop a shared understanding (i.e., style) of how to write code, one that is clear to every member of a particular community. Style allows us to make the perplexing character of code intelligible, since a developer, while reading source code, *discovers* meaning through particular details and contexts of use. In this sense, addressing the codebase is similar to a language game (Wittgenstein [1953] 2010) that implies creation of conventional systematic practices. A developer always needs to "consult" with the "source" in order to bring his code into correspondence with the codebase, with the "text" of the collective author that constitutes a certain practice.

Thus, working with the code as a learning process has two primary inputs: technology (when one learns the rules of a programming language that constitutes practices) and community (when one learns how to use this programming language according to conventions in the given context of the codebase). Yandex employees need to agree that they mean the same things not because they share the same understanding of how software should be written, but because they are predisposed to have a convention by the need to collaborate. While community conventions are consistent, they are not fixed or standardized, since they depend not only on agreements but also on adjustments that constantly arise. At this point, it is noteworthy to discuss what properties code has that allow it to facilitate the processes of learning and community building.

Code has the performative function that stems from its unique property: "Code is the first language that actually does what it says—it is a machine for converting meaning into action" (Galloway 2004, 166). Adrian Mackenzie (2005, 76) was among the first to discuss the performativity of code. Focusing on the Linux kernel, he suggests that the performativity of code lies in its ability to objectify linguistic praxis through processes of circulation. However, while processes of circulation play a primary role for open source code, such practices of "repeating" and "citing" that, according to Mackenzie, produce performative effects are limited in the case of a company. In this respect, proprietary code is not speech;[12] rather, it takes the form of a "sacred" text that can be accessed only by "elects" (members of a community or, in this case, Yandex developers). Yet it is not a text because it is not a fixed substance but the result of a progressive process of code writing. Indeed, a company gives code its limits, but code also constantly changes and grows with the community. In contrast to open source, one cannot decide what to write and from where to start because the company code is being written "on the shoulders" of peers and precursors, generation after generation. Therefore, a key feature that distinguishes the Yandex community from any other expert community is that developers collaborate virtually with people but practically are engaged with the fruits of their collective labor: *the codebase*.

The codebase is performative by virtue of the fact that it is itself an act of speech—it enacts its own description. Furthermore, the "corpus" encapsulated in the codebase preserves the intentionality of its collective author, since it cannot be detached from the context in which it is written: it is "glued" to conventions that govern code writing, data in data centers, hardware, algorithms, protocols, operating systems, virtual machines—to all the digital, social, and physical elements that are involved in its production. Therefore, such a "corpus" literally shows how the company's software is being written, setting a pattern of code-writing practices. However, while being stable, the "corpus" is not ideal or fixed. In the case of a bug or out of necessity to update or scale certain technologies, the "corpus" is reconsidered and changed in order to bring it to stable form again. When failures in the technological domain happen, the norms and patterns of how to write software are simultaneously being revisited. The "corpus" communicates these changes to its readers and users accordingly. Therefore, it is a "monster" (Haraway 1992) that persistently resists transparency within the community while the community persistently strives to make it transparent. The ability of the codebase to simultaneously absorb and transmit the collective experience makes it a central element of community building and learning, because it facilitates learning-by-doing and learning-as-membership. The access to its knowledge means that newcomers have become a part of the community.

Such a change in approach, from communities of practice to language communities, allows us to treat programming languages and code as sites through which we can explore how training and expertise are transferred. In what follows, I focus my analysis on code and programming languages to capture how Yandex builds a professional community around its codebase.

Using the conceptual lens described above, I argue that Yandex builds its community through the practice of reading the code. Readability of the source code is an important property from the business perspective, since it makes software maintenance easier and less time consuming: the code should remain readable not only to newcomers but also to old-timers, should they have to go back to it at a later date. The emphasis on readability is also important for creating a sense of community: the source code should be readable in order to continue its function as the center of the community, concentrating every employee around it. It is by being clear that the code ensures software quality, while simultaneously creating commitment among employees to the replication of the Yandex community. Therefore, the very first thing every new employee has to learn is how to make code readable and to improve its utility for human readers. At Yandex, I heard several times that code (ideally) should look like it is being written by the same person, and if the code is "unreadable, but working, it is not good code" (Artemiy, aged forty-two). As I illustrate below, this often overlooked practice of engaging with code— "code reading"—is precisely the practice that facilitates the transition from neophyte to professional.

The interviews reveal that during the early stage of their careers newcomers are primarily involved with debugging. One of my informants admitted that if he needs something to work, he quickly writes a working prototype, which is needed before being polished into a production version. Usually this kind of work is performed by less experienced colleagues:

> This is how it works for a while for all newbies: I made them do all the dirty, routine work. Primarily it means that they will have to do a lot of debugging; later on they can be entrusted with fine-tuning and rewriting. From the very beginning they basically only read a lot. This way they can get acquainted with the codebase as it's an essential skill to know how to operate within it. (Denis, aged thirty-seven)

Therefore, debugging proves itself a simple task and an effective means by which newcomers introduce themselves to the company's codebase and acquire all the necessary skills to work with it. This is not only the aim of on-site training but also a necessity for stable software development. Debugging is an essential routine that novices can perform, although they need to understand the corpus of code in the base and navigate freely inside the system. However, even for experienced practitioners it can be difficult to get to know a codebase and understand semantic and structural relationships between various interlinked pieces of code.

Since newcomers are not the authors of the code and they have never before participated in its development, they face the necessity of learning how to read the code and grasp all its essential moments in order to maintain it in future. Therefore, the process of familiarization with the codebase has the following trajectory: first, newcomers learn how to *read* the code (while being relatively passive members of the community); after this, they learn how to *develop* (as they begin transforming into active contributors). Such learning from the inside out comes with an important advantage. In the case of internet-based products that require stable online performance, having novices "on the bench" is potentially a way of keeping the project safe in case key contributors leave[13]; if this happens, they are already familiar with the codebase and able to improve upon it. Once newcomers have familiarized themselves with the codebase, they can avoid inappropriate code duplicates and significant dependencies between code blocks, as well as build software following reusability principles, i.e., performing their tasks as experienced users of the codebase. Therefore, reading is a practical achievement: having the ability itself means that one understands the code and is able to operate with it. I need to note that, obviously, modifying code and then observing what happens next is the best way to learn how to deal with software—by experimenting and testing its capabilities. Yet in the case of corporate software development, programmers are limited in their freedom to "play" with code, as it might cause serious damage:

> You can't introduce any extreme changes, even if they'll improve code performance. Very often you have to sacrifice performance for readability because you need to make sure that others will be able to maintain your code easily. (Evgenii)

In this respect, reading is not a passive act but an element of training, since by reading one prepares for the role of writing, a role that needs to be in sync with collective intention. However, the question of what exactly is to be read in the source code is a topic for further discussion.

In the previous section, I specified that the source code has two parts: human-readable code and comments. Comments that accompany source code should be convertible into documentation to the company's code, and they are written by developers-authors for developers-users. Writing documentation and comments in code is considered to be an important part of corporate software development, because it explains how a program or a system operates and how to use it. Therefore, a developer needs to comment on his code and keep track of it in order to clarify all possible inconsistences.

Comments are used to clarify code, to make it more readable and clearer. However, at Yandex there is a conflicting tradition of not commenting on the company's code. The very presence of comments in the source code is a highly debated issue among Yandex employees. In fact, such controversy represents a conflict of interests.

The practical problem of code without comments is that it creates an uncertainty about its business purpose and direction—whether it should be actively used or removed or, more probably, changed. To put it more directly, comments to some extent justify the presence and usefulness of code. From the business point of view, software companies need documentation because management has to keep track of development. From the practitioner's point of view, comments often create confusion. While many of my informants stressed that it is necessary to write comments in order to have a proper documentation for those "next in line," some of them argue that it is a questionable practice:

> Sometimes it is better not to read comments at all as it could be extremely confusing. Ideally, it serves the purpose of clarifying code; however, as a rule of thumb, it does quite the opposite. For instance, let's say we write down a general algorithm in comments. But we execute its special case. So, what we have: you refer to one thing, while doing another. No details provided. And you have to sit and delve into it really long to figure it out. (Aleksei, aged twenty-six)

Comments can be even more misleading when they state that code is doing one thing while in practice it is actually doing something completely different; relying only on information in comments may lead to serious vulnerabilities in the software later on.[14] This example illustrates an interesting phenomenon: instead of functioning as a device for clarification, comments sometimes produce unexpected output and, in Bruno Latour's (2005) terminology, serve as "mediators. Comments are designed to formalize development, to make it transparent and explicit. Bad commenting or the absence of comments, on the other hand, deprive software of its ability to be universal in its application, to be detached from its creators.

In her study of Indian IT workers, Sareeta Amrute (2014) has shown that if a developer fails to explain the code in comments, he augments his irreplaceability. While such commenting strategies may serve to sabotage corporate rule, at Yandex, as our further discussion will show, the absence of comments has an almost ideological meaning and helps to teach newcomers how to be reliable professionals who care about the community and its replication.

"Brutal" programmers with vast experience rely mostly on technical virtuosity and mastery and do not put comments in the code: "Don't let comments mess with your code. Excess is the enemy of good code. Nothing extra, just the essence. Comments are not necessary: if you are able to write code, you are able to read and understand it without further ado" (Denis). Such styles of coding help to test one's proficiency and sort out candidates with potential. It is similar to what Christopher Kelty (2008, 58) calls "argument-by-technology" and "argument-by-talk," meaning that the process of familiarization with professional practice surrounding technologies is constituted through code, as well as speech. Thus, the Yandex tradition of writing code without comments—a process that requires technical expertise—has become an organizational element that helps transform newcomers into experts. "Argument-by-technology" places initial hurdles before newcomers, requiring them to read the code and understand it:

> You know, our elderly, so to say, generation is against comments in code. I think they believe we [newcomers] should suffer, while reading it [laughing]. Sometimes it's really hard to understand what is in there [in code] without explanations and designations that are usually written in comments. They say, they want to get from us code without redundancy and that we need to learn how to understand it without tips. (Tamara, aged twenty-one)

This does not imply that luminaries in the company do not want newcomers by their side as colleagues; instead, they want them to prove their technical skills—the ability to read the code.

By reading code without comments, newcomers familiarize themselves with the structure of the codebase and the reason behind it in order have the requisite skills to improve it in the future. Thus, instead of simplifying the process of code reading, comments or their absence serve as an effective learning tool. While navigating a codebase, employees encounter difficulties that capture their attention and help them memorize important moments in the code. Also, when newcomers have problems with their stack, their more experienced colleagues ask them if they read the source itself, not the comments. The very need for comments calls the explicitness of code—often hailed as the virtue of the IT world—into question. Yandex's luminaries argue that the answer is always in the code itself. My informants with more than ten years of experience stated: "Read code and everything will be clear."

This motto carries almost biblical connotations in the sense that one should seek all answers in the source. The knowledge of the source and the ability to read it signify that one has become a member of the group: new people join the community by learning how to make sense of the code itself, of the "corpus" encapsulated in the codebase. However, the analogy between the Bible and the codebase lies not only in the fact that both are written by a collective author, but that they both have performative force; that is to say, they cannot be interpreted.

The fact is that the comments are interpretations of actions and the code is itself an action. As noted, comments can be misleading, while the code itself is the ultimate truth: the code is not describing anything, it simply runs. Thus, by reading code without comments, newcomers learn how to understand without explanation, how to grasp the very essence of the code and then write code that literally speaks for itself:

> Code tells you exactly how it was done. Comments explain to you the process or the idea behind the code. If you need to explain, it means you're not sure. Or it means that your code is way too complex to understand. If it lacks certainty and clarity, it's always bad code. You don't have to explain what it is supposed to do, just do it. . . . Actually, I never read comments, as I need to see the result. (Aleksandr, aged twenty-nine)

My informants also noticed that sometimes newcomers use comments in order to "hide" ambiguities in their code, to cover their lack of experience by using comments as a "crutch": "They often try to explain in comments what was meant to be done, instead of actually making the code to do that" (Denis). Also, such "crutches" often lead to bugs that, if detected in the main branch of the code, become not individual mistakes but mistakes of the collective author. In order to prevent such "shared" bugs, comments are often discouraged.

The absence of comments in code at Yandex provides its community with stability and ensures high-quality software by pushing newcomers to write as clearly as possible and not rely on comments as descriptions or interpretations. The absence of comments can be seen not as a drawback but as a practical necessity that meets the requirements of professional practices. In "industrial coding" the very skill of reading lines of code written in different languages and in different styles is crucial. By "industrial coding" informants mean the specific style of code writing:

> Any big company, and Yandex as well, is about industrial coding. So, code should be accurate, simple, and readable. It means that when you do industrial coding, you should write it for centuries to come. If it's reliable, durable, then anyone can continue your work, in case you are gone with the wind. But it's not only about us being interchangeable. Also, it's about such situations when other groups need to borrow our code. And they should be able to understand it, if they are going to use it. Basically, if code is written in such a way, it is easier to maintain it in production,[15] when it goes public, already open for users. (Yaroslav, aged twenty-three)

"Industrial coding" implies an opportunity for long-term use and further development. Therefore, by wading through an excessive amount of code lines without comments, newcomers receive training that stems from a hands-on experience of exploring the codebase and results in a set of practices for creating readable and, therefore, reliable code.

CRITIQUING AND CORRECTING

The analysis of how Yandex builds its community through language practices gets more nuanced if we consider peer code review as another technique of training, along with code reading and commenting. Peer code review is introduced in order to detect and fix the vulnerabilities of code, but it also reveals itself as a practice that allows Yandex newcomers to evolve as professionals.

In order to create a stable, consistent, and durable "corpus" of code, its quality needs to be controlled; and peer code review performs this disciplining function. The practice of peer code review has become a key element in software development not only for open source projects,[16] but for proprietary software as well. In particular, all lines of code that are going to be committed to a shared repository must be approved by peer code review. Yet, instead of being centralized and vertical, such control also has a communal nature: it is delegated to coworkers and dispersed among employees. Further, I will explain how peer code review helps Yandex employees to achieve a shared vision on software development.

Peer code review is closely connected to code reading, but while code reading is passive and subject to individual tasks, peer code reviewing is a collaborative practice that facilitates knowledge circulation and sharing. My field research showed that peer code review creates affinity for one another among employees, since, at Yandex, developers are allowed to review all the company's code, regardless of the project they are currently working on. Communicating through peer code review allows different contributors to combine their ideas and track progress in other projects and also helps unite newcomers around practices of development.

Developers pay specific attention to code-writing practices, as they believe that one can evaluate professionalism by observing how the code is written:

> We have a guy; he just recently came to us after his work at a bank. Well. . . . Obviously, he can't write code. It's not surprising, though, as he comes from a bank, but still I'm wondering how can one write so badly?! Noodles everywhere! We can't read his pieces. A total mess! (Anatoliy, aged twenty-six)

This quotation not only highlights the distinction that this informant made between his company and the bank, but also uncovers the ethical rule for "good" code writing, which is accuracy and the necessity that code be "readable" so that everyone is able to work with it. I want to emphasize here that the concept of "good" is not a given, but something that is invented collectively and achieved during systematic examination of each other's code, i.e., peer code review. This practice allows developers to discuss and propose changes to the codebase, as well as negotiate their code-writing practices.

When new employees come to Yandex (both experienced and inexperienced), they start writing code according to their own understanding of software development. According to my informants, code must "express" certain criteria. Usually, they explain what "good" means to them in terms of beauty: "Code might not be written in a conventional way, but if it's still beautiful, then this is good code" (Mark, aged twenty-nine).

Yet while some of my informants defined "beauty" in terms of "nontrivial solutions" inscribed in code, others stated that "accurate design" and simplicity characterize "beautiful" code. These two different understandings of "beauty" represent two conflicting approaches to programming: mathematical and engineering.[17] This is a very rough division, though it illustrates how different understandings of software development result in a variety of possible code-writing practices. Such imposition of a particular understanding on code production is similar to what Michael Lynch (1985) called "disciplining," which is when objects are brought into compliance with a certain scientific vision.

It should be noted that the division suggested above does not necessarily represent educational background, but rather subjective viewpoints on what is considered the best way to write code. In this respect, it is also interesting that Yandex developers have different preferences for using particular programming languages. Usually, but not necessarily, they tend to learn languages that "reflect" their understanding: "mathematicians" prefer high-level languages (e.g., Python) and "engineers" are adherents of low-level languages, especially c++.

Importantly, I am not suggesting that "mathematical" development equals writing code in high-level languages, or that "engineering" development implies writing code in low-level languages. There are projects at Yandex that are fundamentally engineering, but are written in high-level languages (e.g., intranet services at Yandex are mostly written in Python). Yet, the approach that programmers choose is strongly connected to how they understand development and prioritize objectives.

"Engineers" often use Python as it is a multipurpose language—it is even used at CERN and NASA[18]—with a clear syntax and readability that make it relatively easy to maintain. However, in the case of software production within the context of a large company, an "engineering" mind chooses low-level languages for the sake of performance. Meanwhile "mathematicians" are more inclined to write code in high-level languages, since they are usually more focused on the problem itself rather than on the tools that are required to solve it. Similarly, this may be why "mathematicians" frequently start by writing "dirty," unclear code, as they are more concerned with making it work—with solving the problem—than with long-term maintenance issues. According to my interviews, mathematicians are represented by a number of specialists with different backgrounds who focus on creating solutions that result in sophisticated algorithms. They prefer to use abstract programming languages that are "slow," as a machine needs more time to recognize them, but "fast" in that it is easier to write code on them; they are useful for obtaining quick results during prototyping. The community of engineers unites developers who are focused on the construction of a product's architecture. They prefer to elaborate the design of software and are concerned with how code will work on hardware. For their aims, engineers choose low-level programming languages that are "fast," because machines readily recognize their symbols, while writing on them is "slow" and time consuming: "I like Python as you can write the formula you need with a couple of lines. But in the case of c++, it could take you hours of code lines to write a finished piece" (Mikhail, aged twenty-six).

This example with mathematicians and engineers illustrates the classic differentiation between "us" and "them"; and this division is possible within one company because their coding practices bear the imprint of a certain conception of how code should be written. This conception can exist in a particular community or within a certain discipline. It is often unrelated to the content of practice but closely connected to the way this practice is performed. In this respect, the quality of code is related to its readership, to the target audience that often coincides with a particular community that shares the same understanding. While all my informants denied that their community could be structured according to different languages, software communities often evolve around developers who share the same understanding of how (and which) languages should be implemented.

Therefore, there are a number of crisscrossing communities that vary based on their views about software development, their educational backgrounds, experience, and also the programming languages they use. The only thing that binds them together is the necessity to work toward common objectives. In order to coordinate their actions and make their code readable, developers need to create a convention that will ensure their agreement on meaning and coding style: if one does not follow the rule as described by coding style, others will not understand their code. The control over following such regulations is usually exercised during peer code review. But it is also peer code review that allows such conventions to come into existence in the first place. I want to highlight that such software conventions are unique to Yandex and they are not akin to industry standards since they are created during peer code reviews.

I believe this is why many of my informants admit that at the very beginning of their careers at Yandex, code development rather than code reading seemed easier for them: one is able to write code without following the convention, although it is difficult to read and understand code without knowing the rules that such conventions set.

However, the interviews revealed that code reviewing is a very hectic process that is hard to navigate. Several of my informants mentioned that review comments do not always contain useful advice. As one of my informants elaborated:

Comments in code reviews are often minor and, to be honest, poorly reflect upon shortcomings in code. Sometimes they can even highlight for you a specific place in code and just write "Won't work." That's all. Since brevity is of the essence. . . . And, so, you have to spare no effort in this and rely on yourself. (Aleksey)

Informants also emphasized that one needs to take greater responsibility for all, even minor, changes, as they might result in greater difficulties down the line:

You know, sometimes code will be reviewed after code commit.[19] Well, generally it is before. . . . Well, you know, we usually fight a lot over this: before or after. It is debatable. Anyway, for the sake of time, it might happen after you already entered all your changes. If it has bugs, it might also affect other modules. . . . All that happens next is a horror show: we are trying to rewrite everything around a troubled spot as it all starts crumbling. (Yaroslav)

The quotation above reveals that the consequences of peer code review have often become confrontational, and it pushes newcomers to change. The absence of a conventional approach to peer code review across projects (precommit or postcommit), the habit of providing quick and undetailed review comments, and the scalable character of reviewing practices facilitate professional learning. Thus, peer code review practices force developers to start exploring and learning the company's codebase faster while simultaneously gaining practical knowledge about the corporate environment.

In addition, I want to clarify one more aspect that helps boost the onsite training of Yandex newbies. As previously mentioned, any Yandex developer is able to review all the company's code and write a review of any new piece that appears in the shared repository. Also, it is possible to trace the author of code through an intraorganizational network called "Staff," where one can find employees' profiles along with all their contact information, position titles, and the structure of projects and divisions within the company. Moreover, Yandex has its own system of blogs ("Etushka") with a built-in ranking mechanism: the most popular and widely discussed posts are displayed at the top. Yandex's internal blogs are used to report on various nondisclosure-agreement topics: they discuss their new software releases, beta testing, the company's business strategies and plans, and sometimes things that are not work related. While being a platform able to facilitate knowledge sharing, the system of blogs often serves the function of expressing public shaming:

Code review is a hot topic. It happens very often that somebody posts a piece of code with no comments at all, just lines of code. As a rule, things tend to go south: the authors are publicly accused, made fun of and usually they have to try to explain what they plan to do initially, then fix all the bugs, rewrite a piece, and post a link to the latest review. It is a motive in itself. (Aleksey)

This illustrates the role that the practices of critique and correction play in ensuring the stability of the "corpus," which is central to community building at Yandex. The tradition of criticizing and correcting as part of peer code review creates a unique, constantly changing "corpus" that differentiates the IT community from any other sci-tech community.

Unlike other fields and disciplines, software development as well as computer science do not have a disciplinary core—a solid tradition with "founding fathers" and unity of writing.[20] The algorithms that are created within computer science are constantly revisited and improved. When the algorithms are implemented in the industry they are completely changed by adjustment to specific needs. And software development itself persistently seeks its origin across different approaches and practices. The case of Yandex has shown that software development does not occur in a rarified, abstract world with fixed concepts and rules, which is probably why it is so hard to strictly define its origin. Instead, we can find a number of communities within the field that create their own, unique repositories of knowledge.

The perpetual return to the codebase, which I described earlier, is similar to what Michel Foucault ([1969] 1984) discussed in "What Is an Author?" An important distinction exists though: Foucault argued that such "return to the origin" is what sustains a discipline that is dependent on the work of an individual author. He draws on examples of Marx and Freud, arguing that they have become not just the authors of their own works but "founders of discursivity"; that is, their texts produced "the rules for the formation of other texts" (Foucault [1969] 1984, 114). This also creates a space where, in one's attempt to link oneself to a particular discipline, one cannot go beyond these original texts, since writing has become enabled by the "author function." In this sense, while psychoanalysis and Marxism are "closed" around a fixed original text or corpus written by their founders, the "corpus" at the center of the Yandex community differs in that it remains "open" to criticism and correction. The unity of writing at Yandex is not imposed by the existence of some inceptive work that eliminates contradictions a priori; rather, such unity is achieved by resolving ambiguities on a permanent basis through peer code review. Therefore, Yandex employees have a moral obligation to correct the "corpus" because it ensures the stability of their community.

It is worth mentioning that while writing, according to Foucault, is defined in terms of the absence of the author, at Yandex writing never happens without the collective author, since the community extends into the "corpus" itself. Thus, code writing is the curious form of practice that does not reduce an ongoing process of knowledge production to one finalized text, since it is always tangled into data and context. While most forms of modern knowledge work result in the creation of abstract "immutable mobiles" (e.g., scientific articles) that are the same in different locations and cultural settings (Latour 1990), "corpora" that occur in software production cannot be detached from authors and spaces.

Code exists in and produces around relationships that are both of social and technological nature. However, these relationships, no matter how dispersed or fixed they are, still carry their "situatedness"—imprints of where, how, and by whom they were set in motion. While the Yandex community is built around the codebase, Russian civic hackers studied by Ksenia Ermoshina are mobilized around a different kind of circulating "corpora" of code (Ermoshina, this volume) and the source code at Goldman Sachs is part of relationships between yet other types of technological and social infrastructures. The multipurpose nature of programming languages provides a developer with the potential to implement them everywhere, though the knowledge of how they can be implemented in a particular place or space is what makes code-writing practices intelligible and "located"; therefore, it is possible to argue that they do not travel around countries or companies as easily as we used to think.

CONCLUSION

Drawing from a study of Yandex's practices of training, this chapter has discussed how routine engagement with code serves to transform a diversified body of newcomers with different educational backgrounds into a coherent body of IT professionals. In order to collaborate, employees need to share a common understanding of software development that does not arise from any particular methodology imposed from above; rather, it is achieved and *discovered* through everyday routine processes of engaging with the codebase.

The example of Yandex's codebase has shown that code and the knowledge it encapsulates can no more be detached from machines and technological infrastructure than from the social relationships and practices of Yandex employees. Studying code from the perspective of language allows us to reveal complex relationships of training and skill transfer that the hybrid codebase mediates. A developer needs to write complementary code that reproduces the "rules" of the existing codebase. Such "rules" articulate themselves in meeting the requirements of both the community and the technological environment wherein the code runs. Thus, when one reads the source code one also prepares to perform the role of "writer" by learning the conventions of the community, all of which are inscribed in the source code. Along with code reading, Yandex developers build a community around the company's codebase through peer code review and commenting on code. Such mundane and routine practices, exercised across all the projects and teams at Yandex, allow employees to obtain practical knowledge and gain the shared understanding of how software should be written.

There is one amusing footnote to this study of Yandex. Earlier in the chapter, we discussed that the company's codebase resembles a sacred corpus in the sense that the emphasis is on a textual assemblage whose reading is one of the key "rituals" of the Yandex community. New people join the community by reading and learning how to make sense of this corpus (i.e., the codebase), and it is this corpus that passes on knowledge through the generations and remains after all the current players are gone. But unlike other sacred corpora, Yandex's *accumulates* knowledge and *grows* with the community. If the story of Yandex's creation hadn't started with the Bible search directory, the story would have to be invented; for where two or three have gathered in the name of code, Yandex is there in their midst (Sokolov-Mitrich 2014, 61).

NOTES

1. Yandex (NASDAQ: YNDX) was the first Russian technological company that made its initial public offering on NASDAQ.
2. On the complex technological ecosystem that is behind California's economic success, see Arora, Gambardella, and Klepper 2005; Etzkowitz 2008; Gilson 1999; Kenney 2000; Lerner 2009; and Saxenian 1994.
3. See, for example, Coleman 2013; Coleman and Hill 2004; Kelty 2008; Kogut and Metiu 2001; Singh 2012; Steinmacher et al. 2015; Takhteyev 2012; and von Krogh, Spaeth, and Lakhani 2003.
4. With permission from the public relations and human resources departments of the company, I conducted my field study in Moscow, where the headquarters of Yandex are located. During my fieldwork (from January 15 to March 1, 2014), I carried out twenty-six semistructured, in-depth interviews with developers

and four expert interviews with managers, along with workplace observations during the interviews and follow-up discussions with several informants.

5. On the professionalization efforts in the software industry, see Ensmenger 2001, 2010.

6. On the applicability of Lave and Wenger's model, see also Cox 2005; Kimble 2006; Storberg-Walker 2008; Takhteyev 2009, 2012.

7. Version control systems are used to track changes to software development projects.

8. On comment density, see Arafat and Riehle 2009.

9. In 1984, Donald Knuth, one of the world's preeminent computer scientists, introduced a novel approach to programming, which he called "literate programming" (Knuth 1984). While literate programming has not become mainstream practice, it represents an important shift in attitude: the idea that code is intended for human readers rather than machines.

10. I want to emphasize, though, that under consideration here is the collection of source code without comments. Comments are descriptive notes aimed only at human readers, and they do not "participate" directly in the software production, as they are not enclosed in output (i.e., a program runs regardless of their presence or absence).

11. All interviews with IT workers were conducted in Russian and translated by the author.

12. For more on code as speech, see Coleman 2009, 2013; and Stallman 2002.

13. They are skillful and knowledgeable developers who know all the ins and outs of Yandex technologies. Richard Sheridan (2013) calls such experts "towers of knowledge," meaning that if they leave, a project could fall apart.

14. In addition, my informants told me that commenting strategies may depend on programming language as well. For instance, comments in programs written in high-level languages are always undesirable, because code in such cases should be self-documented.

15. Code in production is the stage when the actual development is finished, the code has been already released, and now it is being maintained.

16. See Eric Raymond's (1999) influential *The Cathedral and the Bazaar*, where he discusses virtues of peer code review.

17. Compare with Thomas Kuhn's (1962) discussion on the role of aesthetic considerations in the acceptance of new scientific paradigms.

18. The Conseil européen pour la recherche nucléaire (European Organization for Nuclear Research) and the National Aeronautics and Space Administration.

19. A "commit" is the making of a set of tentative changes permanent.

20. Debates over relationships between computer science, mathematics, and software engineering, along with discussions about the vague division between theoretical and applied regions of computer science, are an inherent problem within the field. See for example Dijkstra 1976; Graham, Knuth, and Patashnik 1994; Hoffman and Weiss 2001; Knuth 1968, 1996; Mahoney 1992; Priestley 2011; Tedre 2013; and Winograd 1991.

Amrute, Sareeta. 2014. "Proprietary Freedoms in an IT Office: How Indian IT Workers Negotiate Code and Cultural Branding." *Social Anthropology* 22, no. 1: 101–17.

Arafat, Oliver, and Dirk Riehle. 2009. "The Commenting Practice of Open Source." *Proceedings of the 24th ACM SIGPLAN Conference Companion on Object Oriented Programming Systems Languages and Applications*, 857–64.

Arora, Ashish, Alfonso Gambardella, and Steven Klepper. 2005. "Organizational Capabilities and the Rise of the Software Industry in the Emerging Economies: Lessons from the History of Some U.S. Industries." In *Underdogs to Tigers: The Rise and Growth of the Software Industry in Some Emerging Economies*, edited by Ashish Arora and Alfonso Gambardella, 171–206. Oxford: Oxford University Press.

Brown, John Seely, and Paul Duguid. 2001. "Knowledge and Organization: A Social-Practice Perspective." *Organization Science* 12, no. 2: 198–213.

Coleman, Gabriella. 2009. "Code Is Speech: Legal Tinkering, Expertise, and Protest among Free and Open Source Software Developers." *Cultural Anthropology* 24, no. 3: 420–54.

Coleman, Gabriella. 2013. *Coding Freedom: The Ethics and Aesthetics of Hacking*. Princeton, NJ: Princeton University Press.

Coleman, Gabriella, and Benjamin Hill. 2004. "The Social Production of Ethics in Debian and Free Software Communities: Anthropological Lessons for Vocational Ethics." In *Free/Open Source Software Development*, edited by Stefan Koch, 273–95. Idea Group Publishing.

Cox, Andrew. 2005. "What Are Communities of Practice? A Comparative Review of Four Seminal Works." *Journal of Information Science* 31, no. 6: 527–40.

Dijkstra, Edsger Wybe. 1976. *A Discipline of Programming*. Englewood Cliffs, NJ: Prentice Hall.

Ensmenger, Nathan. 2001. "The 'Question of Professionalism' in the Computer Fields." *IEEE Annals of the History of Computing* 23, no. 4: 56–73.

Ensmenger, Nathan. 2010. *The Computer Boys Take Over: Computers, Programmers, and the Politics of Technical Expertise*. Cambridge, MA: MIT Press.

Etzkowitz, Henry. 2008. *The Triple Helix: University-Industry-Government Innovation in Action*. New York: Routledge.

Foucault, Michael. (1969) 1984. "What Is an Author?" In *The Foucault Reader*, edited by Paul Rabinow, 101–20. New York: Pantheon Books.

Galloway, Alexander R. 2004. *Protocol: How Control Exists after Decentralization*. Cambridge, MA: MIT Press.

Gilson, Ronald. 1999. "The Legal Infrastructure of High-Technology Industrial Districts: Silicon Valley, Route 128, and Covenants Not to Compete." *New York University Law Review* 74, no. 3: 575–629.

Graham, Ronald, Donald E. Knuth, and Oren Patashnik. 1994. *Concrete Mathematics: A Foundation for Computer Science*. Boston: Addison-Wesley Professional.

Haraway, Donna. 1992. "The Promises of Monsters: A Regenerative Politics for Inappropriate/d Others." In *Cultural Studies Now and in the Future*, edited by Cary Nelson, Paula A. Treichler, and Lawrence Grossberg, 295–337. New York: Routledge.

Hastie, Shane. 2015. "Linda Rising and Richard Sheridan on Creating a Culture of Joy—Part 2." *InfoQ*, February 25. http://www.infoq.com/articles/singapore-rising-sheridan2.

Hoffman, Daniel M., and David M. Weiss. 2001. *Software Fundamentals: Collected Papers by David L. Parnas*. Boston: Addison-Wesley Professional.

Kelty, Christopher. 2008. *Two Bits: The Cultural Significance of Free Software*. Durham, NC: Duke University Press.

Kenney, Martin, ed. 2000. *Understanding Silicon Valley: The Anatomy of an Entrepreneurial Region*. Stanford, CA: Stanford University Press.

Kimble, Chris. 2006. "Communities of Practice: Never Knowingly Undersold." In *Innovative Approaches for Learning and Knowledge Sharing*, edited by Wolfgang Nejdl and Klaus Tochtermann, 218–34. EC-TEL 2006 Workshops Proceedings.

Knuth, Donald. 1968. *The Art of Computer Programming, Volume 1: Fundamental Algorithms*. Boston: Addison-Wesley.

Knuth, Donald. 1984. "Literate Programming." *Computer Journal* 27, no. 2: 97–111.

Knuth, Donald. 1996. *Selected Papers on Computer Science*. Cambridge: Cambridge University Press.

Kogut, Bruce, and Anca Metiu. 2001. "Open-Source Software Development and Distributed Innovation." *Oxford Review of Economic Policy* 17, no. 2: 248–64.

Kuhn, Thomas. (1962) 2012. *The Structure of Scientific Revolutions*. Chicago: University of Chicago Press.

Latour, Bruno. 1990. "Drawing Things Together." In *Representation in Scientific Practice*, edited by Michael Lynch and Steve Woolgar, 19–68. Cambridge, MA: MIT Press.

Latour, Bruno. 2005. *Reassembling the Social: An Introduction to Actor-Network-Theory*. Oxford: Oxford University Press.

Lave, Jean, and Étienne Wenger. 1991. *Situated Learning: Legitimate Peripheral Participation*. Cambridge: Cambridge University Press.

Lerner, Josh. 2009. *Boulevard of Broken Dreams: Why Public Efforts to Boost Entrepreneurship and Venture Capital Have Failed—and What to Do about It*. Princeton, NJ: Princeton University Press.

Lynch, Michael. 1985. "Discipline and the Material Form of Images: An Analysis of Scientific Visibility." *Social Studies of Science* 15, no. 1: 37–66.

Mackenzie, Adrian. 2005. "The Performativity of Code Software and Cultures of Circulation." *Theory, Culture and Society* 22, no. 1: 71–92.

Mahoney, Michael. 1992. "Computer and Mathematics: The Search for a Discipline of Computer Science." In *The Space of Mathematics*, edited by Javier Echeverría, Andoni Ibarra, and Thomas Mormann, 349–65. New York: De Gruyter.

Priestley, Mark. 2011. *A Science of Operations: Machines, Logic and the Invention of Programming*. New York: Springer.

Raymond, Eric. 1999. *The Cathedral and the Bazaar: Musings on Linux and Open Source by an Accidental Revolutionary*. Cambridge, MA: O'Reilly Media.

Saxenian, AnnaLee. 1994. *Regional Advantage: Culture and Competition in Silicon Valley and Route 128*. Cambridge, MA: Harvard University Press.

Shapiro, Stuart. 1994. "Boundaries and Quandaries: Establishing a Professional Context for IT." *Information Technology and People* 7, no. 1: 47–68.

Sheridan, Richard. 2013. *Joy Inc.: How We Built a Workplace People Love*. New York: Penguin Group.

Singh, Vandana. 2012. "Newcomer Integration and Learning in Technical Support Communities for Open Source Software." *Proceedings of the 17th ACM International Conference on Supporting Group Work*, 65–74.

Sokolov-Mitrich, Dmitriy. 2014. *Yandex.Book*. [In Russian.] Moscow: Mann, Ivanov and Ferber.

Stallman, Richard. 2002. *Free Software, Free Society: Selected Essays of Richard M. Stallman*. Introduction by L. Lessig, edited by J. Gay. Free Software Foundation.

Steinmacher, Igor, Tayana Conte, Marco A. Gerosa, and David Redmiles. 2015. "Social Barriers Faced by Newcomers Placing Their First Contribution in Open Source Software Projects." *Proceedings of the 18th ACM Conference on Computer Supported Cooperative Work and Social Computing*, 1379–92.

Storberg-Walker, Julia. 2008. "Wenger's Communities of Practice Revisited: A (Failed?) Exercise in Applied Communities of Practice Theory-Building Research." *Advances in Developing Human Resources* 10, no. 4: 555–77.

Takhteyev, Yuri. 2009. "Networks of Practice as Heterogeneous Actor-Networks." *Information, Communication and Society* 12, no. 4: 566–83.

Takhteyev, Yuri. 2012. *Coding Places: Software Practice in a South American City*. Cambridge, MA: MIT Press.

Tedre, Matti. 2013. "Three Debates about Computing." In *The Nature of Computation: Logic, Algorithms, Applications*, edited by Paola Bonizzoni, Vasco Brattka, and Benedikt Löwe, 404–13. Berlin: Springer.

von Krogh, Georg, Sebastian Spaeth, and Karim R. Lakhani. 2003. "Community, Joining, and Specialization in Open Source Software Innovation: A Case Study." *Research Policy* 32, no. 7: 1217–41.

Winograd, Terry. 1991. Oral history interview with Terry Allen Winograd. Charles Babbage Institute. Accessed July 25, 2018, University of Minnesota Digital Conservancy. http://hdl.handle.net/11299/107717.

Wittgenstein, Ludwig. (1922) 2001. *Tractatus Logico-Philosophicus*. London: Routledge.

Wittgenstein, Ludwig. (1953) 2010. *Philosophical Investigations*. New York: John Wiley and Sons.

CHAPTER THREE

FOR CODE AND COUNTRY

Civic Hackers in Contemporary Russia

Ksenia Ermoshina

I would not call it a revolution. It is more about making the whole system work in balance. If we use a technical metaphor, nowadays in Russia some processes in the system are so heavy that others do not have enough resources to run normally. As computer scientists, what we try to do is to clear cache and restart, so to speak, but without destroying everything.

—ALEXEY P., *computer scientist, developer*

When, in 2010, wildfires started burning near Moscow, governmental agencies were unable to quickly respond to the emergency and the official media simply downplayed or even silenced news of the disaster. Instead, it was the online community that came up with an alternative and efficient handling of the crisis (Asmolov 2010). Developing a web application based on the well-known crisis-mapping platform Usha-hidi, a group of programmers, bloggers, and activists helped thousands of victims of the wildfires by successfully coordinating volunteers from all across Russia and consolidating a self-organized community (Machleder and Asmolov 2011). With about 170,000 unique visitors, it became the first mass-used Russian civic application—one that launched a wave of similar projects aimed at responding to important political, social, and economic challenges with the help of volunteer coders and crowdsourcing technologies.

In 2012 alone, 272 civic applications were developed in Russia.[1] While in the United States and Europe civic software projects are typically part of "open government" programs and are largely supported by the state (Eyler-Werve and Carlson 2012), Russian civic hacking initiatives started as experiments without governmental support; they are bottom-up collaborations of hundreds of volunteer developers, designers, computer scientists, and activists. It is therefore important to understand why, in the particular social and political context of contemporary Russia, civic hackers believe in coding as a way to "fix the system" without governmental support. Many political and cultural commentators stress the existence of an apathy and distrust toward political participation in contemporary Russia (Erpyleva and Magun 2014; Kharkhordin 2011; Zhuravlev, Savelyeva, and Erpyleva 2014).

However, that does not apply to Russian civic hackers. Conscious of the failures of the Russian government and well aware of the problems of corruption, inefficient city services, and electoral fraud, they actively discuss politics online, propose their own solutions, and even put forward visions of political parties driven by "geeks."[2] They refuse to engage in traditional forms of protest like rallies, strikes, and petition campaigns (which they consider to be inefficient), trying instead to invent, experiment, and tinker with new tools—assemblages of programming code and law—that have the potential to fight political apathy and improve the everyday lives of Russian citizens.

It would be wrong, however, to see civic hackers as revolutionaries or radical activists. A phrase found on a programmers' forum—"We do not need revolutionaries, we need legitimacy"[3]—could function well as this movement's motto. Civic hackers operate clearly within the legal arena, developing civic apps as techno-juridical instruments aimed at raising government transparency to compel municipal civil servants to respect the law. Paradoxically, however, the demand for transparency is itself a radical act within the Russian context. Giving citizens the ability to surveil and control the administration, civic apps provoke strong and controversial reactions from governmental institutions, ranging from hostility to collaboration.[4]

The Russian civic hacking movement is a complex and changing network of people, machines, servers, cables, NGOs, and administrative institutions. It is highly decentralized, with several active centers (IT communities and specialized NGOs) but no lead institution. As the interviewee quoted in the epigraph puts it, the Russian civic hacking movement "is not a revolution"— an observation we need to keep in mind to avoid all the possible romantic, nihilist, and maximalist connotations of terms like "hacker" and "civic." First of all, in this context "hacking" is not about coding complex systems, inventing new languages, or committing cybercrimes. Here hacking stands for tinkering and experimenting, a meaning close to that of the French word bricolage; the Russian term smekalka captures it as well. Derived from an old verb, smekat' ("to understand" or, colloquially, "to get it"), smekalka is a quality that Russians claim for themselves. Part of the "national character," it is often mentioned in fairy tales, where it functions almost as a preternatural power to find a solution quickly, in very tight spots, when one has no proper tools or means and can only use what is at hand. Civic hackers are those who can quickly invent a new, intelligent, and cheap way to solve social problems by means of information and communications technology (ICT).

As I will discuss in a moment, civic applications are often based on the integration of existing platforms, the reuse of existing texts (in particular legal texts), and pieces of code. Useful and popular civic applications successfully translate a feeling of social injustice (a "trouble") into a public problem, and then match it with a suitable techno-juridical solution.

The Russian civic hacking movement is not about "geeks only." Unlike computer science, which is rarely open to non-tech-savvy actors, the civic hacking movement is a hybrid field where subject-matter experts (NGO activists, legal experts, journalists, urbanists, or what Harry Collins [2002] calls "experience based experts") can contribute to the production of software. What Collins called the "core-set" is thus relatively open to new kinds of publics, previously kept outside computer science and coding activities. All the Russian civic applications that I have studied are the result of collaborations of tech and social experts. They involve amateurs, beta testers, reviewers, and active users who contribute to the improvement of the software with their user experience, feedback, evaluation, and volunteer coding. While focused on very specific problems, these new networks have far-reaching effects: they restructure Russian civil society, help to overcome the isolation of tech-savvy people, and raise the computer literacy of social activists.

This chapter describes the civic hacking scene and its practices, but also its tensions and limits. Contrary to the belief in a general "apptivization" of societies, there cannot be an app for everything: Russian computer scientists and developers engaged in coding civic software often fail to produce significant social changes with their tools. Still, even if not all civic applications are ultimately successful, the civic hacking community is having an important impact on both Russian society and Russian computer science. Through the proliferation of different civic software projects, Russia can be seen as a political laboratory, where civic hackers experiment with proposing new technical solutions to social challenges and collaborate with new formats of political movements. Thus, two of the most used civic applications have been launched and financed by Putin's chief antagonist, Alexey Navalny. In the last five years, this movement has managed to build an active and prolific community of activists, developers, designers, geeks, and lawyers who contribute to create value, share skills, democratize code, and engage coders in social issues.

While the diaspora of Russian computer scientists seems to actively reclaim its "Russianness," Russian civic hackers refer to the transnational culture of free and open source software (FOSS) developed beyond national borders and identities. Programming languages are believed to be a universal grammar that can help to solve any kind of problem: "The whole world speaking one language—that is the power of digital code" (Joyce 2010). Many of the Russian civic hackers I have met connected their inspirations to the FOSS culture. Vitaliy V., the organizer of the annual hackathon "Spb Data Hack" and a computer scientist from ITMO University, attributes the very idea of using code to solve social problems to FOSS culture, quoting Don Tapscott and Anthony D. Williams's *Wikinomics* (2006) as the main source of inspiration for his own work as a civic hacker: "It is about crowdsourcing and how a large number of people can help you to solve your challenge when you share your knowledge with others. Since I've read it, I started being interested in open innovation and in civic activism." Most of the civic application projects relied on decentralized teams without physical offices or stable workplaces—in the interview, Vyacheslav K., developer of the RosYama app, called them "virtual teams."[5] All of my interviews took place in cafés or coworking spaces, except for those working with the team of Alexey Navalny.[6] Coders emphasize this extreme mobility and independence from a precise physical location as a positive trend, which they oppose to the conservatism and stagnation of Russian society. A particular "imaginary" is thus being produced where Russian administration and its slow and complicated procedures are contrasted with a "new" global society without borders, where people, objects, skills, and ideas can circulate freely, just as software does within the FOSS culture. Within this imaginary, their modern, user-friendly applications contrast with the endless dusty paperwork of the Russian bureaucracy:

> I feel pity for my parents who are stuck in these conditions [they live in the town of Bryansk]. There's nothing there. When I go to see them in Bryansk, they say there's nothing new going on. And I feel a bit ashamed to talk about my trips to the USA, Thailand, or Bali. . . . I think life is hell in the [Russian] provinces. And my goal is to show, on my own example, how people live in the contemporary world, one can work without being attached to a precise place, it is an incredible freedom, you can be everywhere and work from anywhere. (Tatyana, UX designer, WebNabludatel app)

My interviewees are inspired by foreign civic hacking examples, quote details and figures of foreign social innovation projects, and are curious about the latest examples of successfully functional civic apps. They claim to have good contacts with colleagues working in Kenya (with the Ushahidi project) and to participate in different IT events in India, Europe, and Canada. Some even collaborated with the hackers from the Indignados movement in Spain.

Code circulates between projects, and—in accordance with the culture of sharing of the FOSS movement—there are direct and indirect borrowings of pieces of code between Russia and the world. For instance, the founders of RosYama claim to have been inspired by the Fix My Street application that was launched in 2007 in Great Britain, giving citizens the ability to report urban problems to their municipalities. As an open source product, this application was installed in seven countries and credited with the solution of more than 250,000 problems. RosYama, an open source project itself, was developed in Russia, but as a result of being made openly accessible on GitHub, its code was rapidly borrowed by activists in the Ukraine, Belorussia, and Kazakhstan. It is said to have helped fix more than twenty thousand potholes across the former Soviet Union. Krasivyy Peterburg (KP), the application that helps report on different kinds of urban problems, has also been reused in more than twenty Russian cities. One of the developers on the KP team explains the importance of open source to civic innovation:

> To keep the code open means that your product can always be improved, anytime, by anyone. You win from it, because some guys just come and say—I see you have a bug here, I can fix it, just for fun. And they can also borrow your code and bring it to their country and do some good. The social good can't have an owner, it would be absurd not to share your code with someone who wants to improve people's life.

Special events are regularly held to bring coders, activists, and politicians from different countries to work together on major global challenges. Since 2010, events like hackathons (forty-eight-hour coding competitions) or barcamps (informal conferences of IT professionals and entrepreneurs) have become more and more popular in Russia. In September 2011, a binational hackathon "Code for Country" was held simultaneously in Moscow and Washington, DC, co-organized by Russian and American partners. On the American side, it was Emily Parker from the US State Department who organized the competition, presenting it as part of a project to "come up with creative ideas for digital diplomacy, looking for opportunities for Russia-US cooperation" (Emily Parker, interview conducted by the author). The theme of the hackathon was "transparency and corruption," expecting teams from both countries to code applications that could creatively respond to those challenges. In contexts like these, programming code becomes a tool of diplomacy and peace building, an instrument that can effectively work beyond the dominant geopolitical power relations.

It was at "Code for Country" that Alexey P., head of the IT company Progress Engine, worked on a civic project for the first time, providing "the first bifurcation point that converted [Alexey] into doing civic apps." Months later, he developed the WebNabludatel mobile application for the monitoring of elections (Ermoshina 2014b). While the applications prototyped during this event were not released on app stores, they had an important impact on the Russian civic hacking community by helping to establish connections between civic activists and developers.

Since 2012, dozens of other civic hackathons have been held all around Russia, both in Moscow and Saint Petersburg as well as in the provinces, in an effort to decentralize and democratize innovation. They include "Hack against Poverty," "Hack against Corruption," "Social Impact Hack," "Crowdlab," "Apps 4 All," and others. Unlike high-tech industry in the regions of Kazan or Siberia (Alina Kontareva, Andrey Indukaev, this volume), where decentralization happens via a state-driven process, through an important governmental intervention, in the case of civic apps an effort to bring social innovation to the remote regions of Russia has been pushed forward by NGOs. For instance, Teplitsa Sotsial'nykh Technologiy (the Greenhouse of Social Technologies) organized civic hackathons in the cities of Vladivostok, Krasnoyarsk, Yekaterinburg, Kazan, Barnaul, Samara, Ulyanovsk, Novosibirsk, Penza, and so on. These civic hackathons build an all-Russian network of IT volunteers, connect civic activists, tech entrepreneurs, and coders, and establish direct links between programming code and problem solving. This results in a peculiar sociotechnical network that operates in parallel to the state using code as a means of coordination. The organizers of these events believe that code can and should be used to address problems that have been previously delegated to human agents, social movements, or traditional political institutions. As Lilly Irani has argued, the civic hacking movement is not only about producing software prototypes but also about developing a specific "ethos": "They manufacture urgency and an optimism that bursts of doing and making can change the world . . . and imagine themselves as agents of social progress through software" (Irani 2015). But is this "optimism" enough of a motivation to work for free? Indeed, a question quickly arises: who pays for civic apps? What is the economic context of their production?

CODING UTOPIAS: CIVIC HACKERS IN SEARCH OF AN "OTHER RUSSIA"

According to Nicolas Auray, the free and open source software movement is marked by a "massive and brutal rejection of commercialization of social relations. For these hackers the basic organizational factor in their lives is not money or work but their passion for code and the desire to create with others something that has a social value" (Auray 2002). Vyacheslav K., developer of the widely used mobile application RosYama, agrees with Auray:

> We always wanted to create something for ourselves, even if this may seem naive, we wanted to be useful to society . . . because our commercial projects are very cool, we can eat thanks to these projects, but sometimes one needs to build something "for the soul," we wanted to bring our little contribution. And we worked on this project for free. It is, so to say, a gift to society.

All civic applications I observed were developed as side projects: developers worked on them apart from their official jobs as programmers. This particular mode of existence refers back to the specificities of Russian technological entrepreneurship mentioned in the introduction to this volume, with its characteristic "gap between the level of available mathematical, technical, and coding skills and the familiarity with entrepreneurial practices and culture." Only when projects become very successful, and an environment is set up with a proper entrepreneurial infrastructure, can a developer be paid to work full time on a civic application. This requires the intervention of a new kind of third-sector organization, which acts as an "incubator" for civic technologies. Such is the case with the Foundation against Corruption (Fond Bor'by s Korruptsiyey), the NGO founded by Alexey Navalny, today one of the main opposition leaders, which has several developers on staff for the maintenance and updates of their three civic apps: RosYama, RosPil, and RosZKH. These developers, however, are paid not for coding a product from scratch, but for technical maintenance, bug fixing, and updates.

It is interesting that the professionalization of civic hacking tends to occur when the innovation has become more or less stable; when it has already found loyal users it can rely on. However, in the early stage, civic projects emerge and are built on a volunteer basis, as "stigmergic collaborations" (Eliott 2006)—a concept used to describe a spontaneous self-organization within open source and civic-hacking communities based on indirect incentives and mutual support (Eliott 2006; Gregorio 2002; Heylighen 2007b; Parunak 2006; Robles, Merelo, and Gonzalez-Barahona 2005). The projects I have studied were launched as decentralized collaborations of individuals through GitHub, HabraHabr, Stake Overflow, Livejournal, mailing lists, groups in Vkontakte, and other online ecosystems, without a predetermined technical task or a strict division of labor. Typically, an idea is proposed on a blog, a team is quickly formed, a page on GitHub is opened, and the work starts with crucial input from the broader IT community. Users and testers become coproducers and participate in the maintenance and improvement of the project.

The collaborative and stigmergic nature of civic software extends to its business model. The apps I have studied were either supported by crowdfunding (RosYama, RosZKH, RosPil), grants and prizes (Krasivyy Peterburg, which won the Kudrin's Innovation Prize), or financial support from IT entrepreneurs. Globally, no efficient and sustainable business model has yet been found for civic applications. This supports the thesis on "lack of conditions that facilitate technological innovation" outlined by Marina Fedorova in her chapter on Yandex (this volume). Instead, the civic hacking scene operates on "enthusiasm." My respondents claim to work "for themselves" and "for the soul," but also "for the country" and "for the people." For instance, Timofey T. (the backend developer of WebNabludatel) explains:

> I thought it was the best thing I could do to fight against . . . how to say . . . the regime. Really, without joking. I could have said that it was just for fair elections, but these are just words. It was the only thing I could do to fight against the regime. And I worked for free, I even gave a hundred bucks to pay for the servers.

For others, the motivation comes from a mix of political commitment and technical challenge. The "nonprofit gusto" described by Andrey Indukaev in his chapter on Tomsk (this volume), is a very relevant trait for civic hackers who share with Siberian computer scientists a specific attraction to problem solving, where technical complexity and social importance of a given task constitute a more important value than the monetization of the work. As Alexander M. (developer of OpenSalary, an application that provides information on teachers' salaries) puts it:

I was always interested in treating big data. It is my passion. And I adore maps as well. So I had a big technical interest in this project. When they [the teachers' trade union, "Utchitel"] proposed this project to me, I also wanted to help them because it is a shame that teachers have such miserable salaries and there is no open data on how much they must really earn. I felt pity for them, as they wanted to do something but had no idea of how the code works. And also . . . there are lies everywhere in our country. And I am very tired of this.

Often the coders have difficulty distinguishing between their passion for code, their interest in a technical challenge, and the urgency of a social issue. For them, coding becomes their way to participate in producing social and political change in Russia. This form of engagement through code is also related to a certain mistrust toward traditional forms of public participation. Olga, a former member of Gov2People and manager of several civic IT projects, explains this choice:

I went to some demonstrations but I do not really believe in this kind of actions. People go there to meet other people, to chat with them, to take selfies, this is me with Navalny or this is me with OMON [riot police], and so on. But it does not really change things, that's my opinion. So I prefer coding some projects that can really help people. For example, in 2011 when there were all these big demos, we with Alexey P. made an app HelpWall that aggregates tweets and helps people who get arrested to get legal help or food and warm clothes.

While telling me the same story, Alexey P. added: "I do what I know best and if it can help someone in Russia, that's great. Some people are good on the streets, some people are good on their laptops."

Paradoxically, despite the transnational character of FOSS and the civic hacking movement, the Russian civic hacker community shares a certain type of patriotism: a loyalty to a particular idea of Russia—an idea strong enough to make them code for free for months and even contribute their own money to maintain the servers and update the applications. Civic hacking can thus be opposed to the "brain drain" trend in a peculiar way: even though civic hackers circulate a lot, they still code "for Russia" from abroad. Inventing new ways to use code to improve life in Russia, developers contribute to coding utopias and sustain their vision of a better Russia. What they share is a will to build a system where law would be respected, where existing public institutions would work properly and without corruption, and where citizens would have a means to control their administrations and make them accountable. They code for the country or for the people, but not for the government:

> Actually what I really want is that institutions work properly, that they execute the functions they have been made for. If it becomes true, if the police work to prosecute real criminals, if the road inspection works to build the roads without spending four times more money than what is needed, and so on. . . . If it works like this, I do not care who our president is because, well, the state is a structure built to serve the people and not vice versa. (Vyacheslav, developer of RosYama mobile app)

Even though civic hacking "is not a revolution," it paradoxically overlaps with antiregime politics. Two of the most used civic apps in Russia (RosYama and RosZKH) are being pushed forward by a politician who is running for presidential elections at the time of writing this chapter. Alexey Navalny is the first political figure who has based a large part of his political capital on these new technologies. RosYama was the first project that made him popular among "lay users," as it addresses a crucial Russian problem known to all citizens: the quality of the roads. Instead of projecting a "big narrative" or global political ideology that could unite people from above, these pieces of software address precise and sometimes seemingly small problems from everyday experience and try to fix them, thus grasping the very particular post-Soviet spirit of "society of repair and maintenance" (Gerasimova and Chuikina 2004). This makes civic apps a very relevant tool in the post-Soviet context with its "distrust" in traditional politics and political ideologies (the feature previously described in this chapter).

PUTTING PROBLEMS INTO CODE

Civic hackers tend to present code as a means to solve the problems of Russian society, but how exactly does the translation from a social cause to strings and functions of Python, Java, or c++ occur? Can we really make an app for everything? And how do apps transform the way citizens define their problems, delegate responsibilities, and communicate with governments?

I followed several civic hacking teams (described in more detail in table 3.1) as they built and tested apps to monitor elections, denounce corruption, send out alerts about leaking roofs, broken street lamps, potholes, and so on. But what do these projects share besides the technical format—the app—through which they are addressed? It was by tracking these projects back to their sources (prototypes, ideas, drafts, discussions) that I discovered some striking similarities—similarities of experience, not structure. All of them started from the experience of a "trouble": electoral fraud, urban problems, leaking roofs, corruption, and so on.

Traditional responses did not, however, give satisfying results, as official institutions proved unable to adequately address the problems. As a result, the authors had to launch an inquiry (in the pragmatic sense of the word) in order to search for a means to redescribe their situations, to reattribute responsibilities, and inscribe troubles into "problematic fields." We can think of this in terms of the micropolitics of trouble as described by Robert Emerson and Sheldon Messinger: the difficulties we face in our everyday lives happen within more or less stabilized "problematic fields," with "typical solutions of typical problems" (Schuetz 1944). However, when these solutions are either no longer accessible or do not work, a "trouble" can progressively take the form of a problem and reassign new solutions and new "troubleshooters" (Cefai 2013). I argue that, starting from the experience of a "trouble," the programmers came up with the idea of coding applications as new tools for the publicization of problems and for communicating with the authorities in contexts wherein the "official" channels were not perceived as working properly. Digital tools, mobile or web applications, should be considered as crystallizations of this collective inquiry:

> Finally after five or six visits [to the municipal council] I decided against going there and found the website of the central city administration on the internet. I started sending them my appeals directly. Actually it turned out to be efficient because when you send letters "up there," they trickle down to local officials, and they are so willing to get a good reputation and are so afraid of their superiors that they start working and remedy your problems. This became the basis of the mechanism that we now use in Krasivyy Peterburg. We are sending everything to the very top—to the mayor of the city—and then they send it to the local administration. (Krasimir V., founder of the Krasivyy Peterburg application)

In contrast to the image of Russian bureaucracy as a slow and inefficient machine, civic apps promise a quick and easy-to-use solution "for everyone": the user has only to choose from a number of "categories of problems," fill in some forms, and take a photo of the problem. The app then generates the text of a complaint using all the necessary bureaucratic boilerplate language, references to applicable laws, and sends everything to the authorities.

Table 3.1. **Case Studies**

NAME OF THE APP	SOCIAL PROBLEM ADDRESSED	AUTHORS	DATE OF RELEASE	TECHNICAL SUPPORT
WebNabludatel	Electoral falsifications	A team of developers (9 persons) under the leadership of Ilya Segalovitch (ex-CTO of Yandex) and a Russian NGO "Golos" specialized in electoral law. No political parties involved	January–February 2012	Mobile app (iOS, Android); and a website with an interactive map (statistics of fraud)
Krasivyy Peterburg	Urban problems (12 various categories)	A group of activists from Saint Petersburg, ex-observers of elections. Worked with several volunteer developers (2 mobile developers, 2 web developers, and a community of beta testers and helpers)	Autumn 2012: first idea for the app appears on a special page on Vk.com. 2013: first version of the web application. February 2014: mobile app (Android, iOS)	Web app (interactive problem mapping, photos of problems, user rating systems); mobile app (Android, iOS); and social network groups
RosYama	Potholes and road quality problems	Alexey Navalny (ideas and funding); Fedor E. (independent developer); Vyacheslav K. (developer of the mobile version); the developers' team of Foundation against Corruption (Alexey Navalny's NGO); and a community of beta testers and active users	2010: web apps and groups on social networks (user forums)—Vk.com, Twitter. 2012: mobile app	Web app (interactive problem mapping, photos of problems, user rating systems), generating the text of complaint, redirecting it to the Road Inspection; mobile app (iOS, Android, Samsung Bada); and social network accounts

RosZKH (formerly "Dom. Dvor. Dorogi")	Problems with communal services (light, electricity, gas, in-house commodities)	First prototype ("Dom. Dvor. Dorogi," or "House. Yard. Roads") in the form of a website was developed by Dmitriy L. (lawyer and activist) with the help of volunteer developers. Second version—a lighter and more functional web application with automatic generation of the texts of complaint—was developed by the Foundation against Corruption.	2012: website of "Dom. Dvor. Dorogi." Late 2012: web app by Foundation against Corruption, and pages on Vk.com (user forums) and Twitter	Web app (proposes about 20 different categories of problems and generates texts of complaints, using the Code of Housing, Administrative and Technical Code, and other normative documents); and groups on social networks (Vk.com, Twitter)
Zalivaet.spb	Leaks in roofs	Fedor G. (student in sociology, developer-amateur) built this web platform after a severe leak in his room	2010	Blog (used as a web application to post personal cases of leaking roofs)
OpenSalary	Inequality of teachers' salaries and corruption in educational institutions	Trade union of teachers "Uchitel," and Alexey M. (developer), with the help of "Teplitsa Sotsial'nykh Tehnologiy"	2012	Web application with a map that reuses and treats OpenData of the Ministry of Education and visualizes teachers' salaries all around Russia; and Twitter

Furthermore, as mentioned by Krasimir, civic apps send the complaints to the very top of the city hierarchy. This creates a situation where city hall or the Inspection Department is obliged to redirect the complaints to the local city workers and delegate responsibilities to the corresponding services. As Fedor, the author of one of the applications, explains, "This algorithm reuses the 'fear of superiors' inherent to Russian administrations: when they see all these signatures and stamps, they can't but react."

Civic applications act as techno-juridical filters that turn personal experiences of trouble into transcoded alerts, which are formatted, translated, and expressed in a specific language. By proposing a standardized classification of problems built on legal texts, civic apps act as translating tools, adapting the language of citizens, their emotions and affects, into a language that is not only comprehensible to the city's civil servants, but written in a form that virtually forces them to act on the complaints. Francis Chateauraynaud and Didier Torny (1999) argue that for the civil servants "it is the code itself that constructs the event," and the app has been precisely coded to enact the politico-bureaucratic code that constructs the event.

Civic applications thus transform the practices of complaint that have been historically central to Russian culture, to the point of constituting a specific literary genre (Bogdanova 2013; Dewey and Kleimola 1970; Lambert 1985). Elena Bogdanova (2013) has claimed that the "textual space of a complaint contains the language of both sides (the author and the addressee)," but the civic apps transform this scenario into one in which the author's language is replaced by that of the machine. The justification is thus transformed from one that mobilizes categories of personal experience to one that relies on legal and technical norms. Forging this interpersonal-technical language is also a necessary step in moving from an experience of trouble (which is inherently personal) to a tool that, instead, can be used and reused by thousands of different citizens.

The WebNabludatel app for electoral monitors illustrates the process of transformation from indignation (experience of a problem) to code. The team that worked on the application was formed ad hoc on the basis of a shared experience. They were all witnesses (either direct or through thousands of YouTube videos) of massive falsifications of the electoral process on December 4, 2011. Given the widespread awareness of the problem, and the fear of a repeat performance at the upcoming presidential elections in March 2012, the idea of a mobile application for election monitors was floated on Habrahabr.ru—the most popular forum for IT professionals in Russia.

It was Ilya Segalovich (one of the opinion leaders of RuNet at the time and the chief technology officer of Yandex, Russian's most popular search engine) who posted the idea of an "electronic observers' diary." Published on December 22, 2011, this post received 117 likes and was commented on 398 times over the next forty-eight hours (Segalovich 2011). The comments included about forty stories by people who were both IT professionals and electoral observers, offering their personal testimonies of electoral fraud and police violence. The following is one example:

USER 1: The cops kicked me out [from the voting station] without any explanation: "first you get out, and then we'll bring you your papers." They wrote me: "Was interrupting the work of the electoral commission. . . . Violation of Federal Law #51." This is certainly a lie. And I had lots of witnesses and a video recording I made.

USER 2: Have you complained about the fraud?

USER 1: Yes, sure. I complained to TEC (Territorial Electoral Commission), to the court, to "Citizen observers" and "Demvybor" [NGOs specialized in electoral observations]. All complaints normally should be addressed to TEC, and they have, according to the law, to treat immediately every complaint they get, as soon as they get it. I brought my first complaint to TEC at noon. They told me they would examine it in one hour. Firstly, I was just naively waiting, than I split and came back to the voting station. When I came to see them next time (at 23:30 in the evening) I found out that they had not treated any complaint and any declaration at all.

(From an online discussion, posted on December 22, 2011, at 14:31)

Accounts of the inefficiency of official institutions responsible for controlling the electoral process (such as the Territorial Electoral Commission) coexisted in the same virtual space—the Habrahabr.ru forum—together with the first spontaneous technical design specifications, ideas for the application's interface, and a checklist. The back-and-forth between stories of fraud and design solutions contributed to building connections between an experience of trouble (the physical and legal reality of electoral observations) and a "user experience" (how to put these heterogeneous accounts into the mobile app). Just a few days after the now-famous post by Ilya Sega-lovich, a working team of twelve active members plus five more in charge of specific tasks such as legal consulting or beta testing was constituted. The story of WebNabludatel's creation thus exemplifies what I call "stigmergic collaboration" (Ermoshina 2014b): It took only one month to go from the first online conversations and elaboration of ideas to the final realization in a digital interface; all coding work was performed on a volunteer basis with everyone working efficiently against a nonnegotiable March 4, 2012, deadline—the day of the presidential elections. In one month this decen-tralized team (everyone was working from their own place) came up with a website and a mobile app for Android and iOS.

The complexity of electoral observation practices and a multitude of pos-sible microsituations of fraud can become obstacles for observers who have no experience or expertise. The mobile app was supposed to serve as a mo-bile guide to help, instruct, and prepare as many independent observers as possible. But how to put fraud into code? How to develop an interface that would take into account different cases of anomalies and illegal situations? The first step consisted of building standardized electoral "scenarios": from the early morning, when the voting stations open, to the late night, when the votes are being counted. To better classify different kinds of fraud and develop the guide, developers worked with legal experts. The team collaborated with "Golos," an NGO that specialized in electoral code and in the training of observ-ers. The digital interface was based on several documents. The first was called the "Roadmap of Observers," a guide printed on A4-size sheets of paper and distributed by NGOs before election day. It served as a base for the WebNab-ludatel team to prototype the "electoral scenario." Another document was the Electoral Code of the Russian Federation, the document that was translated into the final checklist of the app. Tatyana M. explains this translation:

> In the beginning we had a very big text of electoral code that should be about two hundred pages I think. So . . . I and Grigoriy M., a lawyer from "Golos," made a kind of draft of our menu. It had to be easy—imagine, you are an observer, you come to the voting office in the morning, so . . . what should you do right from the start? You should verify that the urns are empty, if the papers are here, and so on. . . . So we made a list of questions for every step. This list was about twenty pages long I think, so I said, "It is not possible to put all this text in a mobile app. A user will just be lost in it." So I worked till I managed to reduce these materials to only six screens with essential questions. Everything in our app is based on the law.

Indeed, Lessig's famous motto "Code is law" becomes particularly relevant in the context of Russian civic applications: it is the language of administrative code, the official technical and legal documents that inspire developers and UX designers to build their interfaces. All four urban civic applications mapped out in table 3.1 reuse legal codes to construct their lists of problems, classifications, and check-lists. For example, in order to build the classification of anomalies and the list of categories to choose from, the developers of RosZKH relied on the text "Norms and Rules for Technical Uses of the Housing Fund":

> Actually, a fault is everything that deviates from the ideal state of things, and this ideal state is very well described in the "Norms and Rules . . ." For example, they specify that all metal door accessories, like door handles or door hinges, must be polished and shiny. So, anything that is not in these norms is a fault and we have the right to report it because we pay for it every month. (Dmitriy L., author of RosZKH)

Similarly, RosYama uses appropriate legal and administrative texts to define which kinds of road defects are categorized as "potholes," that is to say, defects that the city is legally obliged to repair.

As Geoffrey Bowker and Susan Leigh Star (1998, 232) have shown, classifications and standards are important as "sites for mediation between the technical requirements of the systems developer and social and political requirements of the community." Indeed, the categorizations and standardizations at the core of the civic apps were crucially important both technically and politically. Politically, the categorization is important as it translates indignation into an "account" (Garfinkel 1967) that can be transmitted publicly to official institutions or the press. Technically, developers need to have a set of elements to which they can attribute certain values, like "true" or "false." While they cannot code an app "against corruption" in general, they can code a set of small tasks or questions that by answering allows a user to participate in gathering data on corruption. This is what the discourse of crowdsourcing calls "microtasking." The translation occurs when these microtasks are calculated and aggregated by the machine and represented in the same database: every single pothole declared with the help of a mobile app becomes part of a big collaborative map of potholes. By the mechanisms of multiplication and reiteration, an individual problem is inscribed into a more global political context. That is how the struggle against potholes becomes a struggle against corruption (Ermoshina 2014a) and complaint becomes a very specific form of civic engagement.

I have sketched a portrait of Russian civic hackers—coders, computer scientists, UX designers, and geeks—who work on a very specific kind of product: civic mobile and web applications. Though these civic apps are very popular in Russia, it is difficult to speak about Russian civic hackers as a consolidated community; they exist more as a moving, nomadic, and fragile network. Its members are coding for social or common good at the margins of their day jobs as programmers, designers, and scientists. Some may quit civic hacking after having built only one project, while others may instead become "IT volunteers" with a political organization. There is no official membership in this movement; one becomes a "member" by simply hacking and making.

Russian civic hackers' national identities equally fluctuate. On the one hand, they refer to a transnational, borderless FOSS movement, work from abroad, travel a lot, engage in exchanges and conspire with the West, the East, and Africa; but on the other hand, they share a certain form of patriotism. By coding civic software, they produce utopias and advocate situated visions of a "better Russia." These visions are not revolutionary. They are not about overturning the social system or radically changing existing political institutions, but rather about making tools to improve the communication between citizens and authorities concerning specific grievances and points of contention. However, by doing this they produce a very particular, hybrid vision of "common good" (Hemment 2012): the voluntary coding work of civic hackers does not seek monetization but aims at improving public space and public infrastructure—not, however, in compliance with the state. While Western versions of civic apps (such as Fix My Street or Dans Ma Rue) seem to perfectly fit into a neoliberal paradigm of digital labor, where governments and corporations benefit from the efforts produced by coders and users (Eyler-Werve and Carlson 2012), Russian civic applications are not "doing the work of the government." On the contrary, by their very design, Russian civic apps paradoxically become instruments of citizen surveillance and control over the administration. These tools are used to build political capital and are mobilized during electoral campaigns by anti-Putin opposition.

Russian civic hacking is not about breaking the law but about automating respect for it through the translation of legal texts into programming code. Thanks to the performativity of computer code, every user gets access to legal codes and to the ability to mobilize them without having to study or necessarily understand the law. Russian civic hacking is about fixing the system by using its own rules and mechanisms (the pipelines and labyrinths of the notorious "Russian bureaucracy") to make it effective against its own will. It is about the domestication of the Leviathan by means of translating it into many short lines of code and into an easy-to-use interface.

Engagement through an application—"apptivism," as I call it—is a ubiquitous form of political participation. The act of participating is intermediated by the interface and becomes part of day-to-day life. Russian civic applications rethink the communication between citizens and authorities, and in doing so they also rethink the relation between global and local. That a number of civic software projects may die out or prove to be ineffective does not detract from the importance and success of civic hacking as a movement— one that provides alternatives to traditional repertoires of political action (such as street activism, demonstrations, strikes, or petitions, which are either inefficient or forbidden in Russia).

Apptivism enables the innovation of Russian political practices and forms of participation as much as it contributes to the innovation of Russian IT. The interfacing of these two halves of the new "public sphere" relies in part on the work of a new kind of intermediary institution that seems specific to the Russian context, as they tend to compensate for the lack of infrastructure for innovation, already mentioned by several authors in this volume. One example is Teplitsa Sotsial'nykh Tekhnologiy, which identifies its mission as "building bridges between IT-professionals and NGO workers" (Teplitsa, n.d.). In fact, this organization sustains the civic hacking movement by organizing webinars, hackathons, workshops, and other kinds of meetings that promote the use of code to solve actual problems in Russian society. They have also institutionalized the status of the civic hacker with their recent project, "IT-volunteer"—a platform that unites IT professionals willing to collaborate for free on specific tasks proposed by NGOs. This NGO tries to compensate for the absence of conditions for social innovation in Russia and enjoys relative freedom of action because of the lack of governmental control in this field. Neither purely political nor solely technical or commercial, the civic hacking scene constitutes a unique case, even within the scope of this volume: it requires almost no relations with either academia or governmental agencies and is deployed on the margins, in between different fields.

I hope that taken together these examples demonstrate the remarkable, interesting, and emergent qualities of the civic hacking movement and its constitutive connection to both the technical expertise of Russian coders and the specificity of the Russian sociopolitical context. It is literally about code and country.

NOTES

1. According to a study conducted by Alexey Sidorenko, the founder of Teplitsa Sotsial'nykh Tekhnologiy (the Greenhouse of Social Technologies), a Russian nongovernmental organization (NGO) specializing in the promotion of civic applications and computer literacy among social activists.

2. A very interesting example of the political engagement of developers can be found on this forum of programmers working with the "1-c" system: Volshebniy Forum: off Partiya Odinessnikov (The Party of 1C-Workers), n.d., accessed March 16, 2016, http://www.forum.mista.ru/topic.php?id=535190&page=1.

3. Written by user "Krendel," programmer, on February 24, 2011, at 12:47: Volshebniy forum. Accessed March 16, 2016. http://www.forum.mista.ru/topic .php?id=535190&page=1#55.

4. The reaction of authorities to civic software projects is uneven and varies according to city and region. Thus, the city of Moscow—with its trend toward "modernization" and "e-government" launched by Dmitry Medvedev during his presidency—has agreed to collaborate with the project RosYama, an app that generates alerts about potholes. The Road Inspection of Moscow integrated user-generated data from RosYama into their platform. A counterexample is the city of Saint Petersburg that refused to accept alerts sent through the RosZKH application, designed to generate complaints about problems with housing utilities.

5. All interviews quoted in this chapter were conducted in Russian and translated by the author, except for the interview with Emily Parker, conducted in English by the author.

6. Alexey Navalny is a famous Russian blogger, lawyer, and entrepreneur. He is the conceptual author of the RosYama and RosPil apps, and also the founder of the Foundation against Corruption, an NGO that hosts several projects (RosYama, RosPil, RosZKH, Dacha.fbk.info). Navalny had a large office in Moscow where I could observe their work on different apps over the period of a few days.

REFERENCES

Asmolov, Gregory. 2010. "Russia: Online Cooperation as an Alternative for Government?" *Global Voices.* Accessed December 15, 2015. http://globalvoicesonline .org/2010/08/30/russia-online-cooperation-as-an-alternative-for-government/.

Auray, Nicolas. 2002. "De l'éthique à la politique: L'institution d'une cité libre." *Multitudes* 8. Accessed May 16, 2015. http://ses-perso.telecom-paristech.fr /auray/Multitudes8%20CommentaireHimmanen.htm.

Badouard, Romain. 2014. "La mise en technologie des projets politiques. Une approche 'orientée design' de la participation en ligne" [Putting political projects in technology: Design-oriented approach to online participation]. *Participations* 8: 31–54.

Bennett, Elizabeth A., Alissa Cordner, Peter Taylor Klein, Stephanie Savell, and Gianpaolo Baiocchi. 2013. "Disavowing Politics: Civic Engagement in an Era of

Political Skepticism." *American Journal of Sociology* 119, no. 2: 518–48. https://doi.org/10.1086/674006.

Bogdanova, Elena. 2013. "Complaining to Putin: A Paradox of the Hybrid Regime." *Cultures of Grievance* (blog). Accessed March 17, 2016. http://culturesofgrievance.wordpress.com/.

Boltanski, Luc, and Laurent Thévenot. 1991. *De la justification: Les économies de la grandeur*. Paris: Gallimard.

Bowker, Geoffrey, and Susan Leigh Star. 1998. "Building Information Infrastructures for Social Worlds: The Role of Classifications and Standards." In *Community Computing and Support Systems*, edited by Toru Ishida, 231–48. Berlin: Springer.

Bowker, Geoffrey, and Susan Leigh Star. 1999. *Sorting Things Out: Classification and Its Consequences*. Cambridge, MA: MIT Press.

Brabham, Daren C. 2008. "Crowdsourcing as a Model for Problem Solving: An Introduction and Cases." *Convergence* 14, no. 1: 75–90. https://doi.org/10.1177/1354856507084420.

Brabham, Daren C. 2013. *Crowdsourcing*. Cambridge, MA: MIT Press.

Cefai, Daniel. 2013. "L'expérience des publics: Institution et réflexivité. Sur la sociologie des problèmes publics 1/2." *EspaceTemps*. Accessed August 3, 2018. https://www.espacestemps.net/articles/lexperience-des-publics-institution-et-reflexivite/.

Chateauraynaud, Francis, and Didier Torny. 1999. *Les sombres précurseurs, une sociologie pragmatique de l'alerte et du risque*. Paris: Éditions de l'École des Hautes Études en Sciences Sociales.

Collins, Harry. 2002. "The Third Wave of Science Studies: Studies of Expertise and Experience." *Social Studies of Science* 32, no. 2 (April): 235–96. https://doi.org/10.1177/0306312702032002003.

Dewey, Horace, and Ann Kleimola. 1970. "Suretyship and Collective Responsibility in Pre-Petrine Russia." *Jahrbücher für Geschichte Osteuropas* 18: 337–54.

Elliott, Marc. 2006. "Stigmergic Collaboration: The Evolution of Group Work." *M/C Journal* 9, no. 2. Accessed August 3, 2018. http://journal.media-culture.org.au/0605/03-elliott.php.

Ermoshina, Ksenia. 2014a. "Democracy as Pothole Repair: Civic Applications and Cyber-Empowerment in Russia." *Cyberpsychology: Journal of Psychosocial Research on Cyberspace* 8, no. 3, article 4. https://doi.org/10.5817/CP2014-3-4.

Ermoshina, Ksenia. 2014b. "Webnabludatel: A Russian Electoral Observation App." In *Civic Media Reader Project*, MIT Press. Accessed August 3, 2018. http://civicmediaproject.org/works/civic-media-project/webnabludatel-russia.

Erpyleva, Svetlana, and Artemy Magun, eds. 2014. "Politika Apolitichnyh: Grazhdanskiye Dvijeniya v Rossii 2011–2013 godov" [Politics of the apolitical: Civic movements in Russia in 2011–2013]. Moscow: Novoye Literaturnoye Obozreniye.

Eyler-Werve, Kate, and Virginia Carlson. 2012. *Civic Apps Competition Handbook*. Sebastopol, CA: O'Reilly Media.

Farman, James. 2012. *Mobile Interface Theory: Embodied Space and Locative Media*. New York: Routledge.

Felstiner, William L. F., Richard L. Abel, and Austin Sarat. 1980–81. "The Emergence and Transformation of Disputes: Naming, Blaming, Claiming." Special issue, "Dispute Processing and Civil Litigation." In *Law and Society Review* 15, nos. 3/4: 631–54.

Forum.Mista.Ru. n.d. Accessed March 16, 2016. http://www.forum.mista.ru/topic .php?id=535190&page=1.

Fuller, Matthew. 2008. *Software Studies: A Lexicon.* Cambridge, MA: MIT Press.

Garfinkel, Harold. 1967. *Studies in Ethnomethodology.* Englewood Cliffs, NJ: Prentice Hall.

Goody, Jack. 1977. *The Domestication of the Savage Mind.* Cambridge: Cambridge University Press.

Gregorio, Joe. 2002. "Stigmergy and the World-Wide Web." *Bitworking*, December 30. Accessed August 3, 2018. http://bitworking.org/news/Stigmergy.

Gerasimova, Ekaterina, and Sofia Chuikina. 2004. "Society of Repair (Obshestvo remonta)." In *Neprikosnovenny Zapas* 34. http://magazines.russ.ru/nz/2004/34 /ger85.html#_ftn1.

Hemment, Julia. 2012. "Redefining Need, Reconfiguring Expectations: The Rise of State-Run Youth Voluntarism Programs in Russia." *Anthropological Quarterly* 85, no. 2. http://works.bepress.com/julie_hemment/7/.

Heylighen, Francis. 2007a. "Accelerating Socio-technological Evolution: From Ephemeralization and Stigmergy to the Global Brain." In *Globalization as an Evolutionary Process: Modeling Global Change*, edited by George Modelski, Tessaleno Devezas, and William Thompson, 286–335. London: Routledge.

Heylighen, Francis. 2007b. "Why Is Open Access Development So Successful? Stigmergic Organization and the Economics of Information." In *Open Source Jahrbuch*, edited by Bernd Lutterbeck, Mat Bärwolff, and Robert A. Gehring, 165–180. Berlin: Lehmanns Media.

Irani, Lilly. 2015. "Hackathons and the Making of Entrepreneurial Citizenship." *Science Technology and Human Values* 40, no. 5: 799–824. https://doi.org/10 .1177/0162243915578486.

Joyce, Mary. 2010. *Digital Activism Decoded: The New Mechanics of Change.* New York: Idebate Press.

Kittur, Aniket, Ed H. Chi, and Bongwon Suh. 2008. "Crowdsourcing User Studies with Mechanical Turk." *Proceedings of the 26th Annual ACM Conference on Human Factors in Computing Systems*, 453–56. New York: ACM.

Kharkhordin, Oleg, ed. 2011. *Ot obshchestvennogo k publichnomu: kollektivnaia monografiia* [From social to public: Collective monograph]. Saint Petersburg: EUSP Press.

Lambert, Nicolas. 1985. *Whistleblowing in the Soviet Union: Complaints and Abuses under State Socialism.* London: Macmillan.

Machleder, Josh, and Gregory Asmolov. 2011. "Social Change and the Russian Network Society: Redefining Development Priorities in New Information Environments." *Internews Network.* Accessed December 15, 2015. http://www .internews.org/research-publications/social-change-and-russian-network -society.

Nérard, François-Xavier. 2002. "Les bureaux des plaintes dans l'URSS de Staline (1928–1941): La gestion du mécontentement dans un état socialiste." *Revue d'histoire moderne et contemporaine* 49, no. 2: 125–44.

Parunak. 2006. "A Survey of Environments and Mechanisms for Human-Human Stigmergy." In *Environments for Multi-Agent Systems II*, edited by Danny Weyns, H. Van Dyke Parunak, and Fabien Michel, 163–186. Berlin: Springer.

Raymond, Eric S. 1999. *The Cathedral and the Bazaar: Musings on Linux and Open Source by an Accidental Revolutionary*. Sebastopol, CA: O'Reilly Media.

Robles, Gregorio, Juan Julian Merelo, and Jesus M. Gonzalez-Barahona. 2005. "Self-Organized Development in Libre Software: A Model Based on the Stigmergy Concept." *Proceedings of 6th International Workshop on Software Process Simulation and Modeling*. www.libresoft.es/webfm_send/44.

Schuetz, Alfred. 1944. "The Stranger: An Essay in Social Psychology." *American Journal of Sociology* 49, no. 6: 499–507. Accessed August 3, 2018. http://www.jstor.org/stable/2771547.

Segalovich, Ilya. 2011. "Video-nabludenie I Translyatsia Na Izbiratelnom Utchastke" [Video Observation and Broadcasting on Voting Stations]. *Habrahabr*. Accessed January 10, 2016. http://habrahabr.ru/company/yandex/blog/258231/.

Tapscott, Don, and Anthony D. Williams. 2006. *Wikinomics: How Mass Collaboration Changes Everything*. London: Portfolio.

Te-st.ru. n.d. Accessed August 3, 2018. https://te-st.ru/section/teplitsa/.

Zhuravlev, Oleg, Natalia Savelyeva, and Svetlana Erpyleva. 2014. "Apoliticism and Solidarity: Local Activism in Russia." http://www.criticatac.ro/lefteast/apoliticism-and-solidarity-local-activism-in-russia/.

OUTWARD-LOOKING ENCLAVES

CHAPTER FOUR

AT THE PERIPHERY OF THE EMPIRE

Recycling Japanese Cars into Vladivostok's IT Community

Aleksandra Masalskaya and Zinaida Vasilyeva

When viewed from Moscow or Saint Petersburg, the IT industry in Vladivostok does not seem like a remarkable place. Most of our interlocutors from the Russian capitals have no clear idea about the activity of their colleagues on the Pacific coast: located more than five thousand miles away from Moscow and feeling even more remote due to the seven-hour time difference, observers may perceive it as a small and negligible periphery.[1] However, a closer look at Vladivostok's IT community offers a peculiar picture of local IT development, inseparable from the region's geographical and historical context and instructive for understanding post-Soviet transformations.

The IT sphere in the Far East of Russia emerged in the wake of the social and economic crisis created by the collapse of the Soviet Union. Relying on the knowledge and skills acquired by the late Soviet academia and seizing on the opportunities presented by the subsequent turmoil, local experts succeeded in adapting to the new emergent market economy and built their businesses by mobilizing their professional competences, alumni networks, and creative thinking skills. This chapter contributes to the growing literature on emerging ecologies of knowledge and innovation (Arora and Gambardella 2005; Drori, Ellis, and Shapira 2013; Saxenian 1994), the relationship between universities and industry (Chen and Kenney 2007; Kenney 1986, 2000; Kenney and Mowery 2014; Sohn and Kenney 2007), and the role of IT entrepreneurship in promoting regional development (Francis, Bercovitz, and Feldman 2005; Kenny 2000). It also helps to fill a gap in the history of computer science and IT in the late Soviet Union (Gerovitch 2002; Peters 2016; Tatarchenko 2013), a history yet almost unwritten (Tatarchenko, this volume).[2]

The institutional development of academic knowledge in Primorye, which literally means "close to the sea," started early in the Soviet period: in 1923, the Far Eastern Department of the Academy of Sciences (AS) of the USSR was founded. For several decades, it prioritized "studying the productive resources of the Far East for the needs of the people's economy of the region."[3] This regional but also quasi-colonial approach prioritizing the exploration of local natural resources lasted until the 1970s, when the emphasis shifted toward fundamental research in natural and hard sciences and the training of local academicians. Eventually, in the early 1970s, several new AS institutes were established, including the Institute of Chemistry and the Institute of Automation and Control Processes, equipped with a computing center. Following the usual Soviet practice of postgraduate professional placement, new graduates from the country's best universities were assigned to work in the region.

Artur, a sixty-six-year-old researcher at the AS Institute of Applied Mathematics, recalls: "When I came here in 1972 it was a kind of a landing of troops: I was one of a hundred people from the leading universities of Moscow, Leningrad, and Novosibirsk and a few people from Kiev. Well, this group was soon to play its role."

To host the arriving young specialists, often relocating with their families, a new academic campus was constructed in the suburbs of Vladivostok. It soon became a hotspot center of local cultural and public life: "Creating the Far-Eastern scientific center stirred up the cultural life of the city [quite a bit], and [gave rise to] various youth organizations. In the 1970s, enthusiastic scientific workers created a 'Club of friends of cinema,' *Vostok* ('The East'), 'Club of fans of ballet,' and a folk songs movement was expanding. These initiatives mostly belonged to the new-comers" (Kuznetsov 2014, 148). The newly constructed campus was inspired by the model of Novosibirsk Akademgorodok (see Indukaev, this volume) and other late Soviet science cities: they were designed as "green cities" convenient for intensive intellectual life but also suitable for the development of informal, social, and neighborly networks. The memoirs of the former residents of these cities are rich in descriptions about a dense local academic and cultural life.

In the 1970s and 1980s, a community of IT experts emerged in Vladivostok thanks to the institutional and professional interactions of specialists working within the academic context—in the research centers of the Academy of Science and in public universities. These were mainly mathematicians, cyberneticists, and electronic engineers employed within the three main AS centers: the Institute of Automation and Control Processes (1971), Institute of Applied Mathematics (1988), and Institute of Marine Technology Problems specializing in underwater robots (1988).[4] Besides these AS institutes, other important knowledge centers included the Department of Mathematics and Informatics at the Far Eastern State University (FESU) and the Department of Electronics and Instrument Engineering at the Far Eastern State Technical University (FESTU).

Although the research agendas and institutional interests of the Academy of Science and public universities differed considerably, a professional community interested in new calculating machines and computer sciences (*informatika*) emerged and maintained itself through regular informal professional exchanges with colleagues rather than through specific institutional formats. As Tatarchenko explains in this volume, while the state universities "resisted classes in computing" and were busy arguing about the pedagogical agenda and the format of the curriculum, masses of programmers were actually trained on the job by the Soviet computer industry and dispersed through the professional networks. In the case of Vladivostok, for university students interested in IT one way to get introduced to the new field was, for example, to do an internship and/or PhD program at one of the AS institutes, where computers were used for specific research purposes. However, the intellectual and institutional environment of these R&D centers offered very specific settings for IT as an "assistance service" for maintaining concrete and highly specialized activities of the laboratories and, thus, did not often allow for scientific research in computer science (CS) as an independent field.

The massive increase of interest in IT technologies in the Far East in the 1980s was due to the introduction of school computers imported from Japan: the Yamaha MSX. In 1984, a new academic subject—"Fundamentals of Informatics and Computer Engineering"—was introduced throughout the Soviet Union as part of a regular secondary school curriculum in order "to assure the computer literacy of the youth." Moreover, the officials considered the reform to be urgent and "requiring the adoption of immediate measures" (for the genealogy of this reform, see Tatarchenko, this volume).[5] By this time, the Soviet authorities had already given up on the plan to develop national hardware and instead relied on imported machines; so, in 1985–86, a special competition was organized by the state to identify the best computers for educational purposes. In Vladivostok, this resulted in the large-scale centralized purchase of Yamaha MSX-1 kits. Although we lack a detailed history of this reform and a clear account on how the decisions on this purchase were made, we know that the task to provide schools with computers was delegated to local authorities and, therefore, carried out at the expense of large regional enterprises in the framework of Soviet school patronage politics. Hence, one can suggest that the decision in favor of MSX-1 computers (and the next-generation MSX-2) was very much thanks to geography and preestablished contacts between local Vladivostok industries and Japan. Whatever the means used, by the early 1990s, almost all secondary schools in Vladivostok offered computer classes equipped with MSX-1 and MSX-2 computers.

The availability of school computers allowed for more regional organization of computer training on a mass scale. In the Far East, this development is strongly associated with the name of Kirill Fakhrutdinov, then head of Mathematics and Informatics at Far Eastern State University and a former graduate of Leningrad State University. Together with his colleagues and students, Fakhrutdinov initiated training programs for schools and school teachers across the entire Far East region and launched the development of software for the Yamaha MSX-2. The programs developed by this team were widely used after the collapse of the USSR and remained an important educational support in the "times of troubles": students from Vladivostok who participated in and won the All-Russian School Olympiads—annual school competitions in programming—were all trained on MSX-2 machines and Fakhrutdinov's team's software.

This wide computerization of the region with Japanese machines laid the cornerstone for educating the first "computer generation" not only in Vladivostok but in many other Soviet cities as well. An important feature that contributed to the popularity of the Yamaha MSX-2 was that along with educational applications it allowed for computer games and, therefore, opened a new and *playful* modality of appropriating coding skills and tech culture. The Yamaha MSX-2 was a revolutionary machine that even today retains its popularity among former school users and remains one of the most emulated computers. As a participant of the MSX Resource Center Forum writes:

> As soon as I got a Yamaha [computer] I immediately understood everything—assembler language, ASCII codes and C. The MSX computers were obviously ahead of their time. The PCs similar in their multimedia capacities appeared only by 1995. And I'm happy that the oldy-moldy MSX was my real first computer. Investigating all [its features], it was with MSX that

I learned how to write efficient code, compact, fast and one that was able to beat the shit out of that hardware. And this is an art you can't drink away. With such a first experience one can code for any computer and any OS. And what advanced games there were . . . (MSX Resource Center Forum 2009)

THE EMERGENCE OF LOCAL IT BUSINESSES

The fall of the Berlin Wall and the dissolution of the Soviet Union in 1991 resulted in the consequent social and economic crises that profoundly changed the local knowledge ecology in the Far East, as well as in other regions of the country. On the one hand, all public sectors—including the state universities and academic research centers—were suddenly drastically underfunded and left to fend for themselves. On the other hand, the introduction of a free-market economy offered new opportunities outside of academia. As computers became increasingly common, the demand for programmers increased dramatically on the labor market. At the same time, the lack of professionals with relevant competences and experience opened the opportunity to take a job as a programmer not only to graduates from mathematics departments but also to physicists, engineers, and anyone else who felt him- or herself capable of learning computer code. As Dmitriy Alekseyev, a forty-year-old engineer and successful IT entrepreneur, explains:

There is a Department of Electronics and Instrument Engineering, it's not quite a programmers' department, and it's still [designed] for the electronics engineers. . . . But then . . . well, there was high demand for programmers and computer geeks in the '90s, and zero demand for electronic engineers. . . . And it is clear that the graduates were very much focused on this [programmers] community.

The lack of professional programmers on the labor market was significantly escalated by the brain drain migration, well documented for the 1990s (see also Antoschyuk; West; and Fedorova on Israel, all in this volume). As international IT companies came to Russia to investigate a new and promising market and to headhunt for talent, local R&D centers, universities, and academic institutes quickly lost their best specialists, many of whom left to join the commercial sector or relocate abroad or to other regions with their families. For example, Kirill Fakhrutdinov, one of the key IT and computer science persons in the Far East, left Russia for the US in 1997. According to official data, 720,000 people (about 10 percent of the population) left the Far East between 1996 and 2006. These were mostly people of working age and with high qualifications (Resolution of RF Government 1996). The brain drain issue was one of the most sensitive topics in our interviews: Aleksandr, a thirty-seven-year-old IT and computer science expert, recalls:

> When I had been studying, we still had very strong specialists, but they had been leaving right before our eyes. I mean, in my second year, we were taught by a really very famous person, who raised up the whole industry. . . . And he moved away right during my studies. . . . At that time, in the 1990s, this phenomenon was huge, it was just something. . . . In fact, later it relaxed a bit . . . but still from my class [at math school] there remained . . . I don't know, maybe three guys in Vladivostok.

Yet unlike many other regional former Soviet cities, Vladivostok quickly adapted to the new economic logic. The geographic situatedness on the border of the country, local technical experience, and the informal economic networks that had developed in the city during the late Soviet period now became a breeding ground for the emergence of a regional IT market. The weak state control regulations that can be summed up by Yeltsin's formula "Take as much sovereignty as you can swallow"—emblematic for the 1990s—were also a blessing in disguise for the evolution of a competitive environment in the Vladivostok region.

USED JAPANESE CARS AS AN AGENT OF CHANGE

The introduction of market capitalism allowed for a rapid development of border trade with China, Korea, and, most importantly, Japan. As in the late nineteenth century, when Vladivostok was an important gateway of the Russian Empire to international trade across the Pacific, once again it became an important trade route in the 1990s. The fall of the Iron Curtain quickly stimulated a private foreign import trade of Japanese used cars. Owning a private car was the dream of many Soviet people in the 1970s and 1980s; under the crisis state of public transportation in the 1990s, this dream also became a necessity, and the demand for relatively cheap used vehicles soared. Accompanied by many dramatic and even criminal stories, businesses related to the trade in Japanese cars became crucial for the economy of the Far East in the 1990s. Hence, right-hand-drive vehicles spread quickly to Vladivostok, then across Siberia, and into the neighboring countries of Central Asia.

Many of the city's IT companies emerged with the development of the used car import market from Japan. The explosive growth of this commerce stimulated the development of active online trading. The complicated lo-

gistics associated with automobile importing (gathering specific information about the used cars, including photos, making spare parts available,
online tracking of the vehicles, etc.) posed challenges to local IT specialists.
The university training they had received was insufficient to meet market
expectations and—as in many other cases documented in this volume—
many had to retrain themselves on the job. Information technology specialists in Vladivostok seized the opportunity to develop online trade services,
electronic catalogues, search tools, online price calculators, electronic delivery
"trackers," software for stock management, and the list goes on. In the post-
Soviet economic context, this frenetic and creative activity, which emerged
out of a necessity to build one's life in the context of social and economic uncertainty, produced a completely new type of IT business in Russia. Our interlocutors tend to represent that process as the unfolding of a new *industry*: car
importing stimulated local businesses specializing in automobile maintenance
and restoration wherein the old vehicles were repaired, repainted, tuned, and
retrofitted with Russian-language instruments, and adapted for their new lives
in Russia. "Whole software complexes were being developed back then. We've
already developed standards, a common platform, software for companies
which sell or maintain cars, etc.," said Aleksandr.

From the outset, much of this business was conducted online, which placed
a premium on IT competence. In Vladivostok, much earlier than elsewhere
in Russia, virtual business became the norm. Any automobile or parts
trader—when his business had expanded to a certain point—sought not just
representation for his company online but also his own in-house IT studio.
Vadim, a twenty-seven-year-old IT developer, speculates: "Suppose some
companies, selling for instance car tires, achieve a turnover large enough
to buy a whole web studio straight away. It will be creating, say, their website, and their website only. It can employ a dozen workers, usually students.
I mean, as a matter of fact, there's no such thing [anywhere else?] I know
about." The second part of the 2000s was a period of rapid development
for online trade worldwide. It started with the "business-to-business deals"
and quickly spread to wholesale and retail businesses. In Vladivostok, this
trend was further enforced by the urgent need to set up video-mediated
communications allowing Russian customers to participate remotely in car
auctions in Japan and provide semiautomated translations. A command of
virtual communications gave companies an important competitive advantage. In terms of local IT development, this task was a big challenge for the
professional community, as it required sophisticated computer science skills
that Soviet education and training had not provided; back then, the issue of

semiautomated simultaneous translation was on the cutting edge of computer sciences. Typically, this kind of technical expertise was a prerequisite in two kinds of business: the market for automobiles and the market for electronics and domestic supplies. It was precisely within these sectors that the customer base was also most ready to adopt these new online sales practices. Hence, Vladivostok and its region literally drove its "peculiar" right-hand-drive Japanese cars into the computer age.

Used car imports from Japan quickly became the local economy's major branch, impacting Vladivostok and the entire surrounding area. By 2008, the import of Japanese cars had given Vladivostok the greatest vehicle density in all of Russia: 566 cars per one thousand inhabitants (AVTO 2008). Such a concentration of cars had negative effects on urban infrastructure, the ecology, and the health of Vladivistok's residents.[6] At the same time, the burgeoning business related to the import of Japanese cars provided the city with new job opportunities, attracting workers from nearby regions. Port and shipping workers, customer brokers, salesmen, traders, and car mechanics were all in high demand, and both locals and newcomers quickly became integrated into the new economic setting and powered the development of a market economy in the entire region.

THE GROWTH OF IT COMPANIES IN THE VLADIVOSTOK REGION

a) Drom.ru and the FarPost Company

The relationship between the automobile import sector and the growth and expansion of IT knowledge in the region can be well illustrated by two business initiatives undertaken by Yegor Nikolayev, a graduate of the FESU Department of Informatics and one of the main IT stakeholders in the Far East.

Back in 1998, the Drom.ru project started as a web portal dedicated to commerce in Japanese cars.[7] It soon became the most important information hub for car enthusiasts and commercially successful automobile enterprises. Today, Drom.ru is the largest internet community dedicated to cars, counting more than eight million users in the Russian Federation (Drom.ru 2011), and recipient of the highest popular ratings of car websites in Russia. Its most popular feature is the forum where car owners share details of their experiences with various car makes and models.

The commercial success of Drom.ru allowed Yegor Nikolayev and his team to undertake other projects, in particular Vl.ru ("Virtual Vladivostok"), an information-oriented web domain. Vl.ru offers a large spectrum of applications relevant to different aspects of city life, including news, map, a shopping guide, and even a special service for university applicants.[8]

> To some extent, the company informs the life of the city . . . about everything, from nightclubs to political issues. So, it's about cinemas, museums, leisure, but also news, urgent news. . . . When the [disaster] happened with Fukushima, we posted the radiation [level]. When the notorious flood happened in Khabarovsk, we [reported on] the level of water. (Anton, aged twenty-five, IT developer and lecturer at the Far Eastern Federal University [FEFU])

The various projects by Yegor Nikolayev are now united in a single holding called FarPost, which is recognized as a regional leader in internet services and is the local competitor of Yandex, the Moscow-based national internet service (see Fedorova on Yandex, this volume). Through its development of thematic web forums, hosting services, and its own network of banner advertisements, FarPost became the most comprehensive, well-structured, and user-friendly catalogue of internet resources in the Far East region. According to our interviews and field experiences, on the local level FarPost definitely remains the main reference point for regional everyday life, often outperforming Yandex. For instance, Yandex.Map fails to provide a traveler with an adequate map of Vladivostok, while FarPost does. Evidence of this local superiority can be seen even along Vladivostok's major avenues, where huge Yandex.Market billboards tout the company's services with a fervor that suggests the difficulties it has in competing in the Far Eastern market.

A trait of the FarPost holding is its strong regional identity and socially responsible self-presentation. Its ambition was to build a publicly recognized resource and, according to Vl.ru's mission statement, "take [the] business of Vladivostok and the Far East to the Internet, thus making it civilized and [conformant with] global standards" (Businesspress 2002).

b) Rhonda Software

Beginning in the mid-1990s, foreign IT companies eagerly entered the young Russian market and penetrated deep into the Siberian and Ural regions. For instance, by 1995, IBM had opened offices in five Russian cities: Moscow, Saint Petersburg, Vladivostok, Chelyabinsk, and Tyumen (Lyudmirskiy and Malyutin 1995). The potential for collaboration with Western companies can be well demonstrated by the history of Rhonda Software (RS), one regional example of IT business development. Rhonda Software began its collaboration with Motorola early on, signing long-term contracts for the development of pager software by 1999. This contract stimulated reorganization to bring the company up to international standards and it also lifted the business to a new level of quality and global partnership. In 2001, RS was successfully certified for Capability Maturity Model Integration (CMMI) as a Software Engineering Institute Capability Maturity Model (SEI SW-CMM) Level 3 Company; a year later it was reclassified as a SEI SW-CMM Level 4 Company. Then it began developing software for mobile phones and, in 2004, RS became a certified partner of Microsoft. According to CNews, it was on the list of the hundred largest Russian IT companies for three years running (from 2004 to 2006); it was featured twice (in 2006 and 2007) in a rating by the Expert RA rating agency as one of the largest Russian IT companies; and by 2006, the company employed about two hundred workers.

c) DNS

Another example of successful ecommerce in Vladivostok is the DNS company, which owns a chain of supermarkets selling digital goods. Founded in 1998, it has become one of Russia's leading digital retailers, serving more than four hundred cities throughout the country and producing its own laptops, desktops, monitors, uninterruptible power supply, and other computer accessories under the brand names DNS and AirTone.

Although DNS is a national retail company marketing computer supplies, it is also one of the critical stakeholders in Vladivostok's IT market. Moreover, the DNS case highlights the significant presence of engineers in Russian IT. While most other local firms were started by graduates from the FESU Informatics Department, DNS was launched by a group of friends who had graduated from the Far Eastern State Technical University. They were electronic engineers who were extremely well trained but whose skills were not in much demand during Vladivostok's booming IT market of the 1990s. Although most of them became successful programmers, they shared a distinct "manual" technical culture focused on hardware, engineering, and the material side of computers. The company positions itself in the market as a team of practical professionals and practitioners—"fans of the digital lifestyle" and "already something more than just a trade company," as stated on the official website (DNS 2016). With their focus on hardware, they created a digital platform for discussing the newest gadgets and offering advice from enthusiasts and experts alike on purchasing, using, and repairing digital equipment. As a clearinghouse for information on computers, DNS has created a large community of people interested in the newest technologies: today, it hosts more than eighty thousand users. Like Drom.ru (developed by FarPost), the DNS Technopoint.ru website conforms to international technological standards and is the most visited Web-sale platform in Russia.

In addition to its focus on hardware, DNS develops software for corporate use and is one of the biggest employers of graduates from the IT departments of local universities. Today, it employs around 150 IT professionals supporting online trade across Russia. The company's cofounder, Dmitriy Alekseyev, is one of the most respected IT experts in Vladivostok and an enthusiastic promoter of robotics.

d) Kama Games

Finally, we discuss the case of a successful local company, Kama Games, a studio specializing in developing games for mobile devices. The story of this firm, however, represents a notorious case within the IT business community because, in local memory, it remains both the most brilliant commercial success and the worst failure in terms of business practices.

In 2010, the multiplayer game *Pokerist Texas Poker* developed by Kama Games suddenly rose into the top-five rankings of Google Play in twenty-five countries; in eighty-nine countries, it rose to first place in the App Store.[9] Unexpectedly large and immediate earnings allowed Kama Games to aggressively "buy up" specialists by offering wages far above the local average, virtually taking over the IT labor market around Vladivostok. Yevgeniy, a thirty-five-year-old IT developer, explains:

> It was decided to hire the best IT specialists in the city. And the firm offered such [high] salaries, that everybody accepted. As I understand, absolutely everybody aspired to get in there. . . . And they really gathered if not all the best . . . then some of the best programmers in the city . . . and for some time it was very comfortable to work there. Even today their office is the best in Vladivostok, if not in the whole Far East.

However, Kama's tactics challenged the local IT community: on the one hand, small studios were not able to keep their best personnel; on the other, even underqualified IT specialists started demanding substantially higher compensation. Moreover, the discussions about the remuneration of the IT labor changed the "mood" of the community and introduced a clear wage-based hierarchy of experts. Rising salary expectations also extended to those who did not have the opportunity or the desire to join Kama Games, making them consider vacancies abroad and triggering yet another wave of emigration. Soon thereafter the owner decided to relocate the company to Moscow, and then later to Dublin. Today, Kama Games has only a minor department in Vladivostok.

In local memory, Kama Games is a negative example of "dirty business," aggressive and incompatible with the ethos of the IT field. To emphasize the distinctively correct and knowledge-based character of IT business and explain the Kama Games anomaly/exception, Vladivostok's IT experts point to the business genealogy of Denis Dranitsyn, the company's owner. Dranitsyn entered the IT market from the construction industry, without being an IT specialist himself. Moreover, in some cases the discussion of Kama Games made our interlocutors speculate about the moral side of the game industry in general, thus revealing the old Soviet juxtaposition of "useful" and "spoiling" leisure practices. Thus, by contrasting styles in IT and construction businesses, IT professionals defend a certain image and morality of their professional activities which they tend to imagine as being based on expertise and social responsibility rather than on contingencies and opportunities of "wild" capitalism.

The companies discussed above (except for Kama Games) are representative of the early days of IT development in Vladivostok when they tended to serve the emerging private computer market. Since the mid-2000s, the focus has shifted toward the IT needs of the state and public institutions: new firms have arisen to specialize in the development of software facilitating integration with federal information systems, such as cryptography, messengers, intranet, and so on (this shift is also noted in Kontareva, this volume). Yet according to our interviews, the most prominent firms today still work for the consumer and business markets, focusing on the development of new web products (FarPost and Drom.ru), outsourcing (Rhonda and small game developers), and online trade combined with internal software development (DNS and Monastyrev-pharmacy).

UNIVERSITY AND BUSINESS: SURVIVAL BY COOPERATION

As in many regions of Russia, the social and economic crises of the 1990s had dramatic consequences in all spheres of public life, including public universities. Due to the lack of funding, Vladivostok technical schools were losing their best teachers through emigration or to the commercial sector. At the same time, although the outmigration from Vladivostok was considerable, the city remained an important regional university city and, thus, kept receiving school graduates coming from the entire Far East region, from South Primorye (on the Korean border) to Yakutiya and Kamchatka.

Under these conditions, the only way to maintain the level of university training was to involve more young professionals in teaching. This problem was particularly topical, as the newly established IT businesses lacked professionals able to deal with complex IT tasks, while local universities failed to provide the market with sufficiently competent workers. The general dissatisfaction with the skills of graduates forced businesses to be in touch with local educational centers and to participate in additional student training. This particular context pushed both sides—universities and industry—to look for common ground and build up cooperation. In many cases, such cooperation was the result of individual efforts undertaken by local experts and enthusiasts. The life story of Aleksandr Klenin, the former head of the Informatics Department at the Far Eastern State University, is emblematic in this respect.

Today, mathematics students at university start working for IT firms by their third year, and quickly gain the kind of professional experience that is unobtainable in academia. Raised in a family of Soviet scholars, Aleksandr started his professional trajectory in IT when he was in the ninth grade. Back then, he was hired as a programmer at one of the recently opened banks, and had to learn everything on the job. A few years later, when he entered university and was formally a freshman himself, Aleksandr continued combining his studies with work in the private sector; moreover, very soon he started to teach at the university:

> You know, when I entered the university, one can say, there were no teachers able to teach us anything new. I mean, there was math analysis, sports, history, but nobody could teach special courses. So, I have been teaching starting from my first year [of university studies]. Of course, this was not official, because officially this would be impossible, and yet. . . . Because nobody was able to say anything new in Vladivostok. Nobody at all. . . . And our best teachers knew that.

Even after his graduation in 1996, when Aleksandr officially became a university teacher and then—later—the head of the department (although he never obtained a PhD degree), he coupled teaching with practical work in the IT industry. Moreover, as head of the department, he always continued to interact with former students while encouraging them to contribute to their alma mater:

We are trying to attract teachers who are practicing programmers. I myself work actively, well, I literally code. Obviously, the university does not
pay [much] money, and everyone earns money outside. This is, of course,
terrible, but if a teacher has managed to survive, this means he can earn
money somewhere else. And it makes a huge difference.

This quote points to a major identity crisis that occurred within the educational system for IT professionals in today's Russia: only someone who
works outside academia is recognized as a qualified teacher, while a full-
time university professor is perceived as a "loser" or, at the very least, an
underskilled practitioner. In the same vein, Andrey Indukaev argues in this
volume that "competences are now concentrated in the IT industry" as opposed to universities. Yet at the same time, the gradual recovery of the regional economy—which took off around the turn of the millennium—and
the growing demand for IT specialists in the labor market helped young
graduates find good jobs and think of themselves as real experts. Put together, this feeling of "being a pro," along with the old-fashioned Soviet prestige
of the university as a temple of knowledge, enticed many recent graduates to
engage in university teaching, although this kind of work was often done on
a quasi-voluntary basis.

Thus, while in many ways deleterious, the immediate departure of the
best IT minds had some positive, though unexpected and underestimated,
side effects. First, it stimulated social and professional mobility for young
graduates; and second, it forced IT companies and universities to collaborate, if for no other reason than as a survival strategy (compare with Drori,
Ellis, and Shapira 2013, who argue that this was also one of the crucial factors
in Israel's technological development).

The university's strategy of cooperation with its alumni turned out to be
crucial for maintaining the level of both theoretical and professional training. Despite the lack of adequate university training and a large outflow of
employees from universities, the departments providing training in programming and computer sciences managed to progress and develop under
conditions of permanent crisis. The active and interested involvement of
practitioners in teaching helped to shape a common understanding of the
IT profession and introduce an industry-oriented approach into education
practices. Local IT practitioners—often the alumni themselves—got involved
not only in teaching but also in revising the academic curriculum and, thus,
played an important role in readjusting university training according to the
expectations of local firms and potential employers. Moreover, profession-

als who combined work in academia and in industry could transmit to the younger generation their understanding of good practices and their styles of coding. Therefore, they helped to develop professional standards and identity as performed through the practices of coding (the issue of style and standardization of coding as a feature of corporate identity is discussed in Fedorova on Yandex, this volume).

A thorough understanding of both sides—university teaching and the demands of the IT industry—allowed Aleksandr Klenin and his former students to build educational "bridges" between academia and business and, hence, to bring their individual efforts to the institutional level. In this activity, the Informatics Department at the Far Eastern State University became the key node in the network between the main IT companies in Vladivostok and the university. Our interlocutors estimate that about 50 percent of practicing IT experts in the Far East, including leading entrepreneurs, passed through this department. Prominent industry representatives feel that graduates from this department are better adapted than before to the requirements of today's business and are thus in the highest demand in the labor market. Aleksandr is regularly contacted to provide information about his former students, which is considered more valuable and useful than any written recommendation.

No doubt, today Aleksandr Klenin is one of the key figures on the IT scene in Vladivostok. In different contexts, he was referred to by our other interlocutors as one of the best IT experts and community leaders. Growing professionally between industry and academia and holding positions on both sides, Aleksandr himself became a "bridge" across the river of IT knowledge and practices. To concretize Aleksandr's trajectory and give another example of "institutional bridging" between the worlds of education and industrial programming, we would like to discuss the role of his mother, Nadezhda Klenina, a mathematician and university teacher.

ACM ICPC Championship in Vladivostok

Being a gifted and engaged pedagogue, Nadezhda has always been interested in early programming and put a lot of effort into promoting programming skills in the region. For instance, she supervises the "Academy for Young Programmers," weekly programming courses for school students set up within the institutional framework of the Informatics Department of the Far Eastern State University. This initiative allows gifted juniors to be trained by the best teachers and practitioners of Vladivostok.

In 1996, Nadezhda was part of Kirill Fakhrutdinov's team who organized the first ACM ICPC championship, thus, putting the Far East region on the map of international IT. While many of the initial ideologists left Vladivostok for good, Nadezhda was the person who maintained the educational tradition. Since 1996, she has annually devoted about two months of her life to organizing the competition. Today, it has become the Russian quarterfinal of the prestigious programming championship for students, which is listed among the most notable networking and recruiting events for the IT business. Most of the teams' coaches are former participants themselves; hence, this regular training and coaching maintains continuity by ensuring the transfer of knowledge and professional skills as well as imparting a corporate understanding of IT labor as highly intellectual, and even "beautiful." Aleksandr, who first participated in the ACM ICPC as a student and, indeed, was part of the team that came in tenth in the All-Russian competition, is now one of the Vladivostok teams' trainers.

The practical side of organizing the championship is also evidence of the entanglements between individual trajectories, IT education, and the IT-industry in Vladivostok. For instance, one of the major sponsors of the ACM ICPC is Rhonda Software, the company consisting of many of Klenin's former students. As Aleksandr puts it:

> Rhonda has always been our sponsor, that is for old times' sake. . . . Because they one and all—from director to our colleague [who combines work for Rhonda and university teaching]—are, in different senses, our graduates.

The ACM ICPC championship is also a remarkable example of a venue, where personal relationships based on friendship and professional solidarity meet business interests. On the one hand, the ACM ICPC is hosted by the Department of Informatics and, thus, operates as an important additional platform for IT training, "bridging" the formal curriculum of the university. The preparations for a competition presuppose year-round training and serve as a kind of semiprofessional disciplinary format: as one of our interlocutors phrased it quite well, "You need to sit down, glue yourself to the chair, and code nonstop." On the other hand, the championship is a venue for performing excellence and up-to-date best practices, and hence functions as an event that literally brings together all the IT experts of Vladivostok. It is a good occasion to meet colleagues and friends and—in addition—to negotiate business with partners and headhunt young participants. Unsurprisingly, for the same reason, many of the local IT companies sponsor the Far Eastern stage of ACM ICPC and other student competitions. By allocating winners' prizes, companies keep an eye out for potential employees while showcasing themselves as good employers (compare with the educational initiatives by Yandex documented by Fedorova, this volume). Igor, a twenty-nine-year-old IT professional, who for seven years (until 2012) combined teaching and industrial programming, describes the competition as follows:

> Look at the championship ACM, for example, which takes place at the university: it usually gathers people to talk—they are not much involved in the jury, and not even necessarily organizers. This championship, watching the competitions, often brings together people who once participated, who are now engaged in professional activities, and still they often show up there. But the main goal of the event, surely, is not in this [networking], even though it serves this task as well.

Thus, the individual efforts by Aleksandr and Nadezhda Klenin and their colleagues indeed created something more than just another local educational project. Their devotion to the IT profession, deep pedagogical engagement with students and alumni, and strong regional identity all greatly contributed to the consolidation and reproduction of Vladivostok's IT community and to the establishment of professional standards of IT knowledge.

Today, almost all local IT companies take part in IT educational projects. For instance, FarPost organizes short-term courses on specific IT topics and offers student internships, often designed around engagement in a concrete project. Recently, within the framework of cooperation with the Far East Federal University, students were involved in developing a university guide app under the leadership of FarPost experts. Such collaboration allowed the university to get a cheap and good-quality app as well as provide students with practical training, while the company contributed to the professionalization of future programmers and was afforded an advantageous recruiting opportunity. FarPost is also one of the regular sponsors of the ACM ICPC championship.

Similarly, Rhonda Software and DNS are regular sponsors of university programming competitions. Moreover, Dmitriy Alekseyev (DNS) has initiated and invested himself in the creation of the Center for the Development of Robotics in Vladivostok.[10] During the interview, he confessed:

> In fact, I did not intend to get myself into education or any children's activities, but step by step. . . . First, I just wanted to support a movement. . . . By the way, I saw how the ACM [championship] had been developing. . . . There is a kind of process, some competitions are going on . . . and I liked it very much there, it's very cool and good. But then I was surprised why nothing similar happens within robotics, where there [are] so many interesting

things? . . . At first, I wanted to help an internal championship but discovered that, in fact, there is no internal championship at all, nothing is run, and that's why there are no teams. Well . . . I tried to organize and motivate, let's say, the bureaucratic machine . . . but then realized it's easier to do everything myself. Looking at results, and applied efforts, it's much more efficient to do it, to do everything myself.

Thus, born amid the social and economic uncertainties and instabilities of the post-Soviet period, a unique IT ecosystem had developed in Vladivostok by the mid-2000s. With its reasonably effective business models and patterns of interactions, this ecosystem proved to be efficient, resistant to crises, and able to sustain itself within the regional economy.[11] Moreover, the critical need to maintain the reproduction of professionals pushed local IT industries to cooperate with public universities and thus compensate for the loss of cadres produced by a massive emigration of professionals. This cooperation helped (at least partly) to adjust public education to industry needs, a major problem still current today. It also, very importantly, allowed symbolic continuities in the process of forming a professional community identity to be preserved.

Nevertheless, all this progress and development in the Far Eastern IT industry went almost unnoticed and, alas, unappreciated by the federal government. Rooted, on the one hand, in the period of weak state regulation in the 1990s and, on the other hand, in the Soviet tradition of supplementary education and early professionalization, the IT industry emerged from the bottom up. Its emergence was due to local initiatives and individual efforts, and ingrained with a strong sense of regional particularity in the face of suspicion and hostility from and toward the center.

RECONFIGURATIONS AFTER 2008

The automobile business paradise tumbled down in December 2008, when the Russian government introduced a new policy that doubled customs duties on imported cars older than five years.[12] This decision was to protect Russia's automobile industry, which could not compete with foreign used vehicles. Most of Vladivostok's companies specializing in the car trade, including online trading, could not survive under the new policy and either closed or significantly curtailed their businesses.

As an act of resistance, local car dealers started to import cars as kits of spare parts that could be checked and approved by customs on the border as spare parts rather than vehicles. Such kits—remembered in Vladivistok as *konstruktory* and in Japan as *matreshkas*—were afterward reassembled by local handymen into functioning cars and sold. Although matreshkas enjoyed a good reputation for their quality, which is indicative of the high level of Vladivostok craftsmanship, the police authorities were reluctant to register them as vehicles. Nevertheless, this semilegal trade persisted until 2010–11 (Motoi 2013).

The economic pain caused by the new policy was felt well beyond the car import market, affecting hundreds of thousands of people and triggering mass protests throughout Russia, particularly in its Far East region, from late 2008 until the spring of 2010. The first protest actions started spontaneously. On December 14, 2008, hundreds of people took to the streets in Vladivostok to appeal to regional and federal authorities on behalf of the Japanese car industry: "Almost 1500 people participated in the demonstration. We haven't seen such an abundance of people in a long time. The Vladivostok folks not only supported the All-Russian action, but became its main driving force" (Zagoruyko 2008).

Other regions besides the Far East that relied on the import used-car market were also harshly affected by the new policy. The same day, parallel demonstrations occurred in many cities across Siberia and the Urals (Drom. ru 2008), and this unrest spread all the way to Moscow and Kaliningrad, near the Polish border. In Vladivostok, the protests were poorly coordinated but managed to avoid any violence and vandalism. A massive collection of signatures "in defense of the right steering wheel" resulted in large-scale public participation in the protests. While the first demonstrations focused strictly on economic grievances, the claims were soon reformulated in political terms: the new—and this time unauthorized—gatherings on December 20 and 21, 2008, were accompanied with slogans demanding the dismissal of local authorities and even the impeachment of the president of Russia.[13] The political "smell" of events, however, allowed the federal authorities to react with force: on December 21 an unauthorized gathering was dispersed with help of the Special Police Force brought in from the Moscow region (according to media sources, local police refused to act against the protestors since, as local residents, they supported them). Up to two hundred participants were wounded. Officially, all protests that were related to car imports were interpreted as riots organized by destructive forces and financed from abroad. In January 2009, the Analytical Department of the State Duma sought to identify foreign agitators and its think tanks denounced the protests as part of an attempt at another "color revolution" (as in the Ukraine and Georgia) aimed at separating the Far East from the Russian Federation (State Duma 2009).

To respond to the economic complaints of protesters, federal authorities have undertaken several measures. First, a special regulation was introduced to provide state compensation for transporting cars by train produced in the European part of the country.[14] Second, in the following years, a new car assembly plant was built in Vladivostok; since 2010, it produces the Korean car SsangYong, the Japanese Mazda and Toyota, and the Russian truck UAZ (RIA Novosti 2014).

However, it would be wrong to analyze this case exclusively in terms of protecting the national car industry. Since the middle of the 2000s, the federal government has increasingly focused on the development of the Far East region, which again was recognized as a place of strategic and economic importance. For instance, since the 1990s, Russian energy corporations have been investigating the potential of the oil and gas fields near Sakhalin Island, situated on the border between the Sea of Okhotsk and the Sea of Japan, only five hundred miles from Vladivostok. In 2008—the same year as the car customs clearance policy—Sakhalin Island became home to a wholly owned subsidiary of Gazprom and a new natural gas liquification plant; in 2013, Vladivostok also hosted a daughter company of Gazprom.

The decision to hold the 2012 APEC summit in Vladivostok, made as early as September 2007, exemplifies the longer-term federal strategy regarding the Far East region. This resolution set the stage for the most important reorganization of the city in its entire history and attracted significant federal funds to the region. Importantly, these projects responded to the urgent need of urban infrastructural development, thus making some of the local population support the federal government. Indeed, the large-scale highway development and the construction of bridges across the Golden Horn Bay and the Eastern Bosporus Strait have significantly improved transportation in the city, helping to connect the city center to relatively close but poorly accessible areas nearby.

The general plan of urban development included the construction of a new university campus on Russkiy Island, designed as a large-scale educational complex with stand-alone infrastructure. The new campus was intended to become home to the Federal University of the Far East, a prestigious new educational mega-institution, created as part of a reform carried out by the Russian Ministry of Education and Science since 2006.[15]

The construction of a new campus was a way to redevelop a rundown area. Located in Peter the Great Bay in the Sea of Japan, some distance from

Vladivostok, Russkiy Island was the site of an important Soviet military base. Since then, it has been largely abandoned and isolated from the mainland. At the time of construction, only a ferry service existed between the island and the city, making it virtually isolated from urban life. Building a brand-new campus there necessitated, inter alia, the construction of a new bridge and the expansion of the urban infrastructure to accommodate it. It was also assumed that the relative distance between campus and city would further enable the development of the area as a coherent ensemble of educational and residential buildings.

However, as the budget allocations for this expensive university construction project were folded into the preparations for the APEC summit of 2012, its architecture and urban design were ultimately subordinated to the requirements of this mega-event. Unsurprisingly, this rendered the educational and research needs of the university campus relatively unimportant in comparison with the goal of creating a spectacular and prestigious showcase site for the international forum. Today, the new campus occupies a vast and scenic territory with spacious and externally impressive buildings; on the inside, however, oddities abound. In the interviews, we were told about nonworking electrical outlets, stairs leading nowhere, classroom blackboards that cannot be erased, to name just a few examples of many serious infrastructure problems highlighted by our interlocutors. But most egregiously, it was only after the move to Russkiy Island that it became apparent that no public transportation routes to and from the island had been put in place, or even planned; however, a bus service was later provided.

The relocation of the university from the city to Russkiy Island took place in 2013–14, and remains a popular topic for our interlocutors, who often said that the physical remoteness of the new campus was an obstacle. On the one hand, it is now harder to attract industry professionals to part-time (and quasi-volunteer) teaching roles, as it takes up to an hour to drive or commute to Russkiy Island. On the other hand, students also feel themselves disadvantaged as the distance between campus and city limits their access to part-time jobs and internships that used to be available when the university was part of the urban fabric. While this may not be a problem in other professions, familiarity with industrial realities is a necessary part of the training of young IT graduates. Prominent industry representatives feel that the level of experience and training of FEFU IT graduates has significantly declined in recent years, along with the disengagement of the IT practitioners from teaching. Finally, this isolation of students from the IT labor market had the most devastating impact on small local IT companies,[16] as they cannot afford to attract "expensive" professionals, either from Vladivostok or other parts of Russia. Thus, Boris, the director of a small IT studio, complains:

> Now that they moved the university to the island, locked all the students there, good luck hiring a student from the fourth or fifth year! . . . We cannot hire students because they do not commute to us. Hence, well, I think we lose very much of development potential, we have no way of updating staff, training them. Well, that's all—and it turns out that they, too, are losing their opportunity since they do not have access to the experience, to the real market. (Boris, aged thirty-four)

However, not all are critical about the relocation of the university from the city to Russkiy Island. Some argue that early professionalization of programmers prevents students from deeply engaging with their studies, and hint at precarious jobs in Vladivostok's IT market.

The topic of the university relocation appears to be particularly sensitive, as it merges with the painful experience of the federal university reform, which greatly disturbed the local IT community. First, the reform was accompanied by the assignment to all federal universities of so-called "top-priority research directions" (i.e., research emphasizing the specificities of their respective regions). For instance, while IT-related sciences were identified as "priorities" for many other federal universities, this was not the case for Vladivostok, which was prescribed to concentrate on "resources of the world ocean," "energy resources and energy saving technologies," "industry of nanosystems and nanomaterials," "transport and logistics complex," "cooperation of Russia and the Asian-Pacific Region," and "biomedicine."[17] Federal funds were of course distributed accordingly. In fact, this has made the needs of the IT departments virtually invisible to the FEFU administrators who report on their progress as per government priorities.

Second, the institutional restructuring disrupted old educational traditions. In Vladivostok, the FEFU was created through a mechanical administrative merger of four institutions of higher education: the Far Eastern State University (FESU), the Far Eastern State Technical University (FESTU), the Pacific State University of Economics, and the Ussuriysk State Pedagogical Institute. Due to this restructuring, all former faculties (*fakul'tet*) from the four distinct (though now decapitated) local universities have been transformed—through a mechanically administrative "mix-and-match" reordering—into big newly established administrative units called "schools."[18] This translated the traditional three-tiered structure of "university–faculty–department" (*kafedra*) inherited from the Soviet era into a two-level structure of "school (consisting of several former faculties)–department." In practice, this abolished the old kafedras, which were the main research and innovation incubators of the universities and consisted of ten to fifteen faculty members who worked closely together. In their place, large academic units—"schools" with fifty to a hundred faculty members—were created and incorporated faculty members from previously independent institutions. Our interlocutors describe new "schools" as amorphous collectives functioning without a coherent educational program and clear research agenda, largely because their faculty members come from different universities with various teaching traditions and priorities. Unsurprisingly, the restructuring also affected academic hierarchies. For example, Aleksandr Klenin has not received any administrative status within the new system, because he does not hold an academic degree. Nevertheless, he is still one of the main people cited when local IT experts speak about the university.

Finally, the reform was carried out hastily and without consulting the local scientific community, which naturally provoked sharp criticism. For instance, contrary to university practice dating back to the tsars, all new academic and administrative positions were filled without an open competition.[19] While many newly created academic vacancies were given to professors who had taught at the old local universities, all of the top management positions were given to administrators appointed from the federal center, from Moscow. To placate local academic elites, the former rectors were offered "emeritus" status or became vice-rectors. One of the results was a considerable expansion of the academic bureaucracy. This provoked much criticism, and the new administrative system was ridiculed as *kormleniye* (which literally means "feeding"). This alludes to the medieval Muscovite practice of taxing towns and rural districts to support and "feed" the government officials who ruled them, often Muscovite nobles.

Thus, the second half of the 2000s was marked by an increased presence of the federal government, whose authority had previously been felt only distantly in the Far East. By suppressing the car protests and directing funds to the region, the state demonstrated its power as the master who came to "restore order." In other words, the development program for Primorye can be described as an imposed deal where, at the price of the loss of political autonomy, urgently needed infrastructural renovations were undertaken (compare with mega-events in Kazan' described in Kontareva, this volume). But for the local IT community, the cost was high. First, the whole business landscape was dramatically disrupted, since many of the companies dependent on the Japanese car trade were shut down. Moreover, 2008 was the year of global economic crises, which affected companies relying on foreign capital. For instance, in that year Motorola closed down projects with Rhonda, thus making more than two hundred highly qualified professionals unemployed. All this resulted in yet another wave of migration and emigration and restructured the local IT community considerably. One local expert noted that many of those who did not survive the year 2009 left for Cisco, Google, Samsung Electronics, Texas Instruments, and other international companies.

Second, the effects of the federal reform on the existing system of IT professional training in Vladivostok proved controversial. What emerged from our interviews was that the so-called "optimization" of regional educational institutions has so far produced the opposite result from its intended effect. The reforms were aimed at strengthening the ties between federal universities and the real economies of the region; though, in the case of Vladivostok's IT, they have in fact damaged the ecosystem that professionals and enthusiasts had been developing for the last ten to fifteen years.

VLADIVOSTOK IT MOBILIZATION

We can, however, find a silver lining: life under permanent crises rendered the local IT community relatively flexible and resistant to risks. While the community reliant on trading old cars could not survive after the introduction of the 2008 policy and was partly absorbed by the new car-assembly industry, the biggest IT business players proved to be able to adapt to a new economic and political situation. Moreover, in some cases they did so with a quite independent political agenda. For instance, FarPost openly positions itself as an independent information portal, and discusses sensitive corruption-related stories about the new federal university and local politicians and bureaucrats quite openly and freely. Others took advantage of the situation: Kama Games, which emerged in 2008–9, clearly benefited from hundreds of unemployed highly qualified programmers who remained in Vladivostok. Finally, many of the less ambitious professionals were happy to occupy apparently stable jobs in newly opened firms working on the maintenance of electronic government and public IT products.

Moreover, the problems caused by the federal university reform and the general dissatisfaction with the current state of affairs pushed the IT business stakeholders to self-organize and engage in regional politics. For instance, in 2014 a group of directors from Vladivostok's most prominent IT companies decided to create the Association of the Technology Industry of the Asian-Pacific Region (ATEIAPR) to help increase the visibility of Far Eastern

IT in both federal and foreign arenas. The association strives to develop the IT sector in the Primorskiy Kray, and in the whole Far East, as well as to strengthen ties between IT companies and universities, especially the FEFU. For the first time, business actors have focused their attention on the FEFU and publicly expressed their readiness to participate in IT training. As Dmitriy Alekseyev explains:

> In principle, you know, it is the first time we succeeded in creating a kind of IT Association in Vladivostok. . . . It always used to break at the moment when someone said, "Well, like, why do we need it?" Right now everyone has agreed on the fact that this is made in order to make somehow the FEFU still pay attention to IT professions. It would be great to have a separate IT school, huh? To somehow take a focused and systematic approach to training IT professionals. The thing is, the FEFU is now saying that they do not have IT in the list of priorities, hence they do not need it. Well, [now] everyone feels it. . . . This fact [forced us to say for the first time in] the twenty years I have been here doing computer business, let us unite for the sake of some idea.

In the fall of 2015, the Far Eastern Federal University officially refused to support the ACM ICPC championship competition, claiming lack of funds. After a series of negotiations and organizational efforts by engaged individuals, the competition took place with the help of local businesses and the Association. Once again, Vladivostok's IT community demonstrated its social commitment and its capacity to resist top-down decisions disrupting the local IT ecology. Unfortunately, such initiatives are rarely supported by federal representatives. As Dmitriy Alekseyev commented on Facebook on November 15, 2015:

> Enthusiasts are the backbone of many things in Russia. Probably it should be this way, but at the same time mechanisms that support those initiatives and make them part of the system are needed. Unfortunately, this rarely happens here. And the example with the sport programming championship comes from the same series. This is a very good championship giving a wonderful experience with algorithm problem solving, and besides—in a team! This is a real programmer's incubator. In addition, the school part [of the championship] is a perfect way to attract and prepare children for university, and student participation is an [important] element of the educational process. You may think that FEFU would be very interested in that process? No, this year the university outright refused to finance

this championship. The two billion [rubles] for a campus—this is a must. One hundred for the championship—no way. That's why I take my hat off to the enthusiasm of Nadezhda Klenina and Alexander Klenin and their team who developed the competition project that has helped to nurture hundreds of Far-Eastern programmers for 17 years already. They are great people and I am proud to stand side-by-side with them and do my best to help in their excellent work.

The example of the IT community in Vladivostok demonstrates that to develop their businesses, Vladivostok's IT leaders need to develop a consensus on regional politics of knowledge and use that consensus to come to terms with the federal government. As happened so often before in Russian history—from the Russian Empire to the Soviet period—Moscow appeared to be inattentive to local developments, while simultaneously asserting itself as the authority best equipped to understand and address them. This attitude was emblematic of the recent federal university reform, where the central government cast itself as the sole decision maker able to identify regional strategic needs and goals, even when the regions concerned may be more than five thousand miles away. In the era of a global knowledge economy, this logic seems outdated and shortsighted.

The case of Vladivostok shows, however, that qualified, active entrepreneurial actors may be able to create local innovation ecology with specific industry-university collaborations even under conditions of a seemingly permanent social and economic crisis. Yet, this time-consuming and complex process can be easily damaged by authoritarian policy decisions that, by disregarding the regional context, end up disrupting the local IT ecology.

Apparently, the strategy of communication with the long-term federal agenda turned out to be beneficial for Vladivostok's IT, at least in some cases. On April 1, 2015, Vladivostok opened the Far East representative office of the Skolkovo Foundation, which aims at developing innovations and high-tech entrepreneurship in Russia (for more details on Skolkovo, see Simonova, this volume). During the first ten months, thirty IT companies from Vladivostok became "Skolkovo" residents, thus claiming a presence for an unexpectedly large IT pool in the Far East. Today, however, it is still too early to evaluate the extent to which this kind of cooperation with federal stakeholders will benefit the local ecology of several independent startups and the whole ecosystem of IT knowledge in Primorye. The risk remains that while the Association was mobilized for the sake of education in the region, it might become a kind of Moscow neoliberal offspring, running in and beyond the local community.

NOTES

This chapter is mostly based on empirical data—interviews, publications, and observations collected by Alexandra Masalskaya in Vladivostok in November 2014—secondary literature, and online publications. In total, sixteen biographical interviews were conducted. The first interviews were conducted thanks to contacts established remotely before arriving in Vladivostok. We thank Daria Savchenko who shared her contacts with professionals from the IT industry. Some of the subjects were discovered thanks to the digital analysis of Web of Science publications: two of them working at research institutes of the Russian Academy of Science agreed to participate in the research and be interviewed. In other cases, we primarily relied on "snowball sampling." Also, several contacts were established via the Facebook communities of Vladivostok residents. We would like to thank Paul R. Josephson, Mikhail Sokolov, and Yuri Takhteyev for their comments on the preliminary draft of this chapter.

1. According to data provided by the Russian Ministry of Digital Development, Communications and Mass Media, in 2014 the Far Eastern region (Primorskiy Kray) hosted 45 big and medium and 346 small IT companies (Ministry of Digital Development 2014). Experts estimate the number of IT professionals in the region to be around two thousand (PrimaMedia 2014). The city of Vladivostok is host to a population of a little more than 600,000 residents. Following our interlocutors, we consider that the number of active members of the IT community roughly corresponds to the number of the participants of the Vladivostok Developers Sabbath conference, an informal, though important, annual professional gathering. In 2014, the year of our fieldwork research, this conference brought together from six hundred to seven hundred individuals. About one hundred among them are considered to be top-level experts.

2. All interviews with IT workers were conducted in Russian and translated by the authors.

3. In 1939, the department included chemical and geological institutes, soil-botanic and zoological sectors, laboratories of fresh- and seawater hydrobiology, mountain-forest and teleseismic stations, natural reserves, a library, and a publishing house (Far Eastern Branch 2017).

4. Although the official dates of funding of these institutes point to the late 1980s, their institutional histories in the Far East can be clearly traced back to the 1970s.

5. In 1985, the official policy entitled "On the Insuring of Computer Literacy of Secondary School Students and Large-Scale Implementation of Electronic and Computing Technologies into the School Education Process" was issued and became law (Postanovleniye CK KPSS i Soveta Ministrov SSSR 1985).

6. The increase in the incidence of tuberculosis has been clearly observed since the beginning of the 2000s; from 2005 to 2009, it exceeded the average rate for Russia by more than 2.5 times. The situation then stabilized and improved in the following years (Abbasova 2014)—most probably, thanks to more medical care and a restructuring of urban traffic and highways.

7. During the first year, this forum ran under the name Avto.vl.ru.

8. The applicant's guide included information on enrollment criteria and procedures, student social services, pictures of student residences, and so on.

9. This game attracted 47 million players.

10. The official website of the center is http://robocenter.org/.

11. On the crucial role of entrepreneurs for the formation of technological clusters, see Francis, Bercovitz, and Feldman 2005. They argue that entrepreneurs exhibit flexibility and a high capacity to adapt to crises and grasp newly opened opportunities.

12. To a much lesser extent, the same policy affected the import of new vehicles.

13. Anastasia Zagoruiko, a journalist and one of the protest activists, later recalled that "this protest was largely supported by ordinary people, whose interests were very seriously touched upon. Nobody was going to make politics, and on December 14th there were no political parties among the organizers. They came up later, because it was a shame to miss such an opportunity to gain points for themselves" (RK25.ru Shturman Primorya 2013).

14. This measure, however, did not help much. According to 2018 statistics, the Far East residents remained faithful to Japanese cars: three first lines out of five top bestsellers are occupied by different "Toyota" models (Autostat 2018).

15. The reform was designed in response to multiple critics of the level of higher education in Russian regions. The new "federal universities" were thought to become a network of top-level regional mega-institutions embracing the best local educational centers funded through "federal districts" (a new type of territorial and administrative unit introduced in 2000 by President Vladimir Putin and governed by his appointed officials. This new arrangement replaced the locally elected governors who had previously held authority in the regions). The FEFU was founded in 2009–10 and became the third federal university after the Siberian Federal University (in Krasnoyarsk—two thousand miles away from Vladivostok) and the Southern Federal University (in Rostov-on-Don and Taganrog—more than 5,500 miles from Vladivostok). In the following years, federal universities expanded to cover the Ural and Arctic regions, North Caucasus, North East (Yakutiya), Kazan,' and Crimea.

16. According to the local Department of Information and Telecommunications, in 2014 there were forty-five large and medium-sized IT businesses and 346 small enterprises in the region (Ministry of Digital Development 2014).

17. Technically, the fifteen-year university road map was developed within the walls of the university. However, our interlocutors emphasized that it was realized by bureaucrats coming from Moscow who have not really consulted with local experts. Therefore, in many respects, the current university agenda corresponds to Moscow reformers' scenarios rather than to local educational traditions.

18. In its traditional form, a *fakul'tet* was mainly an administrative unit responsible for student recruiting, educational curriculum, and hosting several "departments" (*kafedra*), which were, in turn, small but highly specialized units responsible for problem-oriented teaching and research, and relatively free of administrative work. The administrative responsibilities were primarily imposed on the faculty's staff. However, under the new system these administrative responsibilities have been redistributed among all faculty members, while specialization and research are now subordinated within overgrown new "departments."

19. In the Soviet system of education, all academic positions (including the rector and deans) were elective and, to some extent, guaranteed democratic and meritocratic principles. All vacancy competitions were open and had to be publicly announced in advance and published in local newspapers.

REFERENCES

Abbasova, Yelena I. 2014. "Epidemiologicheskiye aspekty zabolevaemosti tuberkulezom v Primorskom kraye" [Epidemiological aspects of tuberculosis in Primorskii Krai]. *Zdorov'e: Meditsinskaya ekologiya: Nauka* 4, no. 58: 118–22.

Arora, Ashish, and Alfonso Gambardella, eds. 2005. *From Underdogs to Tigers: The Rise and Growth of the Software Industry in Brazil, China, India, Ireland, and Israel.* Oxford: Oxford University Press.

AVTO@mail.ru. 2008. "Nazvany samyye avtomobil'nyye goroda Rossii." ABTO@ mail.ru. September 25. Accessed July 30, 2018. https://auto.mail.ru/article/26736 -nazvany_samye_avtomobilnye_goroda_rossii/.

Autostat 2018. "TOP-10 samykh prodavayemykh novykh avtomobiley na Dal'nem Vostoke." Autostat. Analytic Agency. July 2. Accessed August 1. https://www .autostat.ru/news/34857/.

Belov, Oleg. 2012. "V Primorye samoe bol'shoe kolichestvo avtomobiley v DVFO." *Kommersant*, February 10. Accessed July 31, 2018. https://www.kommersant.ru /doc/1869261.

Businesspress. 2002. "'Farpost'—Pervoprokhodets v virtual'nom labirinte Dal'nego Vostoka." *Businesspress* 6, no. 106 (February 15). Accessed July 31, 2018. http://www.businesspress.ru/newspaper/article_mId_1904_aId_102043.html.

Capua, Michelangelo. 2006. *Yul Brynner: A Biography.* Jefferson, NC: McFarland & Co.

Chen Kun and Martin Kenney. 2007. "Universities/Research Institutes and Regional Innovation Systems: The Cases of Beijing and Shenzhen." *World Development* 35–36: 1056–74.

DNS. 2016. "Forum." Accessed January 31, 2016. http://club.dns-shop.ru/forum.

Drom.ru. 2008. "V Rossii proshli aktsii protesta protiv povysheniya poshlin na inomarki." Drom.ru, December 21. Accessed July 31, 2018. https://news.drom.ru /11803.html.

Drom.ru. 2011. "Levorul'nykh otzyvov uzhe bol'she, chem pravorul'nykh." Drom. ru, October 1. Accessed January 17, 2016. http://forums.drom.ru/blogs/281341 -drom-ru/6697.html.

Drom.ru. 2012. Forums. Pirotehnik.alex: 1431 (number of entry). March 25. Accessed 1 August 2018. https://forums.drom.ru/honda-odyssey/t1151449439-p72 .html.

Drori, Israel, Shmuel Ellis, and Zur Shapira. 2013. *The Evolution of a New Industry: A Genealogical Approach*. Stanford, CA: Stanford Business Books, an imprint of Stanford University Press.

DV-Rating. 2013. "Mikrogosudarstvo dal'nevostochnogo internet-portala 'Far-Post.'" DV-Rating, April 9. Accessed July 31, 2018. http://dv-rating.ru/premia /primorskij-kraj_09.04.2013_4999_mikrogosudarstvo-dalnevostochnogo -internet-portala-farpost.html.

Far Eastern Branch of Russian Academy of Sciences. 2017. Official website. Accessed July 31, 2018. http://old.febras.ru/history/history3239.html.

Francis, Johanna, Janet Bercovitz, and Maryann P. Feldman. 2005. "Creating a Cluster while Building a Firm: Entrepreneurs and the Formation of Industrial Clusters." *Regional Studies* 39, no. 1: 129–41.

Gerovitch, Slava. 2002. *From Newspeak to Cyberspeak: A History of Soviet Cybernetics*. Cambridge, MA: MIT Press.

Ikonnikova, Tat'yana. 2012. "Oformleniye otnosheniy s konsul'skim korpusom v Priamurskom general-gubernatorstve (1908–1912)." *Rossiya i ATR* 1: 26–34.

Kenney, Martin. 1986. *Biotechnology: The University-Industrial Complex*. New Haven, CT: Yale University Press.

Kenney, Martin, ed. 2000. *Understanding Silicon Valley: Anatomy of an Entrepreneurial Region*. Stanford, CA: Stanford University Press.

Kenney, Martin, and David C. Mowery, eds. 2014. *Public Universities and Regional Growth: Insights from the University of California*. Stanford, CA: Stanford Business Books, an imprint of Stanford University Press.

Kuznetsov, Anatoliy M. 2014. "Vladivostok. Diskoteka ('Disco'). 1970s." *News of the Eastern Institute* 1, no. 23: 146–52.

Lyudmirskiy, Dmitriy, and Aleksandr Malyutin. 1995. "Posledniy inostranets." *Kommersant*, February 4. Accessed July 31, 2018. http://www.kommersant.ru /doc/101251.

Ministry of Digital Development 2014. "Mark Shmulevich obsudil razvitiye informatsionnyh tekhnologiy na Dal'nem Vostoke." Ministry of Digital Development, Communications and Mass Media of the Russian Federation. March 21. Accessed August 1, 2018. http://minsvyaz.ru/ru/events/30122/.

Morgun, Zoya. 1999. "Yapontsy vo Vladivostoke v gody grazhdanskoy voyny i interventsii (1918–1922 gg.)." *Rossiyskoye Priamurye: istoriya i sovremennost': Materialy nauchnogo soveshchaniya-seminara, posvyashchennogo 350-letiyu pokhoda E.P. Khabarova na Amur i prisoyedineniya Priamurya k Rossii*, 263–68.

Motoi, Kavao. 2013. "Dal'nevostochnyy rynok yaponskih poderzhannykh avtomobiley: chto zhdet ego, kogda minovala zolotaya pora." [Translated from Japanese.] *Nippon*, October 1. Accessed July 31, 2018. http://www.nippon.com /ru/currents/d10011/#auth_profile_0.

MSX Resource Center Forum. 2009. "Istoriya poyavleniya YAMAHAMSX V SSSR." Section: Multilingualforums. Discussion in Russian. October 1. Microcomputer

and Related Culture Foundation. Accessed August 1, 2018. http://www.msx.org
/node/35521?page=2.

Peters, Benjamin. 2016. *How Not to Network a Nation: The Uneasy History of the Soviet Internet*. Cambridge, MA: MIT Press.

Postanovleniye Soveta Ministrov SSSR. 1960. "O razvitii goroda Vladivostoka." January 18.

Postanovleniye CK KPSS i Soveta Ministrov SSSR. 1985. "O merakh po obespech-eniyu kompyuternoy gramotnosti uchashchikhsya srednikh uchebnykh zave-deniy i shirokogo vnedreniya elektronno-vychislitel'noy tekhniki v uchebnyy protsess." No. 271. March 28.

PrimaMedia. 2014. "Perspektivy razvitiya IT-tekhnologiy na Dal'nem Vostoke ob-sudili vo Vladivostoke." March 21. Accessed August 1, 2018. http://primamedia
.ru/news/344583/.

Resolution of Russian Federation (RF) Government. 1996. *Rossiyskaya gazeta*. Documents, No. 480. April 15, 1996, including changes and amendments 2010–12. Accessed August 1, 2018. http://www.rg.ru/1996/05/16/dv-zabaykal
-dok.html.

RIA Novosti. 2014. "Zavod 'Sollers' v Primorye v 2013 uvelichil proizvodstvo avtomobiley." *RIA Novosti*, January 14. Accessed August 1, 2018. https://ria.ru/vl
/20140114/989069766.html.

RK25.ru Shturman Primorya. 2013. "Pravorul'nomu buntu v Primorye ispolni-los' 5 let." Regional Primorye information platform, December 17. Accessed August 1, 2018. http://www.pk25.ru/news/primorye/17_12_13_pravorulnomu
_buntu_v_primore_ispolnilos_5.html.

Saxenian, AnnaLee 1994. *Regional Advantage: Culture and Competition in Silicon Valley and Route 128*. Cambridge, MA: Harvard University Press, 1994.

Similar Web 2017. "Top Sites Ranking in All Categories in Russian Federation." Accessed August 1, 2018. https://www.similarweb.com/top-websites/russian
-federation.

Sohn, Dong-Won and Martin Kenney. 2007. "Universities, Clusters, and Innovation Systems: The Case of Seoul, Korea." *World Development* 35, no. 6: 991–1004.

State Duma. 2009. "K voprosu o massovykh aktsiyakh protesta v Primorye." Analiticheskaya zapiska. Informatsionno-analiticheskiye materialy Gosudarst-vennaya Duma (State Duma). January. Accessed August 1, 2018. http://iam
.duma.gov.ru/node/8/4668.

Tatarchenko, Ksenia. 2013. "A House with the Window to the West: The Akademgorodok Computer Center (1958–1993)." PhD diss., Princeton University.

Zagoruyko, Anastasiya. 2008. "Takogo bunta Vladivostok ne videl mnogo let." *Novaya Gazeta*, December 18. Accessed August 1, 2018. https://www
.novayagazeta.ru/articles/2008/12/18/35390-takogo-bunta-vladivostok-ne-videl
-mnogo-let.

CHAPTER FIVE

KAZAN CONNECTED
"IT-ing Up" a Province
Alina Kontareva

The Russian economy was in constant turmoil during the 1990s. Following its stabilization in the early 2000s, the new Russian leadership placed a high priority on developing an innovative economy and domestic high-tech industry that could supersede the previous one, based on extractive industries and natural resources. Since the 2008 announcement by former Russian president Dmitry Medvedev of a major initiative to modernize the Russian economy, high-tech and information technologies have been a priority for federal and local authorities alike, leading to policies for the development of innovative clusters, special economic zones (SEZs), and federal projects for the development of technoparks across the country. The Republic of Tatarstan and its capital Kazan were selected to become one of these innovative centers.

Located in Southwest Russia, only a two-hour flight from Moscow, Kazan has aspired to be the premiere Russian center for innovation. It is already one of the leading educational and research centers in the Russian Federation, with a special emphasis on mathematics and computer science. The city is home to thirty-five institutions of higher education, including a federal university and other public and private institutions (Ministry of Science and Education 2015), which provide IT training at both undergraduate and graduate levels. While being one of the oldest cities in Russia, with more than a thousand years of history, Kazan is now promoted as "the capital of the Russian IT industry"—a place where federal and local authorities are working hard at establishing an "ecology of innovation." Since the early 2000s, Kazan politicians have been investing in infrastructure, with several technoparks, industrial zones, new universities, and an ambitious new project—Innopolis—a university-centered city for IT specialists.

In addition to local funding, the republic is drawing on private investors and on federally funded programs.

Tatarstan was one of a few places in the country chosen by the Russian government to participate in the federal technopark program. Since 2007, the state has developed technoparks to support innovation and attract highly skilled migration to the region. Once drafted, the policy of infrastructure development had to be implemented in specific regional settings, but not all of the regions selected to take part in the federal program establishing innovation hubs were successful. In 2015, the National Audit Office discovered that some local programs were riddled with corruption, resulting in the inappropriate expenditure of federal funds. At best, technoparks were operating as ordinary business centers. At worst, local authorities had not even begun constructing the necessary infrastructure (Kustikova and Zaslavskiy 2015). Compared to these regions, Tatarstan is a success. Virtually all of the planned constructions and infrastructure were completed and official federal ratings now rank Kazan as the third most innovative region after Moscow and Saint Petersburg (Gohberg 2014).[1]

Innovation studies literature highlights several factors contributing to regional development. Some emphasize the role of military-related R&D (Sturgeon 2000) or other state interventions in fostering and supporting the most promising projects and technologies within a given region (Breznitz 2007). Others focus on the role of venture capitalists (Florida and Kenney 1988) or the rise of an R&D sector that leads to long-term economic growth (Lundvall 1992; Lundvall et al. 2002; Mowery and Rosenberg 1991; Nelson 1993; Rosenberg 1983). Still others focus on sustainable interactions between the state, industry, and universities (Etzkowitz 2008; Etzkowitz and Leydesdorff 2000; Kenney and Mowery 2014). Some of the extensive literature on specific regions draws attention to the social dimension of knowledge production and implementation within regional innovation systems (Asheim 1996, 2007; Asheim, Lawton Smith, and Oughton 2011; Doloreux 2002; Saxenian 1994). These works reveal the cultural, historical, and social contexts that underlie economic development, and that give every case a unique set of properties. The case of Kazan is particularly intriguing because its success does not seem to be reducible to available models.

Different logics stand behind the formation of this ecology, illustrating the interplay between local and federal politics. Unlike other innovative enclaves described in this book (especially in Simonova's chapter), this specific "innovation ecology" has matured not as a grassroots initiative, but as a top-down policy formulated and executed by politicians in Kazan and Moscow—

politicians whose interests came into alignment through this policy. Similar to Vladivostok (Masalskaya and Vasilyeva, this volume), the case of Kazan illustrates the intention of the Russian state to control peripheral regions, especially politically volatile ones like Tatarstan, and reinforce the federal presence there. By funding the development of an IT hub in the Republic of Tatarstan, Moscow has been clearly asserting the presence of the centralized state in an autonomous region. At the same time, local authorities can deploy strong arguments to promote a region that has a proven track record in innovation-related projects. The ways the Republic of Tatarstan has been pursuing federal investments show the importance of a certain kind of "regional branding"—a game of policy visions and mediatic representations aimed at conveying the sense that innovation is "happening" in and around Kazan, where new buildings, technoparks, and infrastructure come together to index the emergence of an "innovative region"—an image that can then be sold as a national template for successful development.

CENTER-PERIPHERY RELATIONS AND THE POLITICAL FRAMING OF INNOVATIONS

The Republic of Tatarstan is one of the country's leading industrial regions in both petrochemistry and mechanical engineering, contributing to the country's economy through gas and oil extraction. With a few major companies like OAO Tatneft, OAO Nizhnekamskneftekhim, and Kazan-Orgsintez OJSC, the local petrochemical cluster is now represented by over five hundred small and mid-sized enterprises. Also, Tatarstan has the second-largest oil deposit in Russia, which produces thirty-two million tons of oil annually, making the republic a very valuable asset of the national economy. This has framed the relations between Moscow and Tatarstan, involving both investments and federal control over a strategic region.

During the chaotic period after the breakup of the Soviet Union, the republic was filled with separatist sentiments fueled by cultural and economic issues: as the majority population of the republic consists of ethnic Tatars and Muslims, the key separatist argument was that the region had a culture, language, religion, and traditions of its own. In addition to this unique regional identity, Tatarstan has always had a strong political elite, which could convert this popular identity into carefully chosen benefits, especially under circumstances where the breakup of the Union was in the air. As the result of informal arrangements with Moscow, Tatarstan retained its status of an ethnic republic within the Russian Federation, and was granted a special tax system designed to keep most of the income from natural resources within the republic from 1994 to 2000. In exchange for these privileges, local elites tacitly agreed to support whichever candidate Moscow favored in the local presidential elections.

The situation, however, has become more convoluted in the last decade, largely due to Vladimir Putin's attempt to reimpose a vertical power structure within the Russian Federation, which led to reconsidering the practice of making special informal arrangements between Moscow and the republics with strong ethnic identities. The independent status of ethnic republics was thus reframed, and many of Kazan's special privileges were rescinded (Nozhenko and Belokurova 2010). Experts now say that, as during the Soviet era, all incomes from gas and oil production in Tatarstan flow again to Moscow, depriving the republic of resources that many feel belong to it.

Moscow and Tatarstan, however, have found other areas of happier collaboration. Federal funds now come in the form of support of large international events that Tatarstan and Kazan in particular are hosting. Participation in federally supported initiatives is also one way of channeling federal funds back to the republic in an effort to assuage local feelings. Kazan's Millennial Celebrations in 2005 and then the Universiada, a major international sporting event held in 2013, necessitated large-scale investments that transformed the city virtually overnight. Kazan's ability to quickly put federal funding to work was further demonstrated by its readiness to host several other large international events, such as the 2015 FINA World Championship (an international swimming competition), and the FIFA World Cup in 2018. These "mega-events," however, are important not just because of the visibility they provide but also because they exemplify a specific long-term strategy aimed at attracting federal and international investments in order to build or improve local infrastructure.

Each new event is associated with major construction projects that create a substantial number of new jobs and opportunities for local workers. For example, hosting the Universiada led to the construction of a whole new residential zone, initially intended as accommodation for the visiting athletes but subsequently repurposed as a new campus for the Kazan Federal University and the IT Institute, the former claiming to be the largest of the newly established federal university campuses in Russia. In addition, substantial funds were invested in the building, repair, and renovation of roads, highway interchanges, an airport, and hospitals. After the event, several Russian newspapers reported that the amount of money spent on these improvements was twenty times higher than that which was spent on the event itself. Participation in a variety of federal programs brings investments into urban development, which explains why Kazan invites new initiatives on a continuing basis. Each of these initiatives burnishes the Kazan "brand," and every new project contributes different forms of capital to the region—not only of economic value but also social and cultural capital, which is then mobilized to attract yet other projects and events.

To impose control over peripheral and politically volatile regions, Moscow has a long history of providing them with generous funding for local development projects. Scholars have identified Tatarstan, Bashkortostan, and Chechnya as the most vivid examples of this kind of "support" (Bulanin and Shcherbak 2005; Starodubtsev 2009). Tatarstan not only receives the funds necessary to host these events, but is also given federal loans to cover the local share of expenditures. Such federal funding is particularly advantageous for the state, since it invests not only in regional high tech but also in the loyalty of local elites and decision makers. These are the people who largely control local politics and can help get Moscow's candidates elected when "elections" occur (Matsuzato 2001).

The "mega-event" strategy seems to apply well to the attempt to build up Tatarstan as an innovative region. The focus on high tech and the promotion of Kazan as an innovative region is mainly associated with two Tatarstan politicians: Rustam Minnikhanov and Nikoley Nikiforov. The story of Kazan as a high-tech region originates from their successful implementation of e-government projects within Tatarstan's local administration. The federal government had singled out e-government as the first necessary step to make Russia both "modern" and "democratic," making the relationships between the state and its citizens more transparent and effective (Administration 2015). Rustam Minnikhanov, the former prime minister and current president of the Republic of Tatarstan, announced as early as 2005 that all civil servants needed sufficient competence in information technologies so as to use electronic government platforms and e-document flow (Ismagilova 2010). Nikiforov, a Kazan State University IT graduate, became the official advisor to Minnikhanov. His job was to focus specifically on information technologies and he was among the initiators of the e-government program, which involved connecting municipal services and institutions, and digitizing their document flows.

The e-government project had several important consequences for the region. That Kazan's administration had managed to turn digital long before the rest of the country helped the city present itself as a prototype for IT innovation. Furthermore, the strong demand for IT technologies and skills generated by the e-government initiative greatly enlivened the local technological market, providing incentives for IT companies focused on the implementation of state orders and electronic data protection to emerge (Kontareva 2015). As for Nikiforov, as a reward for his work, he was promoted to the position of Tatarstan minister of telecommunications.

This new emphasis on large high-tech projects supported by federal investments aligned with the interests of local politicians, who channeled this momentum toward greater investments in local higher education and human capital. Thanks to the collaboration between Nikiforov and Minnikhanov, the federal government has subsequently supported several other initiatives in Tatarstan, mostly involving large-scale constructions. According to the official web page of the Investment and Venture Fund of the Republic of Tatarstan, the region can now claim to be Russia's largest special economic zone, with at least four new industrial parks, a new technopolis called Himgrad (an acronym for "chemistry city"), and fourteen new technoparks. The special relationship between the republic and Moscow is thus key to the promotion of Tatarstan as the place where innovation thrives.

Nikiforov was not the sole member of the regional government advocating for the development of an IT industry, but his story became legendary among young local IT specialists. Again and again in my interviews with local programmers, Nikiforov surfaced within their narratives of the local professional community. Many pride themselves on having graduated from the same university he attended, some saying that Nikiforov was a "rising star" since his days in primary school. They also recount how even in middle school he was recognized for his talents and ability to organize IT projects among his classmates. They see him as personally responsible for projects such as the IT parks in Kazan and the city of Naberezhnye Chelny, the local IT lyceum, and the IT department at Kazan Federal University. His association with these projects garnered his appointment to the post of minister of telecom and mass communications of the Russian Federation in 2012. At only thirty, he became the youngest minister in Russian history and his promotion was exploited in the effort to craft Kazan's local brand.

Thus local IT projects supported by Moscow have a strong political dimension. In this sense, innovation-ecology building in Kazan resembles investments into the other republics' projects in Russia, such as in Dagestan and Chechnya—places where separatism is still considered an issue and Moscow feels the need to exert control. It is no coincidence that right after the annexation of Crimea, authorities in Moscow proposed establishing an IT cluster there as well, holding out hope of creating the Russian analogue of

Silicon Valley in that region. The citizens of Kazan are only the indirect beneficiaries of these initiatives, in the form of better highways and other urban infrastructure. The real targets of this largesse are the authorities, whose loyalty is purchased through the sponsorship of large, visible, and prestigious projects. One substantial downside for the republic is its debt obligation to the federal government that it has to assume as part of these projects, giving Moscow a greater degree of control over local affairs. Yet, whatever the political motivations of Moscow may ultimately be, the fact that Tatarstan is a relatively independent republic has contributed to the success of these federal programs. It is clear that the achievements in Kazan largely depend on the interests of local and regional politicians in the development of an IT sector. At the same time, because the region does not feature the same convoluted multilayered hierarchical relations that characterize the administration of other regions, Kazan might actually be a promising place to implement new IT initiatives.

BRANDING KAZAN: A CITY ON DISPLAY

When I was planning my first trip to Kazan to interview local IT specialists, my colleagues—fellow sociologists who had recently returned from their own fieldtrips in the region—were not impressed with what they had seen in Kazan. They assured me that the city center was not a real downtown area but an assemblage of streets covered with mud, flooded, without sidewalks, and with piles of bricks randomly dumped here and there. The city, I was often told, is reminiscent of a typical Russian village where something is always under construction, where all needed materials are collected on-site but without any visible sign that something is *actually* being built.

Arriving there a few months later with this picture in mind, I was surprised by what I found. The city center with its old traditional wooden houses was completely restored and Baumana Street (the central pedestrian zone) could easily have been located in any European city, with gift shops and cafés full of tourists. And, as it turns out, the Kazan administration was able to undertake these drastic upgrades and transform the place into a city that is attractive not only to Russian visitors but also international tourists in a surprisingly short period of time. Because Tatarstan is not the only ethnic republic in Russia dependent on federal support, it has to compete with other regions to receive funding from the federal government. Though it has been suggested that "success in competing for federal funds is largely politicized and depends primarily on the ability of local politicians to negotiate and bargain with Moscow" (Kinossian 2006, 334), the promotion of Tatarstan remains crucial for the local economy by showcasing the favorable condition of the region and reassuring Moscow that Tatarstan is worth investing in.

In addition to the federal government, the other targets of regional branding are the high-tech specialists whom the local authorities are trying to attract. Since the collapse of the Soviet Union, the migration of highly skilled Russian specialists has been a worrisome problem for the government. Thousands of IT specialists left the country, likely never to return. Investments into branding, material infrastructure, and renovation in Kazan are meant to prevent or at least decrease the level of emigration, creating within the country the same kinds of opportunities that exist abroad. Kazan is a relatively small city in size and population, having only a tenth of Moscow's population. Larger cities like Moscow or Saint Petersburg are certain to attract the best human resources and skills, but a peripheral city like Kazan has historically lacked this kind of magnetism. However, the way the Kazan administration is currently marketing this place represents an aggressive effort not only to compete with these capital cities but to reproduce in the provinces the same conditions that exist there, and even rival those found abroad. This branding strategy turns Kazan's weak points into strengths. Opposite to Moscow and Saint Petersburg, Kazan is presented as compact and convenient, with the business center and universities situated just steps away from each other. The streets of the city are relatively uncrowded and its light vehicular traffic produces little air pollution and few traffic jams. Many of these factors encourage locals to compare Kazan to Moscow, and by this comparison the region gains advantage: it is where locals want to live and not from where they wish to emigrate.

For a long time now Russian cities have been competing for recognition as the third capital of the country, after Moscow and Saint Petersburg. Kazan went further, and in 2009 officially trademarked several logos such as "Russia's third capital," in both Russian and English. The location of Kazan in the Federal Volga District, as well as the local heritage of Tatar culture, provide an appealing combination of "East meets West" in Russia. Because of the Muslim culture, the city looks exotic to both Russian and foreign tourists. With the collapse of the ruble against the dollar and euro, international trips have become more expensive for Russian tourists, thereby increasing domestic over international tourism. The 2014 rating on TripAdvisor (the world's largest travel site) helped Kazan become the third most visited city in Russia, after Saint Petersburg and Moscow.

Despite the fact that Kazan is situated away from the western centers of the country, it is trying to construct the image of an international or European city: a successful city, one that is able to host prestigious events, cosmopolitan, or at the very least international. Several times during my fieldtrips to Kazan I heard the city compared to European counterparts, and, truth be told, I also made this comparison. Policy makers and local citizens seem to share an understanding of what international means: according to the city's branding, it is associated with specific architecture, better facilities, and a different lifestyle. A European city has a particular layout and typically a historical center, a set of museums—most likely a historical and modern art museum—pedestrian zones, and neat townhouses along narrow streets. For the general public, Kazan meets these requirements and gives the impression of an inviting and comfortable city, which exceeds your expectations of a place situated at the Russian periphery. "European" also means international, ecologically conscious, and culturally tolerant. Kazan's location, traditions, and ethnicity mark it as a gateway between Western and Eastern cultures. Tatarstan's population is a mix of ethnic Tatars and Russians, which means its culture is a mixture of Russian Orthodox and Muslim traditions. In 2002, Kazan was awarded the UNESCO Cities for Peace Prize for "creating bonds of citizenship" among a diverse cultural and ethnic population (UNESCO 2002). Most of the people with whom I had a chance to meet were proud of this special status as a city of tolerance. Tatar national cuisine, crafts, and souvenirs are everywhere evident with the strong regional culture now being repackaged into a new "European" brand: a local tea room that serves traditional cuisine (*qıstıbí* or *öçpoçmaq*—meat and potato pies) was presented to me as the "Tatar McDonald's."

Signage in the city is translated into Russian, Tatar, and English, and all downtown bus stops are announced in these three languages. While such English translations can be found in the capitals of Russia—Moscow and Saint Petersburg—they are not typical for Russian cities in general. Aspiring to emulate the high standards of a European city, Kazan is developing parks and recreational zones and is working to make the city's facilities accessible for disabled persons. The new buildings, constructed for international events or as part of a new innovation ecology, have had a broad impact on city planning, as illustrated by the remaking of Peterburgskaya Street. Local residents say that until recently this area was a run-down district with wooden houses, most of which were torn down as part of the revitalization project. Several houses were kept as cultural heritage sites but most of the space was rebuilt, first for Kazan's Millennial Celebrations in 2005 and then for the Universiada in 2013. During my fieldtrips to this section of the city (fall 2013, spring and fall 2014) it was still under construction, this time to build a new and attractive high-tech business center. By 2013, several new hotels, a Sberbank building, the Ministry of Youth Affairs and Sport, a technopark called Idea, an Investment and Venture Fund headquarter, and an IT park had all been constructed. This section of the city now serves as a showcase for Kazan's innovative potential, demonstrating that the city's development is real and worth investing in.

Because of Tatarstan's reliance on federal-sponsored projects, and the fact that Moscow prefers to invest in material infrastructures in the regions, massive urban development is the landmark of Tatarstan. The strategy of local authorities to focus on infrastructure of all kinds—from the city transportation system and hospitals to specialized high-tech parks—helps to invest in regional branding. Buildings are tangible and material indicators of money spent correctly; they demonstrate that local politicians are strong and decisive, and amplify high expectations about innovations to emerge, once the infrastructure is established.

INFRASTRUCTURING AN IT ECOLOGY

Kazan's strategy to create an ecology of innovation primarily relies on large construction projects, like the IT park completed in 2009, housed in an impressive five-story building sheathed in glass. At the entrance is a public space that provides free Wi-Fi and free computer access as well as a coffee room. Daylight is abundant, creating a clear and transparent environment that is perhaps a visual metaphor for the "mood" of the work that takes place here. Many of my interviews with local IT specialists took place in the IT park, and the business incubators I visited there have an open-plan layout that encourages residents to interact and flexibly use the space as they see fit. The rest of the building is reserved for the office space of IT park residents, software developers, and tech entrepreneurs. As one of the city's most modern buildings, the space is also extensively used for official events and receptions held for visiting delegations.

Several other new technoparks in Tatarstan—such as the IT park in Naberezhnye Chelny or the Navigator Campus in Kazan—are built in the same fashion. Situated on Peterburgskaya Street, the IT park is close to the local universities, which makes it convenient for students to attend presentations or conferences. The other IT park, in Naberezhnye Chelny, was established in 2012 and also serves as a gathering place for the local IT community, with its business incubator that attracts tech projects from nearby regions.

Situated forty kilometers from Kazan, Innopolis—the newest city in Russia dedicated to high-tech industries—was built in just three years. A leading Singapore architect, Liu Thai Ker, was invited to plan the city. The example of Singapore, famous for its rapid economic growth based on high-tech industries, is often referenced in the discourse of local authorities in Kazan. Tatarstan wants not only to emulate the economic success of this Asian nation but to start this process of emulation at the very beginning, with the foundation: city planning. Innopolis was officially opened in June 2015 and is just beginning to function fully. It now includes a cutting-edge research university, a special economic zone for IT companies, as well as a residential zone. Innopolis seeks to bring together in one location all leading regional IT companies by providing new research facilities and sponsoring interesting and intellectually challenging projects. The city's image is very much one of newness and innovation, which differs substantially from a typical Russian city. It is designed to promote the lifestyle of an emergent technological middle class, enjoying high salaries and access to modern amenities. It offers a revolutionary organization of urban space, with townhouses, bike paths, and an eco-friendly environment. However, at present the city plan remains more a layout than a fully functional city. All the new spaces still wait to be inhabited.

By offering new workspace organization and introducing new living standards, local decision makers are hoping to attract high-skilled specialists. As a local expert explains:

> [The] IT park is a very good project. It is certainly not cheap but it already pays off; it is already profitable and at the same time it has managed to provide a certain beautiful image related to a particular profession, in which Tatarstan invests, want[ing] this industry to develop and bloom here, and has provided the labor conditions where people don't feel worse than somewhere else.[2]

The IT park and the city of Innopolis have been designed to create a "beautiful picture," the image of a high-tech utopia that actually works. They symbolize the commitment of local authorities to invest, develop, and support the local tech industry—something that an old or repurposed architecture cannot convey. Commenting on his IT office in an older building, a local expert suggested that even though it was located in the city center and near Kazan Federal University, it was nonetheless historical, of prerevolutionary design, and therefore unable to project the right image:

This is a good building, it is reliable, everything seems OK with sanitary equipment, but nevertheless it is a usual one. And no wonder that the slogan of the IT park is "think materially." They managed to implement this vector toward attracting young people to IT in Tatarstan into something material. And young people really rushed. They really work there, there are good conditions, there is parking for lots of bicycles, and in this respect everything is fine.

Clearly, this branding appeals to the younger generation of high-tech specialists in Russia who are in their late twenties or early thirties. They were raised in typical Russian cities that bear the architectural heritage both of prerevolutionary and Soviet times. Despite the fact that today these cities are constructing new shopping malls, cafés, and parks, they were built in another time and were designed to fulfill the functions of another era. A good example of this kind of city is the nearby Naberezhenye Chelny, built in the 1960s to house workers for the KAMAZ truck plant. It is a vast complex of apartment blocks laid out along the banks of the Kama River. For its time, the sophisticated architectural plan of a neat industrial city was probably functional, but today it looks and feels very outdated. As a visitor one is confronted by endless rows of identical buildings and today—as a result of the increased vehicular traffic it must now absorb—the city is difficult to navigate. Cities like this have little appeal for young tech specialists; instead, the new generation favors contemporary architectural and urban design that accommodates a twenty-first-century lifestyle. To meet these expectations, Innopolis is styled as a city of the future, keeping up with the times and the latest technologies. Its futuristic orientation is what makes this project look promising: new infrastructure brings new expectations. For instance, the project manager of a local venture company in Kazan says:

> There is going to be a golf [course], you can also ride a bike there, and you can do a lot of things. It is so cool, the project is very ambitious. And every time I tell my friends about it, it is very exciting, because it is so fantastic. And you would want the first stage of development to be completed and the IT crowd to settle there.

Others point out that Innopolis is located in one of the most picturesque places in the region, comparing it with a garden city, where everyone can even grow their own fruits and vegetables. In sum, it is described as the perfect choice for a specialist who wishes to stay in Kazan:

You cannot imagine anything better. And even if we speak of Russia in general, there have been no precedents so far which can be comparable with Innopolis. Only Skolkovo, but Skolkovo comes up very short in comparison to this suburban dream city.

Based on these expectations, Innopolis has put an emphasis on what high-tech specialists are looking for when they migrate, and what Kazan is ready to offer. However, some people feel that this newly constructed reality creates a strange impression, that of an artificial formation disorientingly distinct from the typical social, cultural, and urban Russian context. A recent posting (Polygaeva 2015) on *The Village* (a popular Russian news website) presents Innopolis as an alien, "sterile" reality. In addition to that, the remote location of Innopolis and its incomplete social infrastructure raise serious doubts among specialists, who are reluctant to relocate and inhabit this new space. At this moment Innopolis functions as a university campus, rather than an IT city. In view of this kind of reaction, Kazan may yet have a way to go if it wishes to make its brand acceptable and attractive to the larger public.

Technological entrepreneurship is also connected to these promises of a future replete with better living standards. Compared to other types of entrepreneurship, high-tech business has positive connotations in Russian culture, largely because in this case the entrepreneur sells his knowledge and talents rather than goods or services. During the Soviet era, entrepreneurship was prohibited, although the gray and black markets thrived; then with the collapse of the Soviet Union, "buying and selling goods" became widespread as people struggled to survive financially. Yet even though it was now a legal activity and broadly practiced, it still lacked social respectability. Today, these attitudes persist, and they work to the advantage of IT entrepreneurship, which is perceived as a purer form of initiative free of the taint of selling "things" for profit. Information technology entrepreneurship has other attractive features as well. It is a relatively inexpensive field to enter, since it does not require substantial investments in material infrastructure. In some cases, one person and a laptop suffice. The infrastructure being built in Kazan claims to provide opportunities for just this kind of initiative: that is to say, if you want to start your own tech business, IT parks, tech zones, and industrial parks are ready to support your aspirations. The IT parks in Kazan and Naberezhnye Chelny are experiencing a rush of startuppers applying for business-incubator spots in the hopes of becoming the next new tech star.

As a result, what one sees is local infrastructure actively responding in an attempt to offer a wide range of programs that can sustain the ambitions found in all age groups; for instance, the program "Junior Startup" is organized specifically for children, teaching them how to go about organizing their own startup company. As for the promotion of technological competences, IT parks host Olympiads and computer science competitions. The main purpose of these projects is to attract the local community of all ages into the arena of technological business, assuring them that no special skills are required—just a bright idea and high motivation. One of the IT park managers I interviewed explained that participants can learn by doing, perhaps fail the first time, but then return to try again with new and stronger projects. In this way one begins to see how a "purely" infrastructural project coalesces around itself an ecology that encourages innovative entrepreneurship.

Hosting developmental projects has proven to be a winning strategy for Kazan. It helps the regional government construct an imaginary future for itself, given visible shape by utopian-looking building projects. As a result, Kazan is associated with creativity and innovation, attracting talent from across the country.

THE LOCAL SPECIALISTS' PERSPECTIVE

Interviews with local IT specialists confirm that this regional development may indeed affect both migration patterns within the country and emigration abroad. Because IT work is by nature mobile—to a certain extent these specialists can work everywhere—a high standard of living, good working conditions, and a beautiful contemporary city are factors that weigh in when individuals consider where to work in Russia, or whether to leave the country altogether:

> Why do people leave the country in general? Perhaps, because of the better conveniences and also because of the prevailing ideas, that it is better to live abroad, rather than in Russia. Everything will be just right in this new place—I mean society, governance, state, and something like that. But from the other point of view, for instance, in the realization of your personal potential in IT, I would say that the alternatives are the same—you can do it here, you can do it there. There is not so much difference, where there is a will, there's a way.

On one level, everyday life conveniences may indeed attract specialists to one location as compared to another, but the promise of a locally constructed

IT ecology also enhances the appeal of a place among professionals. In some cases it transforms "brain drain" into "brain circulation," when natives of Kazan return because of opportunities they now see at home. One of the stories I heard was the professional trajectory of an IT specialist from Kazan who moved abroad and then returned to Russia, at first describing Kazan as a "province where [an] IT specialist has nothing to do." It turns out that he was "simply afraid to live in Kazan." At first he did not consider settling there and did not, in fact, even try to find a job in Kazan, going straight to Moscow instead. But after three months he realized that Moscow did not meet his Western-inspired expectations of a place conducive to building a career, which included a workplace within walking distance from home, flexible work schedule, and "something creative" for the content of his projects. So he came back to his hometown, first because of family, friends, and a fiancé, but also because of the promise of a local innovative IT ecology in the making. In general, he described Kazan as a dynamic city that is trying to achieve something unique: Innopolis and the IT park are central to these efforts. Yet some local specialists remain skeptical as they consider the difference between mere infrastructure and the promise of a new ecology that it purports to offer. Despite the enthusiastic reviews, many are withholding judgment. Some computer scientists and local software developers are cautious in their evaluation of the grandiose regional scheme; instead, they speak about specific research facilities, such as the university at Innopolis, or the number of companies that the new economic zone will be capable of attracting. As for the idea of growing and nurturing a new ecology of innovation, one of the local programmers emphasized that "the absence of multinational IT companies proves the inconsistency of the hype over Kazan as an IT capital, that it can be in any way comparable with Silicon Valley." Thus, for people like this, Kazan still has a long way to go to prove that its aspirations can be realized. Besides, there may be a downside to the extensive branding strategy of local policy makers. The invention of a "new Kazan" can appear artificial. An IT specialist who migrated to Saint Petersburg from Kazan told me:

> Kazan has changed a lot since the thousand-year anniversary. It was one of the criminal hot spots in Russia. And they [regional authorities] managed to pave it all over with asphalt and make roads everywhere. They really took it seriously—even built a subway. Nowadays, it is all about IT. Every time it is something new and nothing is left from the Kazan of the old days. Does it mean that there was nothing good in it to save? It means that Kazan is something artificial now, something which is constructed from scratch and based on these new technologies.

That is to say, marketing Kazan based on "regional specificity" or "European style" imparts a certain strangeness to the region when viewed from a Russian perspective. High-tech and business people from Saint Petersburg and Moscow perceive Kazan as having a culture all its own: "Kazan is different"; "People in Kazan do things in their own way"; Kazan is an "other" to which outsiders sometimes have difficulty relating.

EXPERIMENTING WITH INNOVATIONS

Starting with the e-government project, the way in which Kazan is reinventing itself as "the capital of Russian IT" has enabled it to promote itself as the leader in implementing pilot projects for federal programs and testing different forms of innovative policy tools for the whole country. The ability of the region to experiment and test successfully is now part of the "Kazan brand," which helps the regional administration to funnel federal money to Tatarstan. For instance, the notion of the technopark, launched in 2004, was a pioneering "federal experimental platform" that stimulated the development of business incubators in other Russian regions. The technopolis Himgrad took part in the development of standards that are now applied to all industrial parks in Russia, and its experience was used for the development of new industrial parks in Ukraine, Kazakhstan, and Azerbaijan. In 2010, the two technoparks in Kazan, Idea and Himgrad, were chosen to be the platforms for the establishment of a new nanotechnology center. One of my interviews with a project manager of the Kazan IT park business incubator revealed its experimental nature as a place where specialists and managers are testing different ways of achieving the goal of growing domestic high-tech startups.

As the result of this experimental framing, Kazan's ability to cast itself as a place where new policies and initiatives can be tested *does not require it to prove that those innovative projects were necessarily "successful."* Therefore, the notion of "testing" changes the focus from innovations per se toward experimentation, using a variety of means to achieve innovation goals. And if specific experiments do not work out, at least the buildings are something tangible that will exist for a long time and can be used for other purposes.

As for the region's future outlook, a combination of existing favorable characteristics will help local politicians adjust their branding strategy to whatever agenda the federal state will have to offer. In the summer of 2014, Nikolay Nikiforov, the minister of telecommunications of the Russian Federation, declared it necessary that the country have complete information sovereignty (Ministry of Telecom 2014). In this context, sovereignty stands for the replacement of all foreign software with domestically produced analogues: "Russian software" designed by Russian IT companies. According to Nikiforov, "It's highly possible, because Russia has always been known for the high qualification of its programmers. We have worldwide famous IT companies, such as Yandex, Mail.ru, and others. We are preparing a complex of measures on substituting imported software with domestic." He also added that Russia will need at least one million programmers to accomplish this, in comparison with the estimated 350,000 IT specialists currently working in Russia.

Rather than consuming foreign products, the Russian state has set out to revolutionize the domestic IT market. This process begins with military, defense, and government operations, where the choice of "Russian" technologies is especially important. In regard to the civilian market, "digital sovereignty" means the development of Russian search engines, email systems, and electronic government—the digitalization of domestic administration. This updated agenda of the Russian state was met locally with support. The idea of the local authorities to become a regional center for import replacement came as a response to Nikiforov's initiative. By the time Nikiforov declared his vision of full informational sovereignty for Russia, Tatarstan had already adopted a special focus on testing electronic government platforms and producing software for state operations. While informational sovereignty was met with criticism among IT experts, its implementation is certain to have a strategic impact on many federal and local initiatives.

CONCLUSION

This chapter has described the strategy of the federal and regional state to establish an ecosystem of innovation in Russia. The Kazan model offers a different approach to design innovation ecology, based on urban development. According to this strategy, its ultimate measure of success lies in the establishment of new buildings—infrastructure, tech parks, and other tangible material forms. And Kazan has mastered it well. All of that considered, it is true that innovations—the development of new technologies and products—are in fact not the focus of this regional ecology. This kind of strategy is not even specific to IT and could also be applied to other high-tech industries, such as robotics or aeronautics. The strategy seems to be the same: a region establishes a new entity funded by state initiative, thereby providing the institutional setting for a new project, designating it the new technopark or business incubator. Then the building begins. The Kazan story also shows that a great deal of money and effort—in the form of highways, buildings, housing, new universities, and research facilities—had to be invested in the region before it could even begin to build a viable high-tech center.

While everything must begin with construction, the creation of a truly successful environment for creative work involves larger-scale processes of development. It requires a broad improvement of urban spaces, which includes social and cultural transformations; the project needs to be appealing to investors, migrants, and locals alike. While the federal government can build infrastructure, the real work of innovation has to be carried out by people on the ground; the efficiency of these organizations largely relies on the competence and expertise of local decision makers and specialists. However, these issues are not considered within this model of innovation, based on square-footage development. It is fair to say that the local ecology of innovation in Kazan remains an experiment, exactly how it was envisioned by the local administration.

On the local level, the establishment of an IT hub enhances the authority of local officials. In a similar study, Nadir Kinossian (2006, 334) analyzes two major programs of urban development in Kazan, which are "Slum Clearance and Modernization of Slum Blocks in Kazan 1995–2005" and "Preservation and Development of Kazan Historic Center 2001–2005." He concludes that "the programme outcomes can therefore be better explained by bureaucratic procedures, politics and the rational behavior of the local political elites rather that by cooperation between the public and private sector." A similar conclusion can be made about the intention of the Kazan politicians to establish a high-tech center. "Ecology of innovation" is yet another appealing scheme to generate investments into the local economy from federal sources, so as to strengthen the relationships between Moscow and Tatarstan and to assert the authority of the local government. Whatever local improvements are made and whatever the result in terms of actual IT innovation, it may be that the chief beneficiary of this policy is the central state. Information technology investment in outlying regions is an ideal vehicle for the enhancement and extension of state authority. For this reason, these projects are often accompanied by extensive publicity designed to demonstrate to the Russian public that the government is active and forward looking. Thus, the ultimate "success" of these projects may have less to do with whatever IT innovations they actually produce than with the goal of establishing control over the periphery and demonstrating the intention of Russia to achieve digital independence.

1. This evaluation is based on the number of innovative companies and the number of patented and implemented technologies that local companies and the authorities in Kazan claim to have developed.
2. All interviews with IT workers were conducted in Russian and translated by the author.

REFERENCES

Administration of Novosibirskaya Oblast. 2015. "E-government." Official website. Accessed December 22, 2015. http://www.nso.ru/page/2631.

Asheim, Bjorn T. 1996. "Industrial Districts as 'Learning Regions': A Condition for Prosperity?" *European Planning Studies* 4, no. 4: 379–400.

Asheim, Bjorn T. 2007. "Differentiated Knowledge Bases and Varieties of Regional Innovation Systems." *Innovation* 20, no. 3: 223–41.

Asheim, Bjorn T., Helen Lawton Smith, and Christine Oughton. 2011. "Regional Innovation Systems: Theory, Empirics and Policy." *Regional Studies* 45, no. 7: 875–91.

Breznitz, Dan. 2007. *Innovation and the State: Political Choices and Strategies for Growth in Israel, Taiwan, and Ireland.* New Haven, CT: Yale University Press.

Bulanin, Nikita, and Andrei Shcherbak. 2005. "Federal Transfers against Secession: Cases of Denmark and Russia." [In Russian.] *Journal of World Economy and International Relations* 11: 78–85.

Doloreux, David. 2002. "What We Should Know about Regional Systems of Innovation." *Technology in Society* 24, no. 3: 243–63.

Etzkowitz, Henry. 2008. *The Triple Helix: University-Industry-Government Innovation in Action.* New York: Routledge.

Etzkowitz, Henry, and Loet Leydesdorff. 2000. "The Dynamics of Innovation: From National Systems and 'Mode 2' to a Triple Helix of University-Industry-Government Relations." *Research Policy* 29: 109–23.

Florida, Richard, and Martin Kenney. 1988. "Venture Capital, High Technology and Regional Development." *Regional Studies* 22, no. 1: 33–48.

Gohberg, Leonid, ed. 2014. *Rating of Innovative Development of the Russian Regions.* 2nd edition. Moscow: National Research University High School of Economics.

Horne, John, and Wolfram Manzenreiter. 2006. "An Introduction to the Sociology of Sports Mega-Events." *Sociological Review* 54, no. 2: 1–24.

Ismagilova, Elmira. 2010. "Rustam Minnikhanov: The President in the Style of High-Tech." *Vesti.ru.* Accessed December 22, 2015. http://www.vesti.ru/doc.html?id=349287&p=7&sort=1&cid=1.

Kenney, Martin, and David C. Mowery, eds. 2014. *Public Universities and Regional Growth: Insights from the University of California.* Stanford, CA: Stanford University Press.

Kinossian, Nadir. 2006. "Urban Redevelopment Programmes in Kazan, Russia." In *The Urban Mosaic of Post-Socialist Europe*, edited by Sasha Tsenkova and Zorica Nedovic-Budic, 319–36. Amsterdam: Physica-Verlag HD.

Kontareva, Alina. 2015. "State Orders and Innovation System Development of a Russian Region: The Case of the Tatarstan Republic." [In Russian.] *Sociology of Science and Technology* 6, no. 4: 164–77.

Kustikova, Alisa, and Iakov Zaslavskii. 2015. "In between Silicon Valley and Zhigulevskaia Valley." *Novaia Gazeta*. Accessed December 22, 2015. http://novayagazeta.spb.ru/articles/9971/.

Lundvall, Bengt-Ake. 1992. *National Systems of Innovation: Towards a Theory of Innovation and Interactive Learning*. London: Pinter.

Lundvall, Bengt-Ake, Björn Johnson, Esben Sloth Andersen, and Bent Dalum. 2002. "National Systems of Production, Innovation and Competence Building." *Research Policy* 31: 213–31.

Matheson, Victor A., and Robert A. Baade. 2004. "Mega-Sporting Events in Developing Nations: Playing the Way to Prosperity?" *South African Journal of Economics* 72, no. 5: 1085–96.

Matsuzato, Kimitaka. 2001. "From Ethno-Bonapartism to Centralized Caciquismo: Characteristics and Origins of the Tatarstan Political Regime, 1900—2000." *Journal of Communist Studies and Transition Politics* 17, no. 4: 43–77.

Ministry of Science and Education of the Republic of Tatarstan. 2015. "The List of Educational Institutions (Higher Education) in the Republic of Tatarstan." Accessed December 9, 2015. http://mon.tatarstan.ru/rus/vuz.htm.

Ministry of Telecom and Mass Communications of the Russian Federation. 2014. "Nikolay Nikiforov Addressed the Participants of the Youth International Forum 'Tavrida-2014.'" Accessed December 9, 2015. http://minsvyaz.ru/ru/events/31483/.

Mowery, David C., and Nathan Rosenberg. 1991. *Technology and the Pursuit of Economic Growth*. Cambridge: Cambridge University Press.

Nelson, Richard R., ed. 1993. *National Innovation Systems: A Comparative Analysis*. New York: Oxford University Press.

Nozhenko, Maria, and Elena Belokurova. 2010. *North-West of Russia: Region or Regions?* [In Russia.] Saint Petersburg: Norma.

Polygaeva, Daria. 2015. "How Does the Youngest City in Russia Live?" *The Village*. Accessed December 22, 2015. http://www.the-village.ru/village/city/places/222053-innopolis.

Roche, Maurice. 1994. "Mega-Events and Urban Policy." *Annals of Tourism Research* 21, no. 1: 1–19.

Rosenberg, Nathan. 1983. *Inside the Black Box: Technology and Economics*. Cambridge: Cambridge University Press.

Saxenian, AnnaLee. 1994. *Regional Advantage: Culture and Competition in Silicon Valley and Route 128*. Cambridge, MA: Harvard University Press.

Starodubtsev, Andrei. 2009. "Political and Socio-economic Factors of Regional Politics Realization in the Russian Federation." [In Russian.] PhD diss., European University at Saint Petersburg.

Sturgeon, Timothy J. 2000. "How Silicon Valley Came to Be." In *Understanding Silicon Valley: The Anatomy of an Entrepreneurial Region*, edited by Martin Kenney, 15–47. Stanford, CA: Stanford University Press.

Twenty-Fourth International Specialized Exhibition within the Forum of Tatarstan Oil, Gas and Petrochemicals. 2017. "Tatarstan Oil, Gas and Petrochemical Industry." Official website. Accessed July 10, 2017. http://www.oilexpo.ru /eng/market/.

United Nations Educational, Scientific and Cultural Organization (UNESCO). 2002. Address by Koichiro Matsuura on the Occasion of the Award of the UNESCO Cities for Peace Prize. Accessed December 9, 2015. http://unesdoc .unesco.org/images/0012/001252/125255e.pdf.

CHAPTER SIX

HACKERSPACES AND TECHNOPARKS IN MOSCOW

Aleksandra Simonova

I started my research on the new Russian technology coworking spaces at a cemetery. Unexpectedly, the Skolkovo "Innovative City," that famous technopark launched by the state for the development of new Russian technologies, was not easy to find. Although not far from Moscow, there were no road signs directing toward it and I had to follow a GPS navigator that gave ridiculous directions. I lost my way, and while standing in front of the cemetery's gates I wondered how many people had abandoned any attempt to find Skolkovo. When I finally reoriented myself and reached the edges of the technopark, I was greeted by a barbed-wire fence and a locked gate. This confirmed my doubts: it would not be easy to enter this place. Behind the fence, there were several gray buildings under construction sporting the letters "Sk," the symbol of Skolkovo, but unable to pass through the gate or find an official parking lot, I left my car in a small lot (where I later found a "No Parking" sign), and managed to flag down one of the official corporate buses—the only vehicles granted access into the premises—which took me into the compound.

The Skolkovo "Innovative City" has been criticized for many things: inefficiency, corruption, high rents, a complicated architectural plan, and a failing program for the support of residential startup companies (Latynina 2013; Reyter and Golunov 2015; Vedomosti 2015). Nevertheless, my experience was that there were two other primary impediments to Skolkovo's success and to the development of the startup companies located therein: first, Skolkovo's geographical isolation from, and lack of robust infrastructural connection to, the city of Moscow; and second, the Innovative City's underdeveloped urban environment.

If my initial impressions of Skolkovo were colored by the difficulties of accessing it, my first experiences at the Moscow hackerspace Neuron were quite the opposite. Due to its location in the Moscow city center it became a place of coworking of independent professionals and startup companies who were eager to find a collaborative environment with appropriate social and highly developed urban infrastructure. Unlike Skolkovo, the hackerspace is part of the self-organized creative quarter Khokhlovka where different initiatives coexist following the vibe of self-organization and grassroots movement. There are no fancy buildings or barbed fences; moreover, the quarter looks quite shabby with old paint on the walls of the buildings, different graffiti, and posters that define the "indie" spirit of the place.

These initial impressions, expanded by months more of ethnographic work at both sites, spoke to a problem often ignored in the analysis of contemporary coworking spaces in Russia: the importance of the broader urban environment, as well as the design and organization of internal office space, to the successful development of these coworking spaces and the companies and projects they foster. By taking Skolkovo's "Innovative City" and the Moscow hackerspace Neuron as indicative contrasting examples, I will attempt to explore these questions of the relationship between spatial organization and the urban environment, and the success of new Russian coworking spaces. In doing so, this chapter will speak to the questions of the relationship between the development of technology startup companies and their proximity to and interconnectedness with, or their separation and isolation from, urban infrastructure, public space, and the forms of sociality such infrastructure and space can foster. Moreover, by taking the urban environment and spatial organization as points of reference, the differences between state-run, top-down organized coworking spaces such as the Skolkovo technopark and independently organized startup spaces such as Neuron can be explored in a new way.

In this chapter, I pursue these questions through ethnographic research at Neuron, where I did four stints of fieldwork from 2013 to 2015, and in Skolkovo, where I spent the summer of 2015. At Neuron, I conducted formal and informal interviews, and monitored internal communications, practices of work and cohabitation, and traced the connections between the hackerspace and the larger urban area in which the hackerspace is located. At Skolkovo, I interviewed workers at residential startup companies, as well as members of Skolkovo's "Skoltech" University and the management of Skolkovo's IT cluster. At Skolkovo, I paid particular attention to the Innovative City's urban infrastructure, as well as to the quotidian dynamics of its versions of coworking environments. Moreover, I observed the day-to-day use of the premises both by members and visitors, which helped me to analyze specific advantages and problems of the site—as well as its contrasts with Neuron.

COWORKING SPACES, THE URBAN ENVIRONMENT, AND THE "CREATIVE CLASS"

Coworking spaces are often defined as shared workplaces for different sorts of knowledge professionals, working in various "creative" industries—a designation generally referring to industries involved in the production and dissemination of knowledge and information services and technologies. In addition to being office-renting facilities where workers can rent a desk and internet connection, coworking spaces are usually places where independent professionals from different creative fields (e.g., computing, design, art, media, science, and social work) work side-by-side with startup companies. In line with this emphasis on the sharing of space, coworking spaces regularly strive to create an environment focused on making connections, fostering collaboration, and sharing knowledge (Gandini 2015; Leforestier 2009), and thus have often located themselves in downtown, urban areas that boast developed infrastructures and the promise of connections with other creative industries and with public spaces and cultural activities.

Starting in San Francisco in 2005, the coworking phenomenon has become a global movement that has grown with each passing year. Coworking spaces have prospered in the so-called "creative" cities such as London, Berlin, Paris, San Francisco, New York, and Moscow. In these cities, creative industries have come to constitute a large part of the local economy. According to *Deskwanted* (an online magazine dedicated to coworking spaces) there were nearly 2,500 coworking spaces in 80 countries by mid-2013: 781 in the United States, 154 in the UK, 95 in Brazil, 44 in Poland, 39 in Russia, and 22 in China (Deskwanted 2013).

The spread of coworking spaces and practices of sharing space while working in different companies and on different projects has followed what Richard Florida has called the "rise of the creative class" (2002). This new social group combines work with leisure time and mixes private and public spheres, thereby creating a new shared environment for individual work. Florida predicted that the creative class would be the anchor of new economic growth in the early 2000s and, indeed, in the 2000s coworking spaces emerged as a part of the development of the postindustrial economy. Yet the rise of coworking spaces also coincided with the global economic crisis of

2007–9, which in turn gave rise to a critique of this new form of work as representative of unstable, project-based employment engaged in by precarious workers dependent upon professional networks as their decisive source of job acquisition (Bandinelli and Arvidsson 2013; Gandini 2015).

Yet even though members of coworking spaces follow strategies of individual entrepreneurship and self-branding, and are embedded within broader neoliberal economic regimes, these spaces are not subsumable within models of hierarchical, post-Taylorist organization. On the contrary, many such spaces oppose hierarchical organization and the sole motivations of profit maximization and efficiency, relying instead on an "open source community approach" to work collaboratively and establish close communication and the open exchange of knowledge within a community based on equal social relations among member-workers (Leforestier 2009). In this sense, collaboration, openness, community, and sustainability have been named as four principles of coworking spaces (Reed 2007).

Hackerspaces have followed this model of collaboration and openness, and have often attempted to provide both a physical and a social space for freelancers and startup companies. There are many hackerspaces around the world, most of which are small-scale grassroots workshops offering not just workspace but an environment where equipment and skills can be shared and various IT and computing projects can be pursued collaboratively. In this way, hackerspaces appeared to be specific instantiations of this global coworking movement, with hackerspaces composed of creative IT professionals and hobbyists who perceive hacking as a form of collective experimentation, sharing skills, tools, knowledge, and encouragement (Kera 2012; Lindtner 2014).

Coworking hackerspaces have thus often become venues for intensive collaboration as a direct result of sharing space, with members benefiting from the forms of knowledge exchange and innovation this proximity can promote. Indeed, even before coworking spaces emerged, the notion of a shared, common workspace had been regarded as important for business development. Scholars claimed that companies located in the same space benefited from "noise in the area" (Grabher 2002), "local buzz" (Storper and Venables 2004), "local broadcasting" (Owen-Smith and Powell 2004), "face-to-face interaction on site" (Iammarino and McCann 2006), or simply the benefits of "being there" together (Gertler 1995).

However, literature on the spatial benefits of working in shared spaces was primarily concerned with the organization of internal workspace rather than as regards the external urban environment in which these offices were located. This lack of focus on the broader urban context is even more surprising since a chief assumption has been that coworking spaces were connected to the rise of the "creative city" and the concentration of creative professionals in such urban environments (Landry 2008). Nevertheless, the urban environment and the choice of location for coworking spaces have received less attention from commentators in considering which factors are most important for the success of these spaces.

While the success of coworking spaces has been largely motivated by the independent, grassroots organization of shared workspaces, the economic importance of the creative sector—and the IT sector in particular—has led many governments to seek to emulate the organizational principles of private coworking spaces in the establishment of state-sponsored high-tech initiatives. One site in which this attempt has been made is in the construction of "technoparks." The term "technopark" is often used to refer to state-sponsored initiatives that attempt to establish collaborative relations between multiple technology companies, working in diverse sectors and often in conversation with local or on-site universities, within a shared territory or "park." The goal of technoparks is generally to facilitate economic development and innovation through such collaboration within a shared locale. Often technoparks provide space for tech companies' offices, coworking spaces for startup companies, as well as industrial sites for small-scale tech production.

Research on technoparks has revealed, however, that the proximity provided by shared geographical space is not a guarantee of cooperation among the firms located therein. For example, only 10 percent of interactions of high-tech firms located in the METU-Technopolis in Ankara, Turkey, took place within the park itself, while the majority of communications were with outside groups, with 64 percent of these interactions taking place either with groups outside of Ankara or with foreign companies (Aslan and Wasti 2015). While the research neither mentioned exactly what prevented companies from interacting within the space of the technopark nor addressed the question of how companies could build ties in the city of Ankara while being located on its outskirts, the implication was that the primacy of the internet for communication reduced the importance of geography and shared space for contact and collaboration.

This implication that new communication technologies reduce the importance of distance and spatial organization for the development of high-tech companies raises the question of whether considerations of spatial organization and urban location still matter for the encouragement of innovation and the overall success of such companies. Yet if such considerations are indeed no longer important, how can we explain the many successes achieved by the model of coworking spaces and the forms of innovative collaboration this model has been able to encourage? Undoubtedly, there are many differences between state-sponsored technoparks and independent coworking spaces, such as the horizontal organization of independent coworking spaces versus the highly regulated, top-down organization of many technoparks. However, another major difference between many private coworking spaces and state-sponsored technoparks lies in where they are located and how they are organized spatially—a difference I will examine below in regard to the Russian technopark Skolkovo and the Moscow coworking hackerspace Neuron.

THE URBAN ROOTS OF RUSSIAN COWORKING SPACES AND TECHNOPARKS

Since the 2010s, the Russian startup movement has been divided between those who chose private coworking spaces and those who opted to work in state-sponsored technoparks (Solodovnikov 2011). Technoparks have been established in many Russian cities to host both IT startups and large technology companies. While there are currently about ninety of them in Russia, most are still in various stages of construction and design and are not yet functional. For instance, in this volume we pay attention to a technopark in the Tatarstan region, an ecosystem envisioned as a site where innovations would thrive by creating a gathering place for the local IT community. The park provided office space for IT park residents (mostly startup companies), independent software developers, and research groups (Kontareva, this volume).

According to research by Ernst and Young and the Russian Venture Company (RVC) (2014, 14) research, 86 percent of those who work in Russian technoparks are concentrated in the sphere of IT and high tech. While operational Russian technoparks demonstrate similar results to their Western counterparts in terms of ensuring the survival of startup companies within a shared environment, the report points out that in many of the technoparks there is "no special space for public events and socialization in an informal atmosphere," which limits development of the companies in many ways. The absence of such spaces prevents startup companies from building informal collaboration.

Furthermore, the report revealed that Russian technoparks are often isolated from outside visitors, with outsiders generally not permitted to access any of the technoparks' facilities, which makes collaboration with outside

groups difficult (Ernst & Young and RVC 2014, 14). For instance, this isolation is visible through the organization and availability of infrastructure. On
the one hand, many technoparks lack technological equipment, the absence
of which prevents or slows down the development of startup companies.
On the other hand, in the technoparks that do have equipment and facilities this infrastructure is often underused by residents. In general, therefore,
Russian technoparks have too often focused on the organization of internal
space (e.g., providing office space and meeting and conference rooms) while
underestimating the importance of urban infrastructure and connections to
the outside world.

On the contrary, successful private coworking spaces in Russia have
tended to be located in developed urban areas and have maintained connections with outside groups in the area. Thus, most Russian coworking spaces
are in Moscow, with the most popular coworking spaces there located in
creative clusters such as Artplay, Strelka, and Winzavod (Dorman 2011). Such
coworking spaces choose their locations based on the comfort, convenience,
and infrastructure of an area, as well as for the cultural activities and social
spaces available there. For instance, the proximity of metro stations and
affordable parking became important factors for the Moscow coworking
space called "#tceh." In their blog, the organizers of this space shared the
story of their search for a location:

> We researched all the factors: simplicity of access (if it is easy to find the
> place for the first time without knowing exactly where it is); the exterior of
> the building (if it is possible to explain even to a foreigner where we are);
> who the neighbors are; if it is possible to arrange collaboration with other
> companies in the area; the view from the windows; proximity to hotels
> and cafes; the possibility for future enlargement of the co-working space;
> proximity to an external conference hall [etc.]. (Tceh 2014)

While this statement testifies once again to the importance of urban
location for coworking spaces, it also speaks to an additional problem faced
by both independent coworking spaces and technoparks: the high rates of
"brain drain" and highly skilled migration among young technology professionals in Russia. As others in this volume have discussed with regard to
Russians leaving the country for the US, Finland, the UK, Estonia, and Israel
(see West; Shatokhina; Antoschyuk; Savchenko; and Fedorova on Israel, all
in this volume), the problem of brain drain has forced Russian-based initiatives to come up with ways to attract such knowledge professionals to either
stay in or return to Russia. This problem of brain drain is exacerbated in the

technology sector as many successful Russian IT startups have proved that their businesses can succeed online, in virtual rather than physical spaces. Without a need for a physical location in Russia, such startups have tended to leave the country, aided by the mobility characteristic of the virtuality of their work environment, by the attractiveness of robust foreign markets, and by the possibility of increased investment and supportive innovation policies in other countries (Appell 2015; Prorokov 2015).

While many studies on emigration and brain drain from Russia have focused on such rationales for and experiences of leaving the country, there has been less attention to those individuals and companies who have decided to stay. In this volume, we make a contribution to this scholarship, as Marina Fedorova does in chapter 2 with regard to one of the oldest Russian IT companies, Yandex, which has proved successful in creating high-quality software and even its own school for programmers while remaining in Russia. In this chapter, I also attempt to intervene in this subject by focusing on Skolkovo and Neuron—both of which were designed to give technology practitioners an incentive to either come back to or refrain from leaving Russia by creating innovative spaces where different specialists, scholars, and teams of startup companies (and in the case of Skolkovo, even investors) can collaborate in a shared space or defined geographical area.

As noted above, Skolkovo was an ambitious state project to promote the development of high-tech industries and modernize the Russian economy. The initiative was criticized from the start: not everyone was convinced by the ambitious plan to build the entire Innovative City on the outskirts of Moscow. In 2010, the main argument against Skolkovo was that while it gestured toward Silicon Valley, it continued to follow the template of the old Soviet "science cities"; yet rather than support existing cities, the state decided to build a new one (Boyarskiy 2010).

While for the last five years Skolkovo has reported the success of its startup companies (SK 2015a, 2015b), one should note that most of them worked outside the technopark because its buildings were still under construction. By 2015, the first group of companies moved into temporary buildings; however, the main building has not yet been completed, due to the "excessive monumentality" of the architectural project (Kosobokova and Petlevoy 2012). Indeed, Skolkovo's management wanted the Innovative City "to be a site of architectural landmarks" (Kochetova 2015) and famous architects participated in a competition to build it. Finally, the French architectural firm AREP was awarded €195,000 for its development. However, the urban specialist Evert Verhagen, who participated in Skolkovo's

City-Planning Council, claimed that while Skolkovo's administration spent a huge budget on attracting famous architects to design the buildings, they did not ask whether the location was suitable for the development of innovative projects and academic institutions (as a new technical university was also to be built on the premises) (Reyter and Golunov 2015). As a result, the long drawn-out construction and the isolated location became significant obstacles to creating a comfortable environment for the development of the startup companies located there.

By contrast, in 2014 the hackerspace Neuron was named one of the best Russian coworking spaces for high-tech startup companies (Grebnev 2014). Aleksandr, one of Neuron's founders, wrote on Facebook: "I was shocked by the success of the hackerspace. The four startup companies that settled there at the beginning already had success in developing into international enterprises. All the companies that have been 'living' with us for several months are rapidly developing as well, even though we don't have any educational programs or special events for startup companies. Isn't it an enigma?"[1] Indeed, the hackerspace has been an outstanding success, though on a small scale—it is a tiny coworking space for the simultaneous work of no more than forty people. Neuron is an example of a coworking space that is attentive to the urban context of its development. It moved into a creative cluster called Khokhlovka and, among other factors, the urban environment supported the hackerspace's community values, such as the open exchange of skills and knowledge, self-organization, horizontal relations within the community, and openness in the development of new technologies.

In the following sections I will examine the differences between Neuron and Skolkovo in more detail, parsing these questions of the relationship between the growth of the technology sector in Russia and the dynamics of spatial organization, urban location, and extant infrastructure, as well as the impact of these on innovation and collaboration within independent coworking spaces such as Neuron and large, state-run technoparks such as Skolkovo.

THE NEURON HACKERSPACE

The Neuron hackerspace was officially founded by two IT professionals, Aleksandr and Alisa. In fact, however, Neuron's establishment was the product of the collaboration of a number of small, independent startup companies that had been trying to create a coworking space for collaborative work. The goal of these original members was to create a shared space that could support collaborative work on various tech projects, with members sharing tools, ideas, and inspiration. This spirit of collaboration and shared space subsequently attracted other startup teams and freelancers to join the hackerspace and become members. Yet even as the number of members has grown, and while the companies and freelancers at Neuron pursue separate projects, they retain this ethos of working together and assisting each other on specific tasks.

Aleksandr explained that there were several reasons to launch Neuron. First, several groups needed a place to work. Prior to settling into Neuron, Aleksandr's own company, Fairwaves, which assembles telecommunication software and equipment, had lacked office space and its members had been forced to work individually at home. But the major reason for founding Neuron was to create an alternative space for IT and engineering startups, with a different culture and ethos from what Neuron's founding members saw as the "boring" IT business scene in Moscow. There was a practical goal as well: to transform informal gatherings of self-avowed computer geeks into a more formalized arrangement in which people could collaborate in order to develop projects that could either remain hobbies or become the basis for launching, as Aleksandr explains, "companies where Russian engineers can work without needing to leave Russia"[2]—the issue of the brain drain of young Russian hackers, scientists, and engineers being one of deep personal concern for Aleksandr and many other members of the hackerspace.

Neuron's physical space consists of eight zones, which are organized in five separate rooms. Three companies (Fairwaves, Cubic Robotics, and Lab3DPrint) have private premises, while other companies share the rest of the space with freelancers and other visitors. This interconnected area has become the main public space, sustaining conversations and collaborations between different companies and their members.

Neuron is a noncommercial space, meaning that its founders do not seek to make a profit from maintaining and renting it to its members, even though it is not officially registered as a nonprofit entity. The studio provides an environment for sharing knowledge and experience while also giving its members access to the tools and equipment (e.g., various electronic components and engineering tools) necessary for their projects. Membership fees provide a budget for communal and administrative expenses, and members pay both a fee to maintain the space and rent that amounts to about 380,000 rubles per month (about $4,500). People in the hackerspace are divided into "static" (more permanent) members who have private desks, and "dynamic" (less permanent) members who do not have their own workspace but rather occupy any vacant table. Static membership costs 10,000 rubles ($130) per month, and dynamic members pay 3,000 rubles ($50) per month. In addition to these membership fees, Neuron sometimes issues one-day passes for people who are nonmembers but want to use the space from time to time. People who are interested in high tech can easily become members but, as Aleksey, a freelancer, explains, any person who disturbs other members will be asked to leave.

Besides providing space for freelancers and startup companies, the hackerspace operates as a sort of social club, hosting a variety of workshops, classes, competitions, and social events for IT professionals and the general public. These activities help to develop collaborative networks and attract potential new members. Hence, the organization of the internal workspace and its utilization for promoting social activities has been an important factor for developing the community and building an appropriate environment for innovation.

THE HACKERSPACE AND THE URBAN CREATIVE QUARTER

Moscow is a global city, and as with any modern city of its size the most active social interactions and resources are in the downtown area. Yet the radial structure of transport flows and areas of mass housing located at the periphery have given rise to several separated "meta-cities," which are self-sustained areas that are relatively unconnected to each other or to the downtown area (Revzin, Tarnovetskaia, and Chubukova 2013). At first, Moscow hackerspaces developed as part of one of these "meta-cities" in the southwest of Moscow, with Neuron initially setting up in 2011 in the Luzhnetskaya embankment, on the edge of the Third Ring Road that now borders downtown Moscow.

While Neuron's founders had been at first attracted to this space further from the city center, they soon realized that the remote location inhibited the development of the community and their members' individual projects. With these considerations in mind, along with the annoyances of a leaky roof and broken heating system, Neuron decided to move downtown to the creative quarter called Khokhlovka, in the Kitay-gorod district. This location was deliberately chosen for its relatively cheap rent and for its location in the heart of Moscow, bordering the city's chain of central squares, most notably the Red Square, just a few blocks from the Kremlin.

The space Neuron moved into is a seventeenth-century palace that was originally built for a diplomat working for the Muscovite tsars. Being an architectural landmark, the surviving part of the palace was painted white with red ornamental framings on the windows. However, the other newer additions to the palace complex fell into disrepair; old brick lost its bright color and the walls were plastered with posters and graffiti. These days, the area exudes an artistic, creative, countercultural atmosphere. The quarter mostly consists of small unmarked cafés, clubs for dancing, studios for drawing and other arts, and vintage stores or tiny shops with handmade products. As Fedor, a startup entrepreneur, put it, "there is an 'indie' spirit here at Khokhlovka." Even though the hackerspace does not share common projects or joint work-related activities with its neighbors, the communal atmosphere, the stream of visitors, and the rhythm of work in the area unites different organizations into one cluster. The clients of these small enterprises could be visitors to the hackerspace as well. The hackerspace chose this location because it shares the spirit of an "indie" movement that takes pride in its self-organization and independence from large institutions and the state. As Fedor explained, Khokhlovka "developed very naturally, organically, as a creative oasis and quarter," without any investment from big corporations and developers, as was the case for the Red October quarter or Flacon in Moscow. Another resident noted that Khokhlovka is a self-organized community; it does not look fancy with its assorted street graffiti, old furniture, and peeling paint on the walls (Narushevich and Dymchishina 2014).

The hackerspace fit well into this independent, countercultural quarter. Neuron was organized as more than just a coworking space: it was intended to be a close-knit community of people with a shared interest in IT and other high-tech projects with a shared DIY (do-it-yourself) attitude. It was important for Neuron's founders that people could drop in after their normal workday and use the office spaces for their own personal projects, and Khokhlovka was the right place because of the nearby Kitay-gorod metro station and the attractiveness of its "indie" culture. For instance, Aleksandr, who is an IT specialist, started to come to the hackerspace as a hobby because he was interested in sound systems and liked coming to the area, but later joined the startup company Cubic Robotics and moved to the hackerspace full-time.

Neuron uses the communally shared courtyard as a space for socializing as well as for work. Its members found ways of exchanging experiences with members of other creative studios located at Khokhlovka. For instance, Nikita, an employee of Lab3DPrint, was able to test his self-made motor kick-scooter in the courtyard without any objections. The courtyard also became the place for common events at Khokhlovka, including a barbecue organized by Neuron with residents of Impact Hub Moscow, a hackerspace for social entrepreneurs.

But even more important for the hackerspace is the shared rhythm of life and work that marks the cluster as a whole: while it opens around noon every day, peak activity is in the evening and you can usually find people still hanging around at midnight. Consequently, Neuron fit comfortably into the cluster and became an integral part of this small community, while also laying claim to being part of the global city around it—a positionality that has facilitated Neuron's development.

Not everybody, however, would consider Khohklovka an appropriate location for a coworking space. Vladimir, who entered the hackerspace on a day pass, confided that for him the coworking spaces at Gorky Park were preferable (Kirillova 2015). He was not comfortable with Khohlovka's vibe and was "afraid to walk in the evening" in these "dark backstreets" because he thought he might be robbed. Vladimir's feeling is emblematic of the fact that people who do not feel the "indie spirit" of Khokhlovka see only shabbiness and do not usually stay in the hackerspace for very long.

In sum, the location of the creative cluster in Khokhlovka influences the shaping of the hackerspace community and the development of its companies and projects. Khokhlovka's location, design, and culture provides the hackers with access to the broader Moscow public and facilitates contact with potential new members who share the same ideals of freedom, creativity, and an exchange of ideas. The downtown location also fosters contact with professional networks in the city, which helps to attract potential clients, workers, and collaborators for startup companies. At the same time, the countercultural feel of the area helps to filter out people with different values and priorities that are not consistent with those of the hackerspace community.

SKOLKOVO'S INNOVATIVE CITY AS EXPERIMENT

A very different, top-down initiative to foster a place for innovation in Russia, Skolkovo was inspired by both foreign and Soviet experiences of science and technology development, and has become the symbol of Russian state-led efforts to promote scientific and technological innovation.

Although it was envisioned as a Silicon Valley–type ecosystem where startup companies could find the right entrepreneurial atmosphere and infrastructure to facilitate their growth, its conceptualization in fact followed old Soviet spatial and organizational models for scientific and technological development. Skolkovo thus appeared to be an echo of the Soviet "science cities" (*naukograd*) that were designed to foster specific scientific fields (e.g., physics, chemistry, biology, aeronautics, etc.) but grew into fully functional small cities with the necessary social infrastructure for scientists and their families (Wade 2013). Indeed, many Russians wondered whether it was necessary to build new cities for technological and scientific development such as Skolkovo when there were still many operating science cities with different areas of specialization all across the country (Boyarskiy 2010). For instance, Zelenograd in the Moscow area and Novosibirsk in Siberia were enclaves for mathematics, electronic engineering, and computer science, and after the collapse of the Soviet Union, scientists there managed to launch high-tech businesses. Yet while such science cities fostered an experimental environment that helped drive successful scientific advances in the Soviet period, many of these cities faced problems integrating themselves into the new market economy after the Soviet Union's collapse (Tatarchenko and Indukaev, this volume). Hence, the various locations of the Soviet science cities were not considered adequate for building the new "Innovative City."

Skolkovo was considered to be a political project of then president Dmitry Medvedev.[3] While Silicon Valley emerged from a combination of many local factors as well as public and private initiatives, its Russian replica was designed by the state. Skolkovo was a central part of an ambitious modernization program that was launched to transform the Russian economy and overcome its dependence on the sale of natural resources. In 2010, Medvedev visited Silicon Valley in order "to see with [his] own eyes the origins of success" (Gorlik 2010). He met the CEOs of major American IT corporations such as Apple, Cisco, and Twitter to establish partnerships and look for the secrets of their business success.

In his programmatic article "Go Russia!," Medvedev declared his economic priorities—the development of a vibrant IT sector among them. This part of the article gained the most attention from both domestic commentators and foreign analysts. Medvedev set the strategic goals for the IT industry's development as, for example, e-governance, educational programs, and the development of a national network of supercomputers (Appell 2015). The goal here was for Skolkovo to become the center of growth for these new IT industries and, consequently, the IT cluster at Skolkovo became one of its leading departments.[4] While some IT startups believed that their business could be developed in any old café as all they needed was internet access

(Slon 2015), Skolkovo's mission was to show how a specialized, centralized location and a collaborative atmosphere could best foster innovation.

The idea of locating the Innovative City at the outskirts of Moscow, removed from existing scientific and business institutions, followed the political will of Medvedev. In fact, Skolkovo became a massive experiment in reforming Russian science and in evolving new technologies and it was envisioned as Russia's fast track to revive its economy, compete globally in the next industrial revolution of science and technology, and wean itself off its reliance on oil and gas.

One of the main elements of the Innovative City is the Skolkovo Institute of Science and Technology (Skoltech). The university was designed by the Massachusetts Institute of Technology (MIT) and it borrowed from MIT's organizational model, which meant interdisciplinary research, the combination of research and education, the fostering of innovation and entrepreneurship, and the involvement of international scholars (MIT 2015). MIT signed up to comanage the creation of the university with a contract of over $300 million, and in 2011 Edward F. Crawley, a professor of aeronautics and astronautics and of engineering systems at MIT, became Skoltech's president.

Skoltech is different from other Russian technology and engineering schools not just in its organizational model but also in how it operates: the new university has less bureaucracy than other post-Soviet universities and it features greater access to modern equipment, higher salaries for professors, and relatively generous fellowships for graduate students (Sitnikov 2014). Despite close collaboration with foreign institutions, Skoltech also strived to repatriate Russia's lost scientific talent. Skoltech's president Crawley estimated that 60 percent of its faculty consisted of diasporic Russians who had returned, while 20 to 25 percent of the institute's faculty were foreigners and only 20 percent had worked at other Russian universities before taking positions at Skoltech (Bodner 2015). Hence, the goal of Skoltech was to replicate a Western university with faculty experienced in foreign educational systems while at the same time luring Russian diaspora scientists back to the country.

Some detachment from Moscow should have allowed foreign professors and students to feel comfortable within this special foreigner-friendly environment. Skolkovo is officially a bilingual space, with all its signs printed in English, and all its staff speak foreign languages. Indeed, scholars were happy to have their labs at Skolkovo, equipped with all the necessary machines for research that could not be funded by other Russian scientific institutions. Additionally, Professor Dzmitry Tsetserukov, who develops IT and robotics at the university, believes that this attractiveness to foreigners and returning diasporic Russians will increase as soon as Skoltech moves to the new, attractive building at the technopark. A small picture of the future university building at Skolkovo hangs on the wall in his office, a promise of the possibilities for Skoltech's future. Nevertheless, with the construction projects ongoing, and this building as yet unfinished, this hope of attracting large numbers of foreign researchers and diasporic Russians is still a work in progress.

Skolkovo was intended to demonstrate a new business model wherein scientific projects developed at Skoltech could become successful startup companies at the technopark, and this ecology of innovation would attract other high-tech companies that might become future Skolkovo residents. Aleksey, Skolkovo's manager, explained that the residents would foster an innovative environment through the exchange of knowledge, the development of common projects, and by collaborating from their private IT and engineering projects to create new innovative products and services.

All the negative effects of a location at the edges of Moscow, transport, and other infrastructural problems should have been compensated for by the development of a professional community within walking distance of each other. Petr, a manager at Skolkovo, believed that the Innovative City would be a site of experimentation to perform the idea of a scientific "gated community," to which only professionals and other targeted audiences would have access. Nevertheless, seven years have passed since Skolkovo was launched and apparently the remote location and endless construction have created more problems than opportunities. Hopes to establish new spaces for technological innovation in Russia faced the dramatic consequences of changing foreign relations and priorities in internal Russian policy. Mutual sanctions between Russia and Western countries following the political crisis over Ukraine provoked economic crisis in Russia and complicated new technology and science development. Many of Skoltech's foreign professors abandoned Russia and Crawley himself announced that he would leave when his contract expired in December 2015. Skolkovo as a project aimed at the integration of Russian startup business into the global market faced serious difficulties. Its manager, Aleksey, claims that internal Russian demand for high tech is too low for the development of a whole new set of high-tech companies, so international cooperation is a necessary backdrop for the operation of Skolkovo's residential companies.

Skolkovo's Innovative City was designed as an experimental site for science and technology development that would provide the grounds for growth of new industries and modernize the Russian economy. The Innovative City was an ambitious initiative to create a favorable working environment for intensive collaboration between the state, the university, startup companies, and big corporations. A remote location and special architectural plan should have become the material context for this new process. This ideal plan faced many unexpected difficulties such as the financial crisis, unstable international relations, and changing internal political priorities, but its weak urban infrastructure and tight regulation of its own territory also became major factors resulting in fewer supporters and private initiatives than were anticipated.

A GLOBAL CENTER IN THE MIDDLE OF NOWHERE

Any person visiting Skolkovo can easily see that the Innovative City has an underdeveloped urban environment and poor infrastructural connection to Moscow. The city is located beyond the Moscow Ring Highway (MKAD),[5] a symbolic border of Moscow, and was built in the countryside, surrounded by an elite golf club and a village called Nemchinovka. Its remote location notwithstanding, it is still fenced off even from this sparsely developed area.

At the time of writing, Skolkovo's buildings remain mostly under construction and visitors can enter the city only on the aforementioned special buses that run across the Innovative City's territory. Even though experts estimate that Skolkovo's territory (which covers 15 square miles)[6] is insufficient for building the entire Innovative City with adequate urban infrastructure (Boyarskiy 2010), at present Skolkovo operates on a much smaller scale than its designers intended. In fact, the complex operates in just a few buildings: four temporary structures that are used for the technopark and the university, and two buildings called Hypercube and Matreshka that were designed for exhibitions and public events. Pavel's company was one of Skolkovo's first residents, but his team was not able to move in until 2015. Construction continues to lag, and since Pavel's company moved in only "a kiosk with an ice-cream stand has been built."

Location and territory are serious issues for Skolkovo because it was envisioned as a destination for thousands of residents, as well as for Skoltech University and offices for large corporations. The failure of this vision is evident in the fact that the majority of the 1,147 putative residents—made up of companies that have gained official status as Skolkovo members—have never been there, while only 81 companies actually rent office space at the technopark as of 2015.[7] Of the 393 residents of the IT cluster, only 21 companies have so far rented office space at Skolkovo and moved in. Yet Skolkovo cannot host all the companies that have committed to relocate there by 2017, and the temporary buildings available have been far too small to provide premises for all the residents.

The inadequacy of the transport infrastructure has likewise become a significant issue, with a large number of workers spending one to two hours commuting each way to the city as the nearest metro station is miles away. While in the past people could go to Slavyansky Bulvar metro station and then catch a special Skolkovo corporate shuttle bus from there, in July 2015 the Skolkovo administration canceled the corporate shuttle service and chose to rely on Moscow public transportation. But, as could have been foreseen, public buses do not run regularly and include many stops along their routes, exacerbating the already onerous commute for many workers. For instance, Aleksey, a Skoltech employee who lives on the opposite side of Moscow, comes to work two hours early in order to avoid traffic jams. He usually arrives at 7:00 a.m. and sleeps at the office until 9:00 a.m. when work begins.

It is not much easier to get to Skolkovo by car. Aside from the city's remote location, the addresses of its buildings are hard to find and GPS systems often display incorrect directions to them. A second problem is parking, which is not easy to find and costs as much as parking in downtown Moscow—a fact that forces workers who cannot afford the high parking rates to leave their cars along the access road under signs that say "No parking." The road infrastructure leading to Skolkovo is likewise a problem: the Innovative City is purposefully designed to accommodate more than ten thousand employees and nearly the same number of visitors per day (Butcher 2015), yet the existing access road is so narrow that two cars can barely pass one another. Easier access may someday be possible, for the plan is to build a regular railroad line to the nearby Trekhgorka railway station, and eventually to build a new metro station at Skolkovo. For the foreseeable future, however, Skolkovo's administration jokes that only helicopters could resolve the current transportation problems. This comment may have had some seriousness to it, however, as I found a helicopter landing pad included in the miniature model of the future corporate building intended for the Renova group that is headed by Viktor Vekselberg, who is also the president of the Skolkovo Foundation.

The four temporary buildings that currently serve the technopark and Skoltech University were never meant to permanently house the university and company offices. As Pavel explained, you cannot find these buildings on the initial plan of the Innovative City because they were built in haste while everything else was under construction. These four buildings are all identical and form squares with an inner courtyard inside each building. They were built on the land of a now defunct resort called Polet, whose land was included in the future Innovative City.

One additional reason for Skolkovo's isolation from Moscow was the hope of creating an "eco city," a new settlement that would be built according to high ecological standards such as energy and water efficiency and the protection of the natural environment (MN 2012). For now, however, the idea of Skolkovo as an "eco city" has not been realized, with companies located there often complaining that installed eco-friendly systems (air, water, heat, etc.) are neither reliable nor user friendly.

The notion that people would love to work in the countryside also remains unrealized. According to my observations, people would appreciate more public spaces rather than the existing narrow paths in the park, which remain from the Polet resort. Currently, the park only amounts to a beautiful view from the windows of some lucky workers, rather than a space that can be shared by most residents. The former resort's cottages and other pavilions are occupied by official services such as a customs office, the police and emergency response divisions, and the construction company currently working on site. Moreover, these extant recreational spaces are not of much real use to Skolkovo workers, who are usually busy from 9:00 a.m. to 7:00 p.m. and need more easily accessible spaces which could be used during work breaks. With such accessible spaces absent, the most intensive social life in the entire complex happens at the entrances to the four temporary buildings, where people gather to smoke.

Another busy public zone is the cafeteria, which is the only place to eat for the many workers located in these buildings. There is also a small café that was envisioned as a meeting place for visitors, yet at any given time only four or five tables are occupied and the rest of the café's premises are empty—a testament to the dearth of visitors to the city. However, it is not that potential clients and partners do not *want* come to Skolkovo, but rather that the city's isolation makes it inconvenient to visit. As Pavel told me, such potential clients and partners "have heard a lot about the Innovative City and would like to see it," but rarely visit more than once, if at all, because they prefer meeting in downtown Moscow. Skolkovo's administration probably foresaw that the remote location could hamper development, so they appealed to large corporations to open on-site offices. They are expecting that international companies like Cisco and Boeing will build their office buildings here, although currently only a few companies such as the Russian trucking company KAMAZ and the Korean company Samsung rent tiny offices in the city.

The lack of connection to Moscow is especially apparent in the evening. All cafés are closed by 6:00 p.m., and in the absence of any grocery stores or supermarkets in the area the only option for food is to walk to the nearby village of Nemchinovka. The manager, Petr, suggested that a night café or even a bar is needed, as while few people are currently interested in lingering at the darkened complex after work hours they still need a place to discuss issues and ideas in an informal setting.

Of course, those who moved to the Skolkovo technopark were to some extent already aware of the transport problems, the poor infrastructure, and the rudimentary nature of public spaces. However, many of them underestimated the impact of these shortcomings on their businesses; they were also misled about the business infrastructure that was promised by Skolkovo's directors. Residents were promised a five-to-seven-year tax holiday; business and technological consulting; extra funding, grants, and investments; public relations support; and lower rents at the Innovative City than in other parts of Moscow. They were also promised enhanced connections with clients both from the government and the business sector that would be facilitated by Skolkovo's administration.

At the beginning, startups did indeed begin flocking to Skolkovo: it grew from 332 resident companies in 2011 to 793 a year later, and to more than a thousand by 2013. However, in 2015, 141 out of 1,351 were deprived of their residential status and it is expected that more will soon have to leave because they did not develop enough new technology to justify the loans and investments given to them at the outset (Appell 2015). Moreover, even more losses are expected by 2017, when all residential companies will be obliged to settle in the Innovative City. Skolkovo obviously has lost its place on the government's priority list since Vladimir Putin became president, and in 2015 it was ordered to cut construction costs by 40 percent—a loss of funding that will have a serious impact on the future of Skolkovo. In 2017 a new financial solution was developed (Vedomosti 2017), with the Russian Venture Company (RVC) taking charge of the creation of venture capital foundations to support the IT sector in Skolkovo (see more about RVC in Indukaev, this volume). It is expected that the foundation will invest 100–200 million rubles in ten to twelve startup companies at Skolkovo. Nevertheless, it is of yet difficult to predict the effects this venture capital investment will have on the development of the technopark and its residential companies.

Residents confirmed that Skolkovo initially provided business support but that the absence of urban infrastructure has impeded the development of their companies. Ilya, a technical director at Nanosemantics, explained that the company had a lot of support from Skolkovo initially, but that the underdevelopment of the area and its location has increasingly become a problem. Furthermore, the rent was recently raised to Moscow levels. Ilya's company is close to the maximum rent it can afford and if the price of office space continues to rise they will leave to find a location with better infrastructure. While Nanosemantics has been waiting for a resolution to these problems, they have hung a huge picture of a city landscape with crowded streets, busy traffic, and high skyscrapers. As one of the managers at Nanosemantics noted, just the image of a city and its high energy seemed to motivate his work.

Perhaps sensing that its efforts to support the business development of startup companies were floundering, the Skolkovo IT cluster decided in 2015 to open a hackerspace as a coworking space for residents who could not afford an office at the technopark. Skolkovo's startup companies are applying for six- or nine-month residencies at the hackerspace with a specific plan for the development of a product that the companies can commercialize. Furthermore, Skolkovo management believes that this coworking space could make the development of new technologies more dynamic through fostering different companies working together in a shared space. However, they appear not to appreciate that an authentic hackerspace is a complex entity that must be rooted in an urban environment and is a social organization that is based on formal and informal communication between its members. "It will not be a place where you can hang out with your friends, drink beer, and assemble some hardware for fun, but it might serve to move forward the development of a special project," Aleksey, the project manager at Skolkovo, explained.

Skolkovo's efforts to create a collaborative atmosphere have also been hindered by odd design and administrative decisions. For instance, the administration building resembles a castle, which seems designed to hide and protect its inhabitants rather than invite visitors. All the doors at Skolkovo are equipped with magnetic locks, yet at the time of my research there the locks functioned only in the building hosting Skolkovo's administration. Even Skolkovo members cannot enter the administrative floors with their keys. The foundation management even disconnected the doorbell, so that all meetings would have to be set up in advance by phone or email. Pavel explained that no casual visitor can enter the floors without a confirmation from Skolkovo's administration. He claimed that Skolkovo has become like a ministry, with its own hierarchy and rigid segregation between the administration and residents. He believes that while it was envisioned as a facility for helping high-tech companies develop and commercialize their products, it gradually transformed itself into a self-sustaining, closed-off structure that exists by itself and for itself. Therefore, there is a certain perverse logic to its location in the middle of a construction site behind impassable forests at the far outskirts of Moscow.

CONCLUSION

While the US has experienced the rise of IT startups since the late 1990s at the intersection of the software, hardware, and internet industries, the Russian startup boom happened much later, in the late 2000s. Russian startup companies were seeking an environment for their development as well as cheap office space in which to place their teams. Most of them found this office space and a surrounding urban environment at coworking spaces and technoparks.

Coworking spaces have become a phenomenon that is strongly connected to the urban environment of Moscow as a global city with developing creative industries. Startup companies found independent coworking spaces particularly useful for the purpose of developing both new IT solutions and their own technologies. At the same time, the Russian state also began creating infrastructure to support startup companies such as technoparks and incubators—facilities that were mostly built at the edges of Moscow's downtown, with budgets and target outcomes under the control of the government.

In this chapter, I have explored how urban spaces can act as an accelerator for the establishment of an environment that facilitates the growth of startup companies. I compared two types of spaces that were initiated for the development of startup companies: the Skolkovo "Innovative City," which was created by the state, and the Moscow hackerspace Neuron. I examined how the urban environment facilitates cooperation in Neuron and development of its startup companies, whereas a lack of urban infrastructure and an underestimation of the importance of such infrastructure has impeded collaboration and hindered the successful development of Skolkovo's residential companies. The everyday rhythms of these two areas are starkly different, and this contrast highlights the importance of accessible transport infrastructure, attractive landscaping, public spaces, and urban design in general, in facilitating the social interaction that is the lifeblood of IT development.

A downtown location with developed transport infrastructure and public spaces such as cafés, shops, and other sites for startup community meetings helps attract a wide range of new members and clients for startup companies at the hackerspace. Neuron chose the Khokhlovka creative cluster for precisely these reasons, seeing the benefits of the area's "indie" culture and the social activities and public spaces that had facilitated the formation of this culture. Khokhlovka's urban environment and location has helped support the values of Neuron's members, which include self-organization, equality, horizontal relations within the community, and the exchange of skills and knowledge—values shared by many other organizations also working in Khokhlovka. Even though members of the Khokhlovka cluster work on their own separate projects, the shared ethos and common daily rhythm of work in the creative cluster reinforces the integration of the community into a creative and dynamic whole.

At the same time, the overall aesthetics of the creative cluster—street art, graffiti, and public spaces for developing art and tech projects—may not appeal to everyone. Thus, self-identification with the creative cluster and its surrounding environment is a prerequisite for becoming a member of the hackerspace. Those who do not feel the "indie spirit" of Khokhlovka usually do not stay at Neuron for long.

Urban infrastructure likewise plays an important role in the organization of Skolkovo's community, albeit in a negative way. Skolkovo's remote location at the edge of Moscow has proved to be one of the primary limitations to its development as an environment that can facilitate the work of its residents. In this way, had Skolkovo worked harder to integrate itself infrastructurally with central Moscow it might have shown more positive results in the development of its resident companies. Yet instead of this, Skolkovo became stuck between an idea of the value of a self-contained and self-sufficient environment promoting collaboration primarily among its internal organizations, and the reality that the Innovative City is a space that can only prosper through maintaining a porous border between the inside environment and the outside world. The dominance of this original idea of self-containment has resulted in a gated community where scholars, entrepreneurs, investors, and state officials could meet and even collaborate but which was almost closed off to outsiders. Moreover, in prioritizing the internal architectural complexity of the Innovative City's buildings above its urban infrastructure, such as a transport system and public spaces, Skolkovo's planners effected an urban structure that has limited the time and space necessary for both informal communication between residents and contact and collaboration with groups outside the city.

This isolation has impacted Skolkovo's residency and the shaping of its community. While Skoltech scholars value the large laboratories, generous supply of scientific equipment and materials, and access to natural sites, they admit that the lack of urban infrastructure limits Skoltech's development. Because of this lack of infrastructure and connection to the outside world, large corporations and startup companies have mostly avoided moving to Skolkovo in recent years, leaving only smaller companies joining because of state administrative support (e.g., tax holidays, PR promotion, business consulting) and funding.

In this chapter I have shown that even though technologies such as the web have both reshaped the meaning of working space, distance, and location and changed the strategies of high-tech companies, infrastructure and the urban environment still influence the development of new technologies and startup companies. Coworking spaces, such as Neuron, rely on connections to transportation infrastructure, public spaces, and the cultural life these foster, which in turn become a central factor in the success of its members' projects. By contrast, disregard for the urban context has produced problems for Skolkovo and its residents. The absence of developed urban infrastructure did not just place a physical restriction on Skolkovo's residents' communication, working processes, and collaboration with non-Skolkovo partners; it also limited the opportunity for the independent development of Skolkovo itself. The top-down organization of the Innovative City's architecture and planning, and the establishment of residents' businesses in the absence of an urban infrastructure, meant that major problems would worsen when state support of Skolkovo decreased. The financial crisis, changing international relations, and a shift from modernization projects to other state priorities have posed perhaps insurmountable difficulties for Skolkovo as it seeks to find resources for future development beyond state support.

NOTES

1. Aleksander Chemeris, Facebook post, September 18, 2014, https://www.facebook.com/alexander.chemeris?ref=br_rs.
2. All interviews with IT workers were conducted in Russian and translated by the author.

3. Even though the state initiated Skolkovo as a specially created nonprofit, Skolkovo Foundation runs the project of the Innovative City development. The Skolkovo project is financed primarily from the Russian federal budget but the Russian oligarch Viktor Vekselberg is the head of the foundation and private funds support Skolkovo as well (Reyter and Golunov 2015).

4. All of Skolkovo's residents are divided among five clusters: IT, Energy, Nuclear, Biomedical, and Space Technologies. The IT cluster has more residents than the others (SK 2015).

5. The MKAD was opened in 1961; it had four lanes of asphalt running 108.9 kilometers along Moscow's city borders. In the 1980s Moscow started annexing territory outside the beltway but MKAD remains a symbolic border of Moscow.

6. In comparison, Zelenograd occupies 14 square miles; Novosibirsk, 194 square miles; and Silicon Valley's territory is estimated at more than 1,500 square miles (Boyarskiy 2010).

7. "90 are Skolkovo participants. The remaining eight are representative offices of Russian and foreign partners of the project and the Centers of Collective Use" (SK 2015).

REFERENCES

Appell, James. 2015. "The Short Life and Speedy Death of Russia's Silicon Valley." *Foreign Policy*, May 6. Accessed December 9, 2015. https://foreignpolicy.com/2015/05/06/the-short-life-and-speedy-death-of-russias-silicon-valley-medvedev-go-russia-skolkovo/.

Aslan, Duygu, and S. Nazli Wasti. 2015. "Space, Interaction, and Innovation: Does Proximity Really Matter for High Tech Firms?" Paper presented at DRUID15, Rome, June 15–17.

Bandinelli, Carolina, and Adam Arvidsson. 2013. "Brand Yourself a Changemaker!" *Journal of Macromarketing* 33, no. 1: 67–71.

Bodner, Matthew. 2015. "Skoltech Strives to Repatriate Russia's Lost Scientific Talent." *Moscow Times*, September 10. Accessed December 10, 2015. http://www.themoscowtimes.com/business/article/skoltech-strives-to-repatriate-russia-s-lost-scientific-talent/529918.html.

Boyarskiy, Alekseĭ. 2010. "Totalitarnaia chastitsa." *Kommersant Den'gi*, April 24. Accessed December 10, 2015. http://www.kommersant.ru/doc/1367681.

Butcher, Mike. 2015. "Russia Hopes the Skolkovo Tech City Will Produce Its Great Leap Forward." *TechCrunch*, May 31. Accessed December 10, 2015. http://social.techcrunch.com/2013/05/31/russia-hopes-the-skolkovo-tech-city-will-produce-its-great-leap-forward/.

Deskwanted. 2013. "The 2013 Coworking Census." *Deskwanted*. Accessed December 10, 2015. http://www.deskwanted.com/coworking/Global-Coworking-Census-2013.pdf.

Dorman, Veronika. 2011. "Art and Design Creative Centres Transform Moscow." *Telegraph*, June 6. Accessed December 10, 2015. http://www.telegraph

.co.uk/sponsored/rbth/culture/8560105/Art-centres-transform-Moscow
.html.

Ernst & Young and Russian Venture Company (RVC). 2014. "Challenges and Solutions: Business Incubators and Technoparks in Russia." *Rvc.ru.* Accessed December 10, 2015. https://www.rvc.ru/upload/iblock/934/201403_Business _incubators_EN.pdf.

Florida, Richard. 2002. *The Rise of the Creative Class: And How It's Transforming Work, Leisure, Community and Everyday Life.* Princeton, NJ: Basic Books.

Gandini, Alessandro. 2015. "The Rise of Coworking Spaces: A Literature Review." *Ephemera: Theory and Politics in Organization* 15, no. 1: 193–205.

Gertler, Nicholas. 1995. "Industrial Ecosystems: Developing Sustainable Industrial Structures Thesis: Technology and Policy Program." Master's thesis, Massachusetts Institute of Technology, Dept. of Civil and Environmental Engineering.

Gorlik, Adam. 2010. "'I Wanted to See with My Own Eyes the Origin of Success,' Russian President Tells Stanford Audience." *Stanford Report*, June 23. Accessed December 10, 2015. http://news.stanford.edu/news/2010/june/president -medvedev-speech-062310.html.

Grabher, Gernot. 2002. "The Project Ecology of Advertising: Tasks, Talents and Teams." *Regional Studies* 36, no. 3: 245–62.

Grebnev, Egor. 2014. "Idei dlī︠a︡ investorov budushchego: vo chto vkladyvat'?" RBC Daily, July 7.

Iammarino, Simona, and Philip McCann. 2006. "The Structure and Evolution of Industrial Clusters: Transactions, Technology and Knowledge Spillovers." *Research Policy* 35, no. 7: 1018–36.

Kera, Denisa. 2012. "Hackerspaces and DIYbio in Asia: Connecting Science and Community with Open Data, Kits and Protocols." *Journal of Peer Production* 2. Accessed December 10, 2015. http://peerproduction.net/issues/issue-2/peer -reviewed-papers/diybio-in-asia/.

Kirillova, Ėlina. 2015. "Rabochaia Stantsia My izbavliaemsia ot slova 'kovorking' v nazvanii." Rusbase, June 16. Accessed December 10, 2015. http://rusbase.com /interview/mihail-komarov/.

Kochetova, Ekaterina. 2015. "Russkoe pole duly eksperimentov." *Izvestia*, November 27. Accessed December 10, 2015. http://izvestia.ru/news/597429.

Kosobokova, Tatiana, and Vitalii Petlevoĭ. 2012. "Vladislav Surkov raskritikoval Skolkovo." RBC Daily, October 8. Accessed December 10, 2015. http://www .rbcdaily.ru/politics/562949984877177.

Landry, Charles. 2008. *The Creative City: A Toolkit for Urban Innovators.* 2nd edition. New Stroud, UK: Routledge.

Latynina, Yulia. 2013. "Konets Skolkovo." *Novaia Gazeta*, October 31. Accessed December 10, 2015. http://www.novayagazeta.ru/columns/60735.html.

Leforestier, Anne. 2009. "The Co-working Space Concept CINE Term Project." *Iimahd*, February. Accessed December 10, 2015. http://www.iimahd.ernet.in /users/anilg/files/Articles/Co-working%20space.pdf.

Lindtner, Silvia. 2014. "Hackerspaces and the Internet of Things in China: How Makers Are Reinventing Industrial Production, Innovation, and the Self." *China Information* 28, no. 2: 145–67.

Massachusetts Institute of Technology (MIT). 2015. "MIT Skoltech Initiative: Guiding Principles and Goals." MIT Skoltech Program. Accessed December 10, 2015. http://web.mit.edu/sktech/sktech-program/.

MN (Moskovskie Novosti). 2012. "Skolkovo mozhet stat' pervym ėkogorodom v Rossii." MN, May 24. Accessed December 10, 2015. http://www.mn.ru/society /eco/132754.

Narushevich, Anastasia, andi Aleksandra Dymchishina. 2014. "ShHourum Xoxlovka Original." *Cozy Moscow*, December 27 Accessed December 10, 2015. http://cozymoscow.me/mesta/shourum-khokhlovka-original .htmlhttp://cozymoscow.me/mesta/shourum-khokhlovka-original.html.

neuronspace.ru. 2014. Accessed December 10, 2015. http://neuronspace.ru/wp /participation.

Owen-Smith, Jason, and Walter W. Powell. 2004. "Knowledge Networks as Channels and Conduits: The Effects of Spillovers in the Boston Biotechnology Community." *Organization Science* 15, no. 1 (2004): 5–21.

Prorokov, Grisha. 2015. "Pereezd v SSHA: Pochemu russkix startapov na samom dele ne sushchestvuet." *Look at Me*, October 15. Accessed December 10, 2015. http:// www.lookatme.ru/mag/live/industry-research/213497-russian-startups-usa.

Reed, Brad. 2007. "Co-working: The Ultimate in Teleworking Flexibility." *Network World* 23, October 23. Accessed December 10, 2015. https://www.networkworld .com/article/2287504/computers/co-working—the-ultimate-in-teleworking -flexibility.html.

Reyter, Svetlana. 2015. "Amerikanskiĭ professor pokinet post rektora v institute 'Skolkovo.'" RBC Daily, September 14. Accessed December 10, 2015. http://top .rbc.ru/technology_and_media/14/09/2015/55f6ec469a7947b356284202.

Reyter, Svetlana, and Ivan Golunov. 2015. "Rassledovanie RBK: chto sluchilos' so 'Skolkovo.'" RBC Daily, March 23. Accessed December 10, 2015. http://daily.rbc .ru/special/business/23/03/2015/5509710a9a7947327e5f3a18.

Revzin, Grigoriĭ, RozaliaTarnovetskaia, and Margarita Chubukova. 2013. *Metagoroda v strane Moskva*. Moscow: Moskovskiĭ urbanisticheskiĭ forum.

Sitnikov, Alekseĭ. 2014. "Iz chego sdelan Skoltex." *Polit*, August 15. Accessed December 10, 2015. http://polit.ru/article/2014/08/15/sk_sitnikov_1/.

SK (Skolkovo). 2015a. "The Residents of Skolkovo's Technopark." SK. Accessed December 10, 2015. http://sk.ru/technopark/residents/.

SK (Skolkovo). 2015b. "Startup Village 2015." SK, July 2–3. Accessed December 10, 2015. https://sk.ru/foundation/events/may2015/startupvillage/.

Slon. 2015. "Startup Karti." *Republic.ru*. Accessed December 10, 2015. https:// republic.ru/specials/startup-map-moscow/.

Solodovnikov, Denis. 2011. "Nastoi͡ashchee i budushchee IT-texnoparkov v Rossii." *Echo*, October 23. Accessed December 10, 2015. http://echo.msk.ru /programs/tochka/823067-echo/#element-text.

Storper, Michael, and Anthony J. Venables. 2004. "Buzz: The Economic Force of the City." *Journal of Economic Geography* 4, no. 4: 351–70.

Tceh. 2014. "About Us." Accessed December 10, 2015. http://tceh.com/.

Vedomosti. 2015. "Fond Skolkovo Teryaet Rezidentov." vedomosti.ru, June 5. Accessed December 10, 2015. http://www.vedomosti.ru/management/articles/2015/06/05/595343-fond-skolkovo-teryaet-rezidentov.

Vedomosti. 2017. "RVC Vneset 4,5 mlrd. Rublei v Tri Novikh Fonda Skolkovo." *vedomosti.ru*, May 29. Accessed December 10, 2015. https://www.vedomosti.ru/technology/articles/2017/05/29/691834-rvk-skolkovo.

Wade, Imogen. 2013. "Science Towns and Science Clusters in the 2000s: An Institutional Comparison of Russia's Obninsk, Akademgorodok, and Skolkovo." Presentation at Triple Helix 2013, London.

CHAPTER SEVEN

SIBERIAN SOFTWARE DEVELOPERS

Andrey Indukaev

To most foreigners, Siberia is a vast, barely inhabited, fatally cold region—an exotic sight best appreciated from the windows of the Trans-Siberian Railway. At the same time, all around the world one can find IT entrepreneurs and managers who see Siberia as a place populated by key practitioners. It is not uncommon for IT firms to have a Siberian subcontractor, a long-term partner, a supplier, or to establish an R&D center in the region. Large international companies as well as small and medium-size enterprises from such places as the US, South Korea, Germany, France, Switzerland, and several former USSR countries rely on their Siberian partners.

The Siberian IT sector may be seen as an exception to the alleged Russian incapacity to gain social and economic benefits out of technology. Loren Graham, a renowned specialist in Russian science and technology studies, suggests in his last major book that for centuries the country's technological development has been plagued by the very same pattern of failure: Russia is able to give birth to outstanding inventions but permanently fails to turn them into innovations, which is to say, to adopt them on a large scale and, in consequence, to reap the technological and economic reward. The author claims that "Russians have never . . . fully adopted the modern view that making money from technological innovation is an honorable, decent, and admirable thing to do," and that this "may be the most important of all" factors that contribute to the unfortunate Russian pattern of failed innovation (Graham 2013, 103). Graham's claim is supported by interviews and conversations with Russian scientists who manifest negative attitudes toward any form of commercial activity as well as by his observation that almost no Russian students in science and engineering have a desire to create a startup.

The present chapter is based on a set of interviews with IT profession-als in two major Siberian cities, Novosibirsk and Tomsk. The collected data may be seen as both confirming and challenging Graham's diagnosis. Former Soviet researchers in Siberia have adopted business logic and are able to run successful companies. However that logic is not the one that Graham and other innovation scholars refer to and which is typically associated with in-novation. Siberian entrepreneurs set themselves apart from startups and ven-ture capital: business models combining extremely high risk with potentially explosive profits. Nevertheless, even if one accepts the idea that only a system that produces startups with exponential growth potential is the key to tech-nological development, the IT firms in Tomsk and Novosibirsk create what is an absolute prerequisite for the appearance of such a system. Venture capital industry is unimaginable without a pool of competent professionals and the basic innovation infrastructure. In Russia that infrastructure is mainly cre-ated within the framework of the state's innovation policy. I will show that Siberian IT firms contribute to the development of the instruments of the federal innovation policy and to the training of a highly skilled workforce.

The chapter starts with an outline of the key features of the IT sector in Tomsk and Novosibirsk and a description of their immediate environment, such as universities and research institutes. Then I show how the key players in the sector, all having backgrounds in Soviet research institutions, combine business logic with a specific professional ethos rooted in their past, valu-ing high technical skill and complex problem solving more than business growth and profit seeking. Finally, I show how the IT firms contribute to local technological development through teaching and through developing local instruments of the federal innovation policy, and argue that this activ-ity is related to the professional ethos of the local community.

THE IT SECTOR IN NOVOSIBIRSK AND TOMSK

Initially labeled a "pseudo-science," computer science struggled during the Soviet era but eventually managed to become a legitimate and active scien-tific and technological domain (Gerovitch 2002; Tatarchenko, this volume). Siberia and especially Novosibirsk played an important role in this process. The computer center situated in Akademgorodok (the "city of science" next to Novosibirsk) was, in the 1980s, one of the largest multiple-access comput-ing centers in the country, with up to 1,300 employees (Ilyin and Marchenko 2014). The programming community in Akademgorodok promoted advanced research and, despite the Cold War climate, was well connected with the broader international scientific community (Tatarchenko 2013). Similarly, computer science developed in Tomsk from the late 1950s on (Yevtushenko 2003), though in a less independent fashion, with programming being closely related to radio physics and applied research for electronic and defense industry needs.

By the time the Soviet Union collapsed in 1991, Novosibirsk and, to a lesser extent, Tomsk were host to a significant programming community distributed over numerous fundamental and applied research teams. However, the following years were characterized by a considerable curtailment of research funding. Along with other scientific fields, the programming community fell on hard times, losing both state support and industry contracts for applied research (Graham and Dezhina 2008); while most of the academic research institutes survived the crisis, an important number of computer scientists emigrated. This chapter does not follow diasporic trajectories and focuses instead on those community members who continued to do research or commercial programming in Novosibirsk and Tomsk.

I will now outline the general features of computer science research in these two cities. The output of scientific activity of computer scientists from Tomsk and Novosibirsk can be assessed by analyzing publication data from the Web of Science database. In general, Russia is not an active source of publications in computer science. Only about fifteen thousand publications in computer science have authors with Russian affiliations, while the US has about half a million publications in the field. Yet by Russian standards, Novosibirsk is an important computer science research center, counting more than sixteen hundred publications, outranked only by Moscow and Saint Petersburg. The first publication listing a Novosibirsk affiliation appeared in 1973. Five hundred and ninety-five computer science articles (40 percent) are cited at least once and ninety-two (6 percent) are cited more than ten times. Tomsk is less prominent but still visible, figuring in the institutional affiliation of three hundred computer science publications. Of those articles, fifty-four (18 percent) are cited at least once and seven (2 percent) are cited more than ten times. It is not surprising that Novosibirsk is ranked ahead of Tomsk as a research site: Novosibirsk is the third-largest city in Russia with about 1.5 million inhabitants, while Tomsk is about three times smaller.

An important feature of Tomsk is that, despite being a relatively small city, it performs quite well as an educational center. The number of students per capita is the highest in Russia, excluding Moscow and Saint Petersburg (Bychkova and Popova 2012, 227). Tomsk State University and Tomsk Polytechnic University hold, respectively, the tenth and twelfth places among Russian universities included in the QS University Rankings for 2014–15, and are out-ranked only by universities from Moscow, Saint Petersburg, and Novosibirsk. The most active research in computer science in Tomsk is carried out by the following universities: Tomsk State University, Tomsk State Polytechnic University, and Tomsk State University of Control Systems and Radio-Electronics (TUSUR). These three institutions generate the majority of the city's publications in the field.

Novosibirsk is also an important educational center, but most of the computer science authors there are affiliated with one of Akademgorodok's research institutes. Local universities also contribute computer science publications, but to a lesser extent. This can be explained by the fact that—in keeping with the initial design of Akademgorodok's education and research system—university faculty were often affiliated with its research institutes. In sum, Novosibirsk is a large city with an important research community in computer science, and while Tomsk is smaller and less active in terms of research metrics, it is still an important training center in the field.

Both cities also feature active private IT sectors. Novosibirsk is definitely an important software development center. According to data presented by Russoft, the city is one of four Russian locations listed in the "Top 100" list of global outsourcing destinations (Russoft 2014). It is known that both Novosibirsk and Tomsk have both been "popular destinations for development centers since the 1990s" (Zhikharevich, this volume). It is difficult to evaluate the size of the IT sectors in Novosibirsk and Tomsk; however, an estimation of the number of developers within a city can be made. According to the Russoft (2014, 43) report, there are about 430,000 software developers in Russia. Russoft estimates that 5 percent of them are in Novosibirsk, which translates to approximately twenty thousand developers (Russoft 2014, 119). Without having such data for Tomsk, one can use the comparative ratio of city inhabitants to estimate the number of programmers at one-third of the population, which equates to approximately seven thousand developers.[1]

ORIGINS AND CHARACTER OF THE SIBERIAN IT SECTOR

Both cities host firms with a strong peer reputation for their professionalism. Most of these firms appeared shortly after the collapse of the Soviet Union, founded by programmers who had previously worked in local research centers and universities. In Novosibirsk, several of these firms play a central role in a nonprofit partnership of IT companies called SibAkademSoft—a well-respected organization that closely interacts with regional authorities and the Academy of Sciences to promote the interests of the IT sector. Among other initiatives, SibAkademSoft played an active role in establishing the local technopark.

While firms that emerged from research institutions are not the only players in the local software sector, they provide an example, or perhaps even an exemplar, for local programmers and entrepreneurs, informing both their business models and ethos. Most of them do not offer products for the "mass market" and individual users, but develop complex customized products for corporate clients (often also in the IT sector), or do software development for other firms (in Russia and abroad), who own and distribute the final product. According to a Russoft (2014, 62) survey, in 36 percent of cases Siberian firms prioritize export over the domestic market, the highest percentage among all Russian regions. This international orientation is, I believe, an index of the quality of Siberian software.

The developers in Novosibirsk and Tomsk often claim that their business model relies on the quality of their work and on the complexity of problems that they can solve. As Irina, the director of a Novosibirsk firm, explains: "It is a high added value, a unique product, normally big projects where we can show off . . . our unique competences." Indeed, Irina's firm works in very specific domains—virtual reality systems for training simulators as well as hardware and software for TV broadcasting—that require high reliability and real-time graphics. In fact, her employees coauthor professional publications with academic and industrial scientists from Stanford University, Sony Pictures Imageworks, NVIDIA, and other leading organizations from industry and academia (Fernando 2004).

Yevgeniy Petrov, the head of another firm in Novosibirsk, also emphasizes their uniqueness and specialization: "We consider ourselves to be rare birds, we do system programming." His firm specializes in compilers, a very specific product for professional programmers that requires a high level of skill to develop. Similarly, Yelena, project manager from another firm, albeit with a less sophisticated specialization—mostly outsource development—still emphasizes the fact that the firm develops projects in specific and complex domains such as bioinformatics and system programming.

Former Soviet research collectives had to significantly change their way of working in order to become successful IT firms. They had to become capable of respecting deadlines and to contain their passion for inquiry in order to provide expected results in a timely manner. That required them to go through quite a challenging learning process. For Irina and her firm it was really difficult to abandon the way of working inherited from their past roles as Soviet researchers:

> It was a tough transition, because people who had joined the company had a researcher's mentality. . . . For them it is not typical to do things in time. They always get absorbed by exploring stuff. That's interesting, but it is difficult to get a result acting this way, and in business you need the result. At our company it was quite painful . . . because when you plan one time frame [for developing a product] but you only manage to make it in a longer time frame, you get low profit.[2]

The understanding of the basic rules of doing business, namely the profitability considerations, created some distance between the former researchers in business and those who stayed in academia. In the 1990s, many of these companies had their office space on the premises of research organizations—a spatial closeness that often continues to this day. However, firm managers do not collaborate much with researchers. In the past, some businesspeople tried to work with academic researchers. For example, Yevgeniy's firm is still located in the building of a research institute, and he mentioned several attempts to work with researchers from the institute, and does not exclude similar attempts in the future. However, there was only one such project, a prototype development for a state enterprise from the space sector, which became profitable but was eventually abandoned by the researchers, who did not have the skills or willingness to handle the clients' demands, or their delays. Yevgeniy appeared to be the most optimistic concerning the collaboration with researchers; most of the respondents believed that research institutes are not of much interest businesswise. So, one could conclude that former Soviet researchers have adopted the business logic of profit seeking and have transformed into innovative businesspeople emancipated from the burden of their past and the critical attitude toward money.

However, the situation seems to be more controversial when one focuses on the IT firms' attitudes to their Soviet past and on their general attitudes toward the research community. For instance, Yevgeniy, despite his negative business experience with researchers, considers himself culturally close to them: "We do not interact with institutes on practical matters; still we have some cultural interaction, we are in the cultural milieu here." This mix of cultural kinship and business distance characterizes almost all the companies I have studied. Some firms build partnerships with academic researchers, but these partnerships are not directly related to business and are not motivated solely by commercially oriented considerations. For example, Yelena's firm developed a bioinformatics project in direct collaboration with local scientists, but in the end the firm had to accept the researchers' mentality rather than the other way around, and the project became almost noncommercial: "One can say it is our scientific hobby." While not all firms in Novosibirsk collaborate with researchers, the proximity to a large research community tends to orient their specialization. In Yelena's words: "Being in Akademgorodok without doing something involving some research element—it would be strange, [as] there are lots of institutes around."

The proximity to the research community also influences the very core of the IT professionals' business specialization which they deduce from their past experience of research work. Irina, Yelena, and Yevgeniy all work for different firms with roots in Soviet research institutes. For them, their firms' origins determine their specialization:

> We have one serious project related to system programming.... It's our subject, because the company's founders are from the [Soviet] supercomputer project. (Yelena)

> Our laboratory [at a research institute] was named "Machine Graphics Laboratory." ... We were specialists in this domain and we keep this specialization. (Irina)

> When you design a computer ... you should [often] create the compiler. K1 group [a group formed around an exploratory chip development project in 1986] worked on it. Its development was continued [by our firm].... It's still our main specialization. (Yevgeniy)

Firms with similar backgrounds and orientations can be found in Tomsk as well. Igor is the head of a company that specializes in video codecs (standard video compression formats), which is well known among professionals worldwide. The firm was founded by researchers from the Special Design Bureau "Optika," which was part of the Academy of Sciences. Stanislav Pavlov, one of its founders, was a researcher in the Laboratory of Digital Television, so the company's specialization reflects, in part, his own academic background. Tomsk's local universities seem to have played the role of "incubators" in equal measure with the research centers, as evidenced by Igor's narrative of the long genealogy of Tomsk's video-engineering community:

> If we talk about the foundations.... The first TV signal was received in Tomsk in 1923. Tomsk was the third city to launch analog television, after Moscow and Saint Petersburg, in 1953. It was done by Polytech

[Tomsk Polytechnic Institute, later becoming University]. Those who did it founded TUSUR and they taught those who taught Stanislav who taught me.

Vitaliy, the head and founder of another Tomsk-based software firm, was trained as an engineer and worked at what, during the Soviet period, was known as the Tomsk Polytechnic Institute. He considers himself to be still working in his degree field: "I was trained as an engineer in circuit design. . . . I am among the rare people who stayed in the field." His firm's specialization is closely related to the research background of its founders and employees, who are also former Soviet applied researchers.

The business specialization of these firms, however, is not shaped exclusively by their founders' scientific backgrounds, their proximity to academic centers, or the perspectives they acquired by being trained in Soviet research institutions. Interviewees often explain such specialization in high-end complex products in terms of what can be seen as a market strategy: firms specialize in complex problem solving to avoid overlap and competition. As the heads of some firms told me:

> By working on a problem that is complex in terms of engineering, we reduce the number of potential competitors. (Igor)

> One cannot be in competition with students; . . . they are ready to create a site for 5,000 rubles. In our case, with rent, officially declared salary, and taxes, it costs us no less than 50,000. So we try to do projects where we can be unique, . . . specialized projects. (Aleksey)

However, we noticed that the specialization of the firm is always presented as something that has an inherent, non-business-related value. Interviewees often describe their jobs as doing work that is "true," "serious," and "interesting." In some cases, programmers state that this abstract "gusto" has a clear priority over profitability:

> We try to make an interesting product, based on in-depth understanding of the domain we work in. It is interesting. And if we see then that our clients are also interested in our developments, we are pleased. And it is also not bad if there are some financial outputs when we release. (Vitaliy)

Many heads of firms contrast their approaches to the more common profit-driven ways of doing business, which some associate with the word "entrepreneur":

So the orientation toward entrepreneurship appeared not because I am inherently an entrepreneur but because we had no job to do [after the drop in
funding for the institute where Vitaliy used to work]. I still perceive myself
more as an engineer than as an entrepreneur. It may explain the orientation of our company. (Vitaliy)

Others contrast their work to that of "young startups":

We do not have a lot of competitors. Because most young and wannabe
startups have the goal of making a fast buck and we do things that required
years of R&D. (Igor)

And yet others explain that a money-driven approach does not fit them:

Doing business only for doing money is not an approach that I support. One
can create a firm of five to ten people and have a great life, have enough
revenue for those ten persons and the firm will be great, while it can be not
worth making it grow to a thousand persons and then sell it. (Irina, addressing students during a public lecture)

What emerges from the interviews is an understanding of a firm's excellence based on the complexity of the problems it solves and the elegance and
quality of those solutions. This goes hand in hand with an explicit refusal of
profit-maximization logic. The firms' roots in the culture of former Soviet
researchers and, to a lesser degree, their ideological proximity to institutes
and universities are among the factors that shape this business approach.

One can clearly see that the Siberian IT businesspeople have not completely abandoned the critical attitude toward profit making, startups, or even
the concept of entrepreneurship—the very attitude that, according to Loren
Graham, may be one of the main reasons for Russia's failure to modernize
its technology and economy. At the same time it is hard to perceive these
successful and respected technological businesses as a threat to Russia's modernization. One of the reasons for that mismatch may lie in the fact that one
should not necessarily embrace the business logic obsessed with explosive
growth in order to contribute to technological development. Due to some
spectacular success that the business model promoted by venture capital has
brought to life in some countries, startups are now seen, by so many, as a key
element of technological development and innovation. Martin Kenney (2012)
suggests that this is the reason why innovation policy today often overlooks
"nice growth firms," that is to say, organizations with business models focused
on competence development and technical excellence rather than strategies

based on a "high risk versus explosive growth" model promoted by venture capitalists. The firms I have described match the "nice growth" model. They produce high-quality software and are integrated into international technological networks, and contribute to the country's technological development at least in this way.

However, those firms could be seen positively even if one adopts the point of view that the only key to technological development is a venture capital model—a system aiming at the endless creation of new business seeking (sometimes with success) explosive growth. Indeed, a historically informed view on the development of the venture capital industry shows that the desired system appears not in a vacuum, but thanks to "a set of conditions that develop in the pre-emergence phase . . . because they provide the resources necessary for the emergence [of the venture capital industry] to be successful" (Avnimelech, Kenney, and Teubal 2005, 197). In the next section I am going to show that IT firms in Novosibirsk and Tomsk contribute to the training of the highly skilled professionals in their field, whose existence is an unquestionable prerequisite for any scenario of the region's technological development. Moreover, these firms not only use the innovation infrastructure created by the state but actively contribute to its efficiency, especially through supporting young businesses. One of the main reasons why IT firms contribute to the region's technological development is their specific attitude to business, rooted in their Soviet past.

FIRMS AND UNIVERSITY TEACHING

The lack of well-trained IT specialists is often presented by IT professionals in Tomsk and Novosibirsk as one of the main challenges that their businesses face. That may be surprising, taking into account that both cities are major educational hubs. However, as Marina Fedorova comprehensively explained in the literature review in her chapter on Yandex, the training of IT professionals is a problem inherent to the domain, where no conventional definition of professional standards exists and on-site training is a crucial part of becoming a programmer. The Siberian IT firms have a solution to this problem that serves as much their recruitment needs as the interests of the community in general.

The firms I have studied do not generally receive a direct technological advantage from their proximity to research organizations. They do, however, still have a close relationship with universities and research institutes, albeit of a specific kind: their employees often teach and supervise students' coursework.

In Tomsk, firm employees are often affiliated with universities, and although many of Novosibirk's software developers are formally affiliated with the local research institutes rather than the universities, they are still involved in teaching because with the creation of Akademgorodok, university teaching is provided by research institute employees. But why do firm employees take on the additional burden of teaching? A possible explanation is that universities seek private-sector specialists to teach up-to-date knowledge to their students. Maksim, an R&D director in a Novosibirsk firm and an administrator and teacher in one of the city's top universities, describes this situation in a very revealing way. For him, the place of researchers in the initial Akademgorodok setting, where "people from science, with real experience, should teach, not full-time teachers," is now taken by people from firms:

> So, a person who is doing research, and now that means can earn money with research, he knows what is needed for it, and he will teach people how to do up-to-date stuff. . . . And taking into consideration the fact that nowadays the informatics in the Academy [Russian Academy of Sciences] is not in a good condition, institutes cannot keep top-level specialists in informatics—there's no money there; with the Academy's salaries, no good programmer will work there.

This quote illustrates the idea that competences are now concentrated in the IT industry. Moreover, it resonates with our description of the local firms' specific attitude toward business. Maksim sees himself and his firm as the heirs of Akademgorodok's important and distinct research tradition, its excellence, its applied orientation, and its engagement in the formation of professionals—researchers in the past and programmers in the present.

It is also interesting to track the reference to "we" in his narrative and, thus, his complex self-identification: "We invite staff to teach students from exactly the same sort of companies as ours. . . . We have people from about ten companies or more teaching at our [university] department." Both "we" and the second "our" most probably refer to the department faculty at a local university, where Maksim teaches. The first "ours" refers to the company where he works. Somehow the role of a company employee and a university administrator are so tightly bound together that it gives the impression that for Maksim the work within a firm and the formation of students belong to the same coherent continuum of activities, as it was at a research institute. And one may extrapolate that such a hybrid role of "business programmer engaged in academic teaching" characterizes not only Maksim's firm but several others, since he mentions "about ten companies or more."

Maksim's complex self-representation does not in any way contradict the fact that people from local firms are active in education also because of their need to identify and recruit competent employees. Given business specialization in complex projects, these companies need highly qualified programmers. In some cases (as with Yandex), such training is primarily provided in-house, while in Novosibirsk it is done at the university, albeit provided by industry specialists. As Maksim explains: "I can teach it only at a university. And it is only me who can do it. I've tried many times to find someone trained as I need, but the science that I need is not taught anywhere."

The described pattern is not exceptional, since there are many cases where IT firms tackle the problem of the lack of a qualified workforce through activities that contribute to the development of the IT community in general. The Yandex Data School is free and open to anyone who can pass the exams; moreover it collaborates with many Russian universities' departments related to IT, contributing to teaching and curricula design. And one does not have to be the Russian Google to adopt this attitude to programmer training—Vladivostok's IT firms, without being industry leaders, were actively involved in teaching (Masalskaya and Vasilyeva, this volume). In Vladivostok's case this spontaneous proximity between industry and education was almost destroyed by the federal government innovation policy. In the case of Tomsk and Novosibirsk the federal innovation policy has not affected the bond between IT firms and education. Moreover, local IT communities contributed to the creation of the instruments of the innovation policy and continue to shape them in such a way that these instruments have become attractive to innovative businesses.

THE SOFTWARE COMMUNITY AND STATE-PROMOTED INNOVATION

The engagement of IT firms of Novosibirsk and Tomsk in education contributes to my argument about the positive effect of the local IT community on technological development. The other achievement of the community is, at first sight, even more spectacular but requires careful examination. The companies that I study are now associated with the relative success of the local state-supported institutions aimed at promoting innovative activity. This success is assessed by official controlling authorities. However, I will show that this assessment, based on performance indicators, may be misleading. Nevertheless, the IT firms I study contribute to the proper functioning of the innovation infrastructure elements created by the state.

In 2004–5, the Russian federal government began to take a more active role in national and regional economies through its innovation and modernization policy. One of the earliest steps was the creation of special economic zones (SEZs) (OECD 2006). When the Ministry of Economic Development and Trade called for SEZ proposals, both Tomsk and Novosibirsk responded, but only Tomsk was selected. The specific SEZ that was awarded to Tomsk is a "Technical Innovation Zone," which gives companies that have resident status tax and custom advantages. Two firms from the sample I studied are SEZ residents.

Yet Novosibirsk's effort to submit a proposal was not in vain. The mobilization of both the local government and the business community eventually gave birth to a different but related project—a technopark—within the framework of a large program supervised by the Ministry of Communications and Mass Media. With the launch of the ministry program in 2006, Novosibirsk's Akademgorodok became a candidate for the location of a technopark, and in December 2007 was selected to host it. The local business community and SibAkademSoft played an active role in the program initiation (Artyushina and Chernykh 2012, 355).

The SEZ in Tomsk and the technopark in Novosibirsk are both part of large governmental programs engaged in many regions throughout Russia. Crucially, in 2014 both projects were officially recognized as the best among their counterparts. The recent report published by the Audit Chamber of the Russian Federation (Schetnaya Palata Rossiyskoy Federatsii 2015) ranked the SEZ in Tomsk as the best among all special zones of its specific type, "Technical Innovation Zones" (Schetnaya Palata 2014, 106). And again according to the Audit Chamber, the technopark in Novosibirsk is the most effective among all the technoparks created in Russia (Schetnaya Palata 2015, 67). However, it is easy to see that almost all metrics that contribute to that are related to one phenomenon: that the SEZ and technopark were able to attract profitable firms employing a significant workforce. Indeed the evaluation is based on indicators such as the revenue of the technopark's residents and also the number of employees. These indicators show that the SEZ and technopark employ a sizeable, highly skilled workforce (up to four thousand in Novosibirsk and one thousand in Tomsk) and are economically viable (218.5 million rubles in tax paid in 2012 by Tomsk SEZ residents, and 823 million rubles collected in 2014 from the residents of Novosibirsk's technopark).

The number of individuals employed by the residents of these organizations is often reported as "the quantity of created jobs." This, however, may be misleading since residents already employed most of their workforce before joining the technopark and SEZ. The taxes paid by the residents and their revenues are also metrics that do not make a distinction between the eventual positive impact of the technopark and SEZ and the economic performance of the residents that is unrelated to activities of those organizations. So there is no precise data about the effect of the technopark and SEZ on local technological development.

However, many facts support the view that these organizations are effective in fulfilling their mission, or, at least, have the potential to do so. First of all, the very fact that active and successful IT firms decided to be associated with the technopark and SEZ signifies that these instruments of the innovation policy are relevant to business needs. This is clearly a good sign, taking into account the troubled track record of many other technoparks and SEZs across Russia and, in general, the Russian tendency to design innovation policy tools in a top-down way, making them irrelevant to business needs, a problem that may in part be illustrated by Skolkovo's mixed performance (Simonova, this volume). Second, at least in Novosibirsk, IT firms are more than mere users of the technopark, but actively shape the way it works.

One of the important elements of Novosibirsk's technopark is the system of support for a new businesses, including a business incubator and a two-week acceleration program (formerly known as Summer and Winter School of Akadempark) taking place twice a year. According to one of the high-ranked managers of the technopark, the acceleration program is "unique . . . because of the size and the composition of the pool of experts, who are practitioners, not business coaches . . . but people who have learned in the school of hard knocks while building their business, and are ready to share their experience" (Petr). Indeed, managers among the techopark's residents, including those who work for IT firms that I study, volunteer as experts for the accelerator, without having such an obligation in the residence agreement. The residents also provide mentorship for startups at the techopark's incubator. According to Petr, the manager cited above, the "mentorship and the support from experts are among the reasons why people come here [to the incubator]." In general, the residents are open to dialogue with startups from the incubator: "If you [a startup] want to communicate with any manager of an Akadempark's resident, we will organize a meeting, no problem" (Petr). This readiness to help the technopark and to contribute to the development of new businesses is, at least in part, related to the general attitude toward local business. Such a situation is possible "thanks to the milieu we have here—at Akademgorodok, at Akadempark," continues Lvov, since "local firms want to develop a technological entrepreneurship milieu here." In the case of Tomsk, I have less evidence on local IT firms' engagement in the development of the SEZ. However, both SEZ residents from my sample are partners of a quite active local business incubator.

As Aleksandra Simonova has shown in her study in this volume, the top-down design of Skolkovo has led to its mismatch with the needs of innovative business, making it difficult for this costly project to become fully functional. The hackerspace Neuron, designed by entrepreneurs, fits their needs and is an example of an active and successful environment for innovative businesses. The case confirms an observation made by many scholars. Indeed, the governments that design instruments aiming at innovative entrepreneurship and technological development in a top-down manner, and without an understanding of the entrepreneurial process, fail to achieve the desired goal. These are reputed to be the two most important pitfalls of the innovation policies in numerous countries (Lerner 2009). While one does not have sufficient proof of the efficiency of innovation infrastructure in Tomsk and Novosibirsk, the very fact that successful local business are closely associated with the technopark and SEZ suggests that these innovation policy instruments have at least avoided those most frequent errors. I suggest that it would not have been possible without a local IT community sharing a particular professional ethos influenced by the Soviet past, especially the "Akademgorodok milieu" in Novosibirsk.

CONCLUSION

The existence and success of the business community observed in this chapter both confirms and questions the diagnosis that Russia's innovation capacity has received from many experts and researchers, most recently Graham (2013). Russians, particularly researchers, may be somewhat critical toward business and that hampers the country's technological development. The IT sector in Novosibirsk and Tomsk may symbolize that Russia is gradually recovering from this old posture. Indeed, many successful and internationally renowned IT firms in these cities were founded by the very same Soviet researchers whose disregard toward commercial activity is believed to hamper Russia's innovation capacity. The founders and managers of these firms take profitability seriously; they have had to adopt a way of working that is clearly distinct from what they were used to while being researchers. They also became aware of the problem Graham has described: that most of their fellow Soviet and post-Soviet scientists are unable to adopt even a tiny bit of business logic.

However, this is only part of the story. It would be misleading to present the IT community in Tomsk and Novosibirsk as the result of a successful emancipation of the former Soviet researchers from the long-lasting aversion that Russians have toward making money through technological entrepreneurship. Despite the lack of business ties with research, many IT firms' founders and employees present themselves as culturally close to the academic community. Also, emphasizing high technical skill and complex problem solving, many IT firms present these both as a business strategy and a value-driven decision, closely related to the roots of the local IT community in Soviet research institutions. For the leaders of the local IT sector, embracing business logic does not mean seeking growth at any price. Many of them explicitly refuse the logic of profit maximization and extensive growth and do not want to identify themselves as entrepreneurs, while in fact managing a successful private firm. Also, they are not very enthusiastic toward what may be called a startup or venture capital business model: high risk with a chance of huge profits.

Business leaders of the IT sectors in Tomsk and Novosibirsk do not fully adopt the attitude that some perceive as the essence of technological entrepreneurship and the main ingredient of the innovation process. However, this does not necessarily mean that IT sectors in those cities are unable to do their part in promoting the country's technological development. First, innovation and technological development do not have to be defined exclusively through successful commercialization following venture capital–prescribed high-risk business models. Second, IT firms that I portray in this chapter have a positive impact on the region's technological development even if one admits the idea that startups and venture capital are the principal sources of the latter. Indeed, the IT community that I describe is actively engaged in the training of highly skilled professionals, this engagement motivated by the community's value-driven attitude toward business and its cultural proximity to research and education. Moreover, the very same professionals took an active role in designing local instruments of innovation policy and contribute to their everyday functioning and, specifically, to the mentoring of local startups, making those instruments adapted to the needs of business, not those of bureaucrats.

By contributing to the training of highly skilled programmers and to the development of the local innovation infrastructure, IT firms in Novosibirsk and Tomsk provide the resources that are an essential prerequisite for what many experts see as a key for technological and economic development and what is a stated goal of innovation policy: a system that sustainably produces new high-technology businesses, some of them manifesting explosive growth. Surprisingly, Siberian IT professionals do this because of the very same set of values originating in the Soviet past that makes them critical toward the logic of profit maximization and the way of doing business associated with venture capital. In a way, the attitude that is supposed to hamper Russia's technological development may actually make it happen. Still, while Siberian IT firms create resources that are essential to that process, one cannot guarantee that it will indeed take place on a large scale—the Russian context is unfavorable to innovation for multiple reasons. But should we put the blame on this peculiar way of doing business that former Soviet researchers have adopted?

NOTES

1. I tested this estimation by looking at the number of users of the popular Stackoverflow website—a "question and answer site for professional and enthusiast programmers." The database of Stackoverflow users developed by our project allows us to count the number of individuals who, when establishing an account, listed Novosibirsk or Tomsk as their location. Novosibirsk hosts forty-six users and Tomsk fourteen; as expected the ratio is approximately three-to-one.
2. All interviews with IT workers were conducted in Russian and translated by the author.

REFERENCES

Artyushina, Anna, and Anna Chernykh. 2012. "Sotsial'nye 'Portrety' Tekhnologicheskikh Predprinimateley: Sluchay Novosibirska I Novosibirskoy Oblasti." Saint Petersburg: Center for Science and Technology Studies, EUSP.

Avnimelech, Gil, Martin Kenney, and Morris Teubal. 2005. "A Life Cycle Model for the Creation of National Venture Capital Industries: Comparing the US and Israeli Experiences." In *Clusters Facing Competition: The Importance of External Linkages*, edited by Elisa Giuliani, Roberta Rabellotti, and Meine Pieter Vav Dijk, 195–214. London: Ashgate.

Bychkova, Olga, and Evgeniya Popova. 2012. "Sotsial'nye 'Portrety' Tekhnologicheskikh Predprinimateley: Sluchay Tomska I Tomskoy Oblasti." Saint Petersburg: Center for Science and Technology Studies, EUSP.

Fernando, Randima. 2004. *GPU Gems: Programming Techniques, Tips and Tricks for Real-Time Graphics*. Boston: Addison-Wesley Professional.

Gerovitch, Slava. 2002. *From Newspeak to Cyberspeak: A History of Soviet Cyber-netics*. Cambridge, MA: MIT Press.

Graham, Loren. 2013. *Lonely Ideas: Can Russia Compete?* Cambridge, MA: MIT Press.

Graham, Loren R., and Irina Dezhina. 2008. *Science in the New Russia: Crisis, Aid, Reform*. Bloomington: Indiana University Press.

Ilyin, Valery, and Michail Marchenko. 2014. "Al'ma-Mater Sibirskoy Vychislitel'noy Informatiki" [Alma mater of Siberian computational informatics]. *Science in Siberia* 21, no. 2956: 4–5, 8.

Kenney, Martin. 2012. "Venture Capital Has a Role, But Do Not Forget Nice Growth Firms." In *Growth Enterprise Review 2012*, edited by Sakari Immonen, 60–72. Helsinki: MEE Publications, 20/2012, Ministry of Employment and the Economy.

Lerner, Josh. 2009. *Boulevard of Broken Dreams: Why Public Efforts to Boost Entrepreneurship and Venture Capital Have Failed and What to Do about It*. Kauffman Foundation Series on Innovation and Entrepreneurship. Princeton, NJ: Princeton University Press.

Organisation for Economic Cooperation and Development (OECD). 2006. *OECD Economic Surveys: Russian Federation*. Vol. 17. Paris: OECD.

Russoft. 2014. "Export of Russian Software Development Industry." Russoft Association. Accessed July 28, 2018. http://russoft.org/downloads/RUSSOFT_Survey_13_en.pdf.

Schetnaya Palata Rossiyskoy Federatsii (Audit Chamber of Russian Federation). 2014. "Otchet O Rezul'tatakh Kontrol'nogo Meropriyatiya 'Audit Effektivnosti Ispol'zovaniya Gosudarstvennykh Sredstv, Napravlennykh Na Sozdanie I Razvitie Osobykh Ekonomicheskikh Zon'" [Report on the audit of spendings of public money on the creation and development of special economic zones]. Accessed on July 28, 2018. http://www.ach.gov.ru/upload/iblock/388/388a2ebb6 9f74390241d6ac0e4aa82d9.pdf.

Schetnaya Palata Rossiyskoy Federatsii (Audit Chamber of Russian Federation). 2015. "Otchet O Rezul'tatakh Kontrol'nogo Meropriyatiya 'Proverka Obos-novannosti, Rezul'tativnosti I Effekt Ivnosti Ispol'zovaniya Byudzhetnykh Sredstv, Vydelennykh v 2011—2014 God Akh Na Realizatsiyu Kompleksnoy Programmy 'Sozdanie v Rossiyskoy Federatsii Tekhnoparko v v Sfere Vysokikh Tekhnologiy'" [Report on the inspection of the effectiveness of utilization of public money on the "Creation of Technoparks in Russian Federation" program in 2011–2014]. Accessed on July 28, 2018. http://www.ach.gov.ru/upload/iblock /f25/f25a17d3f36bb72bdc6214c50f9bc60d.pdf.

Tatarchenko, Ksenia. 2013. "'A House with the Window to the West': The Akademgorodok Computer Center (1958–1993)." PhD diss., Princeton University, NJ.

Yevtushenko, Nina. 2003. "Ob Odnoy Vetvi Tomskoy Kibernetiki" [On one of the branches of cybernetics in Tomsk]. *Tomsk State University Journal* 278: 43–45.

CHAPTER EIGHT

E-ESTONIA REPROGRAMMED
Nation Branding and Children Coding
Daria Savchenko

In 2014, Estonia published its "Vision of Estonian Information Society in 2020," which begins as follows:

> In the spring of 2020 the Estonian President will give an interview to the *New York Times*, citing his reasons why he is proud of Estonia's acumen in developing e-solutions that instill democratic principles to a society that has undergone fundamental technological transformation. The President will recognize the fact that the transition has not been easy for Estonia—following the realization that unmoderated anonymous internet comments, for instance, proved to be a vehicle that was ill-suited for democracy building. (Estonian Association of Information Technology and Telecommunications 2014)

This paragraph is a crude expression of the argument for Estonia's ICT agenda, using popular media discourse: the idea of technology transforming society, the belief in democratic values that can be fostered by technology, and the justification of the idea by the claim that it should be accepted by the international community; hence, the interview in the *New York Times*—a big geopolitical player—lending credence to the political and economic line that Estonia has chosen.

Since gaining its independence from the Soviet Union in 1991, Estonia has rebranded itself into e-Estonia. The country's official website—E-Estonia.com—justifies the "e-" prefix by presenting the new Estonia as a digital society with technologically advanced infrastructure, welcoming entrepreneurs and business from all over the world, while proudly boasting efficient government and forward-thinking education. According to the website, Estonians vote in elections from the comfort of their living rooms, file their income tax in just five minutes, and can sign a legally binding contract over the internet via their mobile phones. The country has an "unprecedented level of transparency and accessibility in government," safe exchange of private, governmental, and corporate data, and "a healthier, better educated population with easy access to social services" (Ministry of Economic Affairs 2015). The internet is presented as a human right of every Estonian in an ultimate "wired" nation and digital society characterized by "transparency, efficiency, and cyber-security."

The dramatic transformation of Estonia since the collapse of the Soviet Union is presented as an illustration of how information technology can enable a country, however small, to quickly catch up in the global "race." Talking about the success of Estonia, President Toomas Hendrik Ilves said: "What made this little former Soviet republic, poor, [in] many ways backwards 25 years ago, an IT power house that everyone sort of [wonders] . . . 'What are you doing?' It's because technology develops so rapidly" (VPRO Backlight 2015, 44:57–45:19). However, the emergence of the e-Estonia "brand" is not just a matter of aggressive digital infrastructure development and the skillful deployment of "cyber talk" in building a place for itself within the geopolitical landscape.

In April 2007, the Estonian government infuriated its Russian ethnic minority by relocating the Soviet war memorial—the Bronze Soldier Monument and the bodies of twelve Red Army soldiers—from Tõnismägi Square in central Tallinn to a military cemetery on the outskirts of the city. The Bronze Soldier Monument is a Soviet World War II memorial symbolizing the Soviet victory over Nazi Germany in 1945 and, thus, the "liberation" of Estonia. However, ethnic Estonians saw it differently, as a symbol of "Soviet occupation," and wanted it removed from Tallinn's city center. This led to mass protests and riots on an unprecedented scale that lasted for two nights, during which one ethnic Russian was killed.

Soon after, a series of cyberattacks (denial-of-service [DoS] attacks) shut down the government website as well as those of banks and financial services—attacks that the media and the government attributed to Russia. This event—which became known as the Bronze Night—was represented by Estonian state officials as an attack perpetrated by Russia and a fifth column of disloyal Russians living in Estonia. However, Estonia's political and military elites also successfully reframed the cyberattacks as the world's first case of cyberwar: warfare waged by one state against another in cyberspace (Kaiser 2012). Seeing this as a great and continuing threat to its security, the Estonian government took measures: First, NATO founded a cyberwarfare think tank in Estonia, to learn from the Bronze Night experience. Second, the Estonian government set up the Cyber Defence League, a network of one hundred volunteers from the cyber sector who formed a kind of territorial army ready for future strife, becoming "a unit of IT people from banks, software companies who in their spare time for one day a week are work[ing] on cyber issues" (Kingsley 2012).

Riots in the streets of Tallinn were organized against the governmental relocation action by Russian-speaking people who were born and raised in Estonia. The subsequent shutdown of websites due to malware, though attributed by some to Russia, cannot actually be attributed to the physical territory from which it came. These two events—the removal of the war memorial and the subsequent riots—were, through discursive manipulation, molded into a geopolitical landscape wherein Estonia became a cyberfrontier: a new imaginary space that became thinkable as events happening in cyberspace were interpreted using conventional geographic or, as in this case, geopolitical reference points. Furthermore, the digital is easily manipulated as it is both highly powerful in today's political discourse and at the same time not easily detectable within physical space. By virtue of these characteristics, the attacks in cyberspace and "the other" (Russia) could be blended into one discursive realm while simultaneously positioning Estonia as an imaginary new cyberfrontier.

Since then Estonia has launched a number of e-related projects, which have resonated throughout global media, such as "Programming Tigers," an initiative launched in 2012 to teach children to code beginning in the first grade. Then, in 2014, media outlets again gave wide coverage to the story of Estonia's move to the Cloud—a plan to store all state and governmental data in the Cloud, using the servers of friendly countries, in response to the ongoing threats and need to protect itself from further cyberattacks. Once again, Russia was the implicit referent for transforming Estonia into e-Estonia.

E-ESTONIA'S MISSING LEGACY

Geographically located in the west of the USSR, Soviet Estonia was—in administrative division and popular perception—put together with Lithuania and Latvia under the umbrella term of the Baltic countries (or Pribaltika), although culturally and ethnically Estonia is more related to Finland. Estonian language, along with Finnish and Karelian, belongs to the Finnic branch, whereas both Lithuanian and Latvian are Baltic languages. During my field trip, a number of officials, ethnic Estonians, talked about perceived kinship between Estonia and Finland. And a significant immigration and emigration movement takes place between these two countries (see the census on Stat.ee).

Estonia, along with the Baltic countries, was on the frontier between the West and the Soviet Union. In the popular imagination of the Soviet people, Estonia's lifestyle, beliefs, and traditions were closer to the perceived West rather than the Soviet Union, in general, and the Russian Soviet Federative Socialist Republic (RSFSR), in particular. Pribaltika was seen to be different from RSFSR as it was more "European": the streets looked different, cafés were existent and open, people were said to be more polite. The perceived divide in popular imagination between Soviet Pribaltika and, say, RSFSR grew wider as the empty shelves of the late Soviet-era food shops (with the exception of Moscow and Leningrad) were countered with relative abundancy on the shelves of Estonian stores.

Soviet Estonia, along with the rest of Pribaltika, was used as a testing ground for many high-technology enterprises and projects. Despite the fact that Estonia uses the idea of "zero legacy" both in IT and software education, there is, in fact, a Soviet Estonian background to contemporary developments; one may say that the very notion of "zero legacy" is a discursive tool used to erase Soviet history. Back in 1960, the Institute of Cybernetics of Tallinn Technical University was founded mostly due to the initiative of Nikolai Alumae, who needed computers for his research on the dynamics of thin shells (submarine hulls). Early computing in Estonia was very much defined by its Soviet military origins. The Institute of Cybernetics became a leading research center in computer science and computer applications in the Soviet Baltic region. Then, due to its proximity to the West, and the 1965 launch of the Helsinki–Tallinn ferry, Estonia became a place where Western and Eastern computer scientists held numerous meetings and conferences (Tyugu 2009, 31–33).

In 1958, when Nikita Khrushchev realized that the USSR needed more computer engineers and mathematicians with computing skills for work in the defense and space industries, several hundred young scientists were sent for reeducation to the Leningrad Technical University and Moscow Institute of Energy. Among these graduates were ten Estonians who, after their training, returned to their home country. One of these was Professor Ülo Kaasik, who introduced computer science education at the University of Tartu (Tyugu 2009, 29–30). In 1961, Kaasik together with Olaf Prinits (a mathematics professor also at the University of Tartu) started the first high school programming classes, in what is today the Hugo Treffner Gymnasium. Because the high schools did not have computers at the time, the programming classes were held at the University of Tartu's computing center. That same year, the ninth-grade student Anne Villems—now a lecturer at the Institute of Computer Science at the University of Tartu—became one of the first students to study programming at high school.

What is perhaps even more striking is that in 1965 a small school in Nõo, in southern Estonia, became the first school in the Soviet Union to have its own computing center. When the University of Tartu received a new Ural-4 computing system, they could no longer keep their old Ural-1, as it occupied too much space, and so they transferred it to the school in Nõo. As Villems recalls: "How they received the permission in Soviet time[s] to open a countryside secondary school with a computing center—I have no idea. Who organized it? Using which kind of lines?—I have no idea, but it was done, and it created the unique, only secondary school with a computing center in the Soviet Union!"[1]

Following the 1985 Soviet educational reform that introduced informatics in secondary and vocational school, Soviet Estonia initiated the production of its own computers: the Juku, Tartu, and Entel. Although the number of computers produced and delivered to schools was much lower than planned, "the number of students who got their first computing experience with Juku was in the tens of thousands—much more, much earlier and more frequently than would have been possible otherwise" (Kanger 2013, 107).

CYBERSECURITY: BETWEEN REAL THREAT AND NATION BRANDING

Since the collapse of the Soviet Union, Estonia has been the subject of many scholarly studies on nation and state building and identity formation (Kuus 2002, 2003, 2012; Noreen and Sjöstedt 2004; Smith et al. 1998; Viktorova 2006–7). Figuring even more predominantly than the eastward expansion of the European Union (EU), Estonia's state sovereignty and national identity was seen in terms of its security. Some studies focused on the transformation of "threat" and its role in international integration, emphasizing that in the political discourse of the early 1990s, Estonia was pushed toward the West by the threat it faced from the "imperial ambitions of Russia" to the east. However, in the late 1990s, Estonia's international integration (its prospective EU and NATO membership) was viewed as being determined by its cultural values and the need to foster and protect Estonia's unique culture (Kuus 2003). In addition, other possible scenarios were developed in the early 1990s whereby Estonia could function as a "neutral meeting point," "a gateway between the West and Russia." In the end, however, the government's active pursuit of NATO membership in the late 1990s put Estonia into a binary framework wherein "Estonia either integrates with the EU and NATO or falls back into the Russian sphere of influence" (Kuus 2003, 579).

A recursive feature in Estonia's political discourse is that the country sits on the frontier between the West and Russia. Samuel P. Huntington's 1999 *The Clash of Civilizations and the Remaking of World Order* was translated into Estonian, with a foreword by the now president of the Republic of Estonia, Toomas Hendrik Ilves. The main thesis of the book—being that the border between the Western and Orthodox worlds ran exactly along Estonia's Narva River—was accepted in Estonia's academic and policy circles (Kuus 2012). Hailed as "common-sense, self-evident and rigorously scientific" (Saar 1998), Huntington's argument was regularly used in political discourse, which it fit like a glove. Frontier discourse and security concerns continue to be central to Estonia's eternal anxiety and to the discourse of its political elite.

The Tiger Leap Foundation (Tiigrihüppe) was founded in 1997, borrowing its name from the Four Asian Tigers (Hong Kong, Singapore, South Korea, and Taiwan) that were then developing by leaps and bounds. The Tiger Leap Foundation was intended to help Estonia demonstrate the same kind of potential. Born in the minds of Toomas Hendrik Ilves and Jaak Aaviksoo, the minister of education at the time, the foundation was to aggressively invest in the development and expansion of computer and network infrastructures in Estonia, particularly in the education sector, bringing the internet into all classrooms and providing teacher training.

Explaining their decision to invest in the digital infrastructure, some Estonian politicians at the time said they were afraid that "Russian armies might take down the TV tower, the central radio station, or newspaper press." The internet, however, would still work, making politicians realize that "this would be a great way of keeping in touch with the world in case of emergency" (Kingsley 2012). As Linnar Viik, the man behind Estonia's internet success, put it: "It seemed then that, had someone attacked us or violated our human rights, then more than NATO tanks or McDonald's investment, Estonian independence would be better guaranteed by transparency and presence in the international media" (EUbusiness 2004).

E-stonia—A Startup Country was posted in June 2015. The video was produced by VPRO, a Dutch public broadcaster, as part of their *Backlight* series that featured current affairs and, according to their website, "balances on the edge of cinematography and journalism," focusing "on our real [globalized] world in which economies, societies, and cultures seek a new equilibrium" (CosmoLearning 2016). The video features some of Estonia's major political and business figures, including long sections of interviews with President

Toomas Hendrik Ilves. Entirely in English, the video is clearly aimed at audiences outside Estonia. It covers important milestones on Estonia's way to becoming a "cyber secure country" and the "digital frontier," and reminds viewers of the success of Skype and TransferWise and of the recently launched project of e-residency and Cloud technologies.

After mentioning that "a great neighbor [Russia] is never far behind" (32:11), the video discusses the events of the Bronze Night. The presenter is quite neutral, but the speaker, Edward Lucas, apparently choosing to present a "Western" point of view on the issue, is not. Lucas is a British journalist and the author of *The New Cold War: Putin's Russia and the Threat to the West* (2008; revised 2014) and *Deception: The Untold Story of East-West Espionage Today* (2012). A strong supporter of Cold War ideology, he is also the first e-resident of Estonia—a status specially granted to him by President Ilves for his friendship and loyalty to the state. When talking about the Bronze Soldier Monument, Lucas unequivocally comments that:

> Well, Estonia was occupied by the Soviet Union in 1940, and the Russian troops didn't leave until 1994, and so for every Estonian this is the geopolitical fact number one, that they have a neighbor who doesn't really recognize their independence, or doesn't respect their sovereignty, and menacing them with propaganda and subversion, and all sorts of other things. (32:41 – 33:01)

The conversation then moves to the subsequent DoS attacks and immediately on to the Cyber Defence League: "a network of hackers and IT specialists who act as a voluntary cyber army" (36:24) and who are meant to protect the country from cyberattacks. (Other media call them the "ponytail army.") The video shows young people (mostly men) coming to an event that resembles a convention, where two girls give them a T-shirt and ask them to step aside so that they can take a picture of them. These images were taken at the Cyber Olympiads organized at the Tallinn University of Technology, where they train and select volunteers "for the virtual front line," "the new soldiers of the front who will defend the country in case of a future cyber attack" (36:15–38:39).

DESIGNING E-ESTONIA

In the globalized world, countries are increasingly competing to be different. The global business of nation branding took off right after the end of the Cold War, with the idea that while people used to believe that nationalism formed the spirit of capitalism, it now seems that capitalism forms the spirit of nationalism. The assumption of nation branding is that nations must embrace the capitalist principles of competitiveness, growth, and profit in order to survive and thrive and provide the social consciousness that gives rise to conditions of belief and belonging (Aronczyk 2013, 128).

From Germany and Sweden to Botswana, Uganda, and Georgia, many countries have in fact used the services of consulting firms to build their "national brands" (Aronczyk 2013; Jansen 2008; Smith et al. 1998). Estonia joined this trend in 2001 when it hired Interbrand, a British consulting agency. Estonia's main incentive for brand building was its aspiration to receive EU membership and join NATO—both goals were achieved in 2004. Interbrand needed to help Estonia convey to the world its legitimacy as a European nation and its openness to world capital. To do so, one of the firm's objectives was "to help Estonia overcome the 'accident of history' that had placed the country in the East rather than the West in the minds of its interlocutors" (Aronczyk 2013, 140). "Putting Estonia on the map," as Interbrand articulated it, was a delicate exercise in spatial manipulation. It meant conceptually annexing the country to Scandinavia, Denmark, and Finland, while severing it from any connection to its Russian past (142). Even more complicated was the attempt to simultaneously place Estonia on the European side of the new cyberfrontier while also presenting it as friendly (and cybersafe) to any kind of businessperson and capital from any part of the globe, including Russia.

Carefully staged, E-Estonia.com features a video about education as a platform to prepare "digital citizens." The notion of "digital society" is still quite new for both Estonians and non-Estonians alike, and can gain meaning only by being linked to related (if equally hazy) concepts like "digital citizens." But digital citizens need to be educated and cultivated and so the website shows images and a video of very small children playing and learning with a tablet PC. How playing on a tablet translates into becoming a digital citizen or what that has to do with programming is not the question here. What matters is the staging of a "digital educational" setting to convey the idea that digital citizens are being produced, which in turn supports the broader nation-branding project. Although branded as "digital," e-Estonia still consists of people, and a country can be branded as "digital" only when its people in some way differ from those that are from "nondigital" countries. Images of small children give an idea of vitality and future-oriented thinking; add a computer to that scene and words like "tech-savvy, forward-thinking, advanced" might come to mind.

For former Soviet republics, to set themselves aside from the solidly forged Soviet identity and carve their own brand in the new geopolitical landscape was not so much a choice of cultural identity but a call urged by socioeconomic necessity (for another example of nation branding, see Kontareva, this volume). For Estonia, a small country of one million people, with the history of tensions and an uneasy relationship with Soviet authorities, situated on the then border between the EU and Russia, nation branding became the key mechanism of building the digital nation of e-Estonia.

MARKETING PROGRAMMING KIDS

Currently, Estonia's biggest challenge is skilled human resources. As the National ICT Policy Adviser Siim Sikkut states: "the country has more ideas and potential than people to carry them out." Since 1990, the population of Estonia has been on a low downward trend, losing about 15 percent of its population (about 230,000 people). In 2013, both natural increase and net migration were negative (-1,740 and -2,614, respectively) (Statistics of Estonia 2014). Though other European countries also have a negative birthrate, Estonia lacks immigration to compensate for it.

However, according to the "Information and Communication Technology Sector's Vision of Estonian Information Society in 2020"—produced in 2014 by the Estonian Association of Information Technology and Telecommunications—the ICT sector is expected to account for at least 15 percent of Estonian GDP by 2020, doubling its 2013 levels. The Ministry of Economic Affairs and Communications' "Digital Agenda 2020 for Estonia" forecasts the same figures. The Estonian government seeks to achieve these goals through the policies set forth in the "Estonian Lifelong Learning Strategy 2020," and by generally promoting careers and training in ICT while raising the quality of higher education in that field. Students, however, do not seem to be heeding the call. According to 2012 data provided by the Ministry of Education and Research, only about 20 percent of university students chose training in technology and the exact sciences, whereas 33 percent go into the social sciences, business, and law, and 13 percent into the humanities. However, between 2007 and 2012 the total number of students receiving ICT-related degrees did indeed increase by about 31 percent (from 2,992 to 3,852), but many students still drop out before graduation. Between 2008 and 2011 only about 12 percent of registered students graduated in those fields (Kori et al. 2014, 1477).

Moreover, many IT specialists go abroad, and several Estonian companies work for other countries, such as Norway or Iceland where operating costs are higher. This creates a tension between the government's policies and the companies' strategic planning. Estonian companies seek to develop a global presence, opening offices wherever they can, but this effectively reduces their investment at home—exactly the kind of investment the government needs to support its much-hyped development of the ICT sphere. Filipp Seljanko, senior program manager at Skype-Microsoft, explains:

> When you build your politics on the IT sphere, you have to realize that it is not a self-sufficient sphere. Of course investing into your own production is more demanding, that's why often they choose the easiest way. Take Nokia. When Microsoft decided to fire twelve thousand employees out of thirty-five thousand, it was a huge blow to the market of the country.... Of course politicians would always root for ICT because they are politicians, but they can't predict what will be in the economy of the country in twenty or even ten years.[2]

The government is employing "pyramid logic": in order to have a certain percentage of people entering the field, it seeks to expand the base of the pyramid starting with primary school education. Discussing the Programming Tigers project, Siim Sikkut explains: "That's why we would like to acquaint them with technology, to hook them early on, because then we have a pyramid working for us, then we have more potential people coming to study ICT, and graduate as specialists as well."

At the same time, ICT skills and programming in schools also become a type of neoliberal political tool. Currently, Estonia is one of the few countries that has such a large number of schools for such a small population: many schools are located in the countryside and others have few students. So in this situation where half of the schools could conceivably be closed due to insufficient student enrollment, programming classes are seen as the way to increase a school's competitiveness and attract students. Estonia being a small country, parents sometimes have the choice of where to enroll their children, for example, in Tallinn or in a smaller place. Ave Lauringson, ICT skills coordinator in the Ministry of Economic Affairs and Communications, provides an example of a small school in a small town called Konguta, where the teaching staff was eager to take part in Programming Tigers and attended all teacher training courses. The result was that before the school added coding to its curriculum, perhaps six or seven new students would join the first-grade class, but the year after it was added seventeen new students applied.

The dynamics of differing views on the initiative are captured in an interview with the IT industry representative Filipp Seljanko, senior program manager at Skype-Microsoft. His idea is that while looking at ICT in Estonia, it is important to understand how political the initiatives are:

Now we are told we need to invest into IT education, but this is just because a person who is in power . . . I'm talking about both the leader of the country, leader of the company, now believes in IT education. But this all can change. From outside it might seem that there is some program and strategy, but this all depends on individuals and it can all change very quickly. . . . To focus the whole economy on ICT just because this is something that they think they have been good at is not a good enough reason.[3]

Some teachers also admit that the ICT focus is a decision made by the people currently in power and that things can change when new people take the reins. That's why, as one of them said, "though I find technology exciting, I do with the students only exciting things connected with technology but [I'm] definitely not going to do any dramatic overhaul of the lesson plans, because in [the] next couple of years the curriculum can change [again]."

Just as has often been the case in other countries, technology education can be used as a crutch for problems such as teacher shortage, poor test results, and lack of enthusiasm on the part of students. Teachers, realizing that there would be job cuts as the number of students declined, thought that colleagues with fewer hours, like art or music teachers, would better secure their jobs by taking on ICT, with the resultant perception that, "we can't expect so much quality out of that." Moreover, as one of the teachers admits, there is lobbying both from the IT industry and from the government to introduce more ICT into the curriculum at the expense of other subjects, and some teachers have been complaining that the curriculum has been dumbed down.

In 2012, Estonia entered the spotlight when English-speaking media started flashing headlines such as "Guess Who's Winning the Brain Race with 100% of First Graders Learning to Code?" (O'Dell 2012), "Estonia Reprograms First Graders as Web Coders" (Finley 2012), and "Why Estonia Has Started Teaching Its First-Graders to Code" (Olson 2012). However, people in Estonia admit that the reputation is a bit unearned, as the Programming Tigers project was conceived as a pilot project and not as a mandatory part of the curriculum. Still, despite the fact that the pilot program was never available outside of a few schools, it provides very powerful rhetoric and imagery that continues to be used in media and government discourse.

While Programming Tigers is the most visible, it is only one of many IT-related initiatives in Estonian schools. Although various initiatives to teach programming to young children exist in other parts of the world, Estonia received most of the attention. This is due in part to the country's nation-branding efforts and its global promotion of good practices, which had already placed Estonia on the global map of digital innovations through e-voting, Skype, and other ICT innovations. However, it is also because, as Ave Lauringson, the cofounder of Programming Tigers, admits, Estonia took a very clever lead by saying it would teach first-graders to code—not intending to awaken worldwide interest but simply to announce the start of its pilot project—a lead that would definitely grab attention. Right after that, the Programming Tigers started getting emails and phone calls from across the globe, and the BBC set off to Estonia to make a video about "first-graders coding." A few days later, when they performed a Google Analytics analysis of their website, only Greenland, China, and some parts of Africa did not have a connection to the site; the rest of the map was green.

A TV crew in Gustaf Adolf Gymnasium in Tallinn, while making a video for a news piece on "first-graders coding," kept saying: "Show us the kids! No, no, we want much smaller students, even if they don't do anything behind the screens." The hyped-up media idea of "first-graders coding" and programming being the second literacy is something that travels extremely well in the world of political and state discourse—likely also supported by the media as it feeds into sweeping expectations that ICT will bring paradigm-shifting changes in everything, including education.

The idea that children should and are able to learn how to program a computer is by no means a new one. In the United States starting in the late 1960s, thanks to Seymour Papert, what was originally part of an instrumental application to teach mathematics (and part of a state-sponsored project with the Naval Ministry to develop the new LOGO programming language) was pushed beyond its original parameters, making LOGO a tool that would improve the way children think and solve problems (Papert 1980). Papert talked about "epistemological perestroika" and "megachange" in education, arguing that technological revolution required a revision of the definition of the human being, and that the new programming language LOGO could help children learn and relate to real life. In the Soviet Union, Andrey Ershov (1981a), who was head of the programming group in Novosibirsk Akademgorodok and an active proponent of school computer education, summarized his vision in the lecture entitled "Programming, the Second

Literacy," arguing that learning how to program is not only a necessity but a virtue that would help overcome the threat of modern society's "escapism and passivity." In his opinion, children should learn how to program in order to become active participants of the new era of technological revolution, computerization, and automation (Ershov 1981b). In France, Jean-Jacques Servan-Schreiber viewed a computer not as an instrument but as a way to multiply the capacity of each person to develop, to learn, and to create; therefore, he saw it as the main element in developing what he called *la resource humaine*, and established a special institution, CMI (Centre mondiale informatique), to realize these goals. Servan-Schreiber believed that computer literacy would help develop the mind of the French citizen, which would, in turn, help that person realize their potential and increase their skills, thereby increasing their opportunity to have a job in and contribute to tomorrow's society.

What unites these initiatives that aspire to use technology (and today's IT) in education and to suggest new education initiatives and reforms in curricula is that they employ ambitious grand-scale goals that are phrased in public discourse using rather abstract yet emotional, moving, and hence often manipulative language and images. They do this in service of a call to change the individual, who or which is often not seen as a human being but as a citizen, a unit with the potential to be employed, pay taxes, guarantee the security and well-being of the state—or, in an even more abstract sense, is seen as a "new man" that contributes to the new life of the country (Tatarchenko, this volume). Moreover, the idea of a metaphoric race between countries toward some digital future is continuously employed or implied through phrases such as being "in the vanguard of the digital economy" (Osborne 2013) or catching up to other countries that have outpaced them.

An important thing to note about the concept of "coding" or "programming," as it is used in education and political or economic discourse, is that although most people would agree that coding relates to our everyday life—as all the technologies we use today are programmable—it remains something that is hidden and can be visualized only on the computer screen. Therefore, by virtue of being both fundamental to the functioning of technologies and hidden from public view, it becomes the easiest concept to manipulate and a very powerful tool in developing technocratic discourse. Moreover, unlike similar projects in the past, today's IT technologies—in particular the internet—allow information to spread almost instantaneously, resulting in an information overload and hype that travels so fast it is almost impossible to identify the actual information, backed up by sources.

Estonia metamorphosing into e-Estonia is a story of a country reimagining itself while also advantageously turning unpredictable events into powerful chapters in a narrative of transformation. Since gaining independence in 1991, Estonia has prioritized the development of its digital infrastructure, simultaneously aiming to be more independent from and secure against Russia, while moving closer to its Scandinavian neighbors. The events of the Bronze Night revealed certain tensions within the country; tensions that did not fit the image that Estonia had hoped to promote. Still, the country managed to turn the cyberattacks to its own advantage, playing down the ethnic tensions within its population while focusing on its ability to successfully defend itself against such attacks. It then mobilized that (real or perceived) success to brand itself (despite its diminutive size) as a global resource: a cyber expert to the rest of the world.

The idea (or perhaps the "meme") of "first-graders coding" became a crucial element in Estonia's nation-branding strategy, as it not only supported the country's claim to digital excellence but also helped its citizens relate to and adopt the new image of their country as e-Estonia, doing so even against substantial evidence that undermined this image or vision: high levels of emigration, young people's low interest in university-level ICT training, and their alarming tendency to drop out of those programs. Images of smiling children playing with keyboards and the real or imaginary success of the Programming Tigers and Tiger Leap Foundation have been thus mobilized to articulate a future kind of citizenship and sociopolitical sphere while deflecting attention away from Estonia's present difficulties.

NOTES

1. Unless otherwise noted, the interviews were conducted in English.
2. The interview was conducted in Russian and translated from Russian into English by the author.
3. The interview was conducted in Russian and translated from Russian into English by the author.

REFERENCES

Aronczyk, Melissa. 2013. *Branding the Nation: The Global Business of National Identity*. New York: Oxford University Press.

CosmoLearning. 2016. VPRO Backlight profile. Accessed June 10, 2017. https://cosmolearning.org/providers/vpro-backlight-188/.

Ershov, Andrey. 1981a. "Programming, the Second Literacy." *Multiprocessors and Multiprogramming* 8, no. 1: 1–9.

Ershov, Andrey. 1981b. *Programmirovanie—vtoraia gramotnost'* [Programming, the second literacy]. Accessed July 22, 2013. Digital archive. http://ershov.iis.nsk .su/ru/second_literacy/article.

Estonian Association of Information Technology and Telecommunications. 2014. "Information and Communication Technology Sector's Vision of Estonian Information Society in 2020." Accessed March 18, 2015. https://www.itl.ee/public /files/Visioon2020_eng.pdf.

EUbusiness. 2004. "Linnar Viik—Estonia's Mr Internet." *EUbusiness.* Accessed December 15, 2013. http://www.eubusiness.com/europe/estonia/040420021538 .qhs3vusx.

Finley, Klint. 2012. "Estonia Reprograms First Graders as Web Coders." *Wired*, September 4. Accessed December 20, 2013. http://wired.com/2012/09/estonia -reprograms-first-graders-as-web-coders/.

Jansen, Sue Curry. 2008. "Designer Nations: Neo-liberal Nation Branding—Brand Estonia." *Social Identities: Journal for the Study of Race, Nation and Culture* 14, no. 1: 121–42.

Kaiser, Robert. 2012. "Estonia and the Birth of Cyberwar." Presentation abstract. Accessed February 10, 2014. http://www.helsinki.fi/aleksanteri/english/news /events/2012/tiedostot/Kaiser.pdf.

Kanger, Laur. 2013. "Domestic PC Production in the Soviet Baltic States 1977– 1992." PhD diss., University of Edinburgh.

Kingsley, Patrick. 2012. "How Tiny Estonia Stepped out of USSR's Shadow to Become an Internet Titan." *Guardian*, April 15. Accessed December 15, 2013. http://www.theguardian.com/technology/2012/apr/15/estonia-ussr-shadow -internet-titan.

Kori, Külli, Heilo Altin, Margus Pedaste, Tauno Palts, and Eno Tõnisson. 2014. "What Influences Students to Study Information and Communication Technology?" *Proceedings of INTED2014 Conference*, March 10–12, Valencia, Spain: 1477–86.

Kuus, Merje. 2002. "European Integration in Identity Narratives in Estonia: A Quest for Security." *Journal of Peace Research* 39, no. 1: 91–108.

Kuus, Merje. 2003. "Security in Flux: International Integration and the Transformation of Threat in Estonia." *Demokratizatsiya: The Journal of Post-Soviet Democratization* 11, no. 4: 573–85.

Kuus, Merje. 2012. "Banal Huntingtonianism: Civilisational Geopolitics in Estonia." In *The Return of Geopolitics in Europe?: Social Mechanisms and Foreign Policy Identity Crises*, Cambridge Studies in International Relations, no. 124, edited by Stefano Guzzini, 174–91. Cambridge: Cambridge University Press.

Ministry of Economic Affairs and Communications of Estonia. 2014. "Digital Agenda 2020 for Estonia." E-Estonia.com. Accessed July 20, 2014. http://e -estonia.com/wp-content/uploads/2014/04/Digital-Agenda-2020_Estonia _ENG.pdf.

Ministry of Economic Affairs and Communications of Estonia. 2015. "The Digital Society." E-Estonia.com. Accessed July 10, 2015. http://e-estonia.com/wp -content/uploads/2015/02/Digital-Society_ ENG.pdf.

Noreen, Erik, and Roxanna Sjöstedt. 2004. "Estonian Identity Formations and Threat Framing in the Post-Cold War Era." *Journal of Peace Research* 41: 733. https://doi.org/10.1177/0022343304047435.

O'Dell, J. 2012. "Guess Who's Winning the Brain Race with 100% of First Graders Learning to Code?" *Venturebeat*, September 4. Accessed December 20, 2013. http://venturebeat.com/2012/09/04/estonia-code-academy/.

Olson, Parmy. 2012. "Why Estonia Has Started Teaching Its First-Graders to Code." *Forbes*, September 6. Accessed July 10, 2014. http://www.forbes.com /sites/parmyolson/2012/09/06/why-estonia-has-started-teaching-its-first -graders-to-code/.

Osborne, George. 2013. "Technology: Let's Make This Country the Best." *Guardian*, September 1. Accessed May 10, 2015. http://www.theguardian.com /commentisfree/2013/sep/01/george-osborne-technology-make-britain-leader.

Papert, Seymour. 1980. *Mindstorms: Children, Computers, and Powerful Ideas.* New York: Basic Books.

Papert, Seymour. 1987. "Computer Criticism vs. Technocentric Thinking." *Educational Researcher* 16, no. 1 (January/February): 22–30. Accessed July 15, 2015. http://www.papert.org/articles/ComputerCriticismVsTechnocentric.html.

Papert, Seymour. 1994. *The Children's Machine: Rethinking School in the Age of the Computer.* New York: Basic Books.

Prinits, Olaf. 1989. "Matematiikkan opetuksen kehittyminen Virossa" [Development of mathematics instruction in Estonia]. *Dimensio* 53, no. 2: 20–23.

Saar, Jüri. 1998. "Tsivilisatsioonide kokkupõrke teooria retseptsioonist Eestis." *Akadeemia* 10, no. 7: 1512–18.

Smith, Graham, Vivien Law, Andrew Wilson, Annette Bohr, and Edward Ellworth. 1998. *Nation-Building in the Post-Soviet Borderlands: The Politics of National Identities.* Cambridge: Cambridge University Press.

Statistics of Estonia. 2014. "The Decrease in the Population Number Has Slowed Down." Statistics Estonia. Accessed July 15, 2014. http://www.stat.ee/72509.

Tatarchenko, Ksenia. 2013. "'A House with the Window to the West': The Akademgorodok Computer Center (1958–1993)." PhD diss., Princeton University, NJ.

Tyugu, Enn. 2009. "Computing and Computer Science in the Soviet Baltic Region." In *History of Nordic Computing 2: Second IFIP WG 9.7 Conference, HiNC 2007.* IFIP Advances in Information and Communication Technology, Vol. 303. Berlin: Springer.

Viktorova, Yevgenia. 2006–7. "Conflict Transformation the Estonian Way: The Estonian-Russian Border Conflict, European Integration and Shifts in Discursive Representation of the 'Other.'" *Perspectives* 27 (Winter): 44–66.

VPRO Backlight. 2015. "E-stonia - A startup country." Accessed May 10, 2016. https://www.youtube.com/watch?v=9bYpk75JnZU.

PART III

INTERLUDE
Russian Maps

CHAPTER NINE

POST-SOVIET ECOSYSTEMS OF IT

Dmitrii Zhikharevich

The preceding chapters have provided detailed analyses of specific practices and sites of the remarkably heterogeneous populations of Russian IT specialists, software engineers, computer scientists, and civic hackers. I want to complement those portraits with something rather different in content and tone: a broad geographical and chronological map of the Russian IT industry. My aim is to fill in the spaces left unmapped by the previous cases, but also to give a comprehensive picture of the key changes that have affected this industry since the collapse of the USSR, with particular attention to education, economy, policy, and migration. While all dimensions of the cultures of Russian software engineers, computer scientists, and hackers are of interest to STS scholars, the IT industry is the crux of current (and past) policy debates. That's where the brain drain hurt the most, and where the government has sought to intervene. As I sketch out a comprehensive (if still incomplete) map, I try to picture the remarkable geographical differences in the IT industry, the center-periphery relations, as well as the social background and demographic profiles of Russian computer scientists and entrepreneurs.

According to a recent ranking of the five hundred largest Russian companies, in September 2015 the total earnings of the oil sector amounted to 97.7 percent of all listed companies combined. By these standards, the Russian IT industry looks almost negligible, making up only 0.7 percent of total corporate earnings (Miledin 2015). Sometimes, however, small is beautiful.

Unlike India, Ireland, Israel, and China, Russia has not yet leveraged the opportunity represented by the growth in demand for software during the 1990s to develop a sizeable software sector (Arora and Gambardella 2005) and thus join those other countries' transformation "from underdogs to tigers." Yet, it is IT that immediately comes to mind when one thinks about how to wean Russian industry from oil and gas. High-quality human capital is another important asset Russia is famous for and, unlike the oil fields, its future seems to be somewhat more promising. Being one of the most human capital–intensive industries, IT has been repeatedly cited as a key potential area of growth for the country's economy.[1] Russian computer scientists and IT entrepreneurs have already achieved notable successes at home and abroad, and have been able to do so despite the political shakeup and the major outflow of IT cadres from the country in the 1990s.[2]

Having nurtured a considerable diversity of business models from the start, today's Russian IT industry is better organized with several important associations representing its interests before the state and a dense network of partnerships across academia, the private sector, informal learning communities, and public bodies. It coped reasonably well with the global financial crisis of 2008 and by 2013 the Russian information and communication technology (ICT) sector had more than 150,000 active companies, employing 1.3 million people, or 2.8 percent of Russia's private sector workforce. Overall, there are approximately 440,000 software developers in the country, employed in different industries (Russoft 2015a, 127).[3]

Over the last decade, Russian IT exports rose consistently, particularly software, which went from less than $1 billion in 2005 to $6 billion in 2014 (Russoft 2015b, 43), though that still amounted to about 1 percent of world ICT exports.

According to some estimates,[4] there are at least 3,200 stable export software companies in Russia, employing at least 140,000 people (mostly young)[5] in no less than fifty cities across the country (Russoft 2015a, 42). In sum, the IT industry is one of the most important reasons why it is misleading to view the Russian economy as little more than a petrol station. But it would be equally misleading to simply reduce IT to just another industry, as its influence is fundamental in both the economy and society.

PIONEERS: SOVIET IT BUSINESS BEFORE 1991

In 1989, David Yang, a fourth-year undergraduate student at the Moscow Institute of Physics and Technology specializing in general and applied physics, was studying French as a foreign language as part of his curriculum. In the cumbersome process of working with dictionaries, he first thought about user-friendly software that would make it possible to find a target word in seconds. In that same year he met Aleksandr Moskalev, who was working in the "neighboring" Institute of Microelectronics Technology and High Purity Materials of the Russian Academy of Sciences in Chernogolovka, a satellite town near Moscow that since the mid-1950s had grown into a science center for physics. No less importantly, Moskalev was equipped with an IBM PC with color display. Their plan was simple: to write the code in one month and in the following month sell a hundred copies of the electronic dictionary *Lingvo* at 100 rubles each. At the institute, Yang and Moskalev had telephone access to a wide network of some four hundred Soviet R&D organizations and assumed that at least one-fourth of them would buy at least one copy. In reality, the process took nine months and they sold only three copies, but at seven times the original price. Still, as was their initial intention, the venture remained little more than a way to make some extra money while on vacation. The idea to register the company came when Yang and Moskalev realized that the software had become well known in their initial "target market," not least due to pirate copying. While it did not seem to garner much interest from the Russian "violent entrepreneurs" (Volkov 2002a), busy in racketeering more easily understandable businesses, *Lingvo* faced the issue of property rights protection as an unintended effect of its popularity. In 1989, they founded BIT Software (renamed ABBYY in 1997), one of today's leading global text-recognition software companies.

Embarking on their venture at a high point of perestroika—a year after the law on cooperatives (1988) was passed and two years before the disintegration of the Soviet Union—Yang and Moskalev were not alone. In addition to the political rupture of 1991, this year also witnessed the first peak of "entrepreneurial potency" (see Drori, Shapira, and Ellis 2013; Stinchcombe 1965) in the history of the Russian software industry. Some contemporaneous analyses tried to explain the emergence and remarkable successes of the post-Soviet entrepreneurs by looking into the recent Soviet past (Kharkhordin 1994; Yurchak 2002). Such retroactive focus on the period before the country was exposed to capitalist markets and major foreign vendors is especially relevant to Russian software-industry pioneers.[6] One of the notable features of these early days is the immediate presence of highly science-intensive businesses,[7] whose genealogies led back to late Soviet design offices and research institutes. Some of these were compelled to shift their initial foci to accommodate the market transition, while others managed to find or invent market niches for their expertise.

In 1988, the specialized design office (SKB) Kontur was founded in Yekaterinburg as a subdivision of the Komsomol Experimental Scientific-Production Association developing CAD (computer-aided design) projects. However, it quickly became apparent that the industry was not ready for such solutions and Kontur found its niche in accounting software development, seizing the opportunities opened up by the introduction of electronic financial reporting. In 1990, the company signed its first contract with a regional dealer, and in June 1992 became the first Russian IT company to legally register property rights on its software products.[8]

At the same time, on the other side of the Ural Mountains, Aleksandr Golikov and Tetyana Yankina were developing the CAD systems for SM EVM[9] at Konstruktorskoye Biyuro Mashinostroyeniya (KBM, "design office of machine-building" in Russian), based in Kolomna, near Moscow. In 1988, Golikov made Yankina an offer to start a business. Before Yankina resigned from KBM to join Golikov (who had left to get a PhD in Leningrad), they were doing "parallel" development of their first product: the CAD system called Compass. Their business, Ascon,[10] was founded in 1989 when it received its first contract, with Leningrad Metal Plant, and several KBM colleagues joined Golikov and Yankina. Surviving the economic challenges of the 1990s—when some contracts were paid through barter exchange—the firm changed organizational forms from a "science and technology center" to a small enterprise to a limited company. Today, both Kontur and Ascon feature in the list of the largest domestic Russian IT companies.

Similar spin-offs were occurring elsewhere, sometimes as the culmination of even longer genealogies. For example, the Magnitogorsk-based company Compass Plus, which develops IT solutions for the financial industry and now has offices and sales worldwide, was founded in 1989 as the successor of the R&D institute for real-time process control and mission-critical industrial systems established in 1956. And, in 1989, the chair of engineering cybernetics at the Moscow Institute of Steel and Alloys became the parent organization for NAMIP, a company specializing in cross-industrial system integration and automation solutions. In 1993, Cognitive Technologies, one of today's leading software companies, was established by Vladimir L. Arlazarov at the Artificial Intelligence Lab of the Moscow-based Systems Analysis Institute of the Russian Academy of Sciences (RAS), inheriting the core staff and wealth of expertise accumulated since the late 1960s.[11] Some of these organizations kept their initial academic preoccupations, combining them with commercial contracts, such as the Research and Engineering Center founded by researchers from the Leningrad State Electro-Technical Institute in 1990; while others only "parented" new commercial companies, such as the chair of systemic programming at Leningrad State University, which since 1991 is the base for a group of companies called Terkom.

The first Russian IT companies were built by former colleagues from R&D institutes—as in the case of Ascon—and by former students of technical universities—as in the case of Reksoft, one of the largest Russian software development firms, established in 1991 by graduates of Saint Petersburg State University of Aerospace Instrumentation. While some companies, such as Kontur, were directly reorganized from design offices into commercial firms, thus retaining their accumulated expertise, others followed a pattern of capturing the advantages of location, where the "right" people tended to cluster, as was the case with Yang and Moskalev.[12]

It is worth noting that both trajectories were linked to the "two incredibly resilient Soviet infrastructures, the Academy of Sciences and the public education system" (Tatarchenko 2015, 39–40), to which one is compelled to add the state security services. Some of its former officers were instrumental in Russia's emerging market economy, effectively taking on the state's responsibilities of property rights protection and contract enforcement (Volkov 2002b). At the same time, their KGB colleagues trained in cryptography played a similar role in the emerging information security market. Such was the case of the Saint Petersburg–based company Infotecs (1989),[13] which provided security solutions for the Central Bank and several federal ministries; Moscow-based LAN Crypto (1991), founded by former officers of the KGB's Eighth Chief Directorate[14]; and later Kaspersky Lab (1997),[15] which seized the opportunity to enter the global information security market.

The appearance and initial successes of the software industry in post-Soviet Russia were partly due to the advantageous high-quality training received by its pioneers in science-intensive Soviet institutions. In contrast to India, for example, a country that also possessed a large stock of engineers by the beginning of the 1990s (Arora and Gambardella 2008, 11), Russian IT pioneers were not necessarily trained in computer science per se, but were nonetheless able to solve complex programming problems. Another important feature of Russia's emerging software industry was its dual orientation toward both products and services, with many companies focused on the global markets from the very beginning, or entering them as early as the second half of the 1990s. However, more mainstream business models such as software licensing/distribution and offshore programming were also important in the industry's development. Many of today's big players in the Russian IT market have distribution and dealing agreements with foreign software and hardware vendors in their early histories; interestingly, it seems that the offshoring model was adopted somewhat later, in the mid-1990s, partly due to the initial unevenness of internet development (see Kolarova et al. 2006). For example, companies that pioneered offshore development services began their operations aimed at regional markets and acted as distributors/resellers of foreign software—as was the case with Vladimir-based Inreco LAN (1989), an offshore outsourcing company that installed Novell for local networks. Others utilized the advantages of access to a large pool of skilled labor, such as INTRICE (1989) in the Siberian R&D center at Tomsk.[16]

Yet, the story of software development business pioneers is only part of the larger story of the ICT field. In the 2000s, ICT's share of Russia's GDP rose rapidly, growing 3.3 times in the period from 2000 to 2003, peaking in 2004, and stabilizing thereafter as the industry matured and became quantitatively recognizable. While Russia had an early advantage in complex software development, the structure of more mass-oriented segments of the IT market was changing: in the early 2000s, distributors of computer equipment captured the lion's share of the market, but by 2005, they were significantly pressed by companies offering a range of services from the supply of equipment and software to installation to IT infrastructure support. These changes reflected IT's increasing penetration of the broader economy. Having already acquired their computer equipment, businesses began to develop a more sophisticated view of their IT needs: IT departments within individual companies were beginning to generate their own profits, as more companies implemented computerized accounting, Enterprise Resource Planning (ERP), and information security systems; a broad range of business activities were now becoming dependent on technical support and IT consulting, thus creating demand for IT services. In fact, today's top ten positions are occupied by companies offering a full range of services, from IT consulting to IT outsourcing (Rudycheva 2014b).

The increasing sophistication of business customers and their IT-related needs occurred at the same time as IT began to enter everyday life, exemplified by the takeoff of the internet in the mid-1990s.[17] Between 1999 and 2000, as well as between 2002 and 2003, the number of Russians with internet access doubled, and during the first half of the 2000s the penetration of the internet increased more than sevenfold, jumping from 1.98 percent of the population in 2000 to 15.23 percent in 2005. Today, more than 60 percent of Russians have internet access in their homes; in 2014, Russia accounted for

3.4 percent of the world's internet users and occupied sixth place in the global rankings behind China, the US, Japan, India, and Brazil (InternetLiveStats .com, 2014). In 2012, 93 percent and 87 percent of all organizations were using PCs and the internet, respectively (HSE 2014, 15).

As the IT market grew to a sizeable share of the country's GDP in the 2000s, it attracted the attention of policy makers, who were concerned by the increasing levels of internet penetration and the rapid development of the cell telephone market. Since then, the state has emerged as an active promoter of IT industry development.

INSTITUTIONALIZING THE INDUSTRY: POLICY, STANDARDS, AND ASSOCIATIONS

The pervasiveness of the state has been cited in relation to both the history of Russian technological innovation and its current innovation policy landscape (Graham 2013; McCarthy et al. 2014). The field of IT is no exception, and in recent years the Russian government has been active in setting the policy agenda in this area, with varying degrees of success. In spite of public trust issues,[18] during the last decade and a half the Russian government, on both the federal and regional levels, has utilized different policy instruments embedded in different "political rationalities" (Rose and Miller 2010).

Initially, the state's innovation policies were concerned with such notions as "information society" and "e-government." On a practical level, this largely meant the digitization of bureaucratic procedures within the public sector. In the early 2000s, several normative acts were drafted, notably the federal bill for the legal regulation of the internet and the "Electronic Russia" federal target program (a Russian policy instrument).[19] In the same period, the government began to address the unequal access to digital technology across the country, adopting various measures from increasing the supply of PCs for schools to testing an electronic system for public procurement tenders. As part of the larger agenda of Medvedev's presidency (2008–12)—yet beginning already in the mid-2000s—the focus of policy rationale shifted to the development of IT innovations and a corresponding shift in policy instruments followed. During these years, the first Russian technoparks, business incubators,[20] and other innovation infrastructures and development agencies were established, notably the Russian Venture Company (RVC) founded in 2006,[21] and the development of the venture capital market began.[22] Nowadays the idea of import substitution seems to be framing the policy process; however, the actual measures adopted are only "loosely coupled" with organizing rationales (Rose and Miller 2010) and can differ on the federal and regional levels.[23]

Innovation is an active policy arena in Russia, and the most important players in this policy landscape are the federal ministries,[24] business associations, and development agencies (such as RVC). In recent years, they have collectively put in place several notable initiatives.[25] On the level of general industrial policy, the federal law "On Special Economic Zones" (N116 FZ) was passed in 2005, creating a new policy instrument to support selected territories that are assigned special legal status and tax and economic benefits in order to attract investors and encourage entrepreneurship, and included six special technological economic zones.[26] Another recent reform project is the federal law "On Science and the State Science and Technology Policy" (N254 FZ), passed in July 2011. For the first time, this law codified such notions as "innovation," "innovation infrastructure," "innovative project," and "innovative activity." It also outlined federal measures for support of such activities, including tax benefits, different kinds of financial measures (subsidies, grants, credits, etc.), educational support, fostering demand for innovative products, and so forth, thereby creating common ground to aid in the coordination of different parties. The new law also recognizes the presence of genuine entrepreneurial risk in innovative business, which is taken into account in the guidelines for the assessment of the efficiency of budget expenditures (RVC and E&Y 2014, 21).

In 2008–10, the Ministry of Science and Education also implemented measures to strengthen commercialization of research by granting the status of federal and national research universities to various institutions, thus opening access to a considerable amount of state funding for the creation of laboratories and innovation incubators.[27] In the same period, Law 217 FZ—meant "to be the Russian analogue of the U.S. Bayh-Dole Act"—was passed, with the intention of incentivizing universities to commercialize their basic research and, although still problematic, the law is thought to be "a major stimulus to the national research universities to create incubators for startups and to develop much more sophisticated commercialization and technology transfer capabilities" (McCarthy et al. 2014, 249–50). Finally, IT education[28] and the labor market are two policy arenas where the state is also active. Measures implemented vary from public actions to familiarize school-aged children with the basics of programming,[29] to an increase of budget-funded places in university IT specializations and the monitoring of IT cadres supply and the employment of graduates (Russoft 2015a, 144).

As the state was growing more aware of the IT industry, the late 1990s and early 2000s also witnessed the emergence of further structuring within the industry itself: the emergence of governance structures and rules of exchange, the core elements of the institutional architecture of established markets (Fligstein 2001) as exemplified by business associations[30] and standardization of skills and technologies.[31] It is worth noting that export software developers were the first to consolidate: In 1999, ten Saint Petersburg–based firms formed the "Fort-Ross" consortium, and further developments soon followed. In 2001, leading Russian IT companies created APKIT (Moscow), today considered Russia's most representative IT industry association;[32] and leading software vendors organized NSDA, following the example of India's NASSCOM, which also largely grew out of the needs of the outsourcing and export software development industry.[33] In 2004, NSDA merged with "Fort-Ross," forming Russoft,[34] the largest association of export software developers in the Commonwealth of Independent States (CIS). The fields of domestic software development[35] and hardware[36] witnessed similar developments later in the 2000s.[37] Consolidation of the industry and the establishment of a more conscious government position were followed by the development and implementation of professional standards. The policy of standards development was initiated by the president's decree of May 7, 2012, "On Measures of Realization of Government's Social Policy" (no. 597), which stipulated the development of circa eight hundred professional standards for different industries by 2015. In 2013, drafts of the first standards regulating different IT subfields,[38] developed in cooperation with APKIT, were made available for open access.

Similar to the process in other countries, Russian IT standardization is also shaped by private actors, notably the major multinational corporations (MNCs) that import their technological standards and corporate cultures and socialize Russian IT specialists. Historically, global standards served as an important coping mechanism in relation to the domestic uncertainty of Russia's offshore software developments during the 2000s;[39] nowadays they help emerging professions, like testers, to legitimize themselves (Feakins 2010). Roman Abramov (2016, 102–3) points to the emergence of "certified professionalism" in Russia: in order to legitimize their expertise, individuals tend to rely on corporate certificates and international standards, alongside or instead of their university diplomas.[40] As a result of a global process of credentials' inflation (Collins 2011), Russian technical education also suffers from quality uncertainty (Akerlof 1970);[41] hence, certificates obtained from the leading global companies like Microsoft and Oracle play an important role in recruiting processes (Abramov 2016).

EDUCATION AND TRAINING

Human capital needs infrastructures for its reproduction. As opposed to the Western countries and the US in particular, where corporate in-house training was instrumental for some of the high-tech fields like hardware, in Russia (and in the Soviet Union) the established universities have always been important training hubs, especially in physics, mathematics, and engineering (McCarthy et al. 2014, 247). Russian universities (but also high schools) still produce students who either win or score very high at world programming contests.[42] Thus, as illustrated in the preceding sections of this chapter, while some IT companies originated directly from within the universities themselves, systematic industry-academia cooperations are a more recent phenomenon.

Several Moscow- and Saint Petersburg–based universities consistently feature in the rankings of both employers' satisfaction (IT companies) and top-salaried employees,[43] as do institutions with a more explicit academic focus like the Saint Petersburg branch of the Steklov Institute of Mathematics of the Russian Academy of Sciences (RAS) and the Academic University of RAS, also based in Saint Petersburg, which offer master's-level programs in computer science. A similar pattern can also be observed in other regions: cities with strong universities[44] are typically the major hubs of training for future IT talent.[45]

While the Soviet tradition of technical education is arguably the ultimate driver behind Russia's initial successes in the global IT market, that system was not designed to fit market environments. Historically, Russian universities were not oriented toward industrial R&D and functions of applied industrial research were transferred to specialized institutions such as sectoral R&D institutes and the Academy of Sciences.[46] Loren Graham and his co-authors noted that "Russians historically have been good at invention but poor at innovation, if the latter word is correctly understood as including successful adaptation or commercialization" (McCarthy et al. 2014, 247; see also EUSP 2010; Gladarev et al. 2013; Graham 2013). While one can argue with the specifics of Graham's explanation, he and his collaborators are pointing to a real pattern. According to Russoft, more than 50 percent of IT graduates do not work in their fields of specialization because their training does not satisfy employers (on average in the whole country); Russoft analysts relate

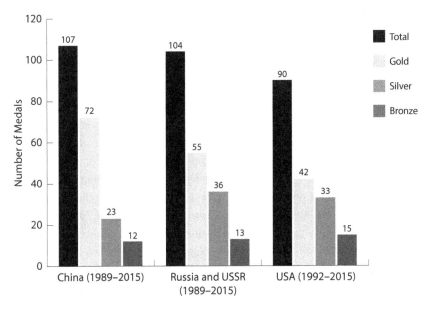

Figure 9.1. International Olympiads of Informatics Statistics. Source: http://stats
.ioinformatics.org/countries/.

this finding primarily to the generally low wages in the field of higher education (Russoft 2015a, 144).

Apart from these inherited specifics, the so-called "demographic gap"
(i.e., the decrease in birthrates during the 1990s) also affected the school
population and, in turn, the contemporary IT labor market.[47] Combined,
these institutional and demographic factors create a situation wherein the
Russian IT market suffers from an undersupply of "common" coders distinct
from the "elite" highly skilled software developers. This means that while
Russia may have an absolute advantage in high-quality, complex (and thus
expensive) programming and a cultural and spatial proximity to the West,
comparative advantage might be more important in the mass market for
standardized IT goods and services, as exemplified by India, with its large
stock of cheaper, if less skilled, software engineers (Arora and Gambardella
2005). In addition, this situation presents challenges for companies within
the domestic market as well: they must compete for the best-qualified employees, increase the overall level of skills and competencies, and provide
opportunities for alternative learning in order to remedy the quality uncertainty of mass IT education (as opposed to the universities with established
IT programs). Thus, in the 2010s, leading Russian private IT companies and

regionally oriented firms with sufficient resources established themselves as major training hubs, often in cooperation with leading universities.[48]

According to Russoft's (2015a, 148) annual member survey, about 50 percent of respondents were engaged in some form of cooperation with universities between 2008 and 2014, most frequently offering internships for students and employment for graduates of the universities they cooperated with. The intensity of industry-academia relations decreases with the size of the company. It is also contingent on business cycles and the general economic situation.[49] Thus, after the 2008 financial crisis many companies began to experiment with other forms of cooperation,[50] like creating endowed chairs and laboratories in universities, offering summer internships for students, organizing theme conferences, offering discounted or free provision of specialized software, opening free training centers for students, organizing competitions and contests, providing lectures by company employees, conducting public events, and so forth.

Last but not least are the more informal initiatives emerging at the intersection between academia and industry, like the creation of the Academy of Modern Programming in Saint Petersburg, which offers a two-year training program in software engineering aimed at complementing a formal education in computer science and providing students with opportunities to practice these skills.[51] It was followed by the Computer Science Club in Saint Petersburg,[52] which organizes free public lecture series on various issues of contemporary computer science,[53] and the Yandex Data School (established in 2007), which offers specialized computer science courses on a free and competitive basis.[54] In 2011, these two organizations, in cooperation with several other institutions, opened the Computer Science Center, which offers two- and three-year courses in computer science, data mining, and software engineering for students and graduates of technical universities. The placement is also free and competitive.[55]

CENTER-PERIPHERY RELATIONS IN THE RUSSIAN IT BUSINESS

In Russia, the center-periphery relations affect the distribution of IT competences and capabilities. Russian regional inequality is significantly shaped by spatial and administrative factors (Zubarevich 2006, 113–16; Zubarevich and Safronov 2011),[56] and partly contingent on the ways in which Russian regions were integrated into the global economy in the 1990s, including the IT market.[57] The latter process moves at a different pace in different regions, being most intense in the dozen largest cities with considerably younger and more educated populations. This configuration of inequality produces hierarchies centered around regional capitals that concentrate both the local labor force and effective consumer demand (due more to their central administrative status than to population size), with higher concentration effects in Moscow and Saint Petersburg, "cities of federal importance" that enjoy the advantages of centrality not only in their respective regions but in the country as a whole.[58] This specific geography intersects with the distributed character of IT business, with the units of its value chain (headquarters, remote development centers, trade and marketing offices, etc.) dispersed throughout these various locations.

In the late 1980s and early 1990s, new IT ventures emerged around Moscow and Saint Petersburg and in the large urban and scientific centers of Yekaterinburg and Perm in the Urals, Novosibirsk and Tomsk in Siberia, and Voronezh and Nizhniy Novgorod in central Russia; some of these cities would come to host champions of the Russian IT industry. However, this geography changed yet again as Russian and foreign companies opened remote development centers in other regions.

The dominance of Moscow and Saint Petersburg is evident in terms of both their shares[59] of the organizational population of Russian IT companies and its density[60] in their federal districts.[61] The two cities also excessively dominate their regions, with around 70 percent of ICT companies located there; however, this pattern is less visible in the Urals, with Yekaterinburg holding a 47 percent share, and in the Volga and Siberian districts no single city has a higher concentration than 30 percent of its regional companies (with Novosibirsk at 29 percent of Siberian ICT firms; based on the data from HSE 2014, 88). Thus, even if every federal district has a center[62]—usually a city with a strong university, more than a million inhabitants, and the densest IT organizational population—the degree of centralization varies considerably, with Moscow and Saint Petersburg home to almost one and a half times more regional firms than the next densest regional center, Yekaterinburg.[63] Similar patterns are discernable in regard to IT labor market size.[64]

Distribution of software developers over the major cities is as follows:[65]

Moscow	35%
Saint Petersburg	15%
Yekaterinburg	5.2%
Novosibirsk	5%
Nizhniy Novgorod	2.5%
Kazan	2.4%
Voronezh	1.2%

In 2014, 76 percent of Russian IT "industry champions" were Moscow-based, with 9 percent coming from Saint Petersburg, 4 percent from Yekaterinburg, and 2 percent each from Kazan and Perm (CNews 2015).[66] Moscow is predictably at the top in terms of financial success as well, with 2014 industry earnings estimated at 866.38 million rubles; moreover, seventeen of the twenty fastest-growing IT firms were Moscow-based, with only two in Saint Petersburg and one in Yekaterinburg (CNews Analytics 2015c). Thus, seen from the financial perspective, the IT industry follows the overall national center-periphery pattern. Moscow is the financial and political center of Russian capitalism, somewhat resembling Fernand Braudel's (2002) image of the central city dominating the entire world economy, the location of the "commanding heights," and the corporate headquarters of capital accumulation.[67] Because of the close proximity to the federal authorities and availability of financial resources, particularly important for emerging growth firms, many regional IT projects are contracted in Moscow, and in 2014 the city was "thought to absorb up to 25% of IT spending in Russia" (PMR 2014). A similar center-periphery pattern emerges in terms of salary distribution: average salaries in Saint Petersburg are around 30 percent less than in Moscow, 40–50 percent less in Novosibirsk and Yekaterinburg (Russoft 2015a, 141–42).

The data on the largest IT firms—while generally providing a fair picture of the industry—does include major legal entities (such as groups of companies) and firms that are headquartered in Moscow in order to take advantage of the capital's "proximity effects," even if the most important units in their value chains are located elsewhere. A slightly more nuanced picture emerges if one looks at the software development industry alone, excluding holdings, but also distributors, hardware, and IT service industries.[68] The concentration effect is observable here too, as Moscow absorbs 60 percent of the largest software developers. However, while among the companies with turnover above $1 billion it faces competition only from the Novosibirsk-based Center of Financial Technologies, it is less represented among firms with turnovers between $50–500 million, and among the smaller ones (with less than $50 million) Saint Petersburg has the highest number of companies;[69] in this latter category Yekaterinburg, Kazan,[70] and Perm also feature prominently. Moreover, many Russian and foreign software firms have remote development centers scattered across the country. Novosibirsk and Tomsk, although less successful in nurturing giant firms, have been popular destinations for development centers since the 1990s. Having hosted some of the early IT ventures, Voronezh and Nizhniy Novgorod later established themselves as important locations for software development, as did Rostov-on-Don, Samara, Saratov, Omsk, and Vladivostok.[71]

IMMIGRATION AND BRAIN DRAIN

Despite the complex history behind and uneven distribution of communities and infrastructures across the Russian territory, mostly clustering around the large urban centers, learning to code or pursuing a degree in a technical field has been an important structural opening for many people in Russia who looked to change their position within the domestic social structure, and perhaps also might hope to find a better future for themselves outside Russia.

In the late 1980s, the term "brain drain" appeared in the public discourse concerning the emigration of scientists from the USSR (Agamova and Allahverdjan 2007, 108). At the beginning of the 1990s, the scale of emigration dramatically increased and again began to receive public attention (Gokhberg and Nekipelova 2001, 177).[72] However, measuring emigration was complicated by several factors, which still make it difficult to broadly assess and more specifically to get isolated numbers for scientists and engineers who left the country.[73] The available data allows only for outlining the major emigration waves, of which the IT specialists are likely to be a part.[74]

The first of these "waves" might be better understood as a peak in the last "long wave" of Soviet emigration during the Cold War era.[75] Before the policy liberalization of the late 1980s and 1990s, Soviet emigration was restricted to ethnic minorities (essentially Jews, Germans, Armenians, and Greeks), who were allowed to leave for purposes of family reunification (Dietz 2000). The first major outflow of scientists and engineers from the USSR was part of this "ethnic migration" that began in the 1960s and continued into the early 1980s, when many Soviet scientists and engineers migrated to the US, Israel, and other countries with strong diasporas, notably Germany (Agamova and Allahverdjan 2007, 136). This wave was mostly shaped by external events[76] and reached its peak in 1979.

By contrast, the second major wave of highly skilled migration from the USSR was internally driven and started in the period of perestroika. Many factors were at play: the easing of the political climate; growing interest for Russian scientists abroad; the increasing openness of the Russian science and technology system to international cooperation; new laws;[77] and, in the 1990s, the worsening social and economic conditions of the disintegrating

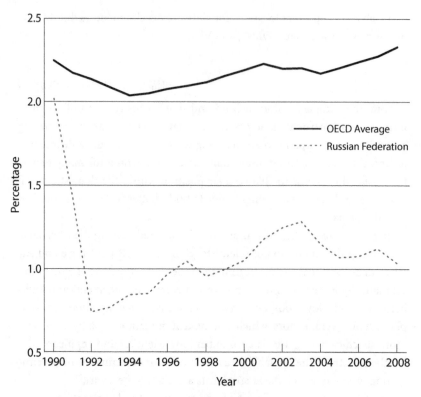

Figure 9.2. Russian Federation—Gross Expenditure on R&D as a Percentage of GDP, 1990–2008. Source: OECD, Main Science and Technology Indicators database, May 2010, http://dx.doi.org/10.1787/888932334830.

Soviet Union, including the drastic decline of R&D spending that fell from 3.5 percent of GDP in the late 1980s in the USSR to about 1 percent in today's Russia, below China (1.3 percent), the US, Korea, and Japan (2–3 percent each), Finland (4 percent), and Israel (5 percent) (Popov 2014, 158).

During this second wave, Germany, the US, and Israel continued to be the most important destinations. Emigration to Israel peaked around 1990–91 (Denisenko 2012), contributing significantly to the evolution of its high-tech industry (Drori, Shapira, and Ellis 2013), while Germany retained its status as the most important destination from 1990 to 1999.[78] The same pattern holds true for Russia:[79] of all 1,079,226 persons[80] who obtained permission to go abroad for permanent residence in the period 1990–2000, approximately 57 percent (618,730) went to Germany, 25 percent (271,057) to Israel, and 11 percent (122,289) to the US, thus leaving less than 10 percent to cover emigration to other countries. Most of the emigrants were adults (70 percent),[81] and about half were employed (see table 1 in Gokhberg and Nekipelova 2001, 179). Overall, various data sources converge on the list of the major receiving countries for the period from the late 1980s through 2000: the US, Germany, and Israel feature most prominently, while Canada and inland emerge as important migration destinations toward the end of the decade (Denisenko 2002; Zayonchkovskaya 2001). Another significant trend is the decrease of the share of migrants leaving large urban centers such as Moscow and Saint Petersburg, and a corresponding increase in the share of those coming from the Russian "hinterland."[82] Finally, an important aspect of the first decade of post-Soviet emigration is its "ethnic normalization" in the sense of getting more evenly distributed across ethnic categories, tending to reflect the actual ethnic composition of the Russian population.[83]

In the period 1992–2000 an average of 8.9 percent of emigrants from Russia had been employed in the science and technology and education sectors,[84] and during the period 1989–2000, 20,200 people employed in the category of "science and scientific services" (including not only researchers but also staff and other sector employees) left Russia.[85] Due to insufficient and/or insufficiently precise categorizations, it is only possible to roughly assess the minimal scale of permanent emigration of scientists and researchers per se, which is estimated at a yearly average of 3,500–4,000 during 1989–2002 (Agamova and Allahverdjan 2007, 111–13). However, foreign exchanges and engagements were more important than permanent emigration,[86] since most scholars went abroad temporarily and on contract (Agamova and Allahverdjan 2007, 111–12), but also mostly to these same emigration destinations. The Center for Science and Research Statistics' (CSRS) 1997–98 survey of scholars working in the Academy of Sciences, universities, and industrial R&D who were abroad temporarily, shows that most of the researchers were members of academic institutes, while those working in universities experienced the most intense movements and exchanges.[87]

Most Russian researchers went to OECD countries and most of them were natural scientists, notably biologists and physicists, with a negligible percentage of engineers, despite their overrepresentation in the domestic stock of researchers (Gokhberg and Nekipelova 2001, 182). The researchers employed abroad were predominantly middle-aged males and possessed much higher qualifications than the average Russian R&D personnel at the time.[88]

While it is impossible to account for the exact number of software developers who were part of the post-Soviet wave, their largest outflow was observed from the early 1990s until the mid-2000s. However, the increase

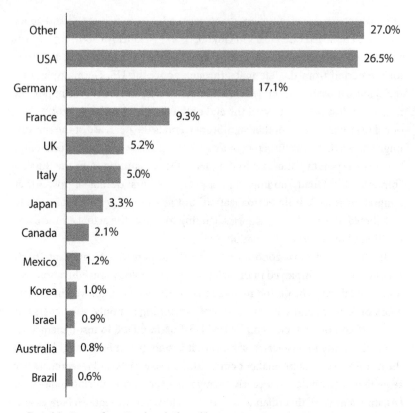

Figure 9.3. Researchers Employed Abroad by Recipient Country, Percentage, 1997–1998. Source: CSRS (Gokhberg and Nekipelova 2001, 183). The "other" category should be the former Soviet countries.

in salaries evidenced between 2005 and 2007 helped change this trend (Russoft 2015a, 127–44), so that migration no longer affects the IT labor market in the same way it did ten to fifteen years ago (Russoft 2014, 94).[89] In general, it seems fair to assume that outflows of IT specialists are associated with salary fluctuations, at least for the period leading up to the mid-2000s, as well as such external events as the increase in H-1B visa quotas in the US or the availability of relatively simple procedures of naturalization for programmers in neighboring countries, such as Finland (Russoft 2010). In the absence of systematically collected data on contemporary Russian IT specialists' motivations to emigrate—with the exception of some polling conducted by human resource agencies[90]—the above-mentioned factors combined with an individual's level of foreign-language competence could be treated as enabling emigration.

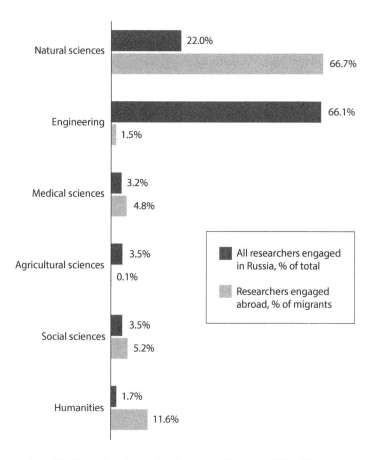

Figure 9.4. Researchers Engaged in Russia and Abroad, by Field of Science and Technology, Percentage of Total, 1997–1998. Source: CSRS (Gokhberg and Nekipelova 2001, 183).

In terms of desirable migration destinations, today's Russian IT specialists typically look to the US and Western Europe, in this sense being not much different from their compatriots engaged in different professions and occupations. Among Russians, generally not eager to emigrate,[91] for those who are considering emigration for permanent residence the most desirable receiving countries remain Germany, the US, France, Italy, the UK, and Canada, sometime joined by Nordic countries such as Finland and Sweden.[92] This list closely matches the potential directions of contemporary IT migration, even though the latter is more inclined to look for Anglo-Saxon destinations.

Top migration destinations being considered by Russian IT specialists are:[93]

US	2.7%
UK	1.8%
Canada	1.7%
Germany	1.1%
Australia	1.0%
Netherlands	0.9%
Spain	0.9%
Belarus	0.9%
Sweden	0.9%
Switzerland and Italy	0.8%

Overall, while the development of ICT may well have signaled "the end of distance" (Kogut 2003, 2), one could argue that rather than eradicating the IT specialists' need for movement it significantly diversified their mobility. Similarly to its effect on the public sphere, where IT enabled new forms of "voice," it has also opened up new channels for "exit." The scope of this diversity may be better exemplified by two contrasting cases, both notably having their roots in the Indian software development industry: one could argue that the multiplicity of choices and forms of mobility of today's IT specialists spans from "virtual migration" (Aneesh 2006), where pieces of code travel from their producers, to "body shopping" (Xiang 2007), whereby the allocation of skills is mediated by the allocation of bodies. Both models serve to sustain the infamous flexibility of the IT labor market and possibly transcend (or articulate anew) the old Marxian distinction between the formal and the real subsumption of labor by capital. However, there is a space between these two extremes, in which an IT specialist or a web developer need not go to a traditional office, but may leave Russia for the far-off shores of Thailand utilizing the flexibility of a remote working regime. Travelable skills may indeed enable their possessors to travel as well, as is the case with intercorporate movements, be it Russian companies opening foreign offices (e.g., JetBrains) or the RCS changing countries while affiliated with a foreign firm.

In sum, post-Soviet migration has become more uniform in terms of sociodemographic characteristics of migrants, and more related to economic motivations, as is the case with much of the world's movements (Collier 2014). That applies to the IT specialists as well, whose diverse forms and channels of mobility have gradually supplanted the narrower vision of "brain drain," causing the government to think about ways of benefitting from as well as exercising influence over its highly skilled pool of expatriates.[94] In fact, it seems that the term "brain drain," having entered the late

Soviet policy discourse in the 1980s, never fully matched the actual migration situation, since the public has always expected it to be worse than it was. As one of the early insider observers argued back in 1995, the post-Soviet scientific and student emigrants' diaspora is probably neither a diaspora nor an emigration (Derluguian 1995). Most of these people, as opposed to those who left the Soviet Union with an intention never to return, can be described as "academic cossaks," that is, relatively young people who decided to stick with academic preoccupations and aspired for a professional recognition, rather than trying to enter politics or business. Under conditions of state disintegration and vanishing opportunities for making a living within academia, they left for abroad without compromising their academic ambitions to explore transnational career openings. However, increased competition, cultural ties, and prospects for domestic social stabilization might well bring them home after some time abroad, depending on the degree of success and professional recognition cycles. Thus, what at first presented itself as "brain drain" might be just the first phase of a longer movement of "brain circulation," whereby Russian brains have not been flying away forever, but rather profitably loaned. Given the travelability of the IT specialists and the fact that post-Soviet emigrants are much less committed to leaving the country forever, but rather looking for better living conditions, the IT "brain drain" is not an unfixable curse. The experience of other developed countries shows, however, that to make this more optimistic vision true would require changes in both domestic policy and politics (Saxenian 2006). The chapters in the following section will analyze distinct scenarios of IT specialists' mobility to show both their variability and their specific roots in the Russian contexts.

NOTES

I want to thank Liliia Zemnukhova and Alina Kontareva, who read the early draft of this chapter and provided generous comments.

1. One of the most recent pronouncements comes from current President Putin, who during the Saint Petersburg Economic Forum held in June 2017 once again resumed the discussion of the importance of IT and digital technologies for the Russian economy. He mentioned various supporting measures for the IT industry to be implemented by the federal state, including support for those companies that trigger cross-industrial improvements (e.g., inter alia, data mining, artificial intelligence, neuro- and augmented-reality technologies), increases in educational placements in the field of IT, funding for universities and startups, as well as improving the digital literacy of the population (RIA News 2017a).

Putin's apparent passion for high-tech was commented upon by First Deputy Prime Minister Igor Shuvalov, who told the press that the president is eager to discuss new technologies and the prospects of digitization of the economy until very late in the night. In an ironical twist, Shuvalov used the Russian verb *zabolet'*: in that context signifying one's deep involvement in something, literally it translates as "being sick"—in Putin's case, sick with new technologies and digital economy (RIA News 2017b).

2. To list just a few, Kaspersky (founded in 1997) and ABBYY (1989) successfully entered the global markets in security and language processing software; and Yandex (founded in 1997 and established as a company in 2000) and Vkontakte (2006) seized the opportunity to become leading search engine and social network providers in the domestic and Commonwealth of Independent States (CIS) markets.

3. The fact that the Russian IT specialist community does not fully overlap with the IT industry has been a notorious problem for analysts. In 2005, the RAND Corporation observed that "much of Russia's IT talent resides not in information technology and services firms but in the IT departments of companies," as opposed to the West, where "organizations seeking IT solutions typically purchase standardized, off-the-shelf products and obtain systems-integration support from an outside consultant. Russian firms typically use in-house IT departments to design, develop, and integrate customized IT solutions by themselves" (Peterson 2005, 14).

4. Russoft, Export Software Development Industry Association. See (Russoft 2015a, 51).

5. In 2008, 54 percent of Russian IT specialists were twenty-six to thirty-five years old and 31 percent were younger than twenty-five; 82 percent were male, 73 percent with higher education, 43 percent with basic English skills, and 8 percent fluent (Zemnukhova 2013, 88). In 2012, around 70 percent of those with education in the IT sector were employed in ICT (HSE 2014, 224).

6. Major foreign vendors included IBM, Sun, Microsoft, and Oracle, among others. Well-educated and ambitious people became entrepreneurs and started to build their own IT companies.

7. For example: IT solutions for medical technologies, computational fluid dynamics, speech recognition, and modal biometry.

8. See the official history (SKB Kontur 2015). The legal complexities of post-Soviet transition cannot be addressed here. Suffice it to say that before the first post-Soviet copyright law in the Russian Federation was established in 1993, the effective legal basis of innovative and creative activities had been parts IV (copyright) and V (patents and inventions) of the Fundamentals of the Civil Legislation, passed in March 1991 by the Supreme Soviet of the USSR, shortly before the latter's disintegration, and scheduled to enter into force in 1992.

9. SM EVM was the general name for several types of Soviet and Comecon minicomputers produced in the 1970s and 1980s. Production began in 1975.

10. Avtomatizirovannaĩa Sistema Konstruirovaniĩa (Automated System of Design).

11. Arlazarov (b. 1939) is a distinguished Russian mathematician and one of the inventors of the Method of Four Russians, famous for his work on the development of winning computer chess programs (ITEP and Kaissa) in the 1960s and 1970s, database management systems, and academic work in systemic programming, artificial intelligence, and game theory.

12. In sum, as Ksenia Tatarchenko observes in this volume, "a half century's worth of Soviet experience with computing did not just disappear; instead, important continuities exist across the 1991 fault line." However, the way these continuities played out after 1991 may be somewhat more complicated than the stories of entrepreneurial individuals converting their skills and "capitals" (cf. Bourdieu 1986) acquired during the Soviet time into opportunities within a market economy. As some of the cases discussed above demonstrate, organizations, and not only individuals, reproduced themselves as the bearers of different kinds of "capital," including expertise, routines, habits of working, etc.

13. According to the official history of the company (Infotecs 2015).

14. The Eighth Chief Directorate was responsible for protection of government communications, cryptologic intelligence, and information security.

15. Yevgeny Kaspersky graduated from the fourth (technical) faculty of the KGB Higher School—which is today called the Institute of Cryptography, Telecommunications, and Computer Science of the Academy of the Federal Security Service of Russia—where he was trained in applied mathematics and cryptography.

16. On Siberian software development, see Indukaev, this volume.

17. This process has been highly uneven, reflecting center-periphery relations within the country and their complex overlaps with the geography of IT activities (see the section of this chapter titled "Center-Periphery Relations in the Russian IT Business"). Both the FIDO network (which has existed in the USSR since 1990) and the internet were initially concentrated around universities and scientific centers and used by students, academics, and technical amateurs for their communications. The first commercial networks appeared in the first half of the 1990s and offered services exclusively to the financial industry. In 1994–95, major Russian networks acquired access to the internet and attention shifted from banks to individuals (Kolarova et al. 2006, 876). Nineteen ninety-four—the year the web browser Netscape launched—marked the "explosion of the Internet onto the business and cultural scene" (Kogut 2003, 2). This same year, the ".ru" domain was registered and the first www.1-9-9-4.ru site appeared in that domain zone, consisting of a gathering of links to other web resources related to Russia. The creation of the first Russian web search engines—Rambler (1996) and Yandex (1997)—marked the beginning of the consumer internet in Russia. Initially concentrated in Moscow and Saint Petersburg only, since 1998 the World Wide Web expanded into the largest cities (with a population of one million and above), reaching the cities with fifty thousand inhabitants in 2000 (Zubarevich 2002, 99) and becoming accessible en masse. Since then, while being somewhat step-like, the figures of internet users and percentage of population connected in Russia demonstrate a steady rise over the last decade and a half (Kolarova et al. 2006, 876).

18. Beyond the issue of a general lack of trust vis-à-vis public authorities and its impact on Russian innovation activities, many key positions in the innovation development agencies are occupied by members of close-knit networks of Russian ruling elites. Suffice it to say that while having been generally positive about the Skolkovo project, back in 2011, shortly after its inception most Russians associated it with the names of Medvedev (6.9 percent) and Putin (5.7 percent), as well as some other prominent members of the country's politico-economic elite who kept their positions since the 1990s: Anatoly Chubais, one of the architects of Yeltsin's privatization and currently the head of the Russian Nanotechnology Corporation (2.1 percent), and the "oligarchs" Viktor Vekselberg (0.4 percent) and Mikhail Prokhorov (0.9 percent). The only exception is Zhores Alferov (1.5 percent), the Nobel Prize laureate in physics (2000) and a visible member of the State Duma (Russian Parliament) (see VCIOM 2011).
19. Among other legislative initiatives, the strategy of "e-government development until 2010" was adopted. Various other projects of informatization and technical upgrades of public services were discussed under the framework of "national projects."
20. The number of functioning business incubators is between one and two hundred, and between eighty and ninety technoparks exist in Russia, mostly in the Central and Northwestern federal districts (RVC and E&Y 2014, 3).
21. The RVC functions as an umbrella foundation (a "foundation of foundations") and a development institute aimed at the creation of a coordinated venture capital market. Other notable entities include: Rusnano (est. 2007) in nanotechnology; Russian Technologies State Corporation (2007) in military technologies; and the Russian Direct Investment Fund (2011) to complement private equity financing. However, it has been observed that their actions are not well coordinated and the agencies have overlapping responsibilities, which leads to internal competition for funding (McCarthy et al. 2014, 249).
22. Including business angels and other segments investing in companies at different growth stages. However, risk aversion and the lack of an adequate legal and tax base impede the development of real venture capital operations, incentivizing sale-exit strategies instead of the entrance into public markets (McCarthy et al. 2014, 251). In Russia, as well as in much of Europe, no strict demarcation is drawn between private equity and "proper" venture capital (Cetindamar 2003, 3).
23. For example, from a regional perspective, Kazan, Kaluga, Stavropol, and Perm outscore Moscow in terms of "innovation policy quality," measured, inter alia, by strategic planning programs adopted and implemented by the regional governments (see HSE 2014, 50).
24. Ministry of Communications, Ministry of Economic Development, and Ministry of Science and Education.
25. Key field-specific documents governing the policy process are: "Federal Strategies of Innovation Development of Russian Federation until 2020"; "IT Industry Development of Russian Federation in 2014–2020"; and a corresponding roadmap entitled "Russia's Science and Technology Development Forecast until 2030." In accordance with the Strategy of Innovation Development 2020, several sub-

programs were developed and a system of development institutes put in place, including Skolkovo (2010), Association of Innovative Regions of Russia (2011), WEB-Innovations Foundation (2011), Russian Foundation of Direct Investments (2011), Industrial Development Foundation (2014), and ESKAR Inc. (2014). In addition, thirty-five technological platforms according to the technological development priorities were declared in the "Federal Target Programme on Priority R&D 2014–2020" (RVC and E&Y 2014, 32–34).

26. These are located in Dubna, Zelenograd (former Soviet *naukograds*, satellite cities of Moscow with established R&D capabilities), Saint Petersburg, Tomsk (one of the largest university cities in western Siberia), and Kazan (Innopolis), aimed, inter alia, at IT development. However, as Alina Kontareva shows in this volume for the case of Kazan, regional policy initiatives designed to promote innovation ecologies might be less connected to modernizing economic visions than to the political logic of keeping highly heterogeneous semiperipheral regions under central control. In that respect, IT innovations may be seen as "a safe, legitimate, and publicly approved means for asserting the presence of the state in volatile regions," the efficiency of which is to be assessed by political, and not economic, calculations.

27. In 2008, the Saint Petersburg and Moscow State Universities were awarded this designation by presidential decree, and in 2009 and 2010—through two competitive processes—another twenty-seven were selected (McCarthy et al. 2014, 250).

28. See next section for a more detailed discussion.

29. In December 2014, the Federal Ministries of Education and Science and Communications and leading IT companies organized the "Code Hour"—a public action. It encompassed more than seven million children from thirty-five thousand schools all across the country. The companies 1C, ABBYY, Mail.ru Group, and Yandex are also cooperating with federal ministries and regional educational authorities in programs to popularize programming and IT.

30. As some insider observers have noted, the processes of industry consolidation were more active in the regions where smaller companies joined together to bid for contracts, and more complicated in Moscow, where large companies were facing difficulties in reaching common ground (Kolesov 2004).

31. Neil Fligstein (2001, 34) defines governance structures as "legal and normative rules by which firms structure themselves and their relations to competitors," helping to stabilize those relations. Governance structures include different forms of organization, such as vertically integrated firms, networks, associations, etc. Rules of exchange "define who can transact with whom and the conditions under which transactions are carried out," encompassing, inter alia, the rules regarding "weights, common standards, shipping, billing, insurance, the exchange of money . . . and the enforcement of contracts," but also "health and safety standards of products and standardization of products more generally" (34–35).

32. Russian Information and Computer Industry Association (APKIT). By many accounts, APKIT members control up to 70 percent of the official market. APKIT acts as an umbrella organization and represents the industry's interests before the

state, cooperating with the Russian Union of Industrialists and Entrepreneurs, OPORA (Russian Nongovernmental Association of Small and Medium-Size Businesses), other industry associations, and Chambers of Commerce, among others.

33. National Software Development Association, the first major business association of software developers, was established in Moscow in 2001 and renamed Russoft in 2002.

34. Russoft promotes Russian and CIS software businesses in foreign markets and lobbies their interests domestically. For example, they lobby tax benefits for software development companies and support active relationships with the Federal Ministries of Economic Development and Communications. Russoft is also a part of APKIT, where it plays the role of Software Development and Export Committee.

35. In 2009, another association of software developers was formed: the Association of Software Product Developers "Domestic Soft" (ARPP), focusing on the developers of applied software (antivirus, linguistic, complex automatization systems, etc.) and promoting software development in the national and regional systems of division of labor as well as IT-enabled development of the social and cultural spheres.

36. In 2007, out of the initiative of twenty-five leading companies, the Association of Producers of Electronic Equipment and Devices (APEAP, АПЭАП) was formed in Moscow, uniting more than forty industrial enterprises and educational institutions in the Russian field of electronics. In 2009, an Association for Open Software was formed in Russia. Suffering from an interorganizational conflict in 2011, when many members left, some to join the National Technological Platform, it is now in a state of gradual renewal.

37. As of yet, no comparable developments occurred on the other side of industrial conflict, besides several attempts to consolidate IT workers into unions (see Nazarov 2013).

38. Among these were: database administration, software architecture, IT technologies and product management, software development, system analysis, information systems development and management, testing, and others (Russoft 2015a, 146).

39. In the early 2000s, this was the case with Saint Petersburg offshore software development firms, which were not embedded in long-standing interfirm networks of partners and used standards. "A boundary of, and entry to, the open market; a qualification of quality through knowledge of international practices, confirmation of current practices, and a template for instantiating quality within firms (even if the verification procedures of official certification are understood to be sometimes fallible)" (Feakins 2007, 1904; see also Feakins 2010).

40. As "a global trend embracing all groups of programmers and technical specialists in Russia and abroad," it finds support among many Russian IT sector employees (Abramov 2016, 103).

41. With the exception of several leading universities.

42. See figure 9.1 for statistics related to the International Olympiad in Informatics (IOI), the annual competitive programming contest for secondary school stu-

dents held since 1989. Five Russian names feature among the thirty-six multiple winners of the IOI in its "hall of fame" (International Olympiad in Informatics 2015). Over decades, Russian universities have consistently featured in the prize tables of the world's major programming contests. In 1999–2015, fourteen Russian universities feature in the prize tables of ACM ICPC, among them Saint Petersburg National Research University of IT, Mechanics and Optics (ITMO) winning thirteen prize places during the entire sixteen-year period, slightly outscoring Moscow State University (twelve), Saint Petersburg State University (ten), and Saratov State University (seven) (data selected from Russoft 2015a, 152). At the high school level, the notable names include the Kolvogorov physics and mathematics boarding school at Moscow State University, the Academic Gymnasium at Saint Petersburg State University, physics and mathematics school named after Mikhail Alekseevich Lavrentyev at Novosibirsk State University, specialized boarding school at Ural State University, lycees at MIPHI, physical-technical school at the Academic University of RAS, mathematical lycees 239 and 30 in Saint Petersburg, and lycees 444 and 1580 at Bauman State Technical University in Moscow. These specialized schools were (and still are) preparing the best pupils to enter the best universities. Moreover, the schools were complemented by informal learning "circles," special popular journals about technology, physics, and mathematics, etc., all calibrated for a school-level audience. In the late Soviet Union this kind of preuniversity training was very important in the technical fields.

43. These universities are: Moscow State (Departments of Computational Mathematics and Cybernetics and of Mechanics and Mathematics); Saint Petersburg State (Department of Mathematics and Mechanics); Moscow Institute of Physics and Technology (PhysTech); Moscow Institute of Engineering and Physics (MIPHI); Moscow State Technical University ("Baumanka"); Saint Petersburg State University of IT, Mechanics and Optics (ITMO); and Saint Petersburg-based Polytechnical University and Electro-Technical University (LETI).

44. Importantly, all of them are Soviet-era institutions, except the Saint Petersburg Academic University of the Russian Academy of Sciences, which was founded in 1997 (officially decreed in 2002) and chaired by the Nobel Prize laureate in Physics (2000), vice-president of the RAS (since 1995) and a visible member of the State Duma (Russian parliament), Zhores Alferov.

45. It must be emphasized that while being highly selective, the Soviet and current Russian systems of higher education are relatively egalitarian, since most of the universities offer admission funded from the state budget, and thus the education is free, contingent upon the student's good performance. However, given the degree of centralization, whereby the best universities are largely concentrated in Moscow, Saint Petersburg, and other large cities, the sheer cost of living in such conditions might be a challenge for families sending their children to study there.

46. In turn, the low volume of industrial R&D projects affects the position of Russian universities in international rankings (Russoft 2015a, 150). On the problems of commercialization see RVC and E&Y 2014.

47. It is thought, according to Russoft, that by 2018 the education system will prepare up to 150,000 IT engineers; however, the industry needs twice as many, so there are hopes of hiring the deficient engineers from other countries (Russoft 2015b, 124).

48. For example by establishing specialized UR (university relations) divisions.

49. Thus, Russoft reports a significant decrease in cooperations in 2014 (Russoft 2015a, 148).

50. On average, 16 percent of Russoft member companies were promoting other forms of cooperation between 2008 and 2014; however, the 2008–14 average is not representative since only 1 percent of companies reported significant cooperation in 2008, but thereafter the popularity of other cooperation formats increased dramatically up to 37 percent in 2014.

51. Organized in 2005 by Andrei Ivanov and Nikolai Pul'tsin with sponsorship from Borland and ITMO.

52. Created in 2007 by Anton Likhodedov (Deutsche Bank) and Yuri Bogdanov (Rigmora Holdings) and supported by JetBrains, Yandex, EMC, Academic University RAS, as well as alumni of the club.

53. In 2010–14 a branch of the Computer Science Center functioned in Ekaterinburg with the support of SKB Kontur, and in 2014 another was opened in Kazan. In 2015, club records estimated its overall audience attendance since it was established in 2007 at fifty thousand.

54. For example: machine learning, computer vision, issues of natural language processing, and other fields of computer science. The school is based in Moscow and has branches in Ekaterinburg, Saint Petersburg, Novosibirsk, Minsk (Belarus), and Kiev (Ukraine).

55. Following the standards of the Borland Academy of Modern Programming and with support of JetBrains, Yandex Data School, Computer Science Club, and the Saint Petersburg branch of the Steklov Mathematical Institute of the Russian Academy of Sciences. A detailed account of Yandex in-house training is provided by Marina Fedorova in chapter 2 of this volume.

56. The so-called "first nature" factors—spatial positive externalities, such as the availability of natural resources or strategic positions in trade routes, and agglomeration effects of the regional capital cities largely driven by their status as administrative centers.

57. With regions rich in natural resources finding themselves in the peripheral but profitable position of raw materials supply; several of the largest cities on the way of inclusion into global urban networks and resembling many features of global cities worldwide (Sassen 2001); and the specific effect of overconcentration of globalization's positive effects in Moscow (Zubarevich 2001, 100–101).

58. Absorbing respectively 60 percent and 20 percent of internal migration.

59. Thirty-five percent of Russian IT companies are registered in Moscow and around 12 percent in Saint Petersburg, and almost every major software company in the two capitals, as well as a considerable number of medium-sized firms, have remote development centers located across the country (Russoft 2015a, 12–13).

60. The Central federal district is the area with the highest density of ICT organizations in the country, amounting to sixty-five thousand in 2012, of which 70 percent were Moscow-based. The organizational population everywhere else is less dense: the Northwestern, Volga, Siberian, and Urals (47 percent in Ekaterinburg) federal districts have between twelve and twenty-two thousand ICT firms in their territories, and the Far Eastern, North Caucasian, and Southern federal districts have around three to eight thousand ICT organizations.

61. Federal districts are groupings of the federal subjects of Russia created in 2000 as administrative units of governance (not provisioned in the Constitution of Russia).

62. Or sometimes several, as in the Volga federal district.

63. Because Perm belongs to the Volga federal district, its share is not included in the Urals statistics. In fact, viewed from a purely geographical and not administrative point of view, the share of Ekaterinburg would be even less than 47 percent.

64. Central and Northwestern federal districts also stand out in terms of their IT labor market size: both have the highest proportion of IT specialists (256 per 10,000 employees, above the national average) and organizations that require IT specialists (46–47 percent of all organizations; HSE 2014, 256). In 2015, 36 percent of job offers for IT specialists were made in Moscow and the Moscow region; 11 percent in Saint Petersburg; and for junior IT specialists, 34 percent and 7 percent respectively (Russoft 2015a, 128).

65. Russoft 2015a, 127.

66. According to CNews' (2015) annual ranking of the largest one hundred IT companies in Russia in 2014. The survey includes the one hundred largest Russian IT companies (in terms of earnings) and is conducted annually by CNews Analytics, a market intelligence division of the major IT and high-tech media of Russia and CIS countries. Other cities include Novosibirsk (a hardware distribution company), Yaroslavl (hardware distribution and IT services), Barnaul (hardware distribution), Irkutsk and Rostov-on-Don (both software distribution), and the Zelenograd Science Center near Moscow (hardware production), each having 1 percent (CNews 2015).

67. Thus, according to the annual survey of Russian software companies conducted by Russoft in 2010–15, while on average around 30 percent of the companies surveyed were headquartered in Moscow, the city was absorbing circa 60 percent of their net income (Russoft 2015a, 12).

68. Russoft Association prepared a more nuanced ranking of the largest Russian software vendors, based on turnover figures but also adjusted to the business models and growth rates/forecasts. This ranking has four groups: A (turnover in billions of US dollars), B ($100–500 million), C ($50–100 million), and D (less than $50 million) (Russoft 2015c).

69. Another notable feature is that eight out of nine Saint Petersburg–based companies and all four Ekaterinburg-based companies represented in the ranking of largest software developers (CNews Analytics 2015b) also feature in the CNews ranking (CNews 2015).

70. The case of Kazan is particularly instructive in terms of the complex entanglements between the political and the economic dimensions of center-periphery structures of Russia. Recent policy efforts to establish the city as a regional IT center on par with the capitals and develop a corresponding identity (a "brand") may be seen, paradoxically, as yet another instrument for the central control over an independent semiperiphery (see details in Kontareva, this volume).

71. On the latter case, see Masalskaya and Vasilyeva, this volume.

72. Russian Centre of Science and Research Statistics public opinion studies, as reported by Gokhberg and Nekipelova (2001, 186), "have highlighted that 51% of the population believe that by leaving the country in the current difficult times, researchers inflict losses on Russia in general and its science base in particular. Only 29% think that going abroad allows researchers to improve their skills, with a promise of returning enriched by their new experiences."

73. Leonid Gokhberg and Elena Nekipelova (2001, 177–78) name the following reasons that also apply to computer scientists–emigrants. Besides the poor organization and lack of resources of border control statistics in the 1990s resulting in an imperfect system of information collection, there have been: a lack of interest in the category "engineers" on the part of national statistics and migration-related bodies and in the educational background of migrants on the part of the Ministry of Interior; incompleteness of Goskomstat data due to the voluntary character of registration for temporary leave; and discontinuity of collecting data on migrants' qualifications since 1997. Some further Russian statistical specifics concern the definition of emigrants as "persons going abroad for permanent residence, not as those who leave the country for over one year," as well as complicated legacies of the Soviet "affirmative action empire" (see Martin 2001) visible in the mundane business of statistical categorization: "Nationality is understood as the ethnic group to which an individual belongs, not the country of birth or citizenship. For example, a person can be a Russian citizen but at the same time belong to a specific 'nationality': Russian, Jewish, Tatar, German, Ukrainian, etc." Moreover, it is impossible to estimate the number of those who left science after emigration, and, finally, in 2002 accounting for those leaving permanently has been stopped (Agamova and Allakhverdyan 2007, 111–15).

74. Available statistics also leave intact the most important questions, such as the long-term effects of the permanent and temporary scientific migration (brain drain or brain circulation?), initial motivation for going abroad, temporarily or permanently (scientific work or general well-being, or both?), trajectories of those who left temporarily but never returned, knowledge and technology transfer enabled by these movements, etc. Moreover, it seems not to be possible to account for IT specialists only (Gokhberg and Nekipelova 2001, 186).

75. Overall this last wave was lighter than the previous two (1917–37 and 1939–47), which had been compelled by the events of the October Revolution, the Civil War, and later World War II. Seen from this perspective, this last wave is quantitatively less impressive, accounting for about 1.1 million people for the entire

period of 1948–90, as compared to 3.5–4 and 8–10 million for the first and second waves respectively (see Zayonchkovskaya 2001).

76. The establishment of the Centre for Absorption of Scientists in Israel in 1973, designed specifically to accommodate hundreds of Soviet Jews, and the Jackson-Vanik Amendment (1974) in the US being its major milestones (Agamova and Allakhverdyan 2007, 110–11).

77. Notably the 1991 Law on Employment permitting Russian citizens to work abroad, and later the 1993 Constitution that granted freedom of movement (Gokhberg and Nekipelova 2001, 177; Zayonchkovskaya 2001).

78. Between 1990 and 1999 it admitted approximately 1.63 million ethnic Germans and 120,000 Jews from the USSR (see Dietz 2000, 649).

79. Nevertheless, there are some subtle differences: The prevalence of Germany in absolute numbers is due to the sheer scale of migration in-flow from the former Soviet Union (FSU) countries; however, in relative terms "relative indicators reflecting the proportion of S&T [science and technology] and education employees in the total number of emigrants by recipient countries are the highest for Canada (13.8%), the United States (11.9%) and Israel (10.9%)" (Gokhberg and Nekipelova 2001, 180). Moreover, countries offering visa quotas for highly skilled IT personnel, like Canada and Australia, have been and still are important destinations for Russian IT specialist migration.

80. According to UNESCO data, 1,072,500 qualified scientists left Russia in the period between 1990 and 2002 (Sadovnichy and Kozlov 2005, 139).

81. Respectively 58.1 percent, 21 percent, and 12.2 percent in 2000 (see table 2 in Gokhberg and Nekipelova 2001, 179).

82. The two capitals accounted for about 40 percent of outgoing migrants in 1992, but only for 18 percent in 1997, and 10.6 percent in 1999 (Zayonchkovskaya 2001).

83. In the period from 1993 through 2000, of all the persons who acquired permission to leave Russia and ceased to be registered as permanent residents, the share of Germans decreased from 47,500 to 22,600, Jews from 14,000 to 4,500, and Russians increased from 21,300 to 34,500 in 1999, and normalized at 25,800 in 2000. According to Goskomstat, in 1993–95 Germans accounted for more than 50 percent of the outflow, and Jews for 13–15 percent, while in 1999–2000 the share of Russians increased to 40 percent, becoming twice as large as the share of Jews even in the Israel-oriented migration (see table 3 in Zayonchkovskaya 2001).

84. According to the data of the Ministry of Internal Affairs; reported in Gokhberg and Nekipelova 2001.

85. Estimates provided by the Center for Science and Research Statistics; reported in Gokhberg and Nekipelova 2001, 179.

86. "The scale of engagement of Russian research scholars in other countries has significantly exceeded the emigration of R&D personnel per se" (Gokhberg and Nekipelova 2001, 177).

87. Only those who had spent more than three months abroad were considered. The duration of temporary work abroad for persons who had returned home prior to the survey was defined as the actual period of time spent abroad. For those

still working abroad, the respective term was identified on the basis of their contracts or declared intentions, as known to personnel officers at responding units. The survey targeted academy and industry R&D institutes, universities, and other equivalent higher education institutions located throughout Russia (Gokhberg and Nekipelova 2001, 182). Statistics for researchers on temporary leave were collected in 1996 and 2002 only: 4,084 and 2,922 Russian scientists were abroad on long-term contracts, making respectively 0.84 percent and 0.7 percent of the stock of scientists in the country (see Agamova and Allakhverdyan 2007, 111–14).

According to the survey's findings, 21.5 percent of the total number of academic institutes sent researchers abroad, versus 13 percent of universities; however, 9.9 percent of university researchers went abroad for temporary jobs, while only 7.6 percent of those working in the Academy of Sciences did (Gokhberg and Nekipelova 2001, 182).

88. Of the researchers, 63.9 percent were thirty to forty-nine years old and less than 25 percent were women, despite their slight overrepresentation in domestic R&D estimated at 57 percent. "Candidates of science represent 19.7% of researchers employed in Russia but 50.3% of those engaged abroad. For doctors of science, these percentages are 4.4% and 19.9%, respectively. Within the latter category, 10% had the status of a professor, whereas corresponding and full members of the Russian Academy of Sciences represented 1% each" (Gokhberg and Nekipelova 2001, 184–85).

89. However, the situation with IT might be different from other fields of science and engineering: "An increasingly important problem of 'brain drain' from Russia requires fastest settlement possible, including as part of implementation of the Strategy for Innovative development. According to Federal State Statistics Service, incomplete year of 2014—from April to December—saw a record outflow in 15 years that has amounted to 203.6 thousand people. Young people with higher education make up the most qualified emigrants. As a rule, these are the most talented specialists that see no outlooks for the development and implementation of their potential in Russia. According to official statistics, up to 60% of winners of international academic competitions go abroad to work and very few come back—9 out of 100" (RVC and E&Y 2014, 26).

90. Thus, according to the ANCOR recruiting company's survey (spring 2011, reported in Russoft 2011), 77 percent of ICT specialists are to some extent ready to emigrate, and 22 percent consider this possibility seriously. Although the study is clearly biased, since it encompasses only Moscow-based job seekers, Russoft characterized the situation as a matter of concern (Russoft 2011, 61–62). In May 2015, according to HeadHunter Group's study, reported by Russoft (2015a), 58 percent of IT specialists based in Saint Petersburg and Leningrad oblast (Saint Petersburg region) conceded the possibility of moving abroad for a good job; however, only 18 percent seriously considered such an option. According to another 2011 poll, among 63.7 percent of Russian IT specialists who were considering an option of permanently or temporarily going abroad for career purposes, they were mostly interested in foreign work experience (44.6 percent), a

high living standard (44.4 percent), and social benefits (42.1 percent), and less in salary per se (26.5 percent) (Russoft 2015a, 134).

91. According to the all-Russian representative opinion polls conducted by the Russian Public Opinion Research Center (VCIOM) in 2011 through 2016, the proportion of people who would like to emigrate has been around 11–13 percent, slightly below the level of 1991 (16 percent). The most common reason for emigration reported by those respondents who are willing to leave Russia is higher living standards (about 50 percent on average), matched by their desire for increased social security and stability (10 percent on average) (VCIOM 2016).

92. The VCIOM polls indicate that in 2016 the most popular migration destinations for Russians have been Germany for 12 percent of respondents (13 percent in 2011, 18 percent in 2008), the US for 7 percent (10 percent in 2011, 14 percent in 2008), France for 5 percent (5 percent in 2011, 6 percent in 2008), the UK for 5 percent (5 percent in 2011, 4 percent in 2008), Italy and Canada for 3 percent (4 percent in 2011, 5 percent in 2008), and 1 percent opted for Finland (1 percent in 2011, 4 percent in 2008) and Sweden (3 percent in 2011, 4 percent in 2008). The data for 2016 are percentages of those respondents who are considering emigration (VCIOM 2011, 2016).

93. Russoft 2015a, 134.

94. For example, in 2014 the Russian government started the "Global Education" program, granting stipends amounting to 1.38 million rubles (around $40 million). In the period 2014–16, the amount of state funding for the "Global Education" program will reach 4.41 billion rubles (RVC and E&Y 2014, 26) allocated for students to study IT in the world's leading universities. The stipend can cover tuition fees, travel, and other expenses. Prospective awardees must hold a bachelor's degree and upon receipt of the funding enter a contract to return and work in Russian firms, universities, or research or medical organizations. Failure to fulfil that obligation can be penalized by double the amount of money received (Russoft 2015a, 145–46).

REFERENCES

Abramov, Roman N. 2016. "Professional'naiaia kul'tura rossiiskikh inzhenerno-tekhnicheskikh spetstsialistov: universal'nye èlementy" [Professional culture of Russian engineering and technical specialists: Universal and local features]. *Sotstsiologicheskie issledovaniyaia* [Sociological studies] 9: 96–104.

Agamova, Natalya S., and Alexander G. Allakhverdyan. 2007. "Utechka umov iz Rossii: prichiny i masshtaby" [Brain drain from Russia: Causes and scales]. *Ross. Khim. Zh. (ZHurnal Rossiiskogo Ximicheskogo Obshchestva im. D.I. Mendeleeva)* [Russian chemical journal (Journal of the Russian Chemistry Society named after D. I. Mendeleev)] 51, no. 3: 108–15.

Akerlof, George. 1970. "The Market for 'Lemons': Quality Uncertainty and the Market Mechanism." *Quarterly Journal of Economics* 84, no. 3: 488–500.

Aneesh, Arnand. 2006. *Virtual Migration: The Programming of Globalization.* Durham, NC: Duke University Press.

Arora, Ashish, and Alfonso Gambardella. 2005. *From Underdogs to Tigers: The Rise and Growth of the Software Industry in Brazil, China, India, Ireland, and Israel*. Oxford: Oxford University Press.

Arora, Ashish, and Alfonso Gambardella. 2008. "IT and Regional Development: Lessons from the Growth of the Software Industry in India, Ireland, Israel, Brazil and China." RICAFE 2 Working Paper 060, London School of Economics and Political Science. Accessed December 1, 2015. http://www.lse.ac.uk/fmg /research/RICAFE/pdf/RICAFE2-WP60-Arora.pdf.

Benkler, Yochai. 2006. *The Wealth of Networks: How Social Production Transforms Markets and Freedom*. New Haven, CT: Yale University Press.

Bourdieu, Pierre. 1986. "The Forms of Capital." In *Handbook of Theory and Research for the Sociology of Education*, edited by J. Richardson, 241–58. New York: Greenwood.

Braudel, Fernand. 2002. *Civilization and Capitalism: 15th–18th Century*. London: Phoenix.

Cetindamar, Dilek, ed. 2003. *The Growth of Venture Capital: A Cross-Cultural Comparison*. Westport, CT: Praeger.

CNews. 2015. "CNews100: Krupneishie IT-kompanii Rossii 2014" [CNews100: Largest IT companies of 2014]. CNews. Accessed December 1, 2015. http://www .cnews.ru/reviews/2014/review_table/af8f66defobe297573c7300de31ae151631ffd 91.

CNews Analytics. 2015a. "Infografika: Regional'nyi IT-rynok v otrazhenii CNews100" [Infographics: CNews 100 reflected by regions]. CNews. Accessed December 1, 2015. http://www.cnews.ru/reviews/2014/articles/infografika _regionalnyj_itrynok_v_otrazhenii_cnews100_1.

CNews Analytics. 2015b. "CNews Analytics: Krupneishie IT-razrabotchiki Rossii" [CNews Analytics: Russia's largest software developers]. CNews. Accessed December 1, 2015. http://www.cnews.ru/reviews/2014/review_table/a49oba9d7 be15140cad95a1efi16c019fo1cef3d6.

CNews Analytics. 2015c. "CNewsFast: Samye bystrorastushchie IT-kompanii" [CNewsFast: Fastest-growing IT companies 2014]. CNews. Accessed December 1, 2015. http://www.cnews.ru/reviews/2014/review_table/479d2334b5677b6e 33c8e5bea91d54d201c4ecc8.

Collier, Paul. 2014. *Exodus: How Migration Is Changing Our World*. New York: Oxford University Press.

Collins, Randall. 2011. "Credential Inflation and the Future of Universities." *Italian Journal of Sociology of Education* 2: 228–51.

Collins, Randall. 2013. "The End of the Middle-Class Work: No More Escapes." In Immanuel Wallerstein, Randall Collins, Michael Mann, Georgi Derluguian, and Craig Calhoun, *Does Capitalism Have a Future?*, 37–69.

Denisenko, M. 2002. "Emigratsiyatsia iz Rossii po dannym zarubezhnoi statistiki" [Emigration from Russia according to the data of foreign statistics]. *Polit*, May 13. Accessed December 1, 2015. http://www.archipelag.ru/ru_mir/volni /4volna/denisenko/.

Denisenko, Mikhail. 2012. "Ėmigratsiia iz Rossii v strany dal'nego zarubezh'ia" [Emigration from Russia far abroad]. *Demoskop* [Demoscope] 509–10 (May 1–20): 1–18.

Derluguian, Georgi. 1995. "Breiin-drein (Mozhno ili nuzhno s nim borot'sia?)" [Brain drain: Is it possible and necessary to fight it?]. *Znanie—sila* [Knowledge—power] 11: 16–21. Accessed December 1, 2015. http://www .archipelag.ru/ru_mir/volni/4volna/brain/.

Dietz, Barbara. 2000. "German and Jewish Migration from the Former Soviet Union to Germany: Background, Trends and Implications." *Journal of Ethnic and Migration Studies* 26, no. 4: 635–52.

Drori, Israel, Zur Shapira, and Shmuel Ellis. 2013. *The Evolution of a New Industry: A Genealogical Approach*. Stanford, CA: Stanford University Press.

EUSP. 2010. *The History of Technological Breakthroughs in the Russian Empire in XVIII–Early XIX Centuries: Lessons for the XXI?* Report for the RUSNANO Corporation, September. Accessed December 1, 2015. http://www.eu.spb.ru/images /projects/istoria_proryrovXVIII-XIX.pdf.

Feakins, Melanie. 2007. "Off and Out: The Spaces for Certification—Offshore Outsourcing in St Petersburg, Russia." *Environment and Planning A* 39, no. 8: 1889–907.

Feakins, Melanie. 2009. "Offshoring in the Core: Russian Software Firms Onshoring in the USA." *Global Networks* 9, no. 1: 1–19.

Feakins, Melanie. 2010. "Local Experiments with Global Certificates: How Russian Software Testers Are Inventing Themselves as a Profession." In *Calculating the Social: Standards and the Reconfiguration of Governing*, edited by V. Higgins and W. Larner, 151–66. Basingstoke: Palgrave Macmillan.

Fligstein, Neil. 2001. *The Architecture of Markets: An Economic Sociology of Twenty-First Century Capitalist Societies*. Princeton, NJ: Princeton University Press.

Gladarev, Boris, Irina Olimpieva, Oleg Kharkhordin, Zhanna Tsinman, Anna Chernysh. 2013. "Vyiavlenie individual'nyx modelei povedeniia (mexanizmov samorealizatsii, strategii dostizheniia uspexa), vliiaiushchix na ėffektivnost' deiatel'nosti innovatsionnyx, vysokotexnologichnyx kompanii" [Exploring individual models of behavior (self-realization mechanisms, success strategies), influencing the efficiency of the activities of innovative high-tech companies]. STS Centre, European University at Saint Petersburg.

Gokhberg, Leonid, and Elena Nekipelova. 2001. "International Migration of Scientists and Engineers in Russia." In *International Mobility of the Highly Skilled*, OECD Proceedings, 177–89.

Graham, Loren. 2013. *Lonely Ideas: Can Russia Compete?* Cambridge, MA: MIT Press.

Infotecs. 2015. "History of the company." *Infotecs.ru*. Accessed December 1, 2015. https://infotecs.ru/about/history/.

InternetLiveStats.com. 2014. "Russia Internet Users." *InternetLiveStats.com*. Accessed December 1, 2015. http://www.internetlivestats.com/internet-users /russia/.

International Olympiad in Informatics. 2015. "International Olympiad in Informatics—Statistics: Hall of Fame." *Ioinformatics.org.* Accessed December 1, 2015. http://stats.ioinformatics.org/halloffame/.

Kharkhordin, Oleg. 1994. "The Corporate Ethic, the Ethic of *Samostoyatelnost* and the Spirit of Capitalism: Reflections on Market-Building in Post-Soviet Russia." *International Sociology* 9: 405–29.

Kogut, Bruce. 2003. *The Global Internet Economy.* Cambridge, MA: MIT Press.

Kolarova, Desislava, Asel Samaganova, Ivan Samson, and Patrick Ternaux. 2006. "Spatial Aspects of ICT Development in Russia." *Service Industries Journal* 26, no. 8: 873–88.

Kolesov, Andrei. 2004. "Konsolidatsiia razrabotchikov PO vhodit v novuiu fazu" [Consolidation of software developers enters a new phase]. *PC Week*, March 30. Accessed December 1, 2015. http://www.pcweek.ru/infrastructure/article/detail.php?ID=67059.

Martin, Terry. 2001. *The Affirmative Action Empire: Nations and Nationalism in the Soviet Union, 1923–1939.* Wilder House Series in Politics, History, and Culture. Ithaca, NY: Cornell University Press.

McCarthy, Daniel J., Sheila M. Puffer, Loren R. Graham, and Daniel M. Satinsky. 2014. "Emerging Innovation in Emerging Economies: Can Institutional Reforms Help Russia Break Through Its Historical Barriers?" *Thunderbird International Business Review* 56, no. 3 (May/June): 243–60.

Miledin, Pavel. 2015. "Ne slezaia s igly: Neft' i gaz obespechili 98% pribyli rossiiskihx kompanii." *RBC*, September 24. Accessed December 1, 2015. http://www.rbc.ru/finances/24/09/2015/560330bd9a794776bcd6c648.

Nazarov, Aleksandr. 2013. "Bor'ba za svoi prava ili kak ya sozdal profsoiuz programmistov" [Struggle for your rights or how I created a union of programmers]. *Habrahabr,* June 6. Accessed December 1, 2015. http://habrahabr.ru/post/182322/.

Peterson, D. J. 2005. *Russia and the Information Revolution.* Santa Monica, CA: RAND Corporation.

PMR Ltd. 2014. "IT Market in Russia 2014—Current Situation and Short Term Outlook." September 19. Accessed December 1, 2015. http://www.ceeitandtelecom.com/analysis/840/it-market-in-russia-2014-current-situation-and-short-term-outlook.

Popov, Vladimir. 2014. *Mixed Fortunes: An Economic History of China, Russia, and the West.* Oxford: Oxford University Press.

RIA News. 2017a. "Putin na PMÈF rasskazal o pod"eme rossijskoj èkonomiki" [Putin told about the upturn of the Russian economy at SPb economic forum]. *RIA*, June 2. Accessed June 30, 2017. https://ria.ru/economy/20170602/1495682313.html.

RIA News. 2017b. "Shuvalov zaiavil, chto Putin 'zabolel' tsifrovoi èkonomikoi" [Shuvalov told that Putin deeply involved in digital economy]. *RIA*, June 2. Accessed June 30, 2017. https://ria.ru/economy/20170602/1495681166.html.

Rose, Nicholas, and Peter Miller. 2010. "Political Power beyond the State: Problematics of Government." *British Journal of Sociology* 61: 271–303.

Rudycheva, Natalya. 2014a. "20 let IT-rynka Rossii: Kak rozhdalis' lidery" [20 years of the IT market: How the leaders were born]. CNews Analytics, April 4. Accessed December 1, 2015. http://biz.cnews.ru/articles/20_let_itrynka_rossii_kak_rozhdalis_lidery.

Rudycheva, Natalya. 2014b. "20 let IT-rynka Rossii: Kak otrasl' stala tsivilizovannoi" [20 years of the IT market: How the industry became civilized]. CNews Analytics, June 25. Accessed December 1, 2015. http://biz.cnews.ru/articles/20_let_itrynka_rossii_kak_otrasl.

Russian Venture Company (RVC) and Ernst and Young (E&Y). 2014. *Scenarios of Innovation Development and Globalization of the Russian IT industry*. Accessed December 1, 2015. https://www.rusventure.ru/ru/programm/analytics/docs/scenarii_innov_razv.pdf.

Russoft. 2010. "Export of Russian Software Development Industry: 7th Annual Survey." Russoft Association. Accessed December 1, 2015. http://www.russoft.ru/files/RUSSOFT_Survey_7_en.pdf.

Russoft. 2011. "Export of Russian Software Development Industry: 8th Annual Survey." Russoft Association. Accessed December 1, 2015. http://www.russoft.ru/files/RUSSOFT_Survey_8_en.pdf.

Russoft. 2014. "Export of Russian Software Development Industry: 11th Annual Survey." Russoft Association. Accessed December 1, 2015. http://www.Russoft.ru/files/RUSSOFT_Survey_11_en.pdf.

Russoft. 2015a. "Export of Russian Software Development Industry: 12th Annual Survey." [In Russian.] Russoft Association. Accessed December 1, 2015. http://www.russoft.ru/files/2015rus.pdf.

Russoft. 2015b. "Export of Russian Software Development Industry: 12th Annual Survey." Russoft Association. Accessed December 1, 2015. http://www.russoft.ru/files/RUSSOFT_Survey_12_en.pdf.

Russoft. 2015c. "Reiting krupneishikh softvernykh kompanii Rossii po versii "RUSSOFT": 56 razrabotchikov s sovokupnym oborotov svyshe $7 mlrd" [Russia's largest software companies ranking, Russoft version: 56 developers with total turnover greater than $7 bln]. *Russoft.ru*, 23 September. Accessed December 1, 2015. http://www.russoft.ru/tops/2733.

Sadovnichy, Victor, and Boris Kozlov. 2005. "The Russian Federation." In *UNESCO Science Report 2005*, 139–58. Paris: UNESCO.

Sassen, Saaskia. 2001. *The Global City: New York, London, Tokyo*. 2nd edition. Princeton, NJ: Princeton University Press.

Saxenian, AnnaLee 2006. *The New Argonauts: Regional Advantage in a Global Economy*. Cambridge, MA: Harvard University Press.

SKB Kontur. 2015. "History, 1992." *Kontur.ru*. Accessed December 1, 2015. https://kontur.ru/about/history/1992.

Stinchcombe, Arthur. 1965. "Social Structure and Organizations." In *Handbook of Organizations*, edited by J. March. Chicago: Rand McNally.

Tatarchenko Ksenia. 2015. "'I,' 'We' and the EVM: A Plan for the Soviet Future." Unpublished manuscript.

VCIOM. 2011. "Press-vypusk no. 1730: innovacionnyj centr 'Skolkovo': vzglâdy I ocenki rossiân" [Press-bulletin no. 1730: 'Skolkovo' Innovation Centre: Opinions and views of Russians]. Russian Public Opinion Research Center (VCIOM), April 13. Accessed June 30, 2017. https://wciom.ru/index.php?id=236&uid=111523.

VCIOM. 2016. "Press-vypusk no. 3229: Èmigracionnye nastroeniâ-2016: protiv tečeniâ" [Press-bulletin no. 3229: Mood for emigration-2016: Against the current]. Russian Public Opinion Research Center (VCIOM), October 26. Accessed June 30, 2017. https://wciom.ru/index.php?id=236&uid=115921.

Volkov, Vadim. 2002a. *Violent Entrepreneurs: The Use of Force in the Making of Russian Capitalism*. Ithaca, NY: Cornell University Press.

Volkov, Vadim. 2002b. "Security and Enforcement as Private Business: The Conversion of Russia's Power Ministries and Its Institutional Consequences." In *The New Entrepreneurs of Europe and Asia: Patterns of Business Development in Russia, Eastern Europe, and China*, edited by Victoria Bonnell and Thomas B. Gold, 83–104. Armonk, NY: M. E. Sharpe.

Xiang, Biao. 2007. *Global "Body Shopping": An Indian Labor System in the Information Technology Industry*. Princeton, NJ: Princeton University Press.

Yurchak, Alexey. 2002. "Entrepreneurial Governmentality in Postsocialist Russia: A Cultural Investigation of Business Practices." In *The New Entrepreneurs of Europe and Asia: Patterns of Business Development in Russia, Eastern Europe, and China*, edited by Victoria Bonnell and Thomas B. Gold, 278–325. Armonk, NY: M. E. Sharpe.

Zayonchkovskaya, Zhanna. 2001. "Èmigratsiia v dal'nee zarubezh'e" [Emigration far abroad]. *Polit*, August 8. Accessed December 1, 2015. http://www.archipelag.ru/ru_mir/volni/4volna/out-migration/?version=forprint.

Zemnukhova, Lilia. 2013. "IT-rabotniki na rynke truda" [IT workers at the labor market]. *Sociologija nauki i tehnologij* [Sociology of science and technology] 4, no. 2: 77–89.

Zubarevich, Natalya V. 2001. "Izmeneniia v tsentro-periferiinoi konfiguratsii postsovetskogo prostranstva" [Changes in the center-periphery configuration of the post-Soviet space]. *Vestnik Evrazii* [Eurasian herald] 3: 5–21.

Zubarevich, Natalya V. 2002. "Krupneishie goroda Rossii kak 'agenty' globalizatsii" [Russian major cities as "agents" of globalization]. *Rossiia i sovremennyi mir* [Russia and contemporary world] 4, no. 37: 97–101.

Zubarevich, Natalya V. 2006. "Goroda kak tsentry rosta rossiiskoi ėkonomiki" [Cities as the growth centers of the Russian economy]. *Nauchno-prakticheskii zhurnal Severo-Zapadnoi Akademii Gosudarstvennoi Sluzhby* [Scientific and applied journal of the North-Western Academy of Civil Service] 2: 113–18.

Zubarevich, Natalya V. 2012. "Sovremennaia Rossiia: geografiia s arifmetikoi" [Contemporary Russia: Geography and arithmetic]. *Otechestvennye Zapiski* 1: 55–63.

Zubarevich, Natalya V., and Sergey G. Safronov. 2011. "Regional Inequality in Large Post-Soviet Countries." *Regional Research of Russia* 1, no. 1: 15–26. Original Russian text published in *Izvestiya RAN. Seriya Geograficheskaya* 1 (2011): 17–30.

PART IV

BRIDGES AND MISMATCHES

CHAPTER TEN

MIGRATING STEP BY STEP
Russian Computer Scientists in the UK
Irina Antoschyuk

In the '90s we started to accumulate all sorts of Russian people here. But I don't know, if I hadn't got here, maybe there would not be this Russian diaspora.

—YEVGENIY, professor of computer science

The trend toward the internationalization of science is advancing as never before. Research is becoming increasingly collective and collaborative, with more papers produced through cross-border cooperation involving authors from a variety of different countries (Glänzel and Schubert 2005; Leydesdorff et al. 2013; Wagner 2008). The emergence of global networks of scientific collaboration incorporating more and more countries from the developing world is associated (as both cause and effect) with the rise of academic and student mobility and growing flows of academic migration (Kim 2010; Tremblay 2005). Movement is considered a normal and positive element of an academic career. Mobile scholars typically build larger and more diverse collaborative networks and achieve greater scientific productivity and visibility (Scellato, Franzoni, and Stephan 2012; Stephan and Levin 2001). Yet, we know little about academic migrants and scientific migration as a particular stream within highly skilled migration (HSM). If the impact of territorial mobility on scientific work has been a popular research topic, the role of professional contacts among scientists in the migration process has rarely been documented and analyzed in detail. What contacts are utilized by scholars moving from one country to another? What kind of ties are more important in that context? This chapter explores these issues by analyzing the stories of Russian computer scientists (RCS) living and working in the UK, seeking to understand how professional connections are involved in different stages of RCS migration and how they affect migration trajectories and scientific careers.

SOCIAL NETWORKS IN MIGRATION STUDIES

The social network perspective departs from an individual-centered explanation of migration and concentrates on migration as an inherently collective phenomenon deeply embedded in social structures and social relations.[1] Moving beyond its comprehension as the sole result of individual decision or the sole result of economic or political parameters, network framework enables us to reveal the complexity and combinations of structural factors and agency in order to grasp their cumulative interactive outcome (Boyd 1989, 642). A network perspective also compensates for the deficiencies of predominantly economic- or policy-oriented research, focusing instead on the "social foundations of migration" (Massey 1990, 68), which act as an independent force sustaining migration flows even in deteriorating economic conditions and restrictive legal regulations. Social ties transform migration into a self-feeding process as they compose "the social structure needed to sustain it" (69). Migration not only depends on social networks but simultaneously becomes "a process of network building," which "reinforces social relationships across space" (Portes and Bach 1985, 10). Thus, network perspective is based on the vision of social ties as a central social structure in the migration process—its integral part, its driver, and its outcome.

What can network perspective reveal about HSM and academic migration? Steven Vertovec (2002, 5) asserts that networks of skilled specialists are characterized by a "different nature" and lead to "different migratory outcomes" in comparison to migrants with lower qualifications. Qualified professionals are supposed to rely on "networks of colleagues and organizations," whereas kin and family ties are much less utilized, though research produces controversial evidence on this point. Ann D. Bagchi (2001) confirmed the crucial role of formal employment contacts in professional migration of Asian immigrants to the US, but Wilawan Kanjanapan (1995) showed that reliance on formal contacts depends on occupation, with health specialists being more likely to utilize kinship ties in contrast to engineers and computer scientists. Different types of contacts might also be mobilized for different purposes (Johnston et al. 2006)[2] and lead to different occupational outcomes for skilled migrants (Poros 2001). For example, migration of IT professionals through recruitment agencies may be associated with a particular visa status and employment contract in the host country (Xiang

2007). But while more is known about interpersonal contacts, including kin/ household, friends, and community ties, commonly referred to as "chain migration" (Banerjee 1983; Boyd 1989; Johnston et al. 2006; MacDonald and MacDonald 1964; Poros 2001), many issues regarding involvement and use of organizational and professional connections by highly skilled migrants in their transnational movement remain unclear and underexplored. The study presented in this chapter intends to contribute to this discussion, investigating the role of professional connections in RCS migration trajectories and careers.

Ties based on common origin, ethnicity, or nationality are also recognized to be of importance for skilled specialists. Research on transnational intellectual or scientific diaspora networks (Kuznetsov 2006; Meyer and Wattiaux 2006, Meyer 2007) shows that migrant professionals establish collaborative ties and form associations on the basis of their national belonging, striving to benefit their home country. Ethnic networks of technical specialists and scientists also prove serviceable as channels for transnational and regional knowledge exchange (Saxenian 2006), for knowledge diffusion, and innovation transfer (Breschi and Lissoni 2013; Kerr 2008). Examining ethnic ties of immigrants in Silicon Valley, AnnaLee Saxenian (1999) demonstrated that foreign-born specialists engage in local ethnic networks and associations in search of resources for a successful career as well as opportunities for entrepreneurship and business development. A special significance of ethnic/national connections for highly skilled migrants was found to consist in a peculiar coupling of professional ambitions and national feelings. Thus, in the Caldas and SANSA associations scholars observed a process of "re-identification through professional motives" (Meyer 2007, 10); that is, a proactive renewal of a sense of national belonging and reconnection to the home country through participation in professional networks (Meyer and Wattiaux 2006; Meyer 2007). Ethnic professional associations in Silicon Valley revealed a similar merge between the national and professional as they "combine elements of traditional immigrant culture with distinctly high-technology practices: they simultaneously create ethnic identities within the region and facilitate the professional networking and information exchange" (Saxenian 1999, 31). The integration of national belonging and professional aspirations accounted for the proliferation and success of these organizations in the region, showing that professional diasporic ties should be differentiated from other types of connections as they have a special meaning for highly skilled migrants. But even putting ethnic ties between migrant professionals at the core of the analysis, these studies do not discuss their role in HSM and do not question their impact on the migration trajectory of skilled professionals. Departing from their findings, my study seeks to fill this gap: it distinguishes ties based on common origin (diasporic) in a wider network of RCS professional connections and explores the place of RCS diasporic versus nondiasporic contacts in transnational movement.

Research on social networks in academic migration concentrates on its consequences for the evolution of scientific networks and international collaboration. Mobile researchers typically have a greater number of scientific connections covering more countries, including their home country, thus they "contribute significantly to extending the international scope and quality of the research network" (Scellato, Franzoni, and Stephan 2012, 26). Diasporic academics are asserted to occupy a central position in developing global knowledge networks (Larner 2015). Even short-term stays of academics were found to contribute to scientific cooperation between countries (Jöns 2009). But the opposite question—how scientific contacts and networks are involved in the migration process itself—has not yet been properly addressed. In this chapter, I aim to shed some light on this issue, exploring the movement and professional connections of RCS.

Another aim is to characterize academic migration within a larger picture of Russian presence in the UK.[3] Though diverse in terms of ethnicity, language, and religion, the migrant population from the FSU is referred to as the post-Soviet or Russian-speaking diaspora[4] and is supposed to be united by a broad "historically-specific socio-cultural background" rooted in the postwar and late socialist period (Byford 2009, 55). As a country with very restricted entry, the UK accepted a relatively moderate quantity of such migrants for the last twenty to thirty years, represented mostly by highly qualified professionals and scholars (Morgunova 2009; Pechurina 2017),[5] with a considerable share of IT specialists (Salt and Millar 2006). This chapter seeks to highlight the specificity of Russian academic migration in comparison to the movement of specialists for employment in the IT industry, which was found to be largely determined by such push and pull factors as socioeconomic situation in the home country and migration policies in the destination country (Zemnukhova 2015).

The current study is based on semistructured interviews[6] with RCS as a primary source of biographical and migration trajectory data,[7] supplemented by open internet sources[8] and by information on coauthorship from publications on official web pages or specialized databases.[9] I identify RCS by common origin (Russia and FSU republics), Russian language (native speaker/ educated in Russian), and scientific activity in computer science (current research, teaching position, publications). They work in British universities of different rankings, occupying positions ranging from PhD students to professors. Professional connections mean a variety of scientific ties established in the home or destination country, from brief acquaintance at conference meetings to regular scientific collaboration in research projects and joint publications, including ties between fellow students and mentorship relations. Specific attention is paid to diasporic connections defined as contacts with Russian-speaking scientists from Russia and the former FSU republics.[10]

FINDINGS

The study identified two social mechanisms of RCS migration, characterized by a particular configuration and the use of scientific ties in each stage of the migration process. The first mechanism is typical for RCS having moved in the 1990s, while the second is common to the RCS migration of the 2000s. The first mechanism is distinguished by the limited use of nondiasporic professional ties for relocation as well as by the importance of nondiasporic connections for integration into the UK academy. The second mechanism is marked by the utilization of diasporic contacts with UK-based scholars both in migration and afterward. But while being distinct, the two mechanisms are also interconnected. The first is demonstrated by the earliest RCS migrants, who have since gained top positions in British academia, while the second is visible among their successors, now junior researchers, who relied on connections with these first migrants. The two migration mechanisms are analyzed below on the basis of the illustrative case of the RCS community working at an institution I refer to as "M. University."[11] This case was chosen in order to show the functioning of both mechanisms separately and in interaction, as the RCS community at M. University comprises professors— pioneer migrants—as well as junior researchers and PhD students who moved to the UK through their connections with senior scholars.

FIRST MECHANISM: PIONEER MIGRANTS
AND THE ROLE OF NONDIASPORIC TIES

Yevgeniy and Anatoliy, currently professors of computer science, were the first RCS who came to M. University with an ambition to do high-quality science and develop an academic career. Yevgeniy migrated to the UK in 1990, being accepted as a lecturer at a Welsh university for a year. Then, in 1991, he was able to secure a long-term lecturer position at M. University, an institution he found particularly attractive, having held a postdoctoral fellowship there in 1984. Yevgeniy has been working there ever since, being subsequently promoted to reader and then to professor. Anatoliy moved to the UK in 1996, when he joined the department of computer science at M. as a research associate to work on a three-year European research project. But his acquaintance with the university also started earlier, from a postdoctoral internship in 1993–94. From 1996 on, Anatoliy worked at M. University on temporary contracts until he successfully obtained a lecturer position in 2000. After several years and after winning a large European research grant, he was promoted to a professorship.

Anatoliy's biography included multiple relocations across the Soviet Union and beyond before moving to the UK. He was born in 1954, grew up in Kazakhstan, and completed his higher education in Moscow, graduating from Moscow State University with a degree in applied mathematics in 1976. Upon graduation, he was appointed a programmer at Glushkov Institute of Cybernetics in Kiev, where he worked for several years. There, Anatoliy developed a strong interest in computer science, which led him to move to Leningrad to pursue a PhD at the Leningrad Polytechnic University. After defending his thesis, he continued to work there as an assistant professor from 1984 to 1996. He also went to Italy and Switzerland as a visiting researcher in the early 1990s, finally obtaining a one-year postdoctoral fellowship in the UK. Thus, his migration to Britain took place when he was already a mature scientist with a PhD degree, a stable position at a Russian university, and considerable teaching and research experience. Yevgeniy was also an academic with a permanent position in Russia, having several years of scientific and teaching work behind him when he decided to move to the UK. Born in Saint Petersburg in 1956, he received a higher education diploma in 1979,[12] and subsequently defended a PhD in computer science in 1982 at Leningrad Electrotechnical Institute. This became his home institution for thirteen years—from 1977 until moving to the UK—including eight years as an assistant and then associate professor.

A distinct feature of Anatoliy's and Yevgeniy's migration trajectories was their temporary relocation to the UK prior to moving there permanently. In Anatoliy's case it was the Royal Society grant for post-Soviet scientists that enabled him to come to Britain in 1993 as a postdoctoral researcher. For Yevgeniy, it was an exchange program for young postdoctoral fellows conducted by the Ministry of Education in partnership with the British Council. These temporary relocations allowed them to learn the organization of scientific life in a foreign country, the system of research funding, and structure of the academic community. It also helped them to build professional contacts. It became a sort of trial migration: scholars could taste academic life abroad and assess their chances for migration and a career in the UK without leaving their position in their home country, thereby avoiding the risks of failure.

Temporary migration is the starting point for the analysis of RCS professional contacts and their involvement in migration. For Anatoliy, a connection with a famous British scientist turned out to be crucial, as the fellowship program required the applicant to find a host institution and obtain its support. Anatoliy secured such assistance by applying to a scientist at M. University, with whom he had corresponded but whom he did not know personally: "I just had connections here with the main person, who is a major world star, Ben. . . . And we already knew each other somehow through emails. . . . In short, I sent him an email and said that I want to write this [grant], he [said,] 'Fine, write and I'll see.' And that's all, I got this grant."[13]

Other circumstances also led Anatoliy toward a fellowship abroad. His intention to go to the UK and the choice of M. University were affected by his specific scientific background and expertise: "I read a lot of articles and I understood that M. is such a strong world center exactly in the field I was engaged in, and it somehow stuck in my memory." The fellowship was also inspired by Anatoliy's interest in cooperating with European colleagues, his previous short-term visits to Europe, and the contacts he established during those trips: "Then perestroika started, and I tried to make contacts. I wanted to cooperate, in general, with Europe. . . . I built some connections and went to different places a couple of times. But M. was already like a dream, I . . . clearly knew what I would like to do in science, and I had some connections to people there."

Similar circumstances are found in Yevgeniy's story. Explaining his choice of a particular university for his fellowship, Yevgeniy remarks that it "was very well known. K. worked here. I read their articles, I grew up on that when I wrote my PhD." Yevgeniy's application also included a reference to a prominent scholar in the UK, an acquaintance of his supervisor, maintained from his previous research visit to Britain: "In Petersburg, my supervisor, not the last man, well known in many places, had connections in England, he had collaboration with a professor from Edinburgh." Thus, Yevgeniy mobilized a distant nondiasporic tie abroad, but it was mediated by a close professional connection in the home country. The fellowship in Edinburgh did not materialize, but Yevgeniy was accepted at M. University, which he had chosen as a second option because of the high-quality research produced there, despite the absence of any personal contacts. In this way, the scientific expertise and research interests of both scholars directed them toward M. University, acting as a substitute and compensation for the lack of direct professional ties.

In general, temporary relocation was characterized by a rather limited involvement of distant nondiasporic contacts, which served as a formal support or were altogether absent. Their temporary moves became possible largely due to specific institutions and programs for young Soviet scientists, and were prepared by their previous scientific backgrounds, their research experience, and knowledge of European science through journals and conferences. Close engagement with research in Europe contributed to the development of "outward-looking perspectives" making scientists feel "in some sense already abroad" (Biagoli and Lépinay, this volume). Subsequently, it grew into an intensified communication with European colleagues through conference attendance and visits and was followed by temporary migration, signifying a literal movement abroad into the European academic scene.

Long-term migration and permanent residence in the UK is the next stage of the RCS migration trajectory, and is linked to the previous temporary relocation insofar as the nondiasporic contacts established at that time played a significant role in determining the direction of their future movement and the location of their employment. For instance, a postdoctoral fellowship enabled Anatoliy to build a strong professional connection with Ben. The initial supporter of his grant application became his collaborator and colleague. Their cooperation continued upon Anatoliy's return to Saint Petersburg, and was sustained by a UK grant secured by Anatoliy that allowed him to visit regularly and conduct research at M. University. During one such visit, Ben informed him about the vacancy in a European research project and advised him to apply: "When I came next time, the second time, he told me, I have a contract, I have a place for a research associate, and if you apply, there is a chance that you get the position." As a result, Anatoliy submitted the application, passed the interview, and was accepted.

Yevgeniy's migration trajectory was also influenced by his postdoctoral internship. Despite a wide time gap between his first visit in 1984 and his migration in 1990, it was the contacts at M. University that he wanted to renew. He recognizes that he was eager to return to this university as "I had formed many relations back in the '80s" and "in the computer science department there were my own people, my own in a sense, and I was interested in working with them." Being employed in Wales, he sought opportunities to return to M., and having applied for a lecturer position, was successfully appointed there in 1991, where he has since remained.

Professional connections significantly shaped the second stage of RCS migration. They were represented by nondiasporic contacts with UK-based scholars and founded on a substantial experience of cooperation. Short-term scientific work in Britain proved to be of consequence for the subsequent long-term relocation, with researchers showing a strong preference to return and build their academic career in the same institution where they had held previous fellowships. Nondiasporic ties developed through collaborations during the fellowship period became the invisible glue binding the first and the second stage of migration, while being the driving engine of the first mechanism.

The third migration stage of the RCS pioneer migrants involves their settling down in the host country and integrating themselves into the new workplace and academic environment. Anatoliy's and Yevgeniy's experiences demonstrate two ways to establish and mobilize scientific connections. Anatoliy's strategy consisted in the active development of nondiasporic connections with British and European colleagues, especially in the first years after migration. Diasporic collaboration appeared and gradually expanded at a later period and was based on newly established ties. In contrast, Yevgeniy's strategy was to build nondiasporic contacts but combine them with diasporic ties even during the initial period after his move to the UK. His collaborative network was growing more evenly in both directions, increasing the number of nondiasporic as well as diasporic connections.

In Anatoliy's case it was the temporary position of research associate that forced him to realize the need to build up his reputation to obtain a permanent place at the university. His solution was to widen the number and scope of nondiasporic connections, and he started to initiate contacts both inside and outside of his project and his department: "I wrote articles not only with Ben, but with some Germans, with whoever was there. I wrote articles, wrote some grants, got rejected, but I wanted to learn to write grants, so that I can apply on my own, to depend only on myself."

In the first four years of his employment, active collaboration is reflected in Anatoliy's publications: he started with two papers in 1996, but by 2000 he produced ten to eleven articles per year, all in nondiasporic coauthorship. It was a productive strategy as these connections enabled him to prepare a successful grant proposal and secure further funding: "Then I wrote a big European grant, I wrote, but people helped me, they believed in me . . .

and I took the responsibility for writing the big European grant. There were amazingly clever people out there in Europe, but I wrote, it was my project, but, of course, nothing could have happened without them." This proposal brought Anatoliy the lecturer position he strove for and after securing the next large grant he was appointed a professor:

> When I got this big European grant, I made a huge and quick progress through the department's ranks, because I was guaranteed a teaching position, permanent, without time limits, because the department believed in me. It was an important step, not scientific step, but for my position [in] the department. And afterward I got one more European grant, and they made me a professor.

As for diasporic contacts, Anatoliy began to activate them much later. Russian-speaking coauthors started to appear in his publications only in 2000–2001, after he was granted a permanent position. All of them were UK-based scholars with whom Anatoliy had established connections after his move to the country, including Yevgeniy, his colleague at M. Though Anatoliy and Yevgeniy both studied and worked in Saint Petersburg in the 1980s, doing research in different areas of computer science, they never met or collaborated prior to their migration to the UK. They met at M. University and their cooperation started to develop in 2000, when they were both involved in the Tempus project in partnership with K. University in one of the Commonwealth of Independent States (CIS) countries.[14] Their collaboration was made possible by Yevgeniy's connection with a former colleague from Saint Petersburg, at that time the chair of the Information and Computer Technologies Department at K. University. Regular visits led to long-term cooperation and subsequently M. University became one of the major sites for recruiting Russian-speaking PhD students for both Anatoliy and Yevgeniy. Their collaboration served as a source of research staff for their projects in the UK[15] and for the growth of the RCS community at M., across the schools of computer science and electrical engineering. This growth was accompanied by a deepening collaboration among RCS and an increase in joint publications, especially since 2014, when the majority of RCS became involved in a large collaborative research project.

The independent and pioneering moves of Anatoliy and Yevgeniy to the UK and to M. University then led to the development of professional connections between them, which in turn created a framework for the movement of other Russian-speaking junior researchers and their integration into British academia. Thus, diasporic ties between senior RCS formed during the third stage of their migration trajectory became a crucial component in the second mechanism of migration. It is noteworthy that, both in securing and working on large grants as well as in recruiting new students for these projects, Anatoliy and Yevgeniy demonstrated outstanding managerial skills and much organizational effort without losing earnest enthusiasm for the technical content of their research. It surprisingly contrasts to common Russian IT specialists' disinterestedness and avoidance of managerial involvement, perceived as a "sacrifice to technical interest" and explained by the persistent influence of their Soviet work experience (West, this volume; Fedorova on Israel, this volume). Probably, fruitful combination of organizational and technical work became possible because of the specificity of the university as an institutional setting perceived by senior RCS as a totally different sphere of activity as compared to commercial enterprise.

Since 2004, Anatoliy's diasporic connections experienced an active expansion: he attracted his first Russian-speaking PhD student, with whom he published thirty papers, and formed strong ties with Russian-speaking research teams in Ukraine and Finland. Initiated several years after migration, these relations were not rooted in prior contacts in the home country but grew out of conference meetings in the UK or common work on European research projects; these relations have developed into stable and fruitful collaborations that have lasted for more than ten years and generated twenty-eight collaborative publications. Thus, Anatoliy's diasporic connections, characterized by long-term and productive cooperation, made a direct and positive contribution to his scientific activity; however, they hardly served the need of advancing his academic status, as he initiated them while already in a stable university position and continued them after his promotion to a professorship, the latter being largely the result of successful collaborative research with his nondiasporic colleagues. The role of diasporic connections and their meaning for migrant scholars seem to differ from nondiasporic ties, but what this difference consists of requires further elaboration.[16]

Another strategy consists in using both nondiasporic and diasporic ties after migration, relying on collaboration with Russian-speaking scholars in the first few years after settling into British academic life. In Yevgeniy's case, it was the strong connections with former colleagues from his research group in Saint Petersburg that dominated the initial period of his scientific activity in the UK. From his arrival in 1991 until 2000 he published the majority of his papers (30 out of 44, or 68 percent) with RCS from this group.[17] However, only a limited number of papers (13.6 percent) were produced exclusively with Russian scientists. Typically, his publications from that period featured

European, British, and Russian coauthors. Yevgeniy continued to be actively engaged in diasporic collaborations until 2006, generating the majority of publications with other RCS (32 out of 49 papers, or 65 percent). But from 2001 onward, there was a shift from former home-country contacts to new connections in the UK, most of them being colleagues in the same department, including newly recruited PhD students from the former USSR. This shift was also accompanied by an expansion of nondiasporic contacts, which began to grow considerably from 2007 and eventually came to dominate Yevgeniy's scientific activity, accounting for 65 percent of his publications (93 out of 143). In this period, the number of papers with RCS remained at almost the same level (5.5 publications per year in comparison to 4.5 during the previous period).

Thus, Yevgeniy's contacts with Russian researchers maintained from his previous institution played a significant role in the period immediately after migration. They supported his scientific endeavors and allowed him to achieve substantial productivity even when he still had only a few nondiasporic ties in his new academic environment. It helped him to successfully adapt to the new system, fully integrate into the UK academy, and successfully progress to a top position in the university. Continuous collaboration with British and European scholars along with former Russian colleagues and then the proactive establishment of new diasporic connections at his university enabled Yevgeniy to build a large and heterogeneous collaborative network, incorporating colleagues inside and outside of his institution, which resulted in a considerable rise in scientific output and brought him a reputation as an outstanding scholar.

To summarize, the first mechanism of migration is distinguished by several features: (1) nondiasporic professional connections acted as a driving force in the RCS migration process, but their significance varies with the stage of migration; (2) temporary relocation was realized with the limited use of distant nondiasporic connections, while institutional conditions (programs of postdoctoral internships) and RCS scientific expertise and knowledge of European science were more important; (3) the permanent movement of RSC relied much more on nondiasporic contacts, which considerably influenced the choice of migration destination and place of work; (4) the integration stage was marked by expansion and extensive use of nondiasporic ties, enabling RCS to achieve stable positions and build a successful career in a British university; and (5) diasporic connections were also activated and extended, but performed different roles at different periods of the Russian computer scientists' scientific activity.

The second mechanism of migration, typical for the RCS who migrated in the 2000s, differs substantially from the first, both in the conditions surrounding migration and the use of professional contacts. The Russian computer scientists' move to the UK in the 2000s took place directly from their home country, without any prior study or work experience abroad. They entered the UK to pursue a PhD degree immediately after graduation from a university in Russia or one of the CIS countries or, more rarely, after some work experience in their home country. In contrast to the first RCS migrants, these successors had almost no postgraduate research experience, and their development as professional scientists took place in the British academic environment. Their motivation to move was also different: while for the first migrants academic prospects were a priority and they sought an opportunity to do high-quality science, the next wave of junior researchers were not eager to pursue an exclusively scientific career and considered a PhD degree in the UK an advantageous alternative to employment in industry in terms of work conditions, salary, and career prospects. The second migration mechanism is also characterized by a specific use of professional contacts. Migration to Britain was realized through direct personal connections with RCS who had already established themselves in UK universities. It was these pioneer migrants who initially acted as scientific supervisors and afterward became senior colleagues for the newcomers. The stories of two such "newcomers," Leonid and Dmitriy (the first a research associate and the second a senior research associate at M. University), reveal key features of the second mechanism of migration, and its typical outcomes.

Leonid moved to the UK in 2004, to enter a PhD program after completing his higher education in applied mathematics in one of the CIS countries. After a successful defense in 2008, he was offered a research associate position at M. University—a position he has kept in the school of computer science throughout different research projects. Leonid's diasporic connection to Anatoliy (a personal acquaintance through the Tempus project discussed above) played a crucial role in Leonid's move and subsequent career. Meetings at Leonid's university were followed by correspondence, resulting in the offer of a place in the PhD program at M. University. It is noteworthy that Leonid considered various options: a position in a well-known company and a place in the PhD program at a Swedish university. But the crucial factor in deciding to go to M. University was the personal connection to

Anatoliy and the presence of a group of Russian-speaking scientists in the department, including Dmitriy, a young researcher who was an acquaintance from his university:

> I chose M. exactly because I personally met him [Anatoliy], and I liked what he was doing. And as I looked through, in G. [Swedish university] there was no Russian speaker in that group, and it was partly the reason to come here. And I knew Dima[18] personally, he studied in my university. . . . I knew that he went to that university as well. Partly, perhaps, therefore I chose M., though I [hadn't] heard about M. before. Partly because I assumed that there will be a small group of Russians, and it will not be so scary to go.

Dmitriy joined the PhD program at M. University in 2001, where he became the first Russian-speaking student. Similar to Leonid, his decision to migrate was influenced by the contact with Yevgeniy, whom he met through the Tempus project in 2000, when he was a first-year PhD student. Choosing to go to M. (rather than to other universities he had received offers from) stemmed from his personal acquaintance with Yevgeniy and an interest in his new research project. Speaking with other junior RCS at M. University, we find similar scenarios: connections to Anatoliy and Yevgeniy enabled the migration of Aleksey (now a lecturer at M. University), Sergey (a research associate), Semen, Igor, and Mikhail (now working in industry), as well as for Ilya and Vasiliy (who started their PhDs in 2014).

Senior RCS who moved to the UK in the 2000s initiated connections with young Russian graduates as they actively looked for PhD students and researchers. In contrast to the first wave of RCS émigrés who relied on their own resources with limited support from nondiasporic connections, younger scholars had a ready-made migration path that was well structured, clearly organized, and financially affordable: "It was easy for me. . . . I was invited, and I did not have to do anything, and I just took the path of the least effort" (Aleksey). Things looked quite different from the senior Russian computer scientists' point of view, having to work hard to negotiate financial and institutional constraints to attract Russian students. According to Anatoliy:

> It is difficult as here the system does not like foreigners. . . . Therefore we take one by one sometimes, someone who is a very good guy, who is recommended. . . . In the department we have [the] opportunity to save money from our grants, because it is necessary to pay for tuition. . . . Now I have Ilya . . . it is because I have been working on this piece by piece for two

years and I also needed the department to partially reduce the fees. . . . It's very complicated, I had to say: "Do you remember, I had two huge grants and it was so good for the department, could you partially reduce tuition for this man, and I will pay him [a] scholarship from my grant."

What were the reasons that motivated senior scholars like Anatoliy to navigate these difficulties in order to attract students from so far away? As Yevgeniy pointed out, securing funding for research projects is only the first step. Next, one needs to find people:

I had grants and needed to find people, not only research associates, but PhD students. As I was in a computer science department, but was mostly working on electronics, it was difficult to attract computer guys. As a result, I searched through all my acquaintances, through friends from Italy, Spain, with whom I wrote articles, but nothing came out of it.

Seeking Russian students was partly an answer to a shortage of researchers with the right profile for the job, one that straddled the line between software and hardware. Another reason articulated by Anatoliy was his confidence in the high qualifications of Russian students, as well as some feeling of commonality and understanding, which made communication easier and effective:

They are the best, the elite of young people, and I see, they are the same as me. In my time, when I was entering [the university], we had a group of young guys, we read the journal *Quantum* and loved physics and math. These guys are the same, I just see it. When I take PhD students, I understand young Russian guys better, as we have something [in] common. It is very important for my sense with [a] PhD student to totally understand him, not even to trust, but understand all his actions, all his reactions and so there is no resentment . . . and for me it is difficult with Englishmen.

In addition, Russian-speaking students were praised for their deep interest and immersion in research, which manifested itself in persistent work on certain problems and readiness to work overtime and be in contact on weekends. Combined with an inventive turn of mind, the ability to think independently and offer innovative solutions, also much valued by senior RCS, it made Russian-speaking students their preferred and long-term collaborators.

In a few cases, Russian students proactively sought to build ties with Russian professors in the UK. Ilya, for instance, was looking for opportunities to pursue a PhD in the UK and managed to meet Anatoliy through a fellow

Russian student who was already completing a PhD there. Similarly, Vasiliy contacted several professors in the UK during his last year at the Moscow Physical Technical Institute, and Yevgeniy was one of the scholars he got in touch with. As a result, after some correspondence, personal meetings, and a formal test, Vasiliy was offered a position in the project and PhD studentship. The presence of a Russian-speaking community of fellow researchers had an effect on Vasiliy's decision to go to M. University: "I also liked the milieu, and namely the faculty, which consists for the most part of Russian-speaking scientists, because it does not only facilitate communication, but it is also a mentality, [which] is very important, the same as yours, therefore it is easier to establish a dialogue."

Furthermore, Dmitriy and Leonid, the first two Russian PhD students at M., became involved in recruiting new candidates for the PhD program. Similar to the practice of hiring by personal references typical for Russian Jews working in the corporate IT sector in the US (Kurkovsky West, this volume), they used their personal contacts and recommended their friends, acquaintances, and fellow students whose skills and qualities they prized. They also regularly monitored the results of the programming Olympiads in their home country, pointing out students with prominent abilities to their professors. Nontrivial decision-making and the ability to find a unique solution to the problem, trained in such algorithmic contests, proved to be highly valuable skills for academia, aimed at producing new ideas advancing computer science as a discipline, in contrast to industry, which is focused on stability, quality, and maintenance of the product (Fedorova on Yandex, this volume).[19] Still, Dmitriy and Leonid organized and checked testing assignments to ensure candidates possessed the necessary level of qualification. Junior RCS migrants thus not only became involved in diasporic cooperation with senior scholars but developed relations among themselves, mobilizing their own connections and building a professional network of diasporic ties aimed at recruiting more junior RCS.[20] Collaboration and interaction with other RCS effectively frames the early phase of their professionalization and integration into the British academic community and dominates the subsequent years of mature scientific activity. The junior RCS work mostly with colleagues from the same university and, as a result, their networks remain quite narrow, thus maintaining their dependence on senior diasporic colleagues.

The development of Leonid's professional connections illustrates this. From the publication of his first article in 2003 until 2015, the majority of his papers have been published with Russian-speaking scholars (31 out of 41, or 76 percent). His main collaborator is Anatoliy, his supervisor, who is a coauthor in virtually all of Leonid's publications (30 out of 31, or 97 percent). In the first years after migrating to the UK (2004–9), he also cooperated with non-diasporic scientists but within projects headed by Anatoliy, and did not continue the collaboration after the projects ended. Only later was Leonid able to establish independent ties with researchers from the UK and Europe, but it resulted only in a few papers. From the beginning of his studies in the UK, Leonid also started to collaborate with a Russian-speaking group from Finland on a topic that became central to Leonid's interests. He published almost one-third of his papers with them (27 percent) and has maintained this collaboration to the present. But, again, his advisor was guiding this interaction, determining the direction of the work and distributing the research tasks. Though Leonid assumed a more active role, eventually becoming the scientific leader, Anatoliy remained the organizational and financial leader, structuring the workload and securing the funding. Therefore, despite Leonid's participation in the network of diasporic and some nondiasporic scientific ties, his involvement continued to be structured mostly by his supervisor. Even after years of research experience and a number of diasporic professional relations with junior RCs, he did not attempt to organize a research project on his own or develop cooperation independent from his supervisor.

Dmitriy's story resembles Leonid's. Since his first publication in 2003, he has been collaborating predominantly with Russian-speaking scholars within his university. More than half of his articles are coauthored exclusively with diasporic colleagues (14 out of 27, or 52 percent) and the rest with both Russian and non-Russian scientists. When he was coauthoring outside of diasporic networks, it was through the nondiasporic connections of Yevgeniy, his former supervisor. In one such case, Dmitriy collaborated with nondiasporic colleagues from another British university, but these ties ceased with the end of the project in 2009. Yevgeniy remained his main coauthor (25 articles out of 27, or 93 percent), as well as the main influence on his academic career. For instance, it was Yevgeniy's opinion that led Dmitriy to decide to leave the university for a startup company and, when the company collapsed a few years later, it was again Yevgeniy who invited Dmitriy back to the university as a research associate.

This way, compared to senior RCs, Leonid and Dmitriy demonstrated much less interest in organizing their own projects and pushing forward their own research agenda. As described for Russian IT specialists in other regions (Kurkovsky West, this volume; Fedorova on Israel, this volume), they preferred engagement with the technical content of the work, often deliberately distancing themselves from managerial activities. Probably, collaboration with well-established diasporic colleagues enabled followers to achieve sufficient stability already in the position of a research associate and discouraged advancement of their involvement in research management and organization.

However, reliance on diasporic connections may bring about other outcomes. For instance, Aleksey was able to establish himself as an independent scientist, though being also deeply involved in diasporic and intramural collaboration. From 2007 to 2015 he published thirty-five papers, almost all coauthored with other RCS (31 out of 35, or 89 percent), with more than half written exclusively with Russian-speaking scholars (19 out of 35, or 54 percent). But while building his scientific career through diasporic connections, he also strived to achieve more independence. A permanent lecturer position in 2012, granted only three years after his PhD defense, enabled him to apply for grants on his own, winning some of them. He also started to establish his own non-diasporic scientific contacts as well as ties with companies like Microsoft. Additionally, Aleksey began attracting his own PhD students, once again activating contacts with scholars and institutions in Russia.

In sum, immersion in diasporic scientific connections may ensure a smooth entry into the scientific activities of the particular department and research group, learning from experienced scholars, publishing articles soon after arrival, and providing financial support and cultural comfort in the initial years after migration. On the other hand, support may turn into long-term dependence on diasporic connections, especially on senior RCS, thus undermining the breadth and quality of collaborative networks among junior RCS and lowering their chances for establishing their own careers and research programs. Still, those negative outcomes hinge on how effectively a young scientist manages to reduce the role of diasporic connections over time, but there does not seem to be any doubt that such connections can play a positive—indeed crucial—role in enabling young researchers to migrate and start their careers in the UK.

The second mechanism of migration can be thus summarized: (1) diasporic connections were deeply involved in the migration of junior RCS to the UK in the 2000s, and in their integration into British academia; (2) migration itself was marked by a reliance on diasporic contacts with senior RCS, who came to the UK in the 1990s as pioneer migrants, establishing "bridgeheads"—institutional, organizational, and financial opportunities for the migration of the next generation; (3) the growth of the RCS community in the UK in the 2000s was accompanied by the development of substantial diasporic professional networks (primarily, but not exclusively, in the UK), in which junior researchers acted as facilitators for the recruitment of new Russian-speaking PhD students, thus leading to further migration from Russia and CIS countries; and (4) the extensive collaboration with Russian-speaking scholars and intensive reliance on diasporic ties continued after migration, but was associated with different outcomes: either the continuing dependence on senior RCS and lack of independent scientific connections, or the use of diasporic ties as a starting point for establishing one's own nondiasporic professional network.

CONCLUSION

An analysis of the migration trajectories and early career strategies of some RCS community members in a British university has identified two distinct and previously unstudied mechanisms of academic migration. The first is characterized by a virtually exclusive reliance on nondiasporic professional ties, while the second is essentially dependent on diasporic connections, being fully dependent on the previous generation of RCS "pioneer migrants." Another original finding relates to the formation and development modalities of diasporic networks among academics. Building on earlier studies of professional migrant associations (Meyer and Wattiaux 2006; Meyer 2007; Saxenian 1999, 2006), I have shown the special and pervasive significance of ties based on common origins, ethnicity, and nationality for scholars who become highly skilled migrants. Such ties frame their cross-border movement, their training, their professionalization in the scientific community, and their early careers, though with different effects depending on which of the two migration mechanisms is in play. In particular, this chapter has shown that diasporic ties function simultaneously as networks of scientific collaboration and as migrant networks. As such, not only do they generate substantial scientific outcomes but they also create structural opportunities for successive waves of scientific migration from the home country—a brain drain that facilitates further draining. Diasporic or ethnicity-based networks are thus found to be of consequence not only for low-skilled migrants but also for highly skilled and scientific migration. However, migration through diasporic networks should be differentiated from chain migration as they comprise organizational and professional contacts and represent mostly new ties which were established only after movement abroad. In addition, diasporic connections in this case are different from interpersonal contacts in chain migration as they are constructed deliberately and characterized by high selectivity.

What drives the formation and extension of diasporic networks between RCS and holds those networks together? Pragmatic considerations seem to be the most important factor, though another strong influence is the host country's academic environment. By attracting Russian-speaking students to PhD and research associate positions, senior RCS ensure a constant supply of qualified staff for their large-scale research projects, thus securing their status in a British university. Likewise, diasporic collaboration enables junior RCS to start and advance an academic career in the UK, a prospect many find appealing.

The migration of RCS to the UK fits the general pattern of transnational movement and diasporic network development of IT specialists, which is largely determined by migration policies and visa regulations as well as market fluctuations and the needs of multinational corporations. But this pattern extends beyond the IT industry: Russian-speaking scholars also work in the US and UK in other disciplines, such as biology and math, resulting in a brain drain effect for the home country (Allahverdjan and Agamova 2012; Artiushina 2014; Bronnikova 2010). And the similarities and differences in migration and diasporic network formation among these disciplines no doubt reflect both the structural characteristics of each field and the science and research policies of the host countries.

NOTES

1. According to Charles Tilly (1986), migration cannot be reduced to "individual characteristics and intentions" (5) and "isolated individual decision-makers," but is based on "clusters of people bound together by acquaintance and common fate" (3). Individuals migrate "as participants of social processes that extended beyond them"; therefore, "effective units of migration [are] sets of people linked by acquaintance, kinship and work experience" (3).

2. Thus, while "friends and relatives may have provided a great deal of general information and encouragement, most of the participants in the study did not rely on them for migration assistance or to find employment or housing" (Johnston et al. 2006, 1246).

3. Studies of the Russian-speaking population in the UK include research on language communities (Kliuchnikova 2016), friendship connections (Malyutina 2013), Russian diaspora as a performative community (Byford 2014), online community (Morgunova 2012) and even invisible community (Kopnina 2005) as well as Russian identity through homemaking (Pechurina 2010).

4. Though scholars underline the interactional and experiential character of these categories (Byford 2009; Pechurina 2017).

5. Outside of numerous migrants from Baltic countries (Estonia, Latvia, Lithuania) who as citizens of the European Union are subject to a different set of policies and regulations.

6. All interviews with computer scientists were conducted in Russian and translated by the author.

7. Seventeen interviews were conducted in the UK in February 2015. Respondents are males born between 1946 and 1992, who migrated to the UK between 1983 and 2014. They come from the former Soviet Union: Russia, Ukraine, Belarus, and Kyrgyzstan (exclusion: a Bulgarian national, who received higher education in Russia and is Russian-speaking). Some persons had several places of residence in the USSR/CIS before migration (Kazakhstan–Ukraine–Russia; Russia–Estonia–Russia) or migrated to the UK from Europe (Denmark and the Netherlands).

8. CVs, university and personal websites, online professional networks.

9. The DBLP Computer Science Bibliography: last access and calculations were made in August 2015.

10. Nondiasporic connections imply all other professional ties outside of diasporic contacts: thus, they include all non-Russian-speaking members of British and European academia, represented by scientists of British origin as well as by researchers from different European countries and other regions of the world.

11. Currently, the RCS community in M. University consists of eleven scholars and includes two professors, one senior lecturer, two lecturers, one senior research associate, three research associates, and two PhD students. Interviews were conducted with eight scientists, excluding two research associates and one lecturer.

12. This is a so-called specialist degree, a typical five-year higher education qualification in USSR.

13. It should be noted that Evgenii was also indirectly involved in bringing Anatolii to M., as he knew the working scheme of Royal Society grants, and Ben asked for his advice when he got an enquiry from Anatolii.

14. The specific country is not named for anonymity purposes.

15. In total, seven PhD students were found this way, including five currently working at M. University as research associates and lecturer.

16. They may be viewed as more reliable and personal, with diasporic cooperation felt as more comfortable and trustworthy in a highly competitive university environment. For instance, Anatolii remarks that diasporic "connections are maintained even when there are no contracts. They turn into something more . . . into warm relationships. . . . I mean that relationships with Russian-speaking [scholars] become more personal." This perceived difference may be important for understanding RCS migration and collaboration processes.

17. The group was initially based in Saint Petersburg but moved abroad soon after Evgenii left Russia for the UK; still, they managed to sustain collaboration ties for many years after migration.

18. Dima is a short name for Dmitrii, an acquaintance from Leonid's university, mentioned above, Dmitrii's case is discussed at length below.

19. This ability to think nontrivially and independently was often referred to as a specific trait of Russian-speaking students recruited for PhD programs in the UK and was perceived as a necessary element of background for the research work. For instance, comparing students from China and the Middle East to Russian-speaking students, Dmitrii complained that "their mentality is differ-

ent, there is a feeling that they can't think independently, they constantly need professor as God to tell them what to do. . . . They don't have the *dukh research-erstva* [spirit of research work] to try this and that, to compare. . . . They don't have the wit, self-learning, independence." Similar views were expressed by Leonid, Antolii, and Evgenii.

20. It should be noted that similar to pioneer RCS migrants, junior RCS experienced diasporic professional connections as more informal and personal, often involving communication outside the university, including common leisure and family activities (visits, hiking, bicycle rides, etc.) as well as support during the initial period after migration.

REFERENCES

Allahverdjan, Alexander G., and Natalia S. Agamova. 2012. "Russian Scientific Diaspora and the Scientists-Migrants' Mobility to the USA (The End of the XX—Beginning of the XXI Centuries)." [In Russian.] *Sociology of Science and Technology* 3, no. 3: 43–53.

Artiushina, Anna. 2014. "Network Interactions under Conditions of Competition for the Resources in Case of Molecular Biology Laboratories in Russia and USA." [In Russian.] PhD diss., Higher School of Economics, Moscow.

Bagchi, Ann D. 2001. "Migrant Networks and the Immigrant Professional: An Analysis of the Role of Weak Ties." *Population Research and Policy Review* 20, no. 1–2: 9–31. https://doi.org/10.1023/A:1010608225985.

Banerjee, Biswajit. 1983. "Social Networks in the Migration Process: Empirical Evidence on Chain Migration in India." *Journal of Developing Areas* 17, no. 2: 185–96.

Boyd, Monica. 1989. "Family and Personal Networks in International Migration: Recent Developments and New Agendas." *International Migration Review* 23, no. 3: 638–70. https://doi.org/10.2307/2546433.

Breschi, Stephano, and Francesco Lissoni. 2013. "Foreign Inventors in Europe and the US: Testing for Self-Selection and Diaspora Effects." Draft for the 7th Conference on Micro Evidence on Innovation in Developing Economies (MEIDE). http://merit.unu.edu/MEIDE/papers/2013/Breschi_Lissoni.pdf.

Bronnikova, Olga V. 2010. "Formation of 'Professional' Russian Diasporas Abroad: Russian Mathematicians in the UK." [In Russian.] *Diasporas* 1: 142–50.

Byford, Andy. 2009. "The Last Soviet Generation in Britain." In *Diasporas: Critical and Inter-Disciplinary Perspectives*, edited by Jane Fernandez, 53–65. Oxford: Inter-Disciplinary Press.

Byford, Andy. 2014. "Performing 'Community': Russian-Speaking Migrants in Current Britain." [In Russian.] *New Literature Review* 3: 377–95.

Dervin, Fred, ed. 2011. *Analysing the Consequences of Academic Mobility and Migration*. Cambridge: CambridgeScholars Publishing. http://horizon.documentation.ird.fr/exl-doc/pleins_textes/divers13-05/010058370.pdf.

Glänzel, Wolfgang, and András Schubert. 2005. "Domesticity and Internationality in Co-authorship, References and Citations." *Scientometrics* 65, no. 3: 323–42. https://doi.org/10.1007/s11192-005-0277-0.

Johnston, R., A. Trlin, A. Henderson, and N. North. 2006. "Sustaining and Creating Migration Chains among Skilled Immigrant Groups: Chinese, Indians and South Africans in New Zealand." *Journal of Ethnic and Migration Studies* 32, no. 7: 1227–50. https://doi.org/10.1080/13691830600821935.

Jöns, Heike. 2009. "'Brain Circulation' and Transnational Knowledge Networks: Studying Long-Term Effects of Academic Mobility to Germany, 1954–2000." *Global Networks* 9, no. 3: 315–38. https://doi.org/10.1111/j.1471–0374.2009.00256.x.

Kanjanapan, Wilawan. 1995. "The Immigration of Asian Professionals to the United States: 1988–1990." *International Migration Review* 29, no. 1: 7–32. https://doi.org/10.2307/2546995.

Kerr, William R. 2008. "Ethnic Scientific Communities and International Technology Diffusion." *Review of Economics and Statistics* 90, no. 3: 518–37. https://doi.org/10.1162/rest.90.3.518.

Kim, Terri. 2009. "Transnational Academic Mobility, Internationalization and Interculturality in Higher Education." *Intercultural Education* 20, no. 5: 395–405. https://doi.org/10.1080/14675980903371241.

Kim, Terri. 2010. "Transnational Academic Mobility, Knowledge, and Identity Capital." *Discourse: Studies in the Cultural Politics of Education* 31, no. 5: 577–91. https://doi.org/10.1080/01596306.2010.516939.

Kim, Terri, and William Locke. 2010. *Trans-National Academic Mobility and the Academic Profession*. London: Centre for Higher Education Research and Information, Open University.

Kliuchnikova, Polina. 2016. "Linguistic Biographies and Communities of Language of Russian Speakers in Great Britain." PhD diss., Durham University.

Kopnina, Helen. 2005. *East to West Migration: Russian Migrants in Western Europe*. London: Routledge.

Kuznetsov, Yevgeny, ed. 2006. *Diaspora Networks and the International Migration of Skills: How Countries Can Draw on Their Talent Abroad*. Washington, DC: World Bank Publications.

Larner, Wendy. 2015. "Globalising Knowledge Networks: Universities, Diaspora Strategies, and Academic Intermediaries." *Geoforum* 59: 197–205. https://doi.org/10.1016/j.geoforum.2014.10.006.

Leydesdorff, Loet, Caroline Wagner, Han Woo Park, and Jonathan Adams. 2013. "International Collaboration in Science: The Global Map and the Network." *El profesional de la información* 22, no. 1 (January–February): 87–94. http://dx.doi.org/10.3145/epi.2013.ene.12.

MacDonald, J. S., and L. D. MacDonald. 1964. "Chain Migration Ethnic Neighborhood Formation and Social Networks." *Milbank Memorial Fund Quarterly* 42, no. 1: 82–97.

Malyutina, Darya. 2013. "Migrant Sociality in a 'Global City': Friendship, Transnational Networks, Racism and Cosmopolitanism—A Study of Russian-Speaking Migrants in London." PhD diss., University College London.

Massey, Douglas S. 1990. "The Social and Economic Origins of Immigration." *Annals of the American Academy of Political and Social Science* 510: 60–72. http://www.jstor.org/stable/1046794.

Meyer, Jean-Baptiste. 2007. *Building Sustainability: The New Frontier of Diaspora Knowledge Networks.* COMCAD Arbeitspapiere working paper, no. 35, Center on Migration, Citizenship and Development, Bielefeld.

Meyer, Jean-Baptiste, and Jean Paul Wattiaux. 2006. "Diaspora Knowledge Networks: Vanishing Doubts and Increasing Evidence." *International Journal on Multicultural Societies* 8, no. 1: 4–24.

Morano-Foadi, Sonia. 2005. "Scientific Mobility, Career Progression, and Excellence in the European Research Area." *International Migration* 43, no. 5: 133–62. https://doi.org/10.1111/j.1468-2435.2005.00344.x.

Morgunova, Oksana. 2009. "The Present Day: British Russians or Russian Britons?" [In Russian.] *Russian Presence in the UK*, edited by Oksana Morgunova and N. V. Makarova, 37–46. Moscow: Sovremennaia Ekonomika I Pravo.

Morgunova, Oksana. 2012. "National Living On-Line? Some Aspects of the Russophone E-diaspora Map." Working paper for the project *E-Diasporas Atlas: Exploration and Cartography of Diasporas on Digital Networks.* Paris: Edition de la Maison des Sciences de l'Homme.

Pechurina, Anna. 2010. "Creating a Home from Home: Russian Communities in the UK." PhD diss., University of Manchester.

Pechurina, Anna. 2017. "Post-Soviet Russian-Speaking Migration to the UK: The Discourses of Visibility and Accountability." In *Post-Soviet Migration and Diasporas: From Global Perspectives to Everyday Practices. Migration, Diasporas and Citizenship,* edited by Milana Nikolko and David Carment, 29–45. London: Palgrave Macmillan.

Poros, Maritsa V. 2001. "The Role of Migrant Networks in Linking Local Labour Markets: The Case of Asian Indian Migration to New York and London." *Global Networks* 1, no. 3: 243–60. https://doi.org/10.1111/1471-0374.00015.

Portes, Alejandro, and Robert L. Bach. 1985. *Latin Journey: Cuban and Mexican Immigrants in the United States.* Berkeley: University of California Press.

Salt, J., and J. Millar. 2006. "Foreign Labour in the United Kingdom: Current Patterns and Trends." *Labour Market Trends* 114, no. 10: 335–55.

Saxenian, AnnaLee. 1999. *Silicon Valley's New Immigrant Entrepreneurs.* Vol. 32 (1991–2005). San Francisco: Public Policy Institute of California.

Saxenian, AnnaLee. 2006. *The New Argonauts. Regional Advantage in a Global Economy.* Cambridge, MA: Harvard University Press.

Scellato, Giuseppe, Chiara Franzoni, and Paul Stephan. 2012. "Mobile Scientists and International Networks (No. w18613)." National Bureau of Economic Research. https://doi.org/10.3386/w18613.

She, Quianru, and Terry Wotherspoon. 2013. "International Student Mobility and Highly Skilled Migration: A Comparative Study of Canada, the United States, and the United Kingdom." *SpringerPlus* 2, no. 1: 1–14. https://doi.org/10.1186/2193-1801-2-132.

Stephan, Paula E., and Sharon G. Levin. 2001. "Exceptional Contribution to US Science by the Foreign-Born and Foreign-Educated." *Population Research and Policy Review* 20, no. 1–2: 59–79. https://doi.org/10.1023/A:1010682017950.

Tilly, Charles. 1986. *Transplanted Networks*. New York: Center for Studies of Social Change, New School for Social Research.

Tremblay, Karine. 2005. "Academic Mobility and Immigration." *Journal of Studies in International Education* 9, no. 3: 196–228. https://doi.org/10.1177 /1028315305277618.

Vertovec, Steven. 2002. *Transnational Networks and Skilled Labour Migration*. Working Paper for Transnational Communities Programme, University of Oxford.

Wagner, Caroline. 2008. *The New Invisible College: Science for Development*. Washington, DC: Brookings Institution.

Xiang, Biao. 2007. *Global "Body Shopping": An Indian Labor System in the Information Technology Industry*. Princeton, NJ: Princeton University Press.

Zemnukhova, Liliia V. 2015. "IT-Specialists on the Global Market: Migration Strategies and Professional Networks (The Case of Russian IT in London)." *Sociology of Science and Technology* 6, no. 4: 154–63.

CHAPTER ELEVEN

BRAIN DRAIN AND BOSTON'S "UPPER-MIDDLE TECH"

Diana Kurkovsky West

Over the past few decades, the interest in tech creativity and innovation has squeezed out the mid-twentieth-century preoccupation with the ordinary corporate worker. William Whyte's once groundbreaking study *The Organization Man*, depicting the corporate employees in Forest Park, Illinois, as symptomatic of the new landscape of American conformism, seems inapplicable to the new era of tech entrepreneurship stemming from California's Silicon Valley. This tech era, as the story goes, was started in garages by "young engineers who saw themselves as outsiders experimenting with new technology in a new region, far away from the established centers of political and economic power in the United States" (Saxenian 2007, 28). Policy makers around the globe have since wanted to know how to foster dynamic ecologies of innovation and nurture tech mavericks like Mark Zuckerberg or Sergey Brin, investing billions into recreating these environments inside their own countries, whether in Russia, Kazakhstan, or Israel. Deploying Richard Florida's theory of the creative class, along with the Schumpetrian notions of creative destruction, they invest in technoparks, tech accelerators, startup incubators, hackerspaces, and other seemingly indispensable ingredients of tech entrepreneurship. Has the "tech maverick," in his skinny jeans and hipster spectacles, replaced the gray-suited, suburban "organization man"? Did the ordinary process of education, indoctrination, and professionalization traced by Whyte give way to a scene wherein college dropouts turn overnight into nonconformist billionaires? Did American culture, which over fifty years ago was accused of "worshipping" the organization, suddenly reject its values in favor of brilliant "bad boys"? And whatever became of the role of large corporations in shaping America's tech scene?

The focus on Boston's high-tech sector reflects the bias toward the tech maverick in the existing scholarship, which privileges the fast-paced world of tech entrepreneurship and flash flows of capital. This story has dovetailed with discussions of the region's recent biotech renaissance: once a hotbed of corporate giants in the electronics industry, especially along the famous Route 128, the region experienced a slump in comparison to its more successful counterpart in Silicon Valley; however, the reorientation away from electronics toward biotech has reinvigorated the city. In the past decade, Boston's tech innovation scene has shifted toward the city center, precipitating massive redevelopment in once derelict parts of downtown, and a clustering of tech centers, such as the Cambridge Innovation Center near the MIT campus. Initiatives like MassChallenge, Techstars, Y Combinator, and others have capitalized on the abundance of university students and graduates in the area, creating additional incentives for successful regional startups. These accelerators offer seed funding, mentorship, and visibility to startup companies, providing global networks for Boston-area tech entrepreneurs. Boston, one could say, has been actively reinventing its economy by nurturing the tech maverick.

What this picture fails to capture, however, is the strong presence of what this chapter calls Boston's "upper-middle tech." For the thousands of Russian Jewish immigrants arriving in the US in the 1990s, it was precisely the corporate tech sector rather than the risky world of high-tech innovation that became a highly desirable place to seek employment. Between 1971 and 2006, some 700,000 people from the former Soviet Union (FSU) came to America under the Jewish family reunification programs, with the peak of this migration occurring in 1992 and 1993.[1] Of these, an estimated 14,000 to 39,500 Russian Jews settled in Boston, although the number is likely higher if one considers suburbs like Waltham and Newton, well known for their significant immigrant populations from the FSU (Steinhardt Social Research Institute 2006, 24).[2] Many of these Russian Jews came with high levels of technical training, and sought to acquire IT skills in order to succeed not in new entrepreneurial initiatives but rather in large corporations. Careers in various IT sectors were so widespread among Russian immigrants in America that they represented a veritable cultural phenomenon: even the contemporary bard Timur Shaov noted jokingly in his song "Iz Ameriki s liubov'iu" (From America with love) that the Russian American "population is mostly made up of programmers."[3]

While careers in the "upper-middle tech" are largely removed from the preoccupation with startups, seed funding, and "quick returns" innovation, they also make up the majority of what people in IT do. Professionals in this domain are also distinct from the collective company creature described by Whyte: they harbor no illusions about the corporation's loyalty, have likely survived several layoffs, and switch jobs at will, moving from organization to organization. They are often not American or American-born; the corporations where they work are highly internationalized. In the case of the Russian diaspora from the 1990s, the use of the word "programming" applies to a wide range of IT activities, from high-level coding to fairly sophisticated computer science. *Programnirovaniye* was the Russian term widely used by my respondents to identify their computer-related activities, likely because for this generation of immigrants no Russian-language term for IT or computer sciences was in existence. Echoing the language of my respondents, when this chapter refers to programming, it suggests a broad spectrum of middle- to upper-level IT work.

The career trajectories of Russian Jews in American corporations pose numerous challenges to existing assumptions about the phenomenon of human capital flight, often called "brain drain." Scholarship on brain drain often pivots its arguments precisely on the idea that Silicon Valley–style ecologies of innovation prove to be highly attractive to the educated "brains" from all over the world, which flock to these regions for financial and professional fulfillment. For instance, while AnnaLee Saxenian's (2007, 50) *The New Argonauts* challenges the one-way vision of brain drain in favor of global "brain circulation," where the formerly "drained brains" return to their homelands to build new ecologies of innovation, it nonetheless assumes that it is precisely the "growth of regions like Silicon Valley" that "fueled the exodus of talented young adults from poor developing countries." My interviews with Russian Jewish immigrants in Boston, however, suggested a different reality—namely, that it was the stable jobs in large corporations rather than the dynamic innovation scene that proved to be most attractive to large numbers of Russian immigrants employed in the "upper-middle tech."

Although IT jobs were comparatively easier to obtain than positions in the sciences or academia, they nonetheless required significant reprofessionalization for this group of immigrants because programming had not been their primary education in the USSR. Moreover, even in the cases where my respondents had worked in the Soviet computer industry, they had been heavily engaged with the reverse engineering of Western technologies described by Ksenia Tatarchenko in this volume, had worked with either mainframe or analog computers, and few had had any experience with personal computers. The retraining my interviewees underwent complicates another dominant perception of the concept of brain drain, which assumes a kind of inherent and fixed value to the "brains" that leave their homeland, translating as net "gain" to the country where they settle. Brain drain models deal with the potentialities of skilled migrations; namely, the human potential lost to the exporter and gained by the importer, set against economic and educational factors and expenditures. Brain drain assessments of post-Soviet migration usually group all kinds of professionals into the schematic of human capital loss/gain, making no distinction between political refugees and economic migrants (see, for instance, Ganguli 2014). In practice, however, there exists a significant gap between the education levels of the Russian Jewish immigrants and their ability to find correlating employment in the host country. This was especially true for Israel, where thousands of Soviet engineers became employed in low-skilled work (Remennick 2012, 74–80). Similarly, deprofessionalization is a very real aspect of Russian immigration to the US, especially pertinent for doctors and teachers who could not easily obtain the licenses they needed to practice. In fact, for Soviet-trained doctors there was no other option but a complete re-education in the US, and few chose this route. Jobs in IT proved attractive to the numerous Russian Jews living in the Boston area, including people who had never worked in any field related to programming. This was so not because they offered opportunities for entrepreneurship or provided any immediate link to my respondents' preexisting Soviet training; rather, this chapter contends that these jobs were appealing from an organizational point of view. They allowed for financial stability, continual intellectual interest, and relative insulation from management and entrepreneurial activities.

EDUCATION AND RETRAINING

Engineering was a highly popular profession among Soviet Jews, and this had much to do with the history of institutionalized anti-Semitism in the FSU: it was one of the few careers in the Soviet Union that was relatively open to Jews, so the high number of engineers arriving in the US within the Jewish diaspora is not surprising (Remennick 2012, 76–86). Soviet engineering was also open to men and women, with women constituting an estimated 40 percent of all engineers in the FSU (Remennick 2012, 77). The engineering education itself was fairly broad, with heavy emphasis on mathematics and physics, but without much foundation in computers: for instance, according to a study of Russian Jewish engineers in Israel, only 20 percent of older engineers from the FSU had used computers in their work (King and

Naveh 1999; cited in Remennick 2012, 77). Although a certain number of FSU engineers were, indeed, trained in programming, the technologies they were using in the USSR were often significantly outdated by American standards. Even for the highly trained immigrants in the tech industry, the correlation between their education, training, and the ability to secure a job in the IT industry was by no means direct.

Numerous Jews arriving in the US during the 1990s were, however, highly trained in mathematics. Specialized math and physics high schools, called *fizmat*, were created in the late 1950s to advance applied sciences in the USSR and compete with the United States, but they also became islands of intellectual creativity with a certain degree of intellectual freedom (see Kukulin and Mayofis 2015; Kukulin, Mayofis, and Safronov 2015b; Safronov 2015). The fizmat schools became places where students not only received rigorous math training, but also where deep social bonds emerged within the communities of politically liberal students, parents, and alumni. The scholar Slava Gerovitch (2013) has argued that, while by no means strictly Jewish, these high schools created a parallel social structure for Soviet Jews, wherein various math-related communities were formed to circumvent state-sanctioned anti-Semitic practices. Since thousands of Jews immigrated to the US, Israel, and Germany, the fizmat school connections formed new kinds of international social networks both in Russia and abroad: "These classmate ties are as strong as, I would say, a family," Inna, a graduate of one such school now living in Boston, explained. Virtually all my respondents argued that their fizmat training was a key element in helping them acquire new job skills. While the tech boom helped to channel people toward IT, their math school training helped them with learning computer logic: "It's not just the boom, although that helped. But first and foremost, [math school] is where we all studied."

The professional networks that formed around the IT field for Russian Jewish immigrants proved to be a kind of self-fulfilling prophecy, as many immigrants advised their friends to acquire skills that would help them find programming jobs. There was, undeniably, a prevailing notion in this community that programming was a quick and fruitful way to successful careers in the US, as well as the kind of ethnic affinity often discussed in conjunction with the transnational scientific diaspora networks described by Irina Antoschyuk in chapter 10 of this volume. In some cases, the ties of Soviet fizmat school alumni networks functioned in a manner akin to the mechanisms of academic migrations uncovered by Antoschyuk, but in other cases, the mere lore of programming preceded the act of reprofessionalization. The trope of the Russian "programmist" was very much cultivated within the immigrant community, spreading rapidly through the ranks of new arrivals; in some cases, this even encouraged individuals to begin their retraining before immigration. For instance, David, a physicist from Leningrad working in the Soviet polymer industry, was advised by his friends already living in Boston to study computers just before leaving for the US. Knowing that once in Boston he would be looking for a job in IT, he bought a personal computer—which were rare and very costly in late 1990s Russia—and enrolled in computer courses offered by Microsoft. He believes that these courses were very helpful in familiarizing him with the basic tenets of PC use and programming and facilitated his further training in the US.

While David studied computers in Russia for six months prior to arriving in the US, other respondents had to literally learn programming skills on the job. Elena, who was a physics teacher in the USSR, arrived in the late 1990s and was, like David, advised by her Russian émigré friends to look for a position as a programmer. "I didn't even know how to turn on the computer!" she explains. "But I came here, and everyone told me 'You have to become a programmer.'" Elena briefly considered obtaining the certification necessary to continue working as a physics teacher, but decided against it: an émigré math school friend of hers had attempted to do this and confessed that the process was long, strenuous, and resulted in a low salary, and Elena was leery of ending up with no job after the long retraining. Instead, she signed up for computer courses taught at the so-called Russian computer schools, which offered a series of computer courses taught in Russian by Russian émigrés already working in the IT field. In addition to technical skills, these schools offered professional certificates and often provided assistance with finding jobs in IT. She read a book on C++, attended the courses for two months, and quickly grasped the concepts: "My teacher quickly picked me out.... He said I was ready to look for a job." At the same time, a fizmat school friend was leaving her position as a programmer and had recommended Elena as her replacement. She was hired having had no experience whatsoever:

> I was left alone with the code. I had no idea what to do with it—it was very long, and everything was by orders of magnitude more complicated than even what I do now.... I would lose the thread, I couldn't read it from the screen, even.... So I printed it all out.... I decided I'll figure it out in whatever way I could.... I put it on the floor, on the walls, and spent about a week just crawling around the floor, drawing arrows with a marker ... then I began to remove some sheets, it became more compact, I drew myself a diagram from which I could work on the rest of the project.[4]

In the first month of her new job, Elena did not write a single new line of code: "The people who hired me actually understood this. . . . My boss would come by and look at what I was doing. I'd say 'I'm figuring it out,' and he nodded, asked me if I had questions, and left me alone." Elena managed to piece together the code and build upon it, successfully finishing the project.

Retraining was necessary even for people who had worked in Soviet computing, like Marina, a computer scientist now living in the Boston suburb of Waltham. In the USSR, Marina was a systems programmer in a closed government organization, but her experience did not naturally make her able to work as a programmer when she immigrated in 1991. Although her Soviet job involved reverse engineering American computers on the basis of components and software, Marina had never worked on a PC: "I saw a PC in 1990, but no one was allowed to touch it because my boss played video games on it." Upon arriving in the US, she took a job for a Russian-language community newspaper, and this gave her access to a PC, which she studied on her own free time. Once she felt comfortable with what she had learned, she set out to find a job in IT, which she did within two months, not speaking much English (which, by her own admission, remains mediocre even after almost twenty years in the US). In Marina's case, she was hired on the spot for her first job after being asked to reorganize her future manager's desktop display and making useful suggestions.

Like Marina, many Soviet immigrants in tech fields lacked exposure to the technology common in America. Even at the level of engineering training, much of it was very abstract. Yuriy described his education at the Leningrad Polytechnic as mostly paper based:

> For example, in our electronics course we were told to design an amplifier on paper. So the outcome is the diagram of the amplifier. You know, transistors, resistors. I never saw them in real life. I never held them, I never held a soldering iron. What kind of an electronics engineer am I? I can draw something on paper but if someone asked me which one is the capacitor or which one is the resistor, I would not be able to tell.

Sergey also remembered working with analog computers at university in the late 1970s:

> We had computers that essentially looked like large baths. . . . Baths filled with some . . . electrically conductive fluid. . . . You create your boundary conditions using copper sheets with potential to them. And of course the

fluid solves differential equations because electrostatic fields follow the same equations as many other things in nature, so you measure potential of this fluid at different places and basically you collect solutions. And the speed with which it solves those equations is essentially the speed of light.[5]

He recalled other similar analog devices: "by that time, of course, the West was all into digital."

Both Marina and Sergey were familiar with the basics of how computers functioned, and thus retraining did not pose any major difficulties. Their stories serve to illustrate another important feature of the IT profession, which facilitated retraining for Soviet-educated programmers and engineers: namely, the fact that all computer science (CS) professionals are expected to continually acquire new skills to keep abreast of new developments, and are generally offered opportunities by their employers to do so. Courses and certification programs are a routine part of working in a large corporation. Professionals used to working with one kind of platform often find positions in companies that use different ones, and are expected to acquire these skills fairly rapidly. It is standard practice in CS companies to pay for certification courses and even graduate-level training. Hence, significant training is expected even of those with formal education in CS, which worked to the advantage of Russian immigrants with science and engineering backgrounds.

Retraining did not only entail the acquisition of new technical skills. Interviewing itself was a challenging, new process for most Russians who were accustomed to the Soviet practice of being "placed" into industry after graduating from university. Marketing their skills, writing résumés, and going to interviews where they had to speak with various individuals in a language few had mastered was both foreign and difficult. For instance, Yuriy described a particular fear of telephone interviews, explaining that he guided himself through them using a decision tree—a kind of if-then algorithm that he put together in order to anticipate the logic of the questions. New arrivals like David were coached by their friends who already held jobs in the US, as well as by the Jewish Vocational Services, which helped Russian immigrants with writing résumés. Those who attended the Russian computer schools received assistance with this process along with their technical training.

Obtaining new jobs was significantly easier once the individuals developed contacts and experience in the industry. Aleksey, a quality assurance (QA) engineer, explained that although his only training in IT was through the Russian computer schools, the fact that a friend recommended him for his first position made a major difference; this was a specific feature of the period before the tech bubble burst in the early 2000s. He explained: "getting a job was easy. You go to an interview and they ask you if you know where the button is to turn on the computer—well, a little more than that—but if you have someone to vouch for you and say that you're gonna be fine, you're going to get the job." Russian friends in the IT industry recommended Aleksey for several positions he has held, including his current one. He has switched between numerous companies and been through three major layoffs, although he has never stayed unemployed longer than a week. He now interviews many people, and explains that experience and referrals more than educational background continue to be major determining factors for employment. "If you can demonstrate that you can learn on the job, that's the most important thing." This culture of hiring, which privileges and encourages new skill acquisition, was a major facilitator for retraining and a mechanism behind attracting immigrants to IT.

The IT culture of hiring also proved to be highly attractive to some of my respondents who had considered academic trajectories. For instance, Yuriy was a trained physicist in the USSR and had considered entering US academia if he was unable to secure a job: "My general plan was try to find a job here in Boston. If I can't, either go to Silicon Valley and try there, or apply to grad school and get a PhD." Upon arriving in Boston, he sent out forty résumés, received four invitations to interview, and landed a job offer on the second interview. He is content with his career choice and finds the work interesting: "I don't see myself as a scientist even though I worked as one for many years. I see myself as an engineer. And software is a tool that I use." Similarly, David, who was working on his dissertation in physics when the Soviet Union collapsed and his lab was defunded, briefly considered an academic career in physics, but decided against it because CS jobs were more readily available: "The market for programmers cannot be compared to the market for physicists. . . . I can say for sure that I do not regret having switched fields. . . . Looking back on it fifteen years later, I am not sure I would get more satisfaction doing scientific research than from what I'm doing now."

Industry jobs were often more attractive even to those who used graduate education as an entryway into the US. For instance, Boris was admitted to Tufts for graduate school in materials engineering after receiving his undergraduate degree as a mechanical engineer at the Polytechnic University in Saint Petersburg (formerly Leningrad): "It was very popular at the time to invite Russian students to different colleges." Boris found a Russian professor at Tufts who was a friend of his scientific advisor in Leningrad, and who had grant money to sponsor his PhD studies. He spent one year at Tufts but quickly turned to the industry for a job. "I didn't finish my PhD. I spent a year there, I didn't learn anything useful. . . . It was very boring, actually, compared to the job in [the company where he found employment], so I decided to switch." The mundanity of the academic trajectory, where even trained PhDs have to perform routine research tasks, served as an additional deterrent to pursuing an academic career in CS. Boris found his job in "upper-middle tech" more interesting and well paid, with good insurance and excellent benefits. "There was only one minus—I had to work from eight in the morning to twelve in the evening, usually. But that was worth it." He stayed in the firm for seven years, eventually moving on to another position, and founding his own firm in 2004. This firm now has two offices, one in Boston and one in Moscow.

The difficulties associated with the limited job availability in academia also continue to serve as a major deterrent for those looking for academic careers in CS. This is the case with Anatoliy, who also came to the US for graduate study and completed his PhD in computational neuroscience at Boston University. Along with his part-time teaching position, Anatoliy also has a startup, which he is looking to build and expand. To him, a good university position remains desirable, but seems less and less attainable every year: "The problem is that unfortunately my specialization in academia is so narrow that there are probably at most one or two tenure-track positions that I can apply to per year, and there are many more computational neuroscientists that can do it, so . . . I tried for a couple of years, didn't even get an interview." For the past eighteen months, Anatoliy has been primarily focused on his startup: "That's why . . . if [my startup] takes off, I will actually leave academia," he asserted. Since our interview, Anatoliy's startup has received $750,000 in seed funding from a well-known Silicon Valley investor and now has contracts with major government organizations. It is safe to assume that he will not be on the academic job market again in the foreseeable future.

Various industry temptations and the difficulties associated with the American academic job market made academic careers less than desirable for numerous highly educated Russians who, in some cases, already had significant graduate training. At the same time, however, the path into American "upper-middle tech" was by no means a straightforward translation of their Soviet skills; without exception, all of my respondents had to undergo retraining on the level of learning new languages, platforms, technologies, spoken language, and job search skills. What facilitated their transition, however, was the specificity of the field of "upper-middle tech" during the 1990s, which placed less value on formal IT education than on on-the-job acquisition of new skills. In many cases involving Russian immigrants, employers took risks in hiring people who had to learn the basics of coding and programming while already working on projects. Training is also seen as an integral part of this rapidly changing field, and companies rely on personal references in order to secure candidates who are willing and able to learn, rather than those who already possess all the requisite skills.

This feature of the field has the added benefit of creating continued interest on the part of employees who enjoy mastering new technologies. Marina, for instance, switched jobs when she became interested in Cloud computing—she spoke with her manager, who actually recommended that she follow her interests and look for a position that allowed her to pursue them, and even served as a job reference for her. David and Aleksey routinely attend training seminars and certification courses provided by their firms. They also spend time on self-education. Finally, because all companies rely on different platforms, tools, and technologies, as well as provide different kinds of services, there is always new skill acquisition that has to take place. Aleksey explained:

> Because technology changes quickly and you go from one company to another, you're learning new things. I never in my life worked with Mac computers.... Came to this company, they give me a Mac.... [My] previous company was all Microsoft driven, the programming language was C Sharp, Microsoft's language. You came here—it's a different thing: Java, it's all Macintosh, it's all [a] different approach to the things, and I have to learn that, you know.

This does not pose problems for my respondents; on the contrary, it is both an expected element of IT work and something that adds interest to the profession.

BUSINESS AND MANAGEMENT

While IT skill acquisition was possible for many Russian Jewish immigrants, management was something to which they had virtually no prior exposure. Decision-making in the Soviet industry was closely linked with political power, and technical workers were not encouraged to take on this kind of initiative (see Berliner 1988; Lawrence and Vlachoutsicos 1990). Management was inherently political and not seen as suitable for the intelligentsia, who picked careers in technical fields specifically to avoid Soviet ideology and politics. Thus, although the highly educated Russian Jews arriving in Boston found employment in a variety of firms, management proved to be something that was neither intuitive nor an area of great interest to the majority.

Many Russian IT specialists I interviewed, even those in fairly high-ranking positions, describe their disinterest in management—seen as a sacrifice of technical interest in favor of a more authoritarian role—even at the cost of promotion. When Marina's employer asked if she wanted to move into management, she told him, "No, no, please, anything but that!" repeating several times, "I cannot tell people what to do." She wanted to work on the technical part of the project without worrying about anything beyond its content: "Because when my boss comes to me and gives me a piece of paper with nothing but circles and squares on it and tells me that he has a new idea, I can build him a project that everyone will oooh and aaah over. That's the interesting stuff. But not managing someone else." Similarly, David expressed a strong interest in the technical content of his projects instead of managing people: "Someone tells me: 'Here is a problem you need to solve.' I don't need any further direction. I can take the problem, analyze it, find a solution." He, like Marina, believes management is anathema to his personality.

Yuriy explained that his disinterest in management meant that he had to make a conscious decision about limiting the growth of his business: "I don't like to take over somebody's projects, I don't like to pass on the projects that I worked on to somebody else. I like to complete [them] start to finish. But it's just my character. . . . I don't like to delegate, I know I would be a bad manager." He owns two small companies: a consulting firm specializing in system integration and a tech firm designing calorimeters and software for the concrete industry. He hires subconsultants from a small circle of professionals who are at his own level, and on whom he makes no money, because he wants the jobs done without much oversight on his part. His tech firm consists of four full-time employees on whom he can "rely without strong supervision."

Engaging in mostly technical content of projects was part of the Soviet work experience, which entailed lump funding distributed to various industries and strictly hierarchical management structures. Employees were assigned to a workplace after graduating and stayed together as basically the same teams for decades. Yuriy described his lab in the USSR as a place more akin to a family-style gathering than a space of active work on projects:

Our group was great, it had three young men, three young women and our boss, who was ten years older, divorced, very funny guy. It was fun. Everyone did whatever they wanted. One did Zen Buddhism, our boss played golf [at a] very high level. Girls . . . some knitted, some read books. I happen to be interested in engineering, so I grabbed all the equipment, when we got that accounting computer, I grabbed that computer. . . . So I worked not because I had to, I just wanted to learn.

The stated disinterest in management among highly trained IT specialists in Boston's "upper-middle tech" may have to do with a lack of experience in this domain. The strong interest in technical content over and above managing people has remarkable parallels in the way Boris views the culture of his tech consulting firm's branch in Moscow. In his view, Russian tech specialists are often interested mainly in new and technically exciting projects, to the point where they disregard their clients: "They considered clients as second-level persons who are not worth talking to." Boris offered an example typical of this quest for intellectual fulfillment over the needs of clients:

For example: we had a delivery date when the client expected us to deliver an almost final version [of the product]. . . . The night before the delivery it didn't work. When I called Russia and asked them what there were working on, they said "You know, there is a new cursor in Microsoft . . . and we are trying to figure out how to use it." I said: "The product is not working, nothing is working . . . and you're doing this unnecessary stuff." And they said "Yes, but it's much more interesting than fixing bugs."

With the dissolution of the USSR and the rapid change to a market economy, the Russian economic structure transformed quickly, but management culture is taking much longer to cultivate. This applies not only to managing company hierarchies and teamwork but also on the level of business fundamentals. Boris believes one of the problems with Russian business is that "they do not have [a] very good business culture." He explains that the lack of fundamental business etiquette was a major deterrent for Western clients, who construe Russian communication style as rude:

For example: If you send an email to an American guy in business, he will respond to you in a day, or at least acknowledge that he got your letter. When I send emails in Russia, I have no idea where it goes, who read it, if he didn't answer me because he didn't get it or maybe because he didn't read it, or he is not interested, and so on. . . . I actually have a girl who calls people to find out if they got my emails.

He describes the lack of some other etiquette basics, like introducing people to each other at meetings instead of making them guess who is in the room, sending timely communications in case of cancelled meetings or appointments, and not being able to follow meeting schedules. Sometimes, however, the problems are even more basic: "People don't say 'thank you' in emails." In fact, adding words of gratitude to email signatures was one of the things he remembers being taught by his former US employer: "He insisted on reading all emails that I sent, and corrected me every time. It was actually really annoying," explained Boris. "Now I read all emails that my people send to my clients, and insist that they cc me. It's not controlling. . . . Unfortunately, they are just not good communicators [in Russia] . . . especially programmers."

The issue of business culture and basic politesse comes up regularly even in the discussions of American versus Russian American attitudes and behavior in Boston proper. My respondents who worked in American-owned companies tended to be somewhat dismissive of Russian-owned businesses, often citing a lack of respectfulness and friendliness, especially typical of the older-generation immigrants who grew up in the USSR. A particularly telling example of this appeared recently on a Facebook forum for Russians in Boston: in this instance, a young Russian immigrant who owns a business that works mostly with American clients recently began to expand his services to Russian émigré–owned firms. He was sufficiently upset at the difference to create a long post comparing the two experiences. The post was titled "Why I Do Not Want to Work with the Russian Community," and recounted the following differences:

> The majority of American companies that we call are prepared to devote a little time to us in order for us to explain our services and convince them that they could benefit from them. They are prepared to meet (sometimes it takes several weeks to set up such a meeting) and to talk with a smile . . . to discuss and make a decision, even if it is a negative one. My attempts to connect with Americans via LinkedIn and represent my firm almost always receive a reply, or are redirected to the correct respondent. In our community, just the opposite applies. Most often I'm either instantly rejected, or, in the best case scenario, they listen with the expression "Yeah, yeah, we know all this [expletive], don't try to teach me how to run my business." Attempts to connect through LinkedIn are most often ignored, or they inform me they do not need our services, although we never even discussed any services with them.[6]

Interestingly, several replies to his post, all from members of the Russian community in Boston, alluded to a generational difference: "Perhaps we should not forget where we come from and the time we arrived also matters, in my opinion. Our children already treat everything quite differently." Several other replies attempted to suggest special strategies for approaching Russian businesses, explaining that they functioned on tighter budgets and were more suspicious than American companies. A certain self-defeating quality was invoked, and in reply to one of the responses invoking tight budgets, the original poster explained that he was mainly concerned with the fact that "many in our community do not even want to listen to those, from whom they themselves want business." There were, however, a number of Russian business owners who defended themselves by invoking the superficiality of "American smiles." An émigré who explained that he has owned a business for over twenty-four years in the US stated: "It's just that we are different. . . . I don't have this artificial politeness behind which there is nothing, even, in some cases, [there are no] brains. . . . And my education, I'm ready to bet, is several orders higher than any of the 'locals.'"[7] Business culture is still perceived by many in the community as a superfluous and even disingenuous element, which stands in contrast to the real and more authentic "brain power" of Russian immigrants.

A certain generational gap is present with regard to the interest in management that exists among Russian CS specialists. In contrast to the older generation, like David and Yuriy, Aleksey came to the US at the age of twenty-two without any experience in Soviet industry. He has learned most of his technical skills on the various jobs he held during the past ten to fifteen years and is now becoming progressively more interested in management. Recently, he went through a training course in Agile management: Agile is a management approach which—instead of the previously used "waterfall" techniques of task delegation—channels project teams toward decisions rather than having team leaders give them a specific direction. He is very interested in these techniques and enjoys helping teams work toward a consensus. Aleksey's Soviet training was very different from the other respondents: he never studied at university, holds the equivalent of a Soviet associate's degree, and worked as a mechanics engineer in a Soviet factory before immigration. With no preexisting conceptions of how a business or laboratory functions nor a strong culture of technical "purity," such as one finds among Russian techies, Aleksey is comfortable guiding people and understands that management is not simply about telling people what to do.

Yet business etiquette is not the only difference between Russia and the US that the few Russian émigré entrepreneurs in Boston note: they mention the strong technical skills but also a certain lack of understanding about good business planning and a limited sense of the global market among contemporary Russians. Sergey, a graduate of the Sloan School of Management and a VP of a Russian émigré–owned company, coaches Russian startups as one of his professional hobbies. In discussing the startups that approach him for advice, Sergey confessed that one of the biggest problems is that they simply do not have an accurate sense of the market, thinking that if an idea is good technically this in itself will translate into success: "I see executive summaries, business plans for Russians startup[s], probably a couple a day, and they just have no clue how to actually calculate their market. In most of the cases they [envision] a huge market and when you look at that, you understand that the market is at least ten times smaller than they think." Working together with the Russian Venture Company, Sergey and his business partner, also a Russian émigré and a fellow graduate of the Sloan School, bring Russian startups to Boston in order to offer them coaching, mentorship, and professional connections:

> It's one of the other problems with Russian startups. We ask: "Who are your competitors?" And the fairly usual answer [is] "Oh, we don't have competitors yet because we are unique." And when you hear this answer, you know for sure, like a hundred percent sure, that there are two options: one, these guys don't know how to use Google, and two, nobody needs this product.

The technical orientation of the startup culture in itself is not particularly unique to Russia. However, the almost utopian emphasis on the "purity" of technical projects seems specific to a particular generation of Russians who received their schooling in the FSU and especially those who worked in the Soviet industry.

These observations also seem to apply to Russian Jews who become entrepreneurs. Despite the fact that most of the immigrants arrived in Boston during the heyday of the semiconductor field, very few attempted to capitalize on this market. There were, of course, exceptions, but as with management, the immigrants' interest in entrepreneurship seemed to depend on whether they were educated at a Soviet university and had been part of the Soviet technical intelligentsia culture. The case of Vadim illustrates this well: He is dyslexic and colorblind and articulated this as a determining factor in his subsequent career. He never succeeded in formal schooling either in the

USSR or once he arrived in the US in the early 1980s. Taking some extension courses at MIT, however, gave him access to physics labs and scientists, as well as exposure to tech entrepreneurs in the Boston area. He developed a software product that he showed to one of them, got connected with Esther Dyson and other powerful figures in the industry, and has been very much on the forefront of the tech maverick culture ever since. His academic and physical limitations encouraged him to take risks outside the more "accepted" tracks, channeling him toward the culture of tech entrepreneurship and tech startups.

Taking risks, however, was not encouraged in Soviet industry and remains a problem in Russia today. My respondents whose work engages with Russia continue to perceive intolerance of risk as a major feature. In describing how Russia compares with the US and Israel—three markets he knows particularly well—Sergey explained:

> If you look at the ecosystems good for startups, you will figure out that culturally they have a high acceptance of failure. That's one of the big things: in the US it's OK if you failed, it's actually good if you failed. And I know a lot of investors who look at the failure as a positive experience, and if you have on a team at least somebody who failed—it's good.

Failure, however, is not tolerated on the Russian market and businesses that fail tend to be stigmatized. This, for Sergey, is a problem because he sees failing as an essential part of business education. To illustrate this point, he described the story told to him by an investor:

> I have this entrepreneur, who came to me at some point with an idea. I liked the idea, I gave him five million and the company then went bust, and a couple years afterward he came to me with another idea, and again I gave him five million and again it didn't succeed. Now he came with another idea, and again I like the idea, and he needs ten million, and of course I'm gonna give it to him because I already spent ten million on his education.

Invoking his own experience both in Russia and in Boston, Boris notes that it is virtually impossible to get people to make investment decisions in Russia. He told the story of how, after an hour-long presentation to a senior executive of a major US corporation, his Boston firm received a retainer check for $150 million. "In Russia, even Putin will not write you a check on the first meeting. . . . Nobody there wants to take responsibility." This notion corresponds with what various firms observed when they entered the Russian market in the 1990s. The high degree of collectivism encouraged by the Soviet regime created taboos around individual initiative, which translated into what Western firms saw as uncertainty and a lack of risk taking (see, for instance, Elenkov 1988).

As with contemporary Russian startups, Boston's "upper-middle tech" remains marked by the Soviet experience, especially since the members of this population are now middle aged or older and had significant formative experiences in the USSR. Private business in the USSR was entirely illegal, and while numerous people secretly engaged in entrepreneurial activity, this was not seen as acceptable behavior for the intelligentsia. Until recently, words like *delovoy*, signifying "businesslike," were derogatory in Russian, and an entirely new vocabulary has developed since the end of the Soviet Union in order to designate terms from business and management. As Marina Fedorova notes in her chapter on Israel in this volume, much late-Soviet entrepreneurial activity emerged as an antidote to the country's collapsing economy, and the idea of "dishonest speculation" was seen as the predominant form of engaging in business activities. Despite this fact, a number of Soviets found loopholes within the system, most notoriously trading apartments in various cities, subdividing them, and exchanging them for other apartments thereby building small real estate empires.[8] One of my respondents recalled the informal career his grandmother had built in helping people find apartment trades; however, these activities were mostly informal, and were not seen as the domain of professionals. Thus, business practices and the entrepreneurial spirit were foreign to many of the new arrivals in the 1990s. Capitalizing on their math and science training, as well as on the extant tech boom of the 1990s, Soviet émigrés mastered new skills, both with regard to the technical aspects of the field and job search and interviewing techniques. The émigrés often shied away from management roles and found it generally ineffective to pursue academic tracks. Employment in America's "upper-middle tech" proved to be a kind of safe haven, a key to the American dream, that allowed for a comfortable intellectual engagement within a corporate setting.

CONCLUSION: RECONSIDERING BRAIN DRAIN

The financial and professional successes of this community are not to be overlooked. Inna was especially proud to note this in an exaggerated form: "Look around: two houses is the norm [among Russian immigrants]. And not houses just anywhere, but one in Newton and one on the Cape."[9] Confirming this assertion, a 2012 report by the Institute for the Study of Labor stated that unlike most groups classified as refugees, who tend to be less educated than economic migrants in general, Russian Jews were a definite outlier in this trend (Chiswick and Larsen 2012, 4–5). While the levels of language training were as low among Russian Jews upon immigration as with other migrant groups, their training developed much more rapidly with duration in the US, and quickly overtook levels of language development and earnings both among other immigrants and the native born. Overall, the Russian Jewish diaspora is wealthier and better educated than all other immigrant groups, not counting specifically economic migrations (like ones from Southeast Asia) (Chiswick and Larsen 2012, 5). The story of their successes can strike one as highly problematic for Russia, for had all of these talented people stayed in their country of origin, they would ostensibly have been a great asset in the development of the Russian tech industry.

The case of Russian Jewish IT specialists in Boston serves to illustrate that the availability of well-paid positions in the "upper-middle tech," with the potential for intellectual advancement, stability, and opportunities for the acquisition of new skills, made corporate American IT a desirable place of employment for thousands of Russian immigrants. Moreover, even abroad, Russian-owned business continues to be plagued with problems related to management and a poor business culture, which continually diminish its reputation, in some cases turning potential clients away. This is also a problem that was regularly invoked among foreigners seeking to work with businesses in Russia. It is also a systemic problem for the Russian "upper-middle tech."

It has long been the assumption, both in the FSU and now in Russia, that the country was missing a homegrown version of Silicon Valley, and that this was part of the problem it experienced. The Soviets famously tried to build their own region for computing in Zelenograd outside of Moscow (see Usdin 2005), as well as an open city of science and computing in Akademgorodok in Novosibirsk (see Indukaev, this volume). In the post-Soviet years, attempts to encourage startups and the flow of venture capital have resulted in major initiatives like Skolkovo, discussed by Aleksandra Simonova in her chapter, along with numerous other innovation clusters in Russia's various regions, like Tatarstan, described here by Alina Kontareva. The contemporary government's focus on entrepreneurship and startup culture, however, has largely glossed over the critical role of mature corporations for providing funding for basic innovation.[10] Investment numbers indicate that most venture capital goes toward infrastructural development required to grow a business, until a company reaches a sufficient size and credibility to be sold to a corporation

(Zider 1998). But beyond broader theories of economic development, Russian policy makers, eager to reverse brain drain through supporting the tech innovation sector, have entirely neglected the fact that for most highly educated Russian immigrants in the US, jobs in the "upper-middle tech," rather than markets for entrepreneurial activity and/or academic research, proved to be most compelling. If they are to learn from the case of Russian Jewish immigrants in Boston, attention to the creation of a stable, successful, well-managed "upper-middle tech," where employees receive both adequate compensation and intellectual stimulation, may be more fruitful than heavy investments in a startup-driven tech innovation scene.

NOTES

1. The number of people who came to America from the FSU is a matter of some debate. While we do not have statistics available for the entire US Russian diaspora, there exist statistics for the New York City and Philadelphia areas, from which numbers for other cities can be extrapolated. Hebrew Immigrant Aid Society (HIAS) statistics indicated that the Russian Jewish population in the New York metropolitan area totaled about 350,000, approximately 50 percent of the total Russian Jewish population for the United States (Kliger 2004).
2. Benjamin Phillips to Gil Preuss, October 10, 2006; cited in Sarna 2013.
3. "What can I tell you, my dear, about faraway America? / It's large and rich in oil and grain. / There are lots of banks, the climate is warm! The children age quickly, / The population is mostly made up of programmers" (author's translation).
4. All interviews with IT workers were conducted in Russian and translated by the author.
5. Iurii is most likely talking about hydraulic analog computers (hydrointegrators)—a family of analog hydraulic computers developed in the late 1930s and popularly used in the USSR until the 1980s. For a brief history of hydrointegrators see Solovieva 2000.
6. Post accessed on October 2, 2015. I have monitored discussions in this group for nine months in order to track what topics are important to its members. The topics have been quite varied, from advertisement to very personal discussions.
7. Reply to the post added on October 3, 2015, accessed November 12, 2015.
8. In the Soviet Union, apartments could not be bought and sold, but could, rather, be traded if all parties agreed. The system of trading established a kind of implicit hierarchy in terms of location, neighborhood, etc., while some people informally positioned themselves as trading facilitators who went to the trading offices on behalf of their clients and regularly scanned the ads. Additionally, the practice of renovating and subdividing apartments became common; for instance, one could turn a two-room apartment into a three-room by subdividing it, and then trade it for a three-room apartment elsewhere.

9. Newton is a wealthy suburb of Boston, also known for its excellent public school system. Cape Cod is a popular seaside vacation area, where owning a house can be quite costly.

10. For instance, numbers from 2014 indicate that of the record $48 billion venture capital investment, only 1 percent of the money went toward seed deals, while early-stage and expansion-stage funding received 33 percent and 41 percent, respectively (PwC MoneyTree 2014). This indicates that venture capital focuses on financing the expansion of an already-developed idea or product, and thus only encourages innovation after the initial R&D stage.

REFERENCES

Berliner, J. 1988. *Soviet Industry from Stalin to Gorbachev: Essays on Management and Innovation*. Ithaca, NY: Cornell University Press.

Chiswick, Barry, and Nicholas Larsen. 2012. "Russian Jewish Immigrants in the United States: The Adjustment of Their English Language Proficiency and Earnings in the American Community Survey." IZA Discussion Paper, no. 6854.

Elenkov, Detelin. 1988. "Can American Management Concepts Work in Russia? A Cross-Cultural Comparative Study." *California Management Review* 4, no. 4 (Summer): 133–56.

Ganguli, Ina. 2014. "Scientific Brain Drain and Human Capital Formation after the End of the Soviet Union." *International Migration* 52, no. 13: 95–110.

Gerovitch, Slava. 2013. "Parallel Worlds: Formal Structures and Informal Mechanisms of Postwar Soviet Mathematics." *Historia Scientiarum* 22, no. 3: 181–200.

King, J., and G. Naveh. 1999. "The Absorption into Employment of Immigrant Engineers." JDC-Brookdale Institute for Gerontology and Adult Human Development, Jerusalem.

Kliger, Sam. 2004. "Russian Jews in America: Status, Identity and Integration." AJC, paper presented at "Russian-Speaking Jewry in Global Perspective: Assimilation, Integration and Community-Building" Conference, June 14–16, Bar Ilan University, Israel.

Kukulin, I., and M. Mayofis. 2015. "Matematicheskie shkoli v SSSR: genesis institutsii i tipologiia utopii." In Kukulin, Mayofis, and Safronov, *Ostrova utopii*, 241–313.

Kukulin, I., M. Mayofis, and P. Safronov. 2015a. *Ostrova utopii: Pedagogicheskoe i sotsial'noe proektirovanie poslevoennoi shkoli (1940–1980e)*. Moscow: Novoe literaturnoe obozrenie.

Kukulin, I., M. Mayofis, and P. Safronov. 2015b. "Namivaia ostrova: pozdnesovetskaia obrazovatel'naia politika v sotsial'nikh kontekstakh." In Kukulin, Mayofis, and Safronov, *Ostrova utopii*, 5–32.

Lawrence, Paul R., and Charalambos Vlachoutsicos. 1990. *Behind the Factory Walls: Decision Making in the Soviet and U.S. Enterprises*. Cambridge, MA: Harvard Business School Press.

PwC MoneyTree. 2014. "The Technology Q3 2014 MoneyTreeTM Report." PwC
MoneyTree. Accessed November 10, 2015. http://www.pwcmoneytree.com
/Reports/FullArchive/Technology_2014-3.pdf.

Remennick, Larissa. 2012. *Russian Jews on Three Continents: Identity, Integration,
and Conflict.* New Brunswick, NJ: Transaction Publishers.

Safronov, P. 2015. "Ideia politekhnizatsii v otechestvennoi shkol'noi politike: pod-
gotovka reformi 1958 goda i krizis egalitarnoi ideologii." In Kukulin, Mayofis,
and Safronov, *Ostrova utopii.*

Sarna, Jonathan D. 2013. "America's Russian-speaking Jews Come of Age." In
*Toward a Comprehensive Policy Planning for Russian-Speaking Jews in North
America,* 1–27. Jerusalem: Jewish People Policy Institute. Accessed January 16,
2016. http://www.brandeis.edu/hornstein/sarna/contemporaryjewishlife
/russian-speakingjewscomeofage-jppi.pdf.

Saxenian, AnnaLee. 2007. *The New Argonauts: Regional Advantage in a Global
Economy.* Cambridge, MA: Harvard University Press.

Solovieva, O. 2000. "Vodianie vicheslitel'niie mashini." *Nauka i zhizn'* 4. Accessed
January 16, 2016. http://www.nkj.ru/archive/articles/7033/.

Steinhardt Social Research Institute, Brandeis University. 2006. "The 2005 Boston
Community Survey: Preliminary Findings." Report by the Steinhardt Social
Research Institute for Combined Jewish Philanthropies of Boston. Online. Ac-
cessed July 28, 2018. https://cdn.fedweb.org/fed-34/136/2005-Community-Study
-Report.pdf.

Usdin, Steven. 2005. *Engineering Communism: How Two Americans Spied for
Stalin and Founded the Soviet Silicon Valley.* New Haven, CT: Yale University
Press.

Zider, Bob. 1998. "How Venture Capital Works." *Harvard Business Review*
(November–December). https://hbr.org/1998/11/how-venture-capital-works.

CHAPTER TWELVE

JEWS IN RUSSIA AND RUSSIANS IN ISRAEL

Marina Fedorova

My interview with Stanislav, aged twenty-eight, included the following exchange:

> STANISLAV: You've been on Rothschild Boulevard, right?
>
> MARINA: Passing by every day. Buildings, trees, cafés. . . . Why?
>
> STANISLAV: Really? You don't know? It's the Silicon Street. It's the startup community.[1]

I had never heard of Rothschild Boulevard being the most prominent high-tech hub until that moment, and my informants had never heard of the celebrated Russian technical expertise until they met me.[2] As pointed out in the introduction and a leitmotif throughout this volume, Russian computer scientists build successful academic careers outside their homeland, and the best-recognized software brands in the world retain Russian programmers as valuable talent. Yet, surprisingly, the allure around the figure of Russian IT genius does not resonate in Israel.

Back in the 1990s,[3] Israel was still a country specializing in agriculture and gemstones; however, nowadays one may not be able to notice news about the Gaza War or Israeli medical breakthroughs over the sound of record-breaking investments flooding into the country's high-tech sector.[4] Israel stands out as a startup nation, and its citizens engaged in software development are the main asset of many global technological giants—such as Apple, Google, Intel, Microsoft, Amazon, Samsung, and others—which have opened R&D offices there.

High tech has become the driving force of the Israeli economy, and its development coincides with the massive immigration of highly skilled Russian Jews,[5] though the outcome of this wave still remains questionable. The issues that deserve discussion are how immigrants from the post-Soviet countries have fit into the Israeli economy—particularly into the now legendary Israeli high-tech sector—and why nobody in Israel hears the buzz around the virtuosity of Russian programmers. This chapter will address these questions by describing the experiences of two generations of Russians engaged in Israeli high tech for almost a quarter of a century.

HOW TO TRACE RUSSIANS TO ISRAELI HIGH TECH?

The collapse of the Soviet Union opened the gate for those looking for an opportunity to flee the scene of its undoing. Among those unwilling to wait for the dust to settle were many Russian Jews who immediately migrated to Israel. Israel's Central Bureau of Statistics estimates that close to one million post-Soviet immigrants came to Israel through aliyah[6] after the government of the Soviet Union lifted restrictions on movement and choice of residence (Yaffe and Tal 2001). The immigration wave of the 1990s was documented as the largest single wave of Russian Jews immigrating to Israel—after the United States imposed a quota on Soviet Jewish immigrants, making Israel the next most preferable destination (on how Russian Jews settled in the Boston area, see West, this volume).

For Russian Jews, emigrating to Israel is fundamentally different from emigrating to any other country: rather than posing obstacles, the State of Israel actively encourages immigration and not only grants instant citizenship status but also provides tangible assistance to newly arrived immigrants (details are provided later in this chapter). It is also noteworthy that for those who moved to Israel in the 1990s, leaving Russia was not a choice driven by the ambition to seek a career or—as it is true for Russians who relocate to Finland—a leisurely lifestyle (Shatokhina, this volume). Migration to Israel presented Russian Jews with an opportunity to escape anti-Semitism (see, e.g., Blank 1995; Korey 1995; Krupnik 1995; Gitelman 2001; Pinkus 1990) and create an affinity to the Jewish nation:

> I had another kind of sentiment back then. I needed to be among those like me; I needed to feel belonging to this nation, to feel comfortable, to feel that I'm a part of something bigger and to stop hiding. (Stepan, aged fifty-seven)

However, Zionist ideals were a secondary factor in the decision-making process of most Soviet Jews who migrated to Israel in the 1990s. This differed from the first wave of mass emigration during the 1970s, which was a result of Zionist conviction whereby Soviet Jews were "pulled" to Israel for ideological reasons. The second wave, however, was catalyzed by the collapse of the Soviet Union and is often referred to as "pragmatic" (Remennick 2009) or "panic" (Gitelman 2004) immigration. The unstable political situation, the uncertainty regarding economic well-being, and concerns about their children's future were primary factors that set in motion the massive influx of Russians in the 1990s, "pushing" them to Israel. As one of my informants noted:

> The question [of] why we moved to Israel back then seems irrelevant. It was a mass movement, a wave. Everybody was moving: our neighbors were moving to Israel, our friends were moving to Israel, our relatives were moving to Israel, and we did as well. (Georgii, aged thirty-six)

Since these two waves differed in motivation, they produced varying circumstances for the integration of newly arrived Jews. While those who arrived in the 1970s were interested in giving up their former identities and soon integrated into Israeli society, immigrants who came in the 1990s kept positive attitudes toward their former homeland and faced many hurdles during the process of assimilation.

Considering the immigrants' skills and the rapid expansion of the high-tech cluster, one would expect that Russians would be overrepresented in the Israeli software sector.[7] However, immigrants from the FSU experienced a substantial occupational downgrading, gave up their professional ambitions, and were compelled to move to other sectors of the Israeli economy (see Weiss 2000). This controversy makes it even more important to delve into the circumstances of their economic and professional integration.

While it is widely acknowledged by the media that post-Soviet aliyah made an important contribution to the high-tech cluster and educational system of Israel (see, e.g., Gur and Keinon 2009; Maital 2013; Maltz 2015; Sales 2013), scholars often question this opinion held by the public. The role of the post-Soviet immigration wave in the making of the Israeli high-tech cluster is, indeed, mentioned in the literature (Ariav and Goodman 1994; Avnimelech, Kenney, and Teubal 2005; Drori, Ellis, and Shapira 2013; Remennick 2003; Senor and Singer 2009; Trajtenberg 2002), but without a detailed description of their contributions beyond being considered a sustaining force in the sector. There are also a number of studies that claim that the contribution of highly skilled immigrants to the development of the Israeli high-tech cluster is complementary and indirect (Arora, Gambardella, and Klepper 2005; Avnimelech and Teubal 2006; Breznitz 2005b). Most of these studies take economic issues into account when discussing the influence of Russians on Israeli high tech. Yet, I believe that a focus on sociocultural aspects of this phenomenon may enrich our understanding of the role Russian techies have played in Israel and provide us with more insightful analysis.

During my fieldwork, many of my informants explained their professional difficulties through appealing to their "Russianness":

> For them [for native-born Israeli Jews] we are all Russians: Armenians, Belarusians, Georgians, Ukrainians, Baltic people—all who fled from the Soviet Union. It's obvious that we do everything differently, and it's never helped us in our careers. (Andrey, aged fifty-one)

However, this study does not use the word "Russians" as a conventional umbrella term for all FSU immigrants, rather as a concept through which we can explore the Soviet values they share. Using "Russianness" as a research lens helps us to unpack how the career paths of Russian immigrants and their role in the making of the Israeli high-tech industry were mediated by the mental baggage they brought with them from the USSR.

DIFFERENT GAME, DIFFERENT RULES

By virtue of their tenacity in clinging to their culture and customary way of life, Russian engineers and technologists have crafted alternative spaces for themselves within the Israeli economy. When Russians came to Israel in the 1990s, the software industry had started offering promising job opportunities, and technological entrepreneurship was perhaps not as prestigious in Israel back then as it is today, but it was cutting-edge. Also, Israel's absorption policy was able to ease the difficulties confronting immigrants on the capitalist market, since state agencies were actively involved in training,[8] job placement, and the immigrants' overall occupational adjustment, especially for those who were educated (see the detailed discussion in Remennick 2003, 2013). However, Russian Jews were less likely to embark on business ventures and more likely to enter the primary labor market. Instead of adjusting to the emerging startup ecosystem, Russians continued to play by the old rules they had internalized in the Soviet economy. Further, I discuss economic and cultural barriers that prevent the first generation of Russians from being at the forefront of Israeli high tech.

The newly arrived Russian Jews formed the core of the Soviet intelligentsia, and for them, careers in technical fields were particularly attractive, since they had been key to entering the mainstream of Soviet society. One might assume that having arrived in Israel with such training, they were limited only by the process of learning Hebrew and English (the latter being the lingua franca of software development). Yet, the Israeli economy was not able to fully utilize their skills. While some occupations (e.g., engineers, technicians, scientists) are often characterized as highly transferable to the host country of Israel (Mesch and Czamanski 1997; Raijman and Semyonov 1995), it was not easy for highly skilled Russian immigrants to get a position as an engineer or software developer.

Russians who arrived in Israel were exposed to a different environment in relation to the economic structure of production. To be sure, the USSR was neither a country of nimble startups nor did the large public sector enterprises that reigned supreme in Soviet industry reliably provide the expertise required by Israeli companies. The Russian technical elite came to Israel with specializations in relatively low-tech sectors that frequently did not match the needs of Israeli industries. Furthermore, in contrast to the conditions for highly skilled mobility to other countries, migration to Israel allows for entry without knowledge of the language, proof of qualifications, valid work contracts, or binding job offers. As a result, newly arrived Russians struggled with language and their lack of local networks, which are so important in the Israeli economy, and thus faced a very tight job market.

Usually, Russian immigrants who were previously involved in hardware maintenance or programming took retraining courses in order to enter the software niche, and once hired tried to remain in that position, thus limiting their professional mobility. The resistance to changing their workplace and exploring new opportunities was also predetermined by the fear of losing their jobs. Furthermore, they were trying to be loyal to one company; they did this as there was a widely held assumption among Soviet immigrants that hard work provides its own rewards and constitutes a claim in and of itself for being successful. However, while job hopping can be perceived as negative, in Israel, and especially in high tech, it usually means that a person is flexible, eager to obtain new knowledge, and good at networking. Since Russians had a very specific skill set and were reluctant to broaden their skills and connections, one may assume that they occupy a number of specific positions within the market, such as maintaining older computers running COBOL or Assembly languages. Those assumptions, however, were not confirmed by my fieldwork:

You can definitely hear from time to time these stories like someone hired his Russian gardener or pool man (laughing) as a technician to maintain old legacy applications. I personally feel those are exaggerated fairytales about being discovered, though I do believe there is a market for Cobol skills in Israel. And certainly, those who emigrated from the Soviet Union have expertise. But I can't really think of it as a specific niche for Russians. (Ivan, aged thirty-five)

The niche of maintaining old application software and old mainframes had no stable opportunities, and subsequently, it became almost effortless to find a job in this sector after the industry started its transition to newer technologies.

For those who were inclined to carry on their scientific careers inside Israeli academia, the conditions were even more inhospitable. Israeli universities did not have the capacity to integrate all Soviet scientists into their departments.[9] The Soviet Union's traditional strength in the theoretical sciences could have made an important contribution to Israeli academia, yet many of these scientists had difficulty penetrating Israel's scientific communities. Even the most famous scientists and scholars were struggling to find a job. One might think that this was due to the lack of language skills. However, Israeli academia was more concerned with the qualifications and competencies of newly arrived scientists, researchers, and teachers:

If there was a gap in technology, there was a gap in knowledge as well. Russia was thrown back to many years ago. The country used to be closed, there was no internet at that time to communicate, international connections or collaborations were almost nonexistent, and Israel had been successfully catching up with the rest of the world. . . . I was lucky I knew English and I had some publications in English as well, recommendations from the leading American universities. It saved me from unemployment. (Stepan, aged fifty-seven)

Cut off from both the international scientific community and from emergent high-tech consumer technologies, the majority were compelled to either retrain or take lower-ranking and lower-paying jobs, changing their socioeconomic status through a considerable downward occupational shift.

As opposed to the US, Great Britain, and Europe, which all have other sectors intensively using software (e.g., analytics, banking, finance, healthcare), the Israeli market has offered little choice for highly skilled Soviet immigrants, inducing them to move to the private sector and, in particular, to the software industry. To achieve this integration, Israel offered Soviet immigrants retraining courses and set policies to foster technological entrepreneurship.[10] Among all government programs[11] for stimulating the development of the Israeli high-tech cluster, one was specifically designed for Russian immigrants.

The Technological Incubator program was presented as a solution to provide highly qualified Russian engineers and scientists with instant job opportunities and aimed at assisting them in integrating into a capitalist economy. However, those of my informants who were involved in this program during their career path admitted that success stories were rare. Despite government efforts, by 2010 two-thirds of high-tech Incubator companies failed (Grimland 2010). Beginning from this period, Russians came to be labeled as "unable to build business"—a perception shared by most of my informants.

The existing stereotype that Russians cannot run a technological business has evidence to support it. Indeed, a number of works pointed to the fact that the Russian immigration wave of the 1990s failed to produce technological entrepreneurs (Arora, Gambardella, and Klepper 2005; Breznitz 2005b, 2007b; Kapur and McHale 2005). In his study on the career paths of founders of Israeli software companies that went public on foreign stock exchanges,[12] Breznitz came across only one Russian immigrant. He argues that it "points to the difficulties that immigrants from the former Soviet Union have in establishing successful start-ups in a capitalist economy" (Breznitz 2005b, 96).

However, I am not inclined to interpret this state of affairs exclusively as a result of their inability to operate in a capitalist economy due to a lack of entrepreneurial skills. In application to the current research, I would like to discuss this issue from the sociocultural point of view and try to unfold its complexity by taking a look at several dimensions that might have an impact on why Russians are unsuccessful in business.

Given the subtle or open discrimination of Jews in Russia, one might have assumed that immigrants were already prepared to exercise entrepreneurship in Israel as they had had to constantly game the Soviet system, inventing new ways of bypassing intolerance. The immigrants of the 1990s were used to flexibly navigating within the Soviet system in order to access resources that in most cases could only be obtained through *blat*.[13] Therefore, the fact that Russians have not, thus far, appeared to be prominent technological entrepreneurs might not be a result of the lack of entrepreneurial skills—which could have been obtained during their lives under the Soviet regime—but by a desire to finally stop hustling hard, as they had to do back in the USSR in order to survive the regime.

Another reason why Russians often chose not to pursue entrepreneurship, with all its risks and uncertainties, is their perceptions toward business. As a result of institutional restrictions on private property in the USSR, Soviet citizens did not know how to operate beyond the public sector or run a company. Moreover, any attempt at entrepreneurial activity was socially unacceptable, discouraged, or even prosecuted. In addition, the Soviet shortage economy had generated new entrepreneurial groups that adjusted to the economic situation at the time by selling goods illegally and at a higher price, obtaining shadow revenues. This led to the appearance of semilegal entrepreneurs,[14] who were treated as "dishonest speculators," publicly disrespected and "blamed for higher prices and the very intention of private gain" (Barsukova and Radaev 2012, 6). Therefore, entrepreneurial behavior and small enterprises were seen as illegitimate practices from the standpoint of the Soviet citizen. Such attitudes toward doing business might have influenced the choice of some Russians to seek more "regular" jobs with lifetime employment. Indeed, while Israel is often seen as a "nation of entrepreneurs" (Senor and Singer 2009), Russian immigrants do not always fit that description as they may lack flexibility and "entrepreneurial spirit"—cultural traits that are in high demand on the Israeli market. For the first generation of Russian immigrants, working in a small startup or starting their own company was considered risky:

> I started working as [an applied] mathematician, I worked in the field for which I trained, although it was a small firm. . . . Back then I still had the Soviet mentality, I thought that the right thing to do was to work for a big corporation. . . . And when I was offered a job at Israel Aircraft Industry— an enormous firm—I thought: "That's it!" However, I started there not as a mathematician, but as a programmer, though I didn't have any experience in programming. (Liudmila, aged fifty-two)

Liudmila deliberately shifted to another profession for a chance to be hired by a big corporation and to have guarantees. She admitted that it took her several years to realize that she would want "to try to make something of her own":

> Can you imagine such situation: I'm working in a huge corporation in Israel, I finally have stability, I have a newborn on my hands, hence, I can't be fired, I have benefits as a mother, I have high salary and a high position. . . .

And I left it all and opened a new firm on my own. It means my mentality had changed, and I wasn't scared anymore. . . . Although, there are people who would prefer money on a regular basis, stability, peaceful workdays, and then they would go on pension.

This case is an example of how Russian Jews, once they came to Israel, were trying to find stability under the roof of large enterprises. Liudmila also stated that during her work for Israel Aircraft Industry she met many talented Russians engineers, who held very high positions in the company. Another informant also said that usually Russians could be found in big companies, where they have been working for a long time:

I think they [Russians] were successful in engineering positions: they come, they sit, they do their work effectively. . . . And they have positions in Intel, IBM, big companies usually. . . . I think most Russians are less entrepreneurial, and more "sitting at a desk, doing their job" engineer type of people. (Igor, aged twenty-nine)

The lack of the startup ethos among Russian Jews was also highlighted by Diana Kurkovsky West in her study of Russians in the Boston area in this volume. The career strategies that Boston-based Russians have adopted are similar to those described above: Russian Jews both in the US and Israel were longing for stable and hierarchical positions, falling in the division of labor, rather than going for risky jobs.

In addition, all the first-generation informants I met (and even some among the younger generation) admitted that they enjoy a technological challenge and the very process of development, rather than managerial work. It is reasonable to think that such attitudes toward work could also be a part of the Soviet legacy, as the main concern with excellence in the technological part of the job could be a result of the Soviet tradition of technical education. This may partially be explained by the fact that Russians were socialized in government-funded institutions favorable to the performance of technical expertise, rather than to their use by market forces. In this respect, the understanding of professional success for Russians and Israelis is different. While Israelis strive for creating a prosperous business of their own,[15] Russians often prefer the opportunity to perform highly sophisticated technical work, choosing to stay behind the scenes.

The interviews also revealed that the first generation of Russians used to choose international corporations over Israeli firms not only because of the guarantees offered by the brand name[16] and limited local market opportunities but also because of the differences in work culture. One of my informants, who works in the American Israeli company Amdocs, gave an example:

> Sometimes they [Israelis] like to create unnecessary fuss. "Who says what" really matters, the overlap between the personal and the professional—it interferes with work. . . . And all I need is my computer, and I will continue doing my job. When I started working in a big company, it began to feel a lot easier. (Aleksey, aged fifty-one)

In my informants' narratives, the existence of different work styles is often supported by the popular anecdotal evidence that Russian techies are "gloomy" introverts who prefer to work on their own, while Israelis are more comfortable working in teams. Also, those informants who currently run their own companies admitted that if they were to choose between Israeli and Russian, they would, all other things being equal, opt for a Russian candidate because of the easiness in building a rapport.

The difference in working styles is insightful for the current analysis because it illustrates how the structure of an economy informs cultural attitudes toward work. While Russians due to their work culture seem to be more suitable for a job in a large corporation, Israelis prefer smaller organizations and startups. Catherine De Fontenay and Erran Carmel (2004, 52) attribute this difference to the incorporation of values developed during army training and argue that "the organizational skills developed in the military fit a small-to-medium sized operation better than in a large operation." They point to the similarity of functioning within an army unit and a startup and argue that Israeli firms have had difficulty growing because of Israeli organizational culture.

Therefore, despite government programs and policies of assimilation for recent immigrants, many Russian Jews who migrated to Israel feel that their mentality is very much connected to their country of birth. Consequently, their preserved Soviet values affected their professional lives and robbed them of their chances for success in Israeli high tech. While this might be expected for the first generation of Russian immigrants from the 1990s, the next generation of high-tech professionals—or, as they call themselves, the "1.5 generation"—who came to Israel at the age of seven to ten years old, also share these same feelings. This generation of Russians is now the driving force in the Israeli economy as they are currently active on the labor market, but no one speaks of them as technological gurus, as the rest of the world does about Russian immigrants involved in high tech and related fields. One might say that they cannot be considered "Russians" as they were brought up in Israeli society. Indeed, they see themselves as Israeli citizens, who graduated from Israeli universities and are devoted to their country—but are they untouched by the myth of the Russian programmer with world-class technological skills only as a result of successful integration?

EDUCATION, SOVIET STYLE

Who breeds the IT force in Israel? For those who live in Israel, the answer is obvious: the Israeli Army plays a crucial role in the development of the software industry, supplying it with highly skilled labor and technological spin-offs (Breznitz 2005a; Senor and Singer 2009) as well as maintaining a business ecology as effectively as leading universities do in Silicon Valley.[17] However, Russians of the 1.5 generation chose to prioritize education over army service and to socialize professionally in the institutions established by the Russian diaspora. Thus, the greatest strength of the 1990s wave of immigrants—the Soviet tradition of education—has become their greatest weakness. In what follows, I illustrate how the next generation of Russians who stepped into the labor market fell into the trap of their Soviet heritage, just as their parents had.

Graduates of the military technological units gain preferred terms in the business world far beyond Israel's borders. In particular, Unit 8200[18] has developed a reputation as a brand in cybersecurity and, in Israeli terms, service in this unit is equivalent to a degree from MIT or Stanford. When it comes to high-tech jobs in Israel, a university degree is considered to be overrated and much less important than military training:

> The army produces talents that are very competitive with university graduates, in many cases, they are much better, especially in certain fields. Sometimes—for example in security—there can be even a knowledge gap because they actually invent those things in the army: they don't learn how to, they just do. . . . The academia is a self-proclaimed system: they invented their own system of degrees to signal about what you learned. The army doesn't give you a degree, but it's a signal you've already applied what you learned. . . . A person with a degree is going to get a lower salary than someone with experience from the technological unit. (Stanislav)

However, for those Russians who came to Israel as teenagers the only path that seemed intelligible and natural was going to study at a university.

The reason is rooted in their sociocultural profile: Russian Jews, or at least their intellectual elite, are motivated not only to preserve former cultural patterns and values but also to install some of these patterns in their new environment, for example in the area of education. Since their arrival, the Russian immigrants have been dissatisfied with the quality of the Israeli educational system, and this led to the establishment of alternative educational practices (see Horowitz 2005).

The Shevah Mofet science school in Tel Aviv was initially designed by immigrants from the former Soviet Union for their children. Lately, they have developed into a chain of schools or science clubs (*kruzhki*). These learning centers had become hubs for professional training and for Russian-speaking community outreach as they were run by parents with a background in mathematics and physics who volunteered to teach "Russian-style science." Word of mouth had made possible the engagement of Russian parents and children from all across Israel, which helped the Shevah Mofet school system overcome the transition from a local phenomenon to an integral part of state schools. On the one hand, this is a success story of Russian aliyah in respect to the involvement of Russians in Israeli high tech; on the other hand, the language of instruction was Russian as were all the teaching materials, which subsequently led to even more separation and segregation as children's cliques become insular.

Education provided by the Russian community created an alternative framing for thinking about education and career development among Russians, as it cultivated a Russian understanding of vocation specifically in the fields of computer science and software engineering, which in several ways made Russians invisible in developing Israeli high tech. Thus, the 1.5 generation has had its own unique experience: having been raised in Israel and educated in its school system, but still under the influence of the milieu created by their parents.

The influence has cut both ways, however. Israel's educational system has undergone drastic changes through the involvement of Russian immigrants. Initially designed for immigrants, Mofet has become attractive to native-born Israelis as well:

> Mofet is a Russian trend. Although now my daughter has in her class only a couple of Russians, initially such a type of education that specializes in physics and mathematics was introduced by Russians here. In the beginning there were only Russian kids; however, now the overwhelming majority is Israeli. . . . I think, maybe, this was our [Russian] influence, because Israeli kids, as a rule, don't learn so hard at such a young age. (Liudmila)

However, the Russian tradition of education spread beyond the high school classroom. During the middle of the 1990s, Russian immigrant professors were still adjusting to the market and trying to learn the language. Throughout the country there were universities where courses in mathematics and physics were taught in Russian, allowing immigrant students to preserve specific ethics toward study and work.

While native-born Israelis after graduating from school were gaining professional experience during army service, Russians of the 1.5 generation, prejudiced in favor of higher technical education, were still trying to succeed through more classical pathways into professions, that is: finish school, attend university, and then complete compulsory military service:

> It goes without saying that the army service was off the table. There was no doubt I was going to university first. It was mandatory. I just couldn't go to the army as we [family] thought that I must have a degree first. Back in Russia chances were that they would choose a Russian specialist over a Jew for a job. In Israel, when it was that awful situation with unemployment, they would hire a Jewish guy instead of a Russian one. (Georgiï, aged thirty-six)

Such decision-making was driven by the idea of the paramount role of technical education, which is still very common in Russia. It usually comes with the reassurance that your children will always be able to earn their daily bread. For many Russian immigrants, technical education was the only option as they believed that it would safeguard their future:

> At some point, I envied my friend who before his high-tech career went to Oxford and was studying art there. Just because he wanted to do so and his parents were very supportive of him. My parents would never support my obsession with art or philosophy or anything of that kind. And there is no one to help me out, so I had to choose wisely. (Anton, aged thirty-four)

Furthermore, Russians opt for studying theoretical subjects, rather than applied ones. Two of my informants, who work in computer science and software engineering departments, admitted that they almost never see Russians among their students:

> You should look for Russians in the departments of Mathematics and Physics. This is at some point silly and naive as kids still don't understand that: if they want a career in high tech, they should go and become a software engineer. This is simple: to succeed one needs to look for an educational track beyond the fundamental courses. (Maksim, aged fifty-six)

One of my informants also admitted that he would change his mind if he knew that mathematical education would never serve him as a competitive advantage:

That was Russian insanity. Adequate people don't do that. They don't go to universities unless they want to be scientists. So, what we were doing by going to universities first is simply making the distance between us and Israelis even greater. That's why there are so many stereotypes about our inadequacy in business-related or even career-related matters. (Daniil, aged thirty-five)

The conditions listed above substantially decreased chances for Russians to find their first job through personal networks, since they were usually part of the "wrong" crowd. My informants told me that they struggled a lot at the beginning of their careers as their "Russianness," which was very helpful during their studies, proved to be ineffective in moving forward on their career path in Israel. As my informants explained, native-born Israelis tend to "fall into" jobs, asking for referrals from friends and relatives. In addition, one can gain a market advantage by leveraging one's Israeli clique:

We made our startup happen so easily with the help of one simple trick: my cofounder is a native-born Israeli, and his father is an investor. I mean this is his job, and I hope you can imagine how many other investors and people in the industry he knows and outside of Israel as well. That's a key to almost every door, and Russians don't hold such keys on their own. (Anton)

However, not the lack of social networks per se but the lack of local knowledge ("knowing the rules of the game") has influenced the professional development of the 1.5 generation, since the only perspective they had on education revolved around those Russian beliefs on career development that they shared with their parents.

The major obstacle to the success of the 1.5 generation in Israeli high tech was a lack of knowledge about the role of military training. There is a strong link between citizenship in Israel and military service. The Israeli Army represents a shared purpose of "survival," and its soldiers are treated like heroes who guard the safety of the country every single day. It is a special honor to serve in the technological units as the first prime minister of Israel, David Ben-Gurion, declared that in order to survive, Israel must always be technologically superior to its enemies (Avnimelech and Harel 2012). However, there was no way that the first generation of Russians would see the army as a promising career step into high tech. Russians perceive the army very differently: not only is it not considered to be the supreme symbol of civic duty, but it could also be dangerous even in peacetime.

The most obvious concern of every Russian parent is to safeguard their child from army service. In post-Soviet Russia (as well as during the last decades of the USSR) nobody wanted to see their child enter military service: the reason is that recruits face extreme forms of bullying, called *dedovshchina*. This phenomenon encompasses a variety of physical and psychological abuses that sometimes even result in death. Chances are high that children will have a traumatic experience during their military service in Russia—if they simply do not wear the maroon beret[19] or have not got an honor to be in the Presidential Regiment. The perception of the Israeli Army was aggravated by the fact that service is mandatory for women as well as men and that the country, involved in conflicts for decades, is constantly in a state of war. In fact, children of immigrants shared their parents' concerns and attitudes toward military service. Many Russians of the 1.5 generation prioritized getting a degree and postponed their army service in order to invest in higher education. As a result, they turned to an alternative institutional socialization that was not common in Israeli society, but customary for the former Soviet citizens. While for any other profession the sequence does not play a crucial role, for the career track in the Israeli high-tech industry it has significant repercussions, which will be discussed further below.

IF YOU'RE NOT WITH THE ARMY, YOU'RE NOT HIGH TECH

One of the central nodes in the national innovation system of Israel is the military, which facilitates learning, information diffusion, and professional community building (Breznitz 2005a). The Israeli Army provides immigrants with skills that help them to operate within Israeli society in general and Israeli high tech in particular.

A high level of cultural and social integration is the major benefit an immigrant gleans from military service: the army levels the field and provides immigrants with opportunities for developing both skills and contacts (Senor and Singer 2009). Israeli professional networks are often based on relationships formed during army service. All of my informants touched on the topic of the army's role in professional development; in their narratives, they emphasized that often one line on a CV listing service in a unit of the intelligence corps could determine future career prospects not only in Israel but in the US. It is a well-known fact that the development of sophisticated technologies in Israel has stemmed from the existing base of competencies provided by military research in such elite technological units as MAMRAM,[20] Talpiot, Unit 8200, MAMDAS,[21] and Unit 8153. Despite the fact that these units accept recruits on merit, the lack of initial connections nonetheless plays an important role for Russians. In order to get into the technological units, Russians not only need to have clearance and confirm that their time of residence meets the requirements, but they also need recommendations. My informants told me that, in particular, the intelligence corps is notorious for replicating itself and having dynasties on duty:

> I got there based on connections. If it hadn't been for my brother's friend who used to serve in this unit, I would never have gotten there as I didn't have connections of my own. And now I know a lot of my friends bring in their brothers, sisters. Of course, they need to get through the test first, but it's much easier to get through the screening if someone vouched for you. (Igor)

However, army connections come in handy mostly in civilian life. Not only are "graduates" from the technological units better paid, but they also have an easier time finding a job, since they are often recruited by "alumni" of their own "alma mater." The same informant stressed that having connections in the army is "the most important thing in the entrepreneurial world," both skill-wise and in terms of networking:

> University is irrelevant. If I need to hire two more people, then taking people not from our unit is something I don't want to do. I don't hire people from the university unless I don't have a choice. . . . Education in the army is FAR more effective than a degree, ten times more. If I needed to build a new algorithm for something, I would rather take a PhD person. But I need to get things done, and most of the challenges are not that big in software design. . . . And I think most of the people from our units don't do interviews, don't ask for the CV. . . . I know many people in the army that I count on, and I can just ask, who is leaving the army soon and is a strong guy and I will hire him straight away. (Igor)

My informants also recalled a great number of occasions when army friends cofounded a startup. Thus, in Israel military training allows one to be simultaneously a professional in high demand and a thriving entrepreneur without having a degree. Although, interestingly, the absence of a degree indirectly affects the level of migration and keeps the best and brightest in the country:

> The main problem is a visa. It's not that simple to get a US work visa. And for me not having a degree makes it almost impossible to get a work visa there, but if I had a big enough company and I moved it there, then there would be options. (Igor)

Aside from training and building professional networks, the army facilitates the movement of venture capital: the military background of a candidate helps in the process of screening applications, as data on a person's unit is a signal for investors that a person has leadership qualities and relevant experience (Breznitz 2005a). Indeed, both employers and investors look for promising candidates with the managerial skills they receive at a very young age during their army service.

The army forms the "antihierarchical ethos" (Senor and Singer 2009), which follows Israelis into their enterprises and ignites potent startups. Although the Israeli military is far from a small organization, many of its units function rather independently (De Fontenay and Carmel 2004). Due to this relatively flat organizational structure, important assignments are often delegated downward to privates and, consequently, they develop a strong sense of responsibility. The purpose of assignments is to teach soldiers to respond quickly to unpredictable changes, to think strategically, and to be able to communicate their opinions up the chain of command. The ability to come up with solutions and promptly implement them is valued in the Israeli Army, although it requires a high level of organizational flexibility. The Israeli Army had to redefine hierarchy and control to speed up the implementation of innovations. The case of my informant illustrates the military's lack of hierarchy in action:

> I had a startup back in the army. I came up with an idea of how to use artificial intelligence to automatically detect failures of the machine. Typically, in the beginning, a soldier starts with learning how to properly diagnose failures. So, he gets some failures, needs to diagnose and his commander asks him: "Could you tell me what the pressure is there? And what voltage? Do you hear noises? Where are they from?" And he was always right. And I told myself: "Well, if he can do this, the machine must be able to do this as well." . . . Then I built the first prototype, and when a soldier came to diagnose, I told my commander: "Wait, don't tell him, let's use the software." And it worked. It diagnosed the problem. . . . Two months later they told me to stop working on anything else, but this software. I went to pitch to a very high-ranked general, and I prepared the presentation, showing my vision of how they could reduce the number of technicians by 30 percent. . . . They asked me what I needed for this project. . . . I was still the lowest rank in the army but started working with thirty people, some of them were officers. . . . I was a nonofficer leading the team of officers. Nobody prepared them for that. And I said: "Listen, I'm not your commander, we are

a startup." . . . We started working and then we won several national prizes. It shaped me a lot. I know how to dare to deal with things that challenge the status quo. (Stanislav)

The most striking part of this story is that he had to figure out how to make other people do what he wanted without bureaucratic or financial authority and managed to do that. That is why the Israeli Army is rightfully considered to be a hotbed for high-tech entrepreneurs: it provides its "graduates" with the attitude and skills essential for running a technological business.

Another important function of army connections is the creation of dense knowledge networks (Breznitz 2005a). Professional networks are important in the civilian market as they provoke information spillovers between local Israeli firms,[22] creating the circulation of knowledge and successful practices that follow the movement of human capital. At the same time, the army also functions like multinationals in terms of growing the skill base, technology transfer, and setting organizational models and standards for the industry along with being the supplier of spin-offs.[23] These functions that the military performs make an invaluable contribution to the development of the Israeli high-tech industry and are especially important in creating a unified body of professionals.

Indeed, the training offered in the army sets the standards of software development, because the "graduates" of the technological units will use their competencies in the civilian market and will nourish it with the specific techniques they learned. Thus, the army has taken upon itself the role of educating the professional community. One of my informants told me that the high-level quality assurance of Israeli programmers' skills derives from the fact that all army-trained professionals carry out development strictly according to software engineering principles and standards:

> In the army, we were taught that software should be written in a structured way, according to methodologies we were studying. They put a great emphasis on documentation, all those questions of maintaining, like readability and stuff. (Ivan)

The concern about quality is significant in military software development and intensifies the training process as it implies not only professional but also civic responsibility. Recruits learn almost immediately how to deal with technologies and make them bug free and stable, as public safety and the independence of the state are at stake. When graduates of the military technological units enter the civilian market, they spread those techniques and high requirements across the cluster. The military normalizes not only professional but also organizational practices in the Israeli economy. Thus, the country has a relatively homogeneous local market favorable to the military spin-offs or startups founded by graduates, operating in a familiar milieu.

The organizational practices obtained during military service deserve further attention. My informants pointed out that the army provided them with a unique vocational ethos and norms that cannot be replicated anywhere else:

> Each organization has its own culture. And the culture there [in the military] is just right for getting things done. It's really hard to change an organizational culture. Really, really hard. If you take someone who was in the university—a great student and everything—and give him a challenge, something that you yourself don't know anything about, will he be scared or will he say to you, "Hell yeah, let's do this!"? It's also part of the culture. I don't want to educate someone how to operate like this. I will hire a guy who used to work for five years—day in day out—sometimes for forty hours without sleep. (Igor)

In this way, the army provides the industry with technological standards that can be formalized and with more intangible, cultural "standards" that can be obtained only through experience.

Dan Breznitz (2005a, 21–22) made a crucial point about the difference between university and military training, highlighting that they are centered around different approaches to software development. One, he argues, treats software as an academic discipline evolving from mathematics and electrical engineering, while the other treats software as a vocation and trains people to have the skills to write programs providing solutions to specific problems. The notable finding made by Breznitz is that historically vocational training appeared in Israel before the establishment of an academic computer science career path, the latter becoming a complementary training system for software programming in Israel. This transitional, medium-level education makes the Israeli case exceptional in terms of the production of highly skilled professionals. It exemplifies that tertiary education, often neglected, especially in today's Russia, plays an important role in software development, since it has a lot of routine and practical steps that relate more closely to artisanal than to scientific work. Those Russians who were introduced to the academic system first appeared to be trapped in a state of gaining hands-on experience for a much longer period in comparison to their Israeli peers, who were introduced to vocational training. Instead of going from bottom to top in their professional development (the paradigm offered by military training), Russians had to go in the opposite direction, and learn on the job how to apply the knowledge they obtained at the university. This negatively influenced their overall performance and may have reduced their value on the market for a certain period, while they were adjusting their competencies to the needs of the industry. Several of my informants told me that there were even cases when Russians managed to voluntarily skip army service and go straight from university to industry, which is punishable by imprisonment.

However, after finishing an academic degree, Russian graduates could take their chances of getting into one of the technological units, if their area of study lay in a field related to information technology. For those who had a different specialization, but had prior experience in software programming, there was also an opportunity to take several tests and be considered. However, in the early 2000s, such a trajectory required three more years in addition to the compulsory service.[24] This not only postponed their entrance into the civil labor market but also meant they were unable to learn in practice and did not share the work ethic that is cultivated by the military software development. One of my informants explained:

> We just simply didn't know that was possible, that you could choose the army as the educational and career track. Everyone goes to the army, but we simply didn't know about the existence of such schemes, we didn't have such friends who could enlighten us. . . . I would say all of the Russians went straight to university or, at least, all of us were definitely going to. (Daniil)

The process of recruiting for service in the technological units resembles the standard process of applying to the university. Only students talented in sciences or mathematics after passing several exams and going through rounds of selection are admitted to the training programs. As a rule, a special position in the army comes with extensive training, thereby requiring additional years of service for this purpose.[25] Recruits who have previous experience in programming or knowledge in computer science and who successfully pass all the tests can be offered a special service track that results in fewer years of service. Among my informants were several Mofet graduates and some of them served fewer years since they already had certain programming skills at the moment of screening and were able to secure a professional position right away.

However, a six-month preparatory course in the MAMRAM programming school was the main track that Russians were choosing to get into technological units.[26] The important feature of this path is that a candidate should have good potential, but any prior background in programming is not necessary. After graduating, students serve in one of the technological units or may be offered a position in MAMRAM itself. However, this track required two and a half years in addition to compulsory service.[27]

Due to the lack of army experience, the 1.5 generation started their careers later than most Israelis, entering the labor market with fewer chances to compete for lucrative jobs. Yet a lot of Russians often form the intellectual backbone of startup companies, enjoying nonadministrative positions or being technical managers that are usually on the backstage of real success. As they are also lacking in financial and business experience and have homogeneous social networks (most of their friends are usually Russian immigrants like themselves) they hardly ever start a business of their own.

However, today there is a significant shift in attitudes toward work. Many Russians of the 1.5 and the second generations are part of a startup community. If they are not founders, they all are trying to find a job in a startup:

I've been working in the civil sector for fourteen years or so and I've never been a classical employee. Even when our startup died, I didn't see myself at Google, though I had several offers. . . . It's boring and slow. I don't want to be a cog in the machine; I need to see my results, to see that my work has its fruits. You'll never have it, working in a company. (Ivan)

Working in a startup, or at least in a local company, is considered to be more desirable. Moreover, Israeli companies create the chain of supply between the army and industry:

We hire graduates of elite units through recommendations right after their army service. Graduates know our startups and want to work with us [startup founders], rather than with big corporations, like Microsoft. . . . We don't compete for people because big corporations are not trusted that much. (Igor)

In addition, I want to emphasize again the pivotal effect that the first generation of Russian immigrants from the 1990s has had on their children's perceptions toward career choices. The intergenerational transmission of values has a more prolonged effect over time than one might expect. Since the first generation preferred to stay socially and culturally segregated, they were able to translate to their children values that dominated Russian society. Despite the fact that the 1.5 generation of Russian immigrants were raised in Israeli society, one can still detect the cultural footprints of their "Russianness" in their professional biographies. Thus, two generations of

Russian immigrants fell under the influence of Soviet heritage and have preserved certain values toward education and work.

Despite the commonly held opinion about transferability of technical skills, this study has shown that their utilization in the host economy is culturally sensitive. The differences in cultural and professional socialization presented themselves as barriers for Russians to fit into the Israeli software sector.

The economic structure of Israel was not the same as that of the Soviet Union, so that the high level of training acquired in the home country produced negative returns in Israel, as it could not be exploited by local industries. One could argue that Russian techies have not succeeded in Israel because they failed to integrate into the local capitalist economy, but this chapter argues that the issue has multiple layers. On the one hand, Russians could have been deliberately trying to avoid self-employment upon arrival in Israel, as they wanted to find stability that was not available for them under the Soviet regime. On the other hand, the Russian mindset was built on the traditions of Soviet educational excellence, particularly in mathematics and science; therefore, they were more concerned with the technology itself, rather than with learning free-market mechanisms to commercialize it.

The aspiration for educational excellence cultivated by Russian parents pushed many of their children to pursue first an academic track. By going to the university first, many Russians of the 1.5 generation, who are now at the peak of their careers and influence, were socialized into professions and society through an alternative model. While most of them went to universities and studied mathematics, physics, and other exact sciences, thereby respecting the Russian normative priority of education, Israelis went into army service and gained the hands-on experience that is in demand on the Israeli high-tech market. Due to the lack of practical experience—and especially military experience—in dealing with sophisticated technologies, the 1.5 generation started their careers later than most of their Israeli counterparts, entering the labor market with fewer privileges and competencies. As a result, the 1.5 generation, as well as their parents, are not notable in Israel's technological landscape.

The mental baggage Russians brought with them from the FSU has impacted their career paths and the role they play(ed) in the making of the Israeli high-tech industry. However, the effects of Soviet influence on Russians' mindsets has not worn off just yet.

Even now that second-generation Russians are present in the market, few are visible as startup founders. Successful Russian Israeli entrepreneurs I met pointed to cultural aspects to understand this state of affairs. Russians aspire to excellence in a principled and stubborn fashion. Should a Russian entrepreneur notice that his project does not promise great prospects, he will fight until the end, trying to make things work, as Russians usually perceive their startups "as if it were their own child" or as a life project, and often prefer to stay after the acquisition. In the same situation, an Israeli entrepreneur will drop it without hesitation and switch to the next project after the acquisition,[28] since, indeed, "Israel's entrepreneurial culture of exit is blamed on shortsightedness and a focus on immediate monetary return" (Drori, Ellis, and Shapira 2013, 162).

This issue takes us back to Rothschild Boulevard. The street is creating a critical mass of entrepreneurial density. It has gentrified since 2005 and has become one of Tel Aviv's most expensive neighborhoods. Young entrepreneurs flock to the area, opening their offices there so that companies can learn from each other and share resources. One of my informants said that this street is gradually changing Israeli attitudes:

> And now they are building a lot of skyscrapers there for their offices because the demand is crazy. And then, once you have so many acquisitions or exits, all these new millionaires or billionaires, they become investors, so that they fuel the next generation of startups. So now you see different kinds of companies, they are not like those ten years ago. People suddenly wanted to build big companies and long-lasting companies, and they don't want to exit. And it's an interesting question to ask: "Why?" I don't know why: maybe it's a maturity, maybe it's like fashion. . . . I don't know.[29] (Stanislav)

Given the entrepreneurial activity of Rothschild Boulevard, we may be witnessing a new stage in Israel's regional development. And maybe in this emerging culture that aims at creating self-sufficient companies, we will soon be able to find more "Russian" startups.

NOTES

1. All interviews with IT workers were conducted in Russian and translated by the author.
2. During my fieldwork in Israel, I conducted thirty biographical interviews with Russian-speaking Israeli citizens (aged twenty-three to sixty-five) who migrated to Israel from the post-Soviet countries (from 1990 to 2012).

3. This chapter is focused on the 1990s—a period when the software industry in Israel grew at impressive rates and when the biggest wave of Russian aliyah happened.

4. In Israel, they say "high tech" referring to what in Russia we call "information technology." The term "information technology" in Israel does not cover programming/software development as it defines a very specific niche of activities designed to facilitate interactions between "clients" and software developers, e.g., to write functional specifications, to describe systems' design.

5. Hereinafter "Russians." By "Russians" I mean Russian-speaking Jews, who migrated to Israel from the post-Soviet space, according to the Law of Return.

6. Organized immigration of Jews from the diaspora to Israel. The term "aliyah" has a positive connotation and literally means "ascent."

7. The 1990s wave of Russian immigrants was substantially composed of Soviet Jews with academic training: nearly 60 percent of the immigrants received higher education in the USSR, which was higher than the share of people with higher education among Israelis (at 40 percent) (Yaffe and Tal 2001).

8. The Israeli government provides immigrants with free basic training in Hebrew and one free job training program.

9. On how Russians fit into the Israeli academia, see De Fontenay and Carmel 2004; Kheimets and Epstein 2001; Yelenevskaya and Fialkova 2009.

10. It is worth noting that a number of scholars have emphasized that new national priorities emerged with the arrival of Soviet immigrants (Avnimelech and Harel 2012; Avnimelech and Teubal 2006; Breznitz 2007a).

11. Such programs included Inbal, Yozma, Magnet, and Technological Incubators (see Avnimelech and Harel 2012).

12. The difficulty of such analysis is heightened by the fact that most Israeli software startups rely on American investors and shareholders to go global. Israeli companies have adopted the strategy of entering joint ventures with more established US companies (since the establishment of the Binational Industrial Research and Development; see, e.g., Avnimelech and Teubal 2004) or creating alliances with multinational corporations (Breznitz 2005b). Consequently, it has become hard to track the ownership of startups and trace the Israeli roots of their development. It is even more challenging to identify Russian Jews among the founders who, in addition, might have changed their names to Israeli ones. However, during my fieldwork, I met thirteen successful Russian Israeli entrepreneurs from both generations. Still, they remain relatively "invisible," since their companies either have not done an initial public offering yet or were acquired by bigger companies.

13. Blat is the use of informal channels and personal networks to obtain goods and services. For further discussion of blat, see Ledeneva 1998.

14. The best-known examples are small traders (*fartsovshchiki*) and "shuttle traders" (*chelnoki*).

15. The early 1990s brought a cultural shift where entrepreneurship increasingly gained prestige in Israel society (Avnimelech and Harel 2012; Breznitz 2005b).

16. A large number of Israeli technological companies were too small to compete with MNCs (Breznitz and Ornston 2013), thereby threating job security.
17. On how the universities in Silicon Valley create networks of practice and knowledge networks in close reciprocal interaction with the industry, see Saxenian 1994.
18. Unit 8200 is a special unit responsible for collecting signal intelligence and code decryption.
19. In Russia, the maroon beret is the symbol of the elite special forces (*spetsnaz*). It is worn by commandos of the Ministry of Internal Affairs (MVD).
20. Center of Computing and Information Systems. MAMRAM is the software-oriented elite unit, which is part of a bigger parental unit Lotem, the Unit for Telecommunications and Information Technology.
21. Air Force Operational Software and Development Center. Nowadays, MAMDAS is the R&D unit of the Israeli Air Force called Ofet.
22. AnnaLee Saxenian (1994) observed that knowledge spillovers played a key role in the formation of the Silicon Valley ecosystem. Derived from personal connections and interfirm mobility, they promoted the spread of technologies and organizational structures between companies across the cluster.
23. On the role of multinationals, see Giarratana, Pagano, and Torrisi 2005.
24. Nowadays, men serve thirty-six months and women serve twenty-four months.
25. If one wishes to serve in one of the technological units, they have to stay in the army for a longer period. The time of the service above the compulsory period differs across the units. For instance, the Talpiot program for recruits with outstanding potential in science lasts nine years.
26. While there are other technological units that have their own educational programs, only MAMRAM offers a pre-army course.
27. Data from the interviews. Information is relevant for the early 2000s.
28. Israeli culture does not stigmatize failure and repeatedly brings failed entrepreneurs back into the system (Senor and Singer 2009, 20).
29. Compare with Martin Kenney and Richard Florida's (2000) study on the role of venture capitalists in the early history of the Bay Area.

REFERENCES

Ariav, Gad, and Seymour Goodman. 1994. "Israel: Of Swords and Software Plowshares." *Communications of the ACM* 37, no. 6: 17–21.

Arora, Ashish, Alfonso Gambardella, and Steven Klepper. 2005. "Organizational Capabilities and the Rise of the Software Industry in the Emerging Economies: Lessons from the History of Some U.S. Industries." In *Underdogs to Tigers: The Rise and Growth of the Software Industry in Some Emerging Economies*, edited by Ashish Arora and Alfonso Gambardella, 171–206. Oxford: Oxford University Press.

Avnimelech, Gil, and Shai Harel. 2012. "Global Venture Capital 'Hotspots': Israel." In *Handbook of Research on Venture Capital*, edited by Hans Landstrom and Colin Mason, 209–26. Cheltenham, UK: Edward Elgar Publishing.

Avnimelech, Gil, Martin Kenney, and Morris Teubal. 2005. "The Life Cycle Model for the Creation of National Venture Capital Industries: The US and Israeli Experiences." In *Clusters Facing Competition: The Importance of External Linkages*, edited by Elisa Giuliani, Roberta Rabellotti, and Meine Pieter van Dijk, 195–214. Aldershot, UK: Ashgate.

Avnimelech, Gil, and Morris Teubal. 2004. "Venture Capital-Start Up Co-evolution and the Emergence of Israel's New High Tech Cluster." *Economics of Innovation and New Technology* 13, no. 1: 33–60.

Avnimelech, Gil, and Morris Teubal. 2006. "Creating Venture Capital Industries That Co-evolve with High Tech: Insights from an Extended Industry Life Cycle Perspective of the Israeli Experience." *Research Policy* 35, no. 10: 1477–98.

Barsukova, Svetlana, and Vadim Radaev. 2012. "Informal Economy in Russia: A Brief Overview." *European Electronic Newsletter Economic Sociology* 13, no. 2: 4–12.

Blank, Naomi. 1995. "Redefining the Jewish Question from Lenin to Gorbachev: Terminology or Ideology?" In *Jews and Jewish Life in Russia and the Soviet Union*, edited by Yaacov Ro'i, 51–66. Portland, OR: Frank Cass.

Breznitz, Dan. 2005a. "Collaborative Public Space in a National Innovation System: A Case Study of the Israeli Military's Impact on the Software Industry." *Industry and Innovation* 12, no. 1: 31–64.

Breznitz, Dan. 2005b. "The Israeli Software Industry." In *Underdogs to Tigers: The Rise and Growth of the Software Industry in Some Emerging Economies*, edited by Ashish Arora and Alfonso Gambardella, 72–98. Oxford: Oxford University Press.

Breznitz, Dan. 2007a. "Industrial R&D as a National Policy: Horizontal Technology Policies and Industry-State Co-evolution in the Growth of the Israeli Software Industry." *Research Policy* 36, no. 9: 1465–82.

Breznitz, Dan. 2007b. *Innovation and the State: Political Choice and Strategies for Growth in Israel, Taiwan, and Ireland*. New Haven, CT: Yale University Press.

Breznitz, Dan, and Darius Ornston. 2013. "The Revolutionary Power of Peripheral Agencies: Explaining Radical Policy Innovation in Finland and Israel." *Comparative Political Studies* 46, no. 10: 1219–45.

De Fontenay, Catherine, and Erran Carmel. 2004. "Israel's Silicon Wadi: The Forces behind Cluster Formation." In *Building High-Tech Clusters: Silicon Valley and Beyond*, edited by Timothy Bresnahan and Alfonso Gambardella, 40–77. Cambridge: Cambridge University Press.

Drori, Israel, Shmuel Ellis, and Zur Shapira. 2013. *The Evolution of a New Industry: A Genealogical Approach*. Stanford, CA: Stanford University Press.

Giarratana, Marco, Alessandro Pagano, and Salvatore Torrisi. 2005. "The Role of the Multinational Companies." In *Underdogs to Tigers: The Rise and Growth of the Software Industry in Some Emerging Economies*, edited by Ashish Arora and Alfonso Gambardella, 207–35. Oxford: Oxford University Press.

Gitelman, Zvi Y. 2001. *A Century of Ambivalence: The Jews of Russia and the Soviet Union, 1881 to the Present*. Bloomington: Indiana University Press.

Gitelman, Zvi Y. 2004. "The 'Russian Revolution' in Israel." In *Critical Issues in Israeli Society*, edited by Alan Dowty, 95–108. Westport, CT: Praeger.

Grimland, Guy. 2010. "Two Thirds of High-tech Incubator Companies Failed." *Haaretz*, January 5. http://www.haaretz.com/print-edition/business/two-thirds -of-high-tech-incubator-companies-failed-1.260828.

Gur, Haviv R., and Herb Keinon. 2009. "Netanyahu: 20 Years after Iron Curtain Collapsed, It's Clear Russian-Speaking Aliya 'Rescued the State of Israel.'" *Jerusalem Post*, July 9. http://www.jpost.com/Israel/Netanyahu-20-years-after-Iron -Curtain-collapsed-its-clear-Russian-speaking-aliya-rescued-the-State-of-Israel.

Horowitz, Tamar. 2005. "The Integration of Immigrants from the Former Soviet Union." *Israel Affairs* 11, no. 1: 117–36.

Kapur, Devesh, and John McHale. 2005. "Sojourns and Software: Internationally Mobile Human Capital and High Tech Industry Development in India, Ireland and Israel." In *Underdogs to Tigers: The Rise and Growth of the Software Industry in Some Emerging Economies*, edited by Ashish Arora and Alfonso Gambardella, 236–74. Oxford: Oxford University Press.

Kenney, Martin, and Richard Florida. 2000. "Venture Capital in Silicon Valley: Fueling New Firm Formation." In *Understanding Silicon Valley: The Anatomy of an Entrepreneurial Region*, edited by Martin Kenney, 98–123. Stanford, CA: Stanford University Press.

Kheimets, Nina. G., and Alek D. Epstein. 2001. "English as a Central Component of Success in the Professional and Social Integration of Scientists from the Former Soviet Union in Israel." *Language and Society* 30, no. 2: 187–215.

Korey, William. 1995. *Russian Antisemitism, Pamyat, and the Demonology of Zionism*. Jerusalem: Psychology Press.

Krupnik, Igor. 1995. "Soviet Cultural and Ethnic Policies towards Jews: A Legacy Reassessed." In *Jews and Jewish Life in Russia and the Soviet Union*, edited by Yaacov Ro'i, 67–86. Portland, OR: Frank Cass.

Ledeneva, Alena. 1998. *Russia's Economy of Favours: Blat, Networking and Informal Exchange*. Cambridge: Cambridge University Press.

Maital, Shilomo. 2013. "The Debilitating Brain Drain." *Jerusalem Post*, June 2. http://www.jpost.com/Magazine/Opinion/The-debilitating-brain-drain.

Maltz, Judy. 2015. "One, Two, Three, Four—We Opened up the Iron Door." *Haaretz*, February 6. http://www.haaretz.com/st/c/prod/eng/25yrs_russ_img/.

Mesch, Gustavo S., and Daniel Czamanski. 1997. "Occupational Closure and Immigrant Entrepreneurship: Russian Jews in Israel." *Journal of Socio-economics* 26, no. 6: 597–610.

Pinkus, Benjamin. 1990. *The Jews of the Soviet Union: The History of a National Minority*. Cambridge: Cambridge University Press.

Raijman, Rebeca, and Moshe Semyonov. 1995. "Modes of Labor Market Incorporation and Occupational Cost among New Immigrants to Israel." *International Migration Review* 29: 375–94.

Remennick, Larissa. 2003. "Career Continuity among Immigrant Professionals: Russian Engineers in Israel." *Journal of Ethnic and Migration Studies* 29, no. 4: 701–21.

Remennick, Larissa. 2009. "The Two Waves of Russian-Jewish Migration from the USSR/FSU to Israel: Dissidents of the 1970s and Pragmatics of the 1990s." *Diaspora: A Journal of Transnational Studies* 18, no. 1: 44–66.

Remennick, Larissa. 2013. "Professional Identities in Transit: Factors Shaping Immigrant Success on the Labour Market." *International Migration* 51, no. 1: 152–68.

Sales, Ben. 2013. "Two Decades On, Russian Immigrants a Rare Case of Successful Aliyah." *Jewish Telegraph Agency*, December 30. http://www.jta.org/2013/12/30/news-opinion/israel-middle-east/two-decades-on-israels-russian-immigrants-move-from-successful-absorption-to-integration.

Saxenian, AnnaLee. 1994. *Regional Advantage: Culture and Competition in Silicon Valley and Route 128*. Cambridge, MA: Harvard University Press.

Senor, Dan, and Saul Singer. 2009. *Start-Up Nation: The Story of Israel's Economic Miracle*. New York: Grand Central Publishing.

Trajtenberg, Manuel. 2002. "Government Support for Commercial R&D: Lessons from the Israeli Experience." *Innovation Policy and the Economy* 2: 79–134.

Weiss, Yfaat. 2000. "High Skill Immigration: Some Lessons from Israel." *Swedish Economic Policy Review* 7, no. 2: 127–55.

Yaffe, Nurit, and Dorith Tal. 2001. "Immigration to Israel from the Former Soviet Union." Central Bureau of Statistics, Jerusalem.

Yelenevskaya, Maria, and Larisa Fialkova. 2009. "The Case of Ex-Soviet Scientists." In *Transnationalism: Diasporas and the Advent of a New (Dis)order*, edited by Eliezer Ben-Rafael and Yitzhak Sternberg, 613–35. Leiden: Brill.

CHAPTER THIRTEEN

RUSSIAN PROGRAMMERS IN FINLAND:
SELF-PRESENTATION IN MIGRATION NARRATIVE

Lyubava Shatokhina

Information and communication technology specialists are among the most spatially mobile groups in the contemporary global labor market. Russian programmers are no exception; they migrate not only to English-speaking countries such as the US, Canada, the UK, and Australia, but also to Europe and Asia. This chapter looks at how Finland has become a meaningful destination country for Russian programmers. Considering Finland seems at once obvious and counterintuitive. It is clear from migration statistics that Russians represent one of the largest minorities in Finland.[1] Due to their geographical proximity and cultural familiarity with the country, many Russian-speaking professionals end up employed by the Finnish IT sector, reputed to be one of the most developed in the world.[2] In terms of migration, however, Finland is not considered by Russians to be an entirely foreign destination. Russians, especially those from the northwestern part of the country, present their neighbor almost as a part of their native land despite important perceived qualitative differences between Russian and Finnish everyday life and consumer culture (Shatokhina 2014). As one of my informants put it: "Everything is almost the same, but the overall level of the country, its level of civilization is higher [in comparison to Russia]" (Nikolay, aged thirty-five, Espoo).[3]

When comparing migration to Finland and to the UK or Germany, Russian ICT professionals present Finland as something of a compromise destination, almost a quasi-migration. Compared to migration to the US or Canada, moving to Finland is seen as nearly like staying home. If so, why do Russian ICT professionals choose to migrate to Finland rather than stay at home or move to other countries, and how do they explain their choice?

This chapter addresses not the question of migration per se but rather the process through which Russian ICT professionals make sense of their migration to Finland. During my field study in Helsinki in 2013–14, many of the Russian ICT specialists I spoke with relayed surprisingly similar migration narratives. In order to explain this striking consistency, I decided to focus on the values presented by my informants and uncover the reasons for their shared nature.

Generally, Finland is not considered to be a country of mass migration. According to the data of the European Statistical Agency for 2012 (Eurostat 2012), the percentage of the population born outside Finland was 4.8 percent, while in neighboring Sweden it was 15 percent, and in Germany and the UK 12.1 percent. Today the two largest groups of people of foreign descent in Finland come from neighboring Estonia and Russia. Still, despite the relatively small size of these migration flows, Finland is among the top ten countries (Florida 2011) that attract representatives of the so-called global creative class. As Annika Forsander (2009, 10) puts it: "Finland seems to be one of the winners in the global knowledge economy. The explanation for this often points to the combination of a highly developed innovation system that is able to utilize the knowledge economy with the welfare system that offers citizens good services, high-quality education and a safe, equal society to live in." Finland is a country that had (Auto-Sarasmo 2011) and still has (Lisitsyn 2007) a special place in Russian-Finnish high-tech cooperation. Moreover, "the Russian community size in Helsinki in particular is so large by now that it offers cultural and other services as well as a feeling of home to newly arrived Russians" (Forsander and Raunio 2009, 119). Taken together, all these factors make Finland a place that is actively present in the cultural geography of Russian ICT professionals, especially those from Northwest Russia.

The typologies of migration and the explanation of its mechanisms differ depending on both the school of scholarly thought and the specific group of migrants under consideration. For example, popular discourse on migration puts dislocated people into two categories: "migrants" and "expats." Whereas "migrants" are usually seen as members of a disadvantaged group forced to leave their place of origin for economic, political, or other reasons, "expats" are seen as a privileged minority who move to enjoy the benefits of a new location. Professionals in ICT could be categorized as "highly skilled labor migration" (i.e., "expats)," but their migration experience cannot be depicted as unequivocally positive (Xiang 2007). It is clear that the various forms of migration cannot be easily divided into underprivileged "migrants" and prosperous "expats." In this respect, we might need to understand the sense-making narratives produced by ICT migrants in order to shed more light on the migration process from the perspective of its subjects rather than from an external standpoint. The Russian ICT professionals in Finland, for example, cannot be clearly identified as either migrants or expats. Although they mostly present their personal experience in a positive light, they at the same time admit that the experience was not unequivocally positive for their families.

One way to correct classificatory oversimplification is to look not only at the class distinctions between different migrant groups, but also at different values and behaviors within a particular social class experiencing relocation (Scott 2006). In this way, one is able to perceive a highly skilled migrant not only as a representative of the middle-class professional but also to take into consideration his or her specific migration trajectories and the motives behind them. As Sam Scott (2006, 1112) suggests, one can divide skilled migrant populations (in his case the British middle class in Paris) into various lifestyle types that relate to three primary migration motives: "career path," "lifestyle preferences," and "relationships." A more expanded classification is suggested by Annika Forsander and Mika Raunio (2009, 112–13): "global nomads," "career builders," "quality of life seekers," "social relationships," and "adventurers." In this article, I will argue that in the case of Russian-speaking programmers relocating to Finland, it is hardly possible to separate the career path ("career builders") from lifestyle preferences ("quality of life seekers") as a main migration motive, as the two are interconnected and mutually supportive.

It is also important to understand how labor migrants create their own geography based on professional imagination. This approach is particularly productive in the case of ICT professionals who are simultaneously members of a global community of practice and yet deeply incorporated into a specific geographical location (Takhteyev 2012). It is also necessary to understand how professional experience influences the geographical imagination of highly skilled people in different localities, how they see those localities, and how they make sense of the position they occupy there and then. This approach allows us to avoid a simplistic understanding of this group as privileged "expats," as well as an interpretation of migration as driven by a single major reason, simultaneously enabling a more nuanced and complex analysis of the geographical imagination of this migrant group.

Unlike the depiction of migration experience as disruptive often found in the literature (Pine 2014), my research in Finland has indicated that highly skilled professionals who relocate there from Russia tend to present their experience as a generally positive one. The idea of "lifestyle migration" offered by Michaela Benson and Karen O'Reilly (2009, 2) looks especially applicable in this case. According to these authors, "lifestyle migration is the spatial mobility of relatively affluent individuals of all ages, moving either part-time or full-time to places that are meaningful because, for various reasons, they offer the potential of a better quality of life."[4]

The idea of lifestyle as a driving force of career trajectory was also popularized by Richard Florida in his numerous writings about the "creative class." Though an emphasis on lifestyle and spatial mobility was at the forefront of his ideas (Florida 2005), he failed to appreciate variety within the category of lifestyle, thus casting the creative class as homogeneous, even monolithic. In his reading, lifestyle was related neither to the sphere of professional activity, family status, descent, and/or education nor to previous work or migration experience. Instead, I believe that following Max Weber ([1905] 2003) and Pekka Himanen (2001)[5] we should examine in detail what makes people inside the community of practice act and talk in certain ways (Bucholtz 1999; Thompson 2005); that is, how values and norms are provoked by or provoke certain types of conduct, professional activity, and language use. The questions of how new selves are created in specific professional activities (Miller and Power 2013) and how new forms of conduct and professional narratives develop from new kinds of selves (Rabinow 1997) are relevant to understanding the specific features of a professional group. An understanding of the migration of professionals cannot, therefore, be separated from the forms and nature of professional conduct, or from professional identities and their attendant values, norms, and worldviews. For instance, Rebecca Gill and Gregory Larson (2013, 6) have recently addressed the question of "how entrepreneurs [in the high-tech industry] may construct regional identities in ways that are different, unique, resistant and/or similar to the prominent Silicon Valley model." This line of inquiry applies well to Russian-speaking ICT professionals in Finland. Like the entrepreneurs studied by Gill and Larson, the ICT specialists I have interviewed do not feel inclined to conform to the US capitalist system and especially the Silicon Valley model (Saxenian 1996), and have developed an image of Finland as a very specific and more attractive place to work and live. It is particularly interesting since the same holds true for the case of Jewish ICT workers in the Boston area (West, this volume) and in Israel (Fedorova on Israel, this volume).

In this chapter, my place of departure lies within a paradox: though people may find themselves in a new location due to a constellation of highly specific circumstances, they nevertheless strive to make sense of their relocation experience by relating it to a relatively stable set of norms and values that they themselves hold. By addressing this paradox I do not try to answer the question of why people migrate or why they stay in a destination country, but how this experience is used for the purpose of self-presentation and narrativization or legitimization of their life trajectory. In these narratives one can witness a process of selection and assemblage of various elements of mundane migration practices, professional aspirations, and sociopolitical values that result in the production and reproduction of a coherent narrative and coherent narrator's self.

First, spatial mobility is an ever-present ideal model for my informants. Though probably not fully realized in real life, it is seen as an attractive model and a potential future option. Second, I will show how Russians who relocated to Finland try to make retrospective sense of their experience, despite the lack of a conscious and deliberate migration *strategy*. Finally, I look at how these sense-making narratives resonate with the working ethics and lifestyle preferences these practitioners claim to espouse. My analysis is based on twelve interviews with Russian-speaking ICT specialists in Finland conducted during the winter of 2013–14, mostly in Helsinki. Three were conducted outside of Finland as interlocutors had moved either back to Russia or to a third country. The interviews focused on migration, with a specific emphasis on everyday life experience and work-related issues. Most of the informants were found via LinkedIn.[6] All the informants are Russian speakers who have been or were employed in Finland for at least six months. All of them are male, mostly in their early thirties. The majority relocated to Finland with their spouses and sometimes with their children.

Several narratives were strikingly consistent across the interviews. This is an intriguing finding, as I have not managed to trace this back to any kind of shared social community to which my informants belong. Usually they live rather uninvolved lives centered on work and home. They do not tend to associate with the Russian-speaking diaspora widely present in Finland, nor do they build strong ties with either local or foreign colleagues. They are mostly bounded by the limits of their nuclear families and close circle of like-minded friends. At the same time, they are very satisfied with their life in Finland. Their positive migration narratives are only occasionally problematized by the less positive experiences of their wives and children, which however remain external to their own self-presentation strategies.

Most of the Russian programmers I talked to present their migration experience as in keeping with their overall life trajectory. They do not dwell upon their migration experience or present the push-and-pull factors (so common in migration literature) that made them relocate; instead, they see it as a natural step forward that does not need detailed justification. No one recalls any hesitations or conflict at the time they decided to leave Russia for Finland. What is more, there were no extraordinary preparations and the very process of relocation was not seen as a "big deal." Most of them incorporate their migration stories into their career paths without discontinuity. As Alexander (aged thirty-two, Helsinki) explains:

> We started to talk with my wife [about the possibility of relocating], and we already had children by that time. We started to discuss that it would be good to look around, where it would be possible. . . . And I was tired a bit, that is, professional growth had stopped at the place I was then. Everything worked out on its own. And there was no need to search. . . . Well, Finland was close . . . and my wife used to go there.

The idea to relocate to Finland was presented by my informants as an automatic decision, almost a nondecision. Moreover, when answering the question of how they see the future, most of them point to the possibility of further relocations. At the same time, they realize that further relocation is inconsistent with their general satisfaction with life in Finland. They tend to talk about having well-established comfortable routines, if not about having put down roots in their new country. At the same time, many speak about their desire to move to Sweden in particular: "Well, I was thinking about Sweden. If there is any sense in planning while I am here? In the next few years while I am here I will not get citizenship [EU citizenship is often seen as a precondition to further relocation]" (Alexander). Paradoxically, the decisive issue in this choice was that Sweden was perceived as nearly identical to Finland. Thus, the value of further relocation was not perceived in terms of the country of destination but in terms of the process of mobility itself. For these people, the norm of both future career and personal development is in one way or another seen in terms of spatial mobility, be it realized or not.

The way my informants made sense of their life trajectories raises the issue of whether being dynamic is a modus vivendi—a norm for a specific group, in this case a professional one. It would be an overstatement, however, to say that we are dealing with a nomadic tribe. While spatial mobility is definitely perceived as the norm, we must not confuse presentation and reality. Whether the people I talked to will relocate in the future and whether they will do so to Sweden is beyond the scope of this paper. What is interesting is the fact that they prefer to see spatial mobility as an attractive model according to which they are eager to build their professional life narratives.

STORIES OF RELOCATION:
CHOSEN TACTICS AND TAKEN OPPORTUNITIES

While my informants perceive the decision to migrate as "natural" or even inevitable, the question remains as to why they chose Finland? They present several typical routes of how they ended up in Finland. Only one person made a strategic, unequivocal decision to relocate to this country. Other narrators present their experience as ad hoc (de Certeau 1984). Some migrated via student exchange programs; some benefited from having contacts with earlier migrants to Finland; some simply searched online for job opportunities abroad and were interested in large Finnish IT companies. Most importantly, they view any opportunity that they took advantage of as something acceptable, reasonable, and manageable.

One of my initial hypotheses was that my informants would see Russia as a country that stimulates the exodus of highly skilled professionals. Moreover, one would expect that Russian culture's inclination toward a "genre of lamentation" (Ries 1997) would produce a whole range of critical attitudes toward the country of origin, especially from the political and social standpoint. Surprisingly, none of my interlocutors were explicitly or persistently critical of Russian politics,[7] and none considers migration as a forced decision or escape. They do, however, criticize the Russian state for its tendency to underestimate or even neglect the role and the work of well-educated and highly qualified professionals like engineers and scientists: "Forget politics, indeed! What is important is the Gini index. And . . . economics. Well, politics, as we all know, is a servant of economics. Well, in the Russian economy, engineering and the engineering profession—no one needs them, to my mind" (Vladimir, aged thirty-two, Helsinki).

When asked whether he found something dissatisfying about Russia in deciding to emigrate, one of my informants (who used a student exchange program to relocate to Finland) replied:

Far from being unacceptable! It is hard to tell that something was unacceptable at that moment. Because I did not know that it could be different. I mostly was curious, what is it like when it is different? This is more curiosity . . . , a desire to try something else, more than a purposeful undertaking. (Yaroslav, aged thirty-two, Finland, France)

These quotes show that some of my informants have neither a negative attitude toward Russia nor particular feelings toward Finland as a host country. Rather than push or pull factors, "curiosity" or the desire for a "new experience" (that is, mobility in and of itself) were the major factors driving their decisions to migrate.

Another hypothesis suggested by the interview data concerned the economic nature of migration. The Russian-speaking ICT professionals whom I interviewed moved to Finland mostly from large cities such as Saint Petersburg or Moscow, where software engineers are among the top-paid professional groups.[8] Some, in fact, present their migration to Finland as a deterioration of their household's economic position: "On the one hand, objectively the correlation between income and spending—I have even lost a bit. Firstly, because of taxation. Secondly, the housing is very expensive. And I used to have an apartment over there [in Russia]" (Alexander).

Probably the dominant reason for migration choice is the idea of chance or coincidence that decided the future. My informants do not in any way represent themselves as risk takers or adventurers, but narrate their migration to Finland as unplanned and unarranged: "Well, I was not purposefully searching for something in order to leave. But when I saw that option, it occurred to me: 'Why not?!'" (Yaroslav). The way they portray their choice of Finland fits their attitudes to spatial mobility as natural and unproblematic—a sentiment strengthened by the fact that the path between Russia and Finland is well trodden:

To speak of moving to Helsinki, everything is easier, that is, a lot of Russians live here. The man from whom I got a position, he was a Russian who worked for that company. So they [Finns] are friendlier toward Russians and . . . the relocation in this respect is easier. You can ask about all the details. (Andrey, aged thirty, Helsinki)

Preexisting experience and connections mattered:

And . . . there was a need to go international, to go somewhere. I just sent around my cv, and as a result I got two options: either to this country [Finland] or to Sweden. Well, this country was the easy choice. I knew some people here and so forth. (Fedor, aged thirty-two, Helsinki)

The presence of Finland in both the cultural imaginary and real-life experience was particularly true for those Russian ICT professionals who spent time in the Russian Northwest. Unlike those who come to Finland from elsewhere (Forsander and Raunio 2009) and have only a vague image of the country, Russians have their own distinct perception of the neighboring state.

IMAGINING FINLAND: NARRATIVES OF COMFORT

My informants' general feeling about Finland is captured by the term "comfort," which includes pragmatism, predictability, safety, transparency, equality, the human-friendly organization of space, and closeness to nature. Sometimes they contrast these features with their experience in Russia or other countries; sometimes they find these features important irrespective of any comparison. One of their narrative tactics is to present Russian urban life in a dark light, thereby casting Finland in brighter colors and legitimizing their decision to migrate. The Russian cities from which they have relocated are usually depicted as dangerous and disorganized spaces[9]:

> In Russia, when you are leaving home: you open the door and close the door. That is it. Home is left behind. It is already some kind of border crossing, and then you have to . . . watch out and so on. Here, when you leave home, you still feel at home. That means there is no feeling that beyond the doorsteps an alien territory begins. (Alexander)

When talking about Finland, my subjects also contrast it to the US, which they depict as far away, unpredictable, full of stress and challenges, and generally speaking "uncomfortable." While Finland seems to be a "safe choice," the US is a risky one. Though some of my informants have no experience of the US whatsoever, they received vivid images of the country from stories told by colleagues and friends. It is not only the American culture that they find unattractive but also the work ethic: "It is far away and another culture. That is drastically other. It is very different from not only Russian, but European [culture], in terms of work" (Yaroslav). My informants were discouraged by the heavy workload and competitiveness of the American workplace, together with the lack of social security and comfortable work conditions.

Most of the interviewees migrated to Finland with their spouses and often with their children, and greatly value the family-friendly environment. They also emphasize Finland's geographical proximity to Russia as making it possible to remain in touch with their extended families. One of my informants finds the idea of returning to Russia problematic precisely because of a lack of suitable family infrastructure:

> If we arrive in Russia: shortly thereafter we will have to find a place to live, arrange a kindergarten and school for the children, yes . . . and to have a possibility to drive from work to home via kindergarten and school. I think that in Russia this will be hard to organize. That is, firstly, all the waiting lists for kindergartens and schools, for the decent ones. Moreover . . . naturally, more likely, one's job will be only in big cities, i.e., in Moscow, Saint Petersburg. I absolutely do not want to go to the big cities. (Yaroslav).

As in other interviews, what we see here is a statement of lifestyle preferences, not just concerns about social infrastructure and childcare systems.

Finland is seen as an environment that provides all the necessary conditions of what is perceived by my subjects to be a good life: medium-sized cities, accessibility of the outdoors for sports, and a life that is better attuned with nature. Their view of the Finnish public transportation system captures some of this; most of my interviewees are fascinated by it. At first the ubiquity of this topic seemed a bit strange, but I later understood that to them the Finnish public transportation system is a symbol of the predictability, reliability, rationality, and safety they so much value:

> From home to work I was taking a bus. There was a highway and there was not really a traffic jam on this highway but rather heavy traffic, but, however, there was a bus lane and the bus flew down the highway at eighty kilometers per hour. All the distances . . . everything is very close. In Saint Petersburg, I remember, I always was adding something [extra time] to arrive somewhere; all in all, an hour and a half. Because all of this added up, you will get the eventual feeling of discomfort. (Yaroslav)

In fact, this reclamation of time and the attraction of predictability is not simply a matter of comfort but a desire to have agency; that is to say, to act according to one's own will and to control one's own time. Because Russian big cities make people dependent on external structures, they strip inhabitants of their agency, "instituting uncertainty as a rule" (Verdery 1996, 54).

For my informants, comfort, understood in a very particular way, is one of the main reasons to stay in Finland. Interestingly, there is a noticeable uniformity of images and notions that they associate with "comfort," suggesting that despite the lack of a traditional community or diasporic entity connecting my subjects, there is a set of shared values and beliefs. The case of Kazan IT specialists (Kontareva, this volume) reveals a shared pattern, as people who live and work in Kazan hold the same infrastructural and lifestyle preferences: they value a medium-sized city with a bicycle-friendly environment, and proximity to nature impossible to find in large Russian cities.

SELF-PRESENTATION: PRESENTING WORK, PRESENTING THE COUNTRY

There are parallels in the ways people talk about their work and self. Sherry Turkle (2005, 102) has argued that "programming style is an expression of personality style," and that programmers could be distinguished between the "safe" or "racing-car" types: one type is keen on predictability, safety, and control while the other is attracted to challenges and prefers going to extremes. One could draw an analogy between Turkle's findings and the patterns I see in Russian ICT professionals' narratives of work ethic and their image of Finland. In particular, those who relocated to Finland can be presented as belonging to the "safe" group. Also, there is an intuitive feeling that the two categories identified by Turkle may also correspond to two different work ethic paradigms—one that praises risky behavior and individual initiative (i.e., "capitalism") and the other more appreciative of safety and cooperation (namely, "socialism"). It seems fair to say that Russian ICT specialists in Finland gravitate toward the "socialist" end of the spectrum.

The way Russian ICT professionals talk about work and work ethics correlates with the way they talk about Finland. They hardly ever use such categories as career growth, promotion, or search for profit: "It is my firm decision: if my goal was to earn money as much as possible, to do it in Russia is far easier than in Finland" (Vladimir). Most of them seem more interested in working for a company or on a project that is well organized, where one can measure efficiency and see results. This apparent disinterest in money coupled with an interest in productivity and creativity resonates with what Pekka Himanen (2001) sees as a key attribute of the new "hacker ethic"; however, it is also more in tune with social-democratic norms than with the libertarian values and norms Himanen ascribes to hackers. My subjects all display this same moderate interest in financial benefits combined with an appreciation of doing something socially useful. For them, Finnish society is generally calm and welfare oriented: "A small country without big ambitions.

That, according to me, creates a way for it to treat its citizens with more concern" (Yaroslav).

The Russian ICT professionals in Finland occupy very different positions within the various branches of the IT industry; nevertheless, they see work in the IT sector as something that predetermines their everyday life in general. When talking about their life in their new country they suggest that Finland matches their "geekiness"—the "root" of their chosen profession. While they are integrated into Finnish society mostly through their work (Trux 2010), Russian ICT professionals prefer to live rather "asocial" lives, as several of them put it. Most claim that they do not go out or socialize outside the office and prefer to deal with computers rather than human beings. As Alexander says: "I work at the office, then come home and do something for myself at home. The only difference is the computer I use and what I use it for." Most other Russian ICT professionals have told me that they appreciate the Finnish culture of noninterference and privacy, which does not push them to communicate with the outside world when they do not wish to and gives them space to concentrate on what they like to do: programming.

In *Lifestyle Migration*, Benson and O'Reilly (2009) argue that those who relocate in search of a better life usually try to find a better work/family balance. Unlike the Silicon Valley employment model (English-Lueck 2002), where work penetrates all life spheres, the work/family balance in Helsinki is of a different nature. My informants appreciate the fact that in Finland they have more time for both their family and themselves. One interviewee summarized this quite straightforwardly:

> Well, this is one of the reasons why I do not want to go back to Russia. Because here it is easier to find a balance, in Europe [talking about both Finland and France]. That is why I do not want to go, let's say, to the US. Because here it is easier to find a balance between life and work. Because here it is easier with working hours. (Yaroslav)

Those Russian speakers who moved to Finland present their preferred lifestyle as family oriented, and believe in traditional clear-cut boundaries between work and personal life. The postindustrial "flexibility" of working hours that is part of "hacker ethics" (Himanen 2001, 20) is foreign to them.

The absence of risk is another key element of my subjects' narratives. They do nothing to hide the fact that one of their main incentives for moving to Finland is their image of the country as a "safe option." Despite their stated desire to work for a startup or launch their own project, my informants mostly work for big and middle-size companies (as with the Boston "upper-middle tech" case; West, this volume). They admit this contradiction but do not dare to take a risk:

> Well, maybe I am making mistake here, but I somehow do not like to take risks. And because of this I am very critical of [business] ideas. And I, of course, had several [business] ideas. But I was so critical of them. Maybe, in vain, maybe I should have done something. (Vladimir)

My informants do not represent themselves as Schumpeterian entrepreneurs (Schumpeter 1911) or the neoliberal version of that. They do not have a gambler-like attitude toward risk; instead, they fit the profile of the "safe-type" programmer presented by Turkle (2005). But being risk averse does not mean being unappreciative of the quality and professionality of one's work, something they explicitly admire about the Finns:

> Although they are more relaxed, at the same time they are more hardworking. That means they have a desire to get results. They have an interest not only in earning money, but in somehow feeling that they managed to complete their task well. (Andrey)

My interviewees do not see Finland's high taxes as a burden but as a just arrangement for the common good: "Yes, I pay huge taxes. . . . If someone for some reason was taken ill or something else, lost his job, the state supports these people. Partly from my taxes. But I am all for it" (Vladimir). As illustrated by their apparent disinterest in professional promotion and managerial positions, most of the programmers support the idea of equality and economic redistribution. Their attitude toward equality and redistribution both at work and in society at large stands in opposition to capitalistic values of individual profit. Due to the relative social equality in Finland, my subjects find a mental comfort that, while resonating with their search for a better life, also correlates with their more general idea of social justice:

> Well . . . Finland is a more comfortable place, I would say. Here the standard of living is higher. In California you can find a very high standard of living, but at the same time you will be going to work every day and see people with not that high a living standard. This makes your experience of being in a country slightly different. Meaning when you see homeless people on the streets, standing at an intersection with little signs. (Konstantin, aged thirty-six, Helsinki)

Russian ICT professionals in Finland tend to value collectivity, cooperation, and a creative spirit at work and in daily life. However, some apparent tensions can be glimpsed in their commitments: they privilege collective values in comparison with individual achievements but also tend to praise noninterference and the reserved nature of Finnish society. What they value in both the workplace and Finnish society is the opportunity to peacefully coexist according to well-established and -observed rules. "Finns are much more, let's say, formal. I do not mean [this negatively]. . . . Let's say . . . that means that they obey the rules more strictly" (Yaroslav). And at the same time, Finnish society provides a certain degree of freedom, which is so necessary for my subjects: "That means no one breathes down your neck and so forth. There is more respect for private space at your office" (Andrey). Or, as another informant explains: "Finns are very relaxed. They do not bother you, they do not control you like Americans or Russians. They presuppose that you will be productive without anyone hurrying you" (Nikolay). This interesting combination of autonomy and independence while voluntarily following rules resonates deeply with my subjects' own values, tending to present those features of their new place of work and residence that resonate with their understandings of a proper society—a proper programmer and a proper self. In doing so, they implicitly or explicitly compare Finland and their new life with two other sites: their previous life in Russia and the imaginary (potential) experience of life and work in the US.

CONCLUSION

Unlike other chapters in this volume that mostly depict migration trajectories, this chapter has looked at the migration narratives and strategies of self-presentation of Russian ICT professionals in Finland. While it is not possible to argue that my subjects moved to and stayed in Finland because of particular values and lifestyles, these values and lifestyles did become tools and sources for self-explanation and making sense of their own experience in a certain locality. Such narratives are particularly important to ICT specialists who, because of their high level of potential mobility, face the question of whether they should either settle or continue to relocate, and why. In the situation of migration, self-assemblage by making sense of a new milieu becomes especially clear with the appearance of new frontiers for identity re-creation (Barth 1969).

One can paint a rough portrait of my subjects' shared traits.[10] Those Russian-speaking ICT specialists in Finland with whom I talked are pragmatic and moderate; they prefer predictability and safety to risk and uncertainty; and they are team players with larger society-oriented goals. At the same time, they withdraw from the larger society and are bounded by their networks; they value freedom but are eager to play by the rules. In their lifestyle preferences, they appreciate nature and seek a mixture of urban comfort and rural dwelling. Though their narratives are centered around work and professional issues, they emphasize family and define personal comfort from the perspective of a family man.

Surprisingly, identity building and value creation that my subjects demonstrate are similar to those described in the chapters dedicated to Jewish ICT workers from the USSR/Russia who migrated to Boston and Israel (West, this volume; Fedorova on Israel, this volume). Those cases show migration flows that occurred earlier and can thus be more directly explained by the legacy of the Soviet work context and values. However, most of my subjects experienced adulthood in the context of post-Soviet Russia. To my mind, my subjects show not just a simple replication of Soviet practices and beliefs, but more so a particular set of values and lifestyles that can be interpreted as an alternative to the Silicon Valley model of technical entrepreneurship. In this way my study not only explains the Russian ICT case but also casts lights on a global trend among ICT professionals.

EPILOGUE

Recently I attended a conference on applied anthropology in Tartu, Estonia. One of the keynote speakers was a representative of local business, a successful IT entrepreneur from Estonia who now lives and works in Silicon Valley. In his speech, he presented a new platform that his team has been developing. This was a matchmaking site to help talent (mostly highly skilled IT professionals) find a country of possible migration. By way of an algorithm he had developed based on a formalized survey, he claimed that he could find a perfect match between a professional's preferences and the migration country's amenities. When I saw the mockup version of the platform I began to doubt the success of the venture. The list of criteria to choose from was not only limited to ten to twenty options based on the "rational choice" assumption of the platform's developer, but was also strongly dominated by the spirit of the Silicon Valley model. I would argue based on my research that the platform was built on two incorrect assumptions: First, that ICT professionals when faced with migration prospects make rational decisions based on clear-cut preferences they have before relocation. Second, that most of them value a particular lifestyle and share an ethic close to that of the Silicon Valley tech capitalism model. On the contrary, I would argue that discovery and negotiation of an ICT migrant's preferences happens constantly and often as a result of the migration process. Moreover, the entrepreneurial capitalism of Silicon Valley is not the only game in town. Based on the cases presented in this volume, I would offer at least two more ideal type models: one that I would call "corporate capitalist" (risk aversive and profit oriented) represented by the Boston case of "upper-middle tech" (West, this volume), and another I would call "socialist" (risk aversive and social justice oriented) represented in the case of migration to Finland depicted in this chapter.

NOTES

1. Of the total number of people who migrated to Finland in 2011, 18.6 percent came from Estonia and 16.2 percent from Russia (Eurostat 2012).
2. According to the "Global Information Technology Report 2014" provided by World Economic Forum (2014, 7): "Finland tops the rankings with a strong performance across the board. It ranks 1st in the readiness subindex thanks to an outstanding digital ICT infrastructure—the best in the world—and 2nd in both the usage and impact subindexes, with more than 90 percent of its population using the Internet and high levels of technological and non-technological innovation."
3. All interviews with IT workers were conducted in Russian and translated by the author.
4. Paradoxically, however, the term "lifestyle migrant" is used most often to describe the relocation of a nonworking population.
5. Max Weber's *The Protestant Ethic and the Spirit of Capitalism* ([1905] 2003) was built upon by Pekka Himanen (2001) in his work on the hacker ethic.
6. LinkedIn is an international social network that allows professionals to take advantage of the global labor market.
7. It is important to note that most of the interviews were conducted before Russia's annexation of Crimea and the war in eastern Ukraine. I believe that interviews conducted after the annexation of Crimea would have been much more critical and politicized than the narratives I collected.
8. According to most recent surveys conducted in large Russian cities, ICT workers (together with lawyers, sales directors, and chief accountants) are among the highest-paid professional groups.
9. These characteristics partly correlate with what Nielsen (Нильсен 2004) presents as the "limbo state" of Russia during the late Soviet period.
10. The stunning unanimity of their views about Finland and much else remains puzzling. This is not, I believe, a consensus that can be traced back to a single factor: be it Russian descent, age, or professional background. It is rather a mixture of all these and the shared experience of migration that makes their narratives resemble one another. My subjects are not inherently identical at the start, but become more so as they go through similar experiences and fashion similar

narratives in order to make sense of their new predicament and self. I would also argue that it is the very process of narrativization of their experiences in certain circumstances that makes the stories resemble one another. Life narratives are not a string of autobiographical facts but a genre, a mode of narrating the self to construct one. In this case, my subjects' remarkably homogeneous narratives may have also been shaped in response to the narrative genre I offered them— that of the biographical interview—which may have directed them to come up with a more or less coherent story of their migration experience.

REFERENCES

Auto-Sarasmo, Sari. 2011. "Knowledge through the Iron Curtain: Soviet Scientific-Technical Cooperation with Finland and West Germany." In *Reassessing Cold War Europe*, edited by Auto-Sarasmo Sari and Miklossy Katalin, 66–82. New York: Routledge.

Barth, Fredrik. 1969. *Ethnic Groups and Boundaries: The Social Organization of Culture Difference*. Oslo: Universitetsforlaget.

Benson, Michaela, and Karen O'Reilly. 2009. *Lifestyle Migration: Expectations, Aspirations and Experiences*. London: Ashgate.

Bucholtz, Mary. 1999. "'Why Be Normal?': Language and Identity Practices in a Community of Nerd Girls." *Language in Society* 28, no. 2: 203–23.

de Certeau, Michel. 1984. *The Practice of Everyday Life*. Berkeley: University of California Press.

Deleuze, Gilles, and Felix Guattari. 1986. *Nomadology: The War Machine*. New York: Semiotext(e).

English-Lueck, June Anne. 2002. *Cultures@SiliconValley*. Stanford, CA: Stanford University Press.

Eurostat. 2012. Europe in Figures. Eurostat Yearbook 2012. Section 2: Population. Accessed July 29, 2018. http://ec.europa.eu/eurostat/documents/3217494/5760825/KS-CD-12-001-EN.PDF.

Florida, Richard. 2005. *Cities and the Creative Class*. New York: Routledge.

Florida, Richard. 2011. "The World's Leading Creative Class Countries." *CityLab*, October 4. Accessed July 29, 2018. http://www.citylab.com/work/2011/10/worlds-leading-creative-class-countries/228/#slide8.

Forsander, Anika, and Mika Raunio. 2009. *The Welfare State in Competition for Global Talent: From National Protectionism to Regional Connectivity—the Case of Finland. Foreign ICT and Bioscience Experts in Finland*. Bern: Peter Lang.

Gill, Rebecca, and Gregory Larson. 2013. "Making the Ideal (Local) Entrepreneur: Place and the Regional Development of High-Tech Entrepreneurial Identity." *Human Relations* 67, no. 5: 519–42.

Himanen, Pekka. 2001. *The Hacker Ethic and the Spirit of the Information Age*. London: Random House.

Lisitsyn, Nikita. 2007. "Technological Cooperation between Finland and Russia: Example of Technology Parks in St. Petersburg." Working paper, *Electronic Publications of Pan-European Institute*. Accessed July 29, 2018. http://www.utu

.fi/fi/yksikot/tse/yksikot/PEI/raportit-jatietopaketit/Documents/Lisitsyn03_07
.pdf.

Miller, Peter, and Michael Power. 2013. "Accounting, Organizing, and Economizing: Connecting Accounting Research and Organization Theory." *Academy of Management Annals* 7, no. 1: 555–603.

Ministry of the Interior, Finland. 2012. "Annual Report on Immigration." Accessed July 29, 2018. www.migri.fi/download/46518_46515_Maahanmuuton_tilastokatsaus_2012_ENG_web.pdf?da03e85648e0d288.

Pine, Frances. 2014. "Migration as Hope: Space, Time, and Imagining the Future." *Current Anthropology* 55, no. S9: S95–S104.

Rabinow, Paul. 1997. *Making PCR: A Story of Biotechnology*. Chicago: University of Chicago Press.

Ries, Nancy. 1997. *Russian Talk: Culture and Conversation during Perestroika*. Ithaca, NY: Cornell University Press.

Saxenian, AnnaLee. 1996. *Regional Advantage: Culture and Competition in Silicon Valley and Route 128*. Cambridge, MA: Harvard University Press.

Schumpeter, Joseph Alois. 1911. *The Theory of Economic Development*. Cambridge, MA: Harvard University Press.

Scott, Sam. 2006. "The Social Morphology of Skilled Migration: The Case of the British Middle Class in Paris." *Journal of Ethnic Migration and Migration Studies* 32, no. 7: 1105–29.

Shatokhina, Lyubava. 2014. "Rethinking Russian History and Identity through Consumer Culture." In *Handbook of Anthropology in Business*, edited by Rita Denny and Patricia Sunderland, 603–17. Walnut Creek, CA: Left Coast Press.

Takhteyev, Yuri. 2012. *Coding Places: Software Practice in a South American City*. Cambridge, MA: MIT Press.

Thompson, Mark. 2005. "Structural and Epistemic Parameters in Communities of Practice." *Organization Science* 16, no. 2: 151–64.

Trux, Marja-Liisa. 2010. *No Zoo: Ethnic Civility and its Cultural Regulation among the Staff of a Finnish High-Tech Company*. Aalto Print: Aalto University School of Economics.

Turkle, Sherry. 2005. *The Second Self: Computers and the Human Spirit*. Twentieth Anniversary Edition. Cambridge, MA: MIT Press.

Verdery, Katherine. 1996. *What Was Socialism, and What Comes Next?* Princeton, NJ: Princeton University Press.

Weber, Max. (1905) 2003. *The Protestant Ethic and the Spirit of Capitalism*. New York: Courier Dover

World Economic Forum. 2014. "The Global Information Technology Report 2014." Accessed July 29, 2018. http://www3.weforum.org/docs/WEF_GlobalInformationTechnology_Report_2014.pdf.

Xiang, Biao. 2007. *Global "Body Shopping": An Indian International Labor System in the Information Technology Industry*. Princeton, NJ: Princeton University Press.

Нильсен, Финн Сиверс. 2004. *Глаз Бури*. Санкт-Петербург, Алетейя.

IRINA ANTOSCHYUK is a PhD candidate at St. Petersburg State University and a research scientist at the STS Center of the European University at St. Petersburg. Her current research focuses on the migration experience of Russian-speaking computer scientists in the UK and their strategies of integration into academia. Her scientific interests include transnational academic migration, mobility, and scientific networks transformation in the age of increasing internationalization of science and higher education, diaspora networks and ethnic identities in the academic community and their role in the production of scientific knowledge.

MARIO BIAGIOLI is Distinguished Professor of Law and Science and Technology Studies, and director of the Center for Science and Innovation Studies, at the University of California, Davis. He is editor of *The Science Studies Reader* (1998); coeditor (with Peter Galison) of *Scientific Authorship* (2003) and (with Pater Jaszi and Martha Woodmansee) of *Making and Unmaking Intellectual Property* (2011); and author of *Galileo Courtier* (1993) and *Galileo's Instruments of Credit* (2006).

KSENIA ERMOSHINA is a postdoctoral fellow at the University of Toronto, Citizen Lab. She holds a PhD from the Centre de Sociologie de l'Innovation at École des Mines de Paris, France. She has studied the intersection of social activism and coding innovations in hacktivists' communities in Paris and Russia. Her forthcoming book looks at the role in which the design of social mobilization apps have affected the political engagement of activists during the 2011 mass mobilizations in Russia. She is working on the rise of cryptology and privacy issues in the development of personal messaging systems.

MARINA FEDOROVA is a PhD candidate in the School of Information and Computer Sciences at the University of California, Irvine, and a member of the Laboratory for Ubiquitous Computing. Her research lies at the intersection of organizational studies and software studies, with a particular interest in exploring the relationship between code and corporate cultures. She holds an MS in sociology from the European University at St. Petersburg, where she also worked as a research fellow at the Center for Science and Technology Studies.

ANDREY INDUKAEV is a PhD candidate at the École Normale Supérieure Paris-Saclay, France. His research focuses mainly on how scientists embed into their work and careers logics seemingly exogenous to their disciplines or to the academic world in general. His PhD thesis analyzes how market-oriented innovation policy changes academic work and careers in modern Russia. Initially trained as a physicist, he has developed new quantitative methods to explore researchers' careers. He has likewise studied how the structure of interdisciplinary collaborations influences research production dynamics.

ALINA KONTAREVA is Doctoral Research Fellow at TIK Centre for Technology, Innovation and Culture at the University of Oslo and a research fellow at the Center for Policy Analysis and Studies of Technology at Tomsk State University. Her recent positions include Fulbright Visiting Graduate Student at the Department of Human Ecology, Community and Regional Development at the University of California, Davis. Her research interests are in the development of innovative clusters, university-industry relations, innovation policy, and metrics for innovation performance. She is currently working on the emergence and transformation of scientific public policies and innovation systems in post-Soviet countries.

DIANA KURKOVSKY WEST is Mellon Postdoctoral Fellow in Science in Human Cultures at Northwestern University, and formerly the director of the STS Center of the European University at St. Petersburg, Russia. Her research interests include the history of computation, urban planning, industrial design, innovation, and popular science cultures in the Soviet Union. She is currently completing her book manuscript titled *CyberSovietica: Dreaming of Big Data in the Soviet Union*, which interrogates how cybernetics-informed approaches to information validated the Soviet planned economy and offered new techniques of planning and governance throughout the 1960s, '70s, and well into the '80s. In addition to tracing the trajectory of cybernetic thinking in the USSR, the project uncovers a history that helps situate our contemporary discourse on smart cities and big data governance.

VINCENT ANTONIN LÉPINAY is an associate professor and a researcher at the Medialab at Sciences Po in Paris. He is author of *Codes of Finance: Engineering Derivatives in a Global Bank* (2014) and coauthor (with Bruno Latour) of *The Science of Passionate Interests: An Introduction to Gabriel Tarde's Economic Anthropology* (2009). In 2019, he will also publish *Art of Memories*, a study of the cultures of expertise at the Hermitage Museum.

ALEKSANDRA MASALSKAYA was a PhD candiate and a research fellow at the European University at St. Petersburg. Her research interests are in diasporal studies and the anthropology of science and technology. She participated in a large research enterprise on technological entrepreneurship and innovative high-tech companies in South Korea and Primorye.

DARIA SAVCHENKO is a PhD candidate in the Department of Anthropology at Harvard University. She holds a PhD in linguistics from St. Petersburg State University. From 2013 to 2015 she was a research fellow in the STS Center of the European University at St. Petersburg. Her research interests are in the sociology and anthropology of science and technology, education, and nation building. Her current PhD project focuses on various practices that involve robots and robotics in China.

LYUBAVA SHATOKHINA is a senior anthropologist at Gemic, Finland, where her main task is to infuse social theory and ethnographic research methodology into business consultancy. She has also worked as a researcher for the STS Center of the European University at St. Petersburg, where she studied the migration of Russian computer scientists and practitioners to Finland. Her research interests include ethnography, cultural anthropology, Russian consumption culture, and science and technology studies. She is the author of "Rethinking Russian History and Identity through Consumer Culture," in *Handbook of Anthropology in Business*, edited by Rita Denny and Patricia Sunderland (2014).

ALEKSANDRA SIMONOVA is a PhD candidate in social-cultural anthropology at the University of California, Berkeley, working on post-Soviet science cities in Russia. She is a 2016 Wadsworth International Fellow at the Wenner-Gren Foundation. She holds a master's degree in sociology and political sciences from the European University at St. Petersburg and a degree from Strelka Institute in Moscow.

KSENIA TATARCHENKO is a lecturer at the Global Studies Institute, Geneva University, specializing in the history of Russian science and technology. She has held positions as a visiting assistant professor of history at NYU Shanghai and a postdoctoral fellowship at the Harriman Institute, Columbia. She studies questions of knowledge circulation to situate Soviet developments in the global context. With Christopher Phillips, she edited "Mathematical Superpowers: The Politics of Universality in a Divided World," special issue of *Historical Studies in the Natural Sciences* 46, no. 5 (2016). She is currently writing a book on science and innovation cultures in Siberia titled *Science City, Siberia: Akademgorodok and the Late Soviet Politics of Expertise*. Her most recent fieldwork in the Russian Arctic is connected to the new research project: to examine the Cold War interplay between Soviet Arctic and Antarctic research and to question its influence on the ideas about climate change in today's Russia.

ZINAIDA VASILYEVA is PhD candidate at the University of Neuchâtel, working on DIY in post-Soviet Russia. She is an anthropologist interested in historically grounded and ethnographically driven research of postsocialist societies. From 2013 to 2015 she was the executive director of the Russian Computer Scientists at Home and Abroad project at the European University at St. Petersburg. She has participated separately in research projects focusing on consumption, memory, materialities, and urban techno communities. Her field of interests includes anthropology of knowledge and technologies, political anthropology, media and communications, subjectivity, and the post–Cold War politics of knowledge.

DMITRII ZHIKHAREVICH is a PhD candidate in sociology of finance at the London School of Economics. In 2017, he completed a PhD in social theory at St. Petersburg State University. From 2013 to 2015 he was a research fellow at the STS Center of the European University at St. Petersburg, taking part in the Russian Computer Scientists at Home and Abroad research project. His research interests include historical sociology of capitalism, social theory, and science and technology studies.